"Professor Amzat and his team have shown systematic thinking in catching up with contemporary developments in education and teaching while abiding by the core values of Islam. The contributions meet the critical academic standards needed in such an important analysis. The diversity of topics and the deep discourse by the authors from different academic backgrounds and expertise from around the world are indicative of the crucial importance of the book to academia in general and those in education and teacher training in particular. I recommend it highly."

—Assoc. Prof Dr Jabal M. Buaben, formerly of the School of Philosophy, Theology and Religion, University of Birmingham, United Kingdom

"This book by Professor Ismail Hussein Amzat is very important, as it describes pedagogical situations and reforms in the context of Islamic education across the globe. It explores the contesting modernity and traditionality of Islam in terms of pedagogical practices to find more effective solutions to educational problems. It enriches the literary collection about aspects of Islamic schooling, the information of which has been underrepresented in research and publications."

—Dr H. Raihani, Professor of Islamic Education Studies at UIN Sultan Syarif Kasim Riau, Indonesia

"The book is comprehensive and excellent. Its three parts cover a variety of content: knowledge, pedagogy, teaching methods in Part 1; professional development, responsibility and lifelong learning in Part 2; and assessment, Islamic curriculum reform and Islamization of knowledge in Part 3. It will be of interest to all teachers in Islamic schools. The writers—Muslims and non-Muslims—come from different parts of the world with varying experiences in teaching; some represent a majority, while some represent a minority in their respective countries. Hence, each chapter has something new to offer to all readers."

—Rosnani Hashim, Adjunct Prof of Social Foundation of Education, KOED, International Islamic University Malaysia. Founder of the Hikmah (Wisdom) Pedagogy of Philosophical Inquiry

"This is a very courageous book, combining Islamic education with modern pedagogical thought. Personhood formation is emphasized instead of just socialization. It shows best practices for students, as well as the way teachers can sustain via adequate curricula the flourishing of the students."

—Professor Siebren Miedema, Vrije Universiteit Amsterdam, The Netherlands

"This rich book presents an impressive range of studies into teaching in Islamic schools from several continents. It offers a wealth of information for scholars in the field and for other people interested in the current development of Islamic education, its transitions and debates."

—Dr Geir Skeie, UNESCO Chair and Professor of Religious Education, University of Stavanger, Norway

Supporting Modern Teaching in Islamic Schools

Supporting Modern Teaching in Islamic Schools: Pedagogical Best Practice for Teachers advocates the revamp of the madrasah system and a review of the Islamic curriculum across Muslim countries and emphasises training needs for Islamic teachers for modern instructional practice.

Islamic schools across Muslim countries face 21st-century challenges and teachers need continuing professional development to help them keep abreast of modern teaching practice. Books, papers, educators and parents have consistently called for curriculum change to transform teaching and learning in Islamic schools. Divided into three unique parts, Part 1 of the volume focusses on content knowledge, pedagogy and teaching methods; Part 2 highlights professional development, responsibilities, and lifelong learning; and Part 3 comprises chapters on Islamic curriculum review, reform and Islamisation of knowledge.

Scholars from the United States, United Kingdom, Europe, Canada, Australia, New Zealand, Asia and Africa, review the Islamic curriculum to highlight areas for further improvement and provide modern techniques and methods of teaching for pedagogical best practices and effective outcomes in Islamic schools. With these contributions, this volume will be of interest to OIC countries, Islamic student teachers and Islamic teachers who work in international and local settings.

Ismail Hussein Amzat is an Associate Professor, Kulliyyah of Education in the Department of Social Foundation and Educational Leadership at the International Islamic University Malaysia.

Supporting Modern Teaching in Islamic Schools
Pedagogical Best Practice for Teachers

Edited by Ismail Hussein Amzat

LONDON AND NEW YORK

Cover image: © Getty Images

First published 2022
by Routledge
4 Park Square, Milton Park, Abingdon, Oxon OX14 4RN

and by Routledge
605 Third Avenue, New York, NY 10158

Routledge is an imprint of the Taylor & Francis Group, an informa business

© 2022 selection and editorial matter, Ismail Hussein Amzat; individual chapters, the contributors

The right of Ismail Hussein Amzat to be identified as the author of the editorial material, and of the authors for their individual chapters, has been asserted in accordance with sections 77 and 78 of the Copyright, Designs and Patents Act 1988.

All rights reserved. No part of this book may be reprinted or reproduced or utilised in any form or by any electronic, mechanical, or other means, now known or hereafter invented, including photocopying and recording, or in any information storage or retrieval system, without permission in writing from the publishers.

Trademark notice: Product or corporate names may be trademarks or registered trademarks, and are used only for identification and explanation without intent to infringe.

British Library Cataloguing-in-Publication Data
A catalogue record for this book is available from the British Library

Library of Congress Cataloging-in-Publication Data
A catalog record has been requested for this book

ISBN: 978-1-032-04488-0 (hbk)
ISBN: 978-1-032-04486-6 (pbk)
ISBN: 978-1-003-19343-2 (ebk)

DOI: 10.4324/9781003193432

Typeset in Galliard
by SPi Technologies India Pvt Ltd (Straive)

Contents

Lists of Figures	x
List of Tables	xi
List of Contributors	xii
Foreword	xx
Preface	xxii
Acknowledgements	xxvii

PART 1
Content Knowledge, Pedagogy and Teaching Methods   1

1 Sound Pedagogies and Mis-pedagogies in Teaching Islam:
  Learning from Canadian Muslim Educators   3
  CLAIRE ALKOUATLI

2 Are Contemporary Islamic Education and Their Pedagogical
  Approaches Fit for Purpose? A Critique and Way Forward   17
  YAHIA BAIZA

3 Environmental Education and Indonesia's Traditional Islamic
  Boarding Schools: Curricular and Pedagogical Innovation in
  the Green Pesantren Initiative   31
  AHMAD AFNAN ANSHORI AND FLORIAN POHL

4 Developing an Islamic Teacher: Islamic Cultural Contents
  in an ELT Textbook in a Muslim High School in Southern
  Thailand   45
  YUSOP BOONSUK AND ERIC A. AMBELE

5 Islamic Instruction as a Student-Centred Approach   57
  SAMINA MALIK AND NABI BUX JUMANI

viii *Contents*

6 Philosophical Inquiry as a Method for Teaching
Islamic Education 68
WAN MAZWATI WAN YUSOFF, JUHASNI ADILA JUPERI
AND ABDUL SHAKOUR PREECE

7 Technology Infusion in the Design of an Impactful
Islamic Education Learning Experience 81
ROSEMALIZA BINTI MOHD KAMALLUDEEN

PART 2
Professional Development, Responsibility and
Lifelong Learning 95

8 Measures of Physiognomies in Fostering Islamic
Teachers' Professionalism in Selected Al-Majiri Integrated
Model Schools (AIMS) in Sokoto State, Nigeria 97
AHMAD TIJANI SURAJUDEEN

9 Enhancing Professionalism in Teaching Islamic Studies
through Employment of Adequate Instructional Resources 110
JAMIU ABDUR-RAFIU, U. A. AJIDAGBA AND YUNUS ALIYU

10 Improving Islamic Self-Motivation for Professional
Development (Study in Islamic Boarding Schools) 123
MUHAMMAD ANAS MA'ARIF, MUHAMMAD MUTJABA MITRA ZUANA
AND AKHMAD SIROJUDDIN

11 Islamic Teacher Professionalism: The Role of Family
and Society in Teacher Professionalisation 135
ABULFAZL GHAFFARI AND DINA YOUSEFI

12 Teachers' Roles in Making Multiple Intelligences Work in
Indonesian Muslim Schools 146
MUHAMMAD ZUHDI AND ERBA ROZALINA YULIANTI

13 Lifelong Learning among Islamic Studies Teachers: A Path
for Professionalism 157
MERAH SOUAD AND TAHRAOUI RAMDANE

Contents ix

PART 3
Islamic Curriculum Reform, Assessment and Islamisation of Knowledge 169

14 Research-Based Reform of Madrasah Curriculum in
   Bosnia and Herzegovina and Its Implications for Fostering
   Teachers' Professional Development 171
   AMINA ISANOVIĆ HADŽIOMEROVIĆ AND DINA
   SIJAMHODŽIĆ-NADAREVIĆ

15 Arabic Teaching at Australian Islamic Schools: Working
   with Student Diversity and Curriculum Challenges 182
   NADIA SELIM

16 Islamisation of Knowledge: A Critical Integrated Approach 198
   ALHAGI MANTA DRAMMEH

17 Maktab Teachers and Behaviour Education: Ruminations
   from a Teacher Education Programme in the UK 209
   IMRAN MOGRA

18 Islamic Religious Education (IRE) Teachers in the
   Netherlands: From Tradition-Based to Modern Teaching 222
   INA TER AVEST

19 The Role of Supplementary Schools Education in
   Shaping the Islamic Identity of Muslim Youths in Europe 233
   MOHAMMAD MESBAHI

20 Crafting a Strategy to Assess the Learning of Islamic
   Studies in Elementary Schools 245
   TAHRAOUI RAMDANE AND MERAH SOUAD

Index 259

Figures

1.1	An example of students making meaning of Islamic concepts	14
6.1	Summary of a COPI session	73
7.1	Constructive alignment by John Biggs	84
7.2	The ASSURE instructional design model	86
7.3	A screenshot of Quran.com	89
7.4	Link to iCakna Solat YouTube video explanation	90
8.1	Normal probability plot (P-P) of the regression standardized residual	104
8.2	Scatterplot of the model	105

Tables

1.1	Pedagogical recommendations for educators and school administrators	13
4.1	Cultural evaluation in the textbook	51
4.2	Evaluation of cultural contents	52
8.1	Model summary	102
8.2	Coefficients	103
9.1	Branches and divisions of IR	117
14.1	The structure of a research-based approach to madrasah curriculum reform	176
15.1	Examples of activities to help teachers become acquainted with the learners	187
15.2	Encouraging learners to know each other in a Qur'an-inspired activity	188
15.3	Consultation activities for secondary students	190
15.4	Consultation activities for primary students	190
15.5	Ways of encouraging autonomous learning in older learners	192
15.6	Ways of encouraging autonomous learning in younger learners	192
20.1	Assessment methods according to Islamic studies' different segments	254

Contributors

Jamiu Abdur-Rafiu (NCE, B.A. (Ed.), M.Ed, Ph.D.) teaches in the Department of Arts Education, Faculty of Education, University of Ilorin, Nigeria. His research interest includes Islamic studies, religious education, general education, curriculum studies, primary education and Arabic in Islamic studies.

U. A. Ajidagba (NCE, B.A. (Ed.), M.Ed, PGDPA, Ph.D.) is a senior lecturer in the Department of Arts Education, Faculty of Education, University of Ilorin, Nigeria. His areas of research interest include religious studies education, general education, curriculum studies, primary education studies and Arabic in Islamic studies. He is currently the resident electoral commissioner, Independent National Electoral Commission, Nasarawa State Office.

Claire Alkouatli earned a Ph.D. in human development, learning, and culture from the University of British Columbia, in Vancouver, Canada. She is currently serving as an Adjunct Research Fellow at the Centre for Islamic Thought and Education, University of South Australia and Human Development Consultant for the Women's Studies programme at the Vice Rectorate for Postgraduate Studies and Scientific Research, Princess Nourah Bint Abdulrahman University, Saudi Arabia. Her qualitative research focusses on the roles of culture, relationships and pedagogies in human development across the lifespan—particularly imagination, play, dialogue, inquiry and challenge. Claire currently lives between Vancouver, Beirut and Riyadh.

Yunus Aliyu attended University of Ilorin, Ilorin Kwara State, Nigeria and University Kebangsa Malaysia for his undergraduate and postgraduate programmes, respectively. He is a lecturer in the Department of Arts Education, Faculty of Education, University of Ilorin, Nigeria. He has a number of publications in reputable journals. His research interest covers Islamic education, students' academic performance in Islamic studies, female education, among others. He is a member of National Teachers of Arabic and Islamic Studies (NATAIS), a member of the National Association for the Study of Religions and Education and a member of the Teachers' Registration Council of Nigeria.

Contributors xiii

Eric A. Ambele is a lecturer, researcher and member of the Postgraduate (M.Ed. in ELT and Ph.D. in ELT) Board in the Department of Western Languages and Linguistics, Mahasarakham University, Thailand. He holds a Ph.D. in applied linguistics and has published extensively in ISI and Scopus indexed journals. His research interests focus on global Englishes issues; discourse analysis; sociolinguistics; English medium instruction; teacher education, beliefs, attitudes and identity; intercultural communication; and innovative research methodology.

Ahmad Afnan Anshori is a lecturer in religious studies at State Islamic University (UIN) Walisongo, Semarang Indonesia. He is currently a Ph.D. researcher in empirical and practical religious studies at Radboud University, Nijmegen, the Netherlands focussing on religion and ecology. He earned his first master's in comparative religion from CRCS Gadjah Mada University, Yogyakarta, in 2004 and a second master's in human rights education from Curtin University, Perth, in 2009. He also earned a bachelor's in Islamic education from the Islamic University of Indonesia, Yogyakarta, in 2000. His research interests focus on issues of religion and ecology, religion and cross-cultural studies, Islamic education and human rights education.

Ina ter Avest is em. prof. 'Philosophy of Life' of the Inholland University of Applied Sciences and was lecturer 'Interreligious Teaching and Learning' at the Vrije Universiteit Amsterdam. She did her master's at the Radboud University in Nijmegen and graduated as a psychologist of culture and religion. In her Ph.D. research, she focussed on the religious development of pupils (primary school) in an intercultural and interreligious educational context. In her teaching, as well as in her research and publications, (religious) identity development is central: identity development of pupils/students, of teachers and of teams of teachers in schools. In her private practice, she combines the theoretical frame of reference of the dialogical self theory (DST; she was trained as a consultant following the self-confrontation method based on the DST) with her education as a psychodramatist and coaches individuals as well as groups.

Yahia Baiza is a research associate at the Institute of Ismaili Studies in London, United Kingdom. He specialises in education, educational planning, Islamic and Afghanistan studies, as well as the study of refugee and diaspora communities in Europe and manuscript analysis. Dr Baiza is also Bloomsbury Education and Childhood Studies regional editor for Afghanistan. In this capacity, he develops digital resources on education and childhood and youth studies in Afghanistan. He is also an international consultant on various aspects of education, including curriculum and textbook development, and education policy and planning. Dr Baiza is the author of *Education in Afghanistan: Developments, Influences, and Legacies since 1901*, published by Routledge in London and New York in 2013 and 2017, and two forthcoming books, *Education in Troubled* xiv *Contributors*

Times: A Global Pluralist Response (2021) and *The Hazara Ismailis of Afghanistan and Their History* (2022), as well as some 80 academic articles.

Yusop Boonsuk holds a Ph.D. in applied linguistics from the Centre for Global Englishes, the University of Southampton, United Kingdom. He is currently working as an English lecturer/researcher at the English Section, Faculty of Humanities and Social Sciences, Prince of Songkla University, Thailand. His research interest focusses on global Englishes, world Englishes, English as a lingua franca, English as an international language, intercultural and transcultural communication, intercultural awareness, English language teaching (ELT), English medium instruction and English language beliefs, attitudes and identity.

Alhagi Manta Drammeh is an associate professor at Al-Maktoum College. He is trained in both Islamic classical scholarship and social sciences. His academic career started in 1996 at the International Islamic University Malaysia (IIUM). He also taught at the Institute of Human Sciences Wales and moved to work at the Al-Maktoum College of Higher Education Scotland and the Muslim College London. Recognising his expertise, he has been appointed to examine several Ph.D. candidates at various British Universities. He was awarded fellowships at Higher Education Academy and Royal Society of Arts. Drammeh is the author of many publications, including *The Fallacy of the Inevitability of Clash of Civilisations: A Common Ground for Mutual Understanding and Co-existence* (IIUM Press, 2009). Some of his other publications are "Reflecting on Democratic Values and Principles of Governance in Islam" in *International Journal of Muslim Unity*, Kuala Lumpur, International Islamic University; "Islam and Human Dignity: Insights into Muslim Ethico-Philosophical Thinking in Ethical Personalism," Ontos Verlag (Frankfurt am Main); "Methodological Approaches and Implications in Dealing with Qur'an" in Al-Bayan, *Brill*, volume 12/Issue1/2014; and "The Notion of Mutashabihat in the Qur'an and Its Interpretation—The First Three Centuries–1 Ankara".

Abulfazl Ghaffari received his Ph.D. from Tarbiat Madares University (Iran) in philosophy of education. He is currently an assistant professor of education at Ferdowsi University of Mashhad. His research bridges Islamic education, moral education and philosophy of education. He is the manager of the students' Counseling and Empowerment Center of Ferdowsi University of Mashhad.

Amina Isanović Hadžiomerović holds a Ph.D. in social sciences from the University of Kaiserslautern, Germany. She teaches in the Department of Education, Faculty of Philosophy in Sarajevo. Her areas of academic interest encompass adult education, higher education, research methods and methodology. She has published articles and book chapters in journals and publications in B&H and abroad. Two of the recent publications are treating the topic of Islamic education: "Islamic Education in the Balkans" in *Handbook of Islamic Education*, Springer, 2018, and "Publicly Funded Islamic Education in Bosnia and Herzegovina" in *European Perspectives on Islamic Education and Public Schooling*, Equinox, 2018.

Nabi Bux Jumani has been working as vice president and professor of education at the International Islamic University Islamabad, Pakistan. He has also had the privilege of working as acting president of IIUI. He is editor of the *International Journal of Distance Education and ELearning* and chief editor of the *International Journal of Innovation in Teaching and Learning*. He is a member of different national and international professional organisations/associations in the field of education and training like MESH (Mapping Educational Special Know How)—Project of Education Futures Collaboration, United Kingdom; Society for Asian Civilization, Pakistan; and a fellow of the Royal Society of Arts, United Kingdom. He received the Best University Teacher Award from the Higher Education Commission, Pakistan, for the year 2015. He is working on various national projects in the field of education and distance education and on an international project for the European Commission Erasmus+ Programme on blended learning for teacher educators in Asia and Europe.

Juhasni Adila Juperi obtained a law degree and a master's degree in education from IIUM. She won the Best Thesis Award in 2011 at the national level in the category of social science and humanities for her master's research entitled "Philosophical Inquiry in Islamic Education and Its Effects on Students' Questioning Skills." Subsequently, she was awarded a scholarship by St Catharine's College, University of Cambridge, where she completed her M.Phil degree in philosophical inquiry in Malaysia. Prior to this, she worked as a secondary school teacher in the subjects of ESL and Islamic studies. More recently, she has been involved in training schoolteachers and postgraduate students in the method of community of philosophical inquiry (COPI) under the Hikmah Pedagogy programme.

Rosemaliza Binti Mohd Kamalludeen has been an assistant professor of instructional technology at the Faculty of Education, IIUM for about six years. She received her doctorate at Virginia Polytechnic Institute and State University (Virginia Tech), USA, in career and technical education. Currently, her research interests are vocational/technical education, effective use of technology to maximise learner involvement in the teaching and learning process and learning facilitation that inspires. Rosemaliza is one of the national trainers for the Educator 4.0: Redesigning Learning nationwide programme, an initiative by the Ministry of Education Malaysia to upskill and reskill tertiary educators with 21st-century trends in teaching and learning. She has also conducted numerous workshops at various institutions of higher learning on technology-enhanced learning, MOOCs and the arts and sciences of facilitating learning.

xvi *Contributors*

Samina Malik has been working as a professor in the Department of Education at the International Islamic University Islamabad, Pakistan. She possesses diversified experience in administration, research and teaching. She has experience in administration as dean of the Faculty of Social Sciences; chairperson of the Department of Education; additional director, directorate of distance education, IIUI; and director, Female Campus IIUI. She is the winner of a national award (HEC 2014) and has 25 years of experience in the field of education. Prof. Malik has been guiding research scholars on the M.Phil and Ph.D. levels in different areas of education. She is an editor for *IJITL* of the Department of Education and the magazine *Educators Pakistan* and managing editor of *IJDEEL* of the Directorate of Distance Education, IIUI. She has completed various national projects in the field of education and an international project for the European Commission Erasmus+ Programme titled "Blended Learning Courses for Teacher Educators between Asia and Europe."

Muhammad Anas Ma'arif, doctor of Islamic education, graduated from Maliki State Islamic University of Malang in 2019. Dr Ma'arif's research concentration is in Islamic education, character education and education about teacher professionalism. Dr Ma'arif is a reviewer and editor of several journals in Indonesia. Every year, Dr Ma'arif receives research assistance from the Ministry. Lecturer of the Institus Pesantren Kh. Abdul Chalim Pacet Mojokerto, Indonesia

Mohammad Mesbahi is interested in topics such as Islamic education in the West and its complexities. Based on his interest in the teaching of Islam in mainstream education, as well as Islamic schools and colleges, Dr Mesbahi has taken part in the development of undergraduate and postgraduate degrees and diplomas under the Middlesex Collaborative scheme. His most recent works going out for publication are "The Mosaic of Muslim Identity in Britain" and "Why Would Muslims Study Theology to Obtain an Academic Qualification?"

Imran Mogra has worked with pupils of all age groups. He has published articles on various subjects and issues. He authored *Jumpstart RE* (Routledge, 2018) to enhance the teaching of religious education in primary schools and *Islam: A Guide for Teachers* (SAGE, 2020) to support subject knowledge of Islam. His recent publication includes Fundamental British Values: Are They Fundamental? Imran is a senior lecturer in professional studies and religious education in several programmes in the Department of Early Years and Primary Education, Birmingham City University, England. He also provides training to madrasah teachers and is currently a reviewer and consultant for a syllabus being developed for Muslim children in England.

Florian Pohl is associate professor in religion at Emory University's Oxford College. A native of Hamburg, Germany, Pohl earned his Ph.D. in religion from Temple University, Philadelphia, in 2007, after completing an

M.A. in religion at Temple in 1998 and a theology diploma at Universität Hamburg in 2001. His research examines publicly and politically influential expressions of Islam in contemporary Indonesia. A focus of his work has been the role of Islamic educational institutions in Indonesia's process of democratic transition and consolidation. He is the author of *Islamic Education and the Public Sphere: Today's Pesantren in Indonesia* (Waxmann, 2009).

Abdul Shakour Preece is currently an assistant professor at the Department of Curriculum and Instruction, Kulliyyah of Education, IIUM. He holds a bachelor's degree in education from Birmingham City University and a master's degree and Ph.D. in education from IIUM. Dr Abdul Shakour has more than 30 years of teaching experience in primary, secondary and tertiary levels of education and has conducted research and training in 'Philosophy for Children' (P4C) at both government and private schools in Malaysia. Areas of expertise include curriculum and instruction, materials development for English as a second language, 'Hikmah' pedagogy, blended learning and flipped classroom method.

Tahraoui Ramdane is a dedicated Algerian educationalist and academic at the Faculty of Education, IIUM. He offers a proven track record of commended performance in teaching, writing, translation and research, with a passion for education and an unwavering commitment to the cause of Islam. His research interests include curriculum studies in Islamic education, comparative educational politics, history of Islamic education and contemporary educational issues. Dr Tahraoui wrote and edited two books, published several articles in scholarly journals and co-authored several chapters in books. He is active in international academic activities, which include reviewing curriculum of universities and schools in South-East Asia and the Middle East.

Nadia Selim is an early career researcher working in the University of South Australia's Division of Education Futures. She is a member of the Centre for Educational and Social Inclusion. Her research and publications focus on Arabic language teaching and learning, with a particular emphasis on the Australian context. Nadia's Ph.D. research explored the learning experiences of some non-Arab Muslim students enrolled in Australian Islamic schools. In addition, she has a master's in applied linguistics. Nadia has presented at several conferences and conducted professional development and cultural awareness sessions for teachers, university staff and staff at other organisations.

Dina Sijamhodžić-Nadarević is an associate professor at the Faculty of Islamic Studies at the University of Sarajevo teaching pedagogy/religious pedagogy courses. Dina holds academic degrees in Islamic theology and general pedagogy received at the University of Sarajevo. She participated in numerous international study programmes, conferences, symposiums in B&H and abroad (Cairo University; United States—Arizona State xviii *Contributors*

University, Kent State University in Ohio, Chicago; England—University in Birmingham; Turkey—Faculty of Theology; Austria—IRPA in Wien, etc.). Recently, she contributed a chapter to the Routledge volume *Rethinking Madrasah Education in a Globalized World.*

Akhmad Sirojuddin is the lecturer at Institut Pesantren KH. Abdul Chalim (IKHAC), Pacet Mojokerto, Indonesia. He earned both his undergraduate (2011) and graduate (2014) degrees at Maliki State Islamic University of Malang (UIN Malang). He has been actively presenting papers at both national and international conferences. He is a reviewer and editor of several journals in Indonesia.

Merah Souad is an Algerian scholar who is currently the head of the Department of Social Foundations and Educational Leadership, Faculty of Education IIUM. She has a vast working experience of 22 years in teaching, administration and training. Her research interests include social change, women's issues, history and philosophy of Islamic education and Islamic thought, methods of teaching and contemporary educational issues. She published many articles in scholarly journals and co-authored several chapters in books. She is active in academic activities, which include curriculum review, designing university courses and training teachers and students.

Ahmad Tijani Surajudeen obtained a B.A. (Ed.) in Islamic studies in 2007 at the University of Ilorin, Ilorin Kwara State, Nigeria. He earned an M.Ed. in teaching of Islamic education and a Ph.D. in education (curriculum and instruction/Islamic education) at the Department of Curriculum and Instruction, Faculty (Kuliyyah) of Education, IIUM, in 2011 and 2016, respectively. He currently lectures, and he is the current head of the Department of Curriculum Studies, Faculty of Education, Sokoto State University, Nigeria. He has published articles in journals, chapters in books, book reviews and conference proceedings. He is a fellow of the International Institute for Muslim Unity Malaysia; a member of the International Association for the Advancement of Curriculum Studies, Canada; and a member of NATAIS, Nigeria.

Dina Yousefi received her B.A. in ELT from Hakim Sabzevari University in 1996. She received her M.A. in general linguistics from Ferdowsi University of Mashhad in 1998. She is currently a Ph.D. student of philosophy of education at Ferdowsi University of Mashhad.

Erba Rozalina Yulianti is a senior lecturer at the Faculty of Education UIN Syarif Hidayatullah Jakarta. She has a doctorate degree in Islamic education with an emphasis on educational psychology. She started her teaching career at the Faculty of Education of UIN Sunan Gunung Jati, Bandung, West Jawa, in 1998 before continuing her career at the Faculty of Education UIN Syarif Hidayatullah Jakarta. In addition to teaching at the university, Dr Yulianti has also produced a number of scholarly works on Islamic education. She is currently serving as a supervisor of *Dar en Niswah* Foundation, which focusses on Islamic schooling in Pekanbaru Riau.

Wan Mazwati Wan Yusoff is a graduate of Eastern New Mexico University, USA, in accounting and holds an MBA. She received her Ph.D. in education, specialising in teaching thinking through philosophy from IIUM. She currently teaches creative thinking and Islamic world view at the Department of Fundamental and Interdisciplinary Studies, Kulliyyah of Islamic Revealed Knowledge and Human Sciences, IIUM. She is a certified trainer of P4C, awarded by the Institute for Advancement in Philosophy for Children, Montclair State University, New Jersey, in 2006 and is now attached to the Centre for Teaching Thinking at the Kulliyyah of Education, IIUM, which promotes P4C for the enhancement of excellent thinking among youth and students in Malaysia. Currently, Wan Mazwati is active in conducting research about the application of hadith in education, psychology and communication. She is also involved in developing teaching materials that employ philosophical inquiry in Islamic education to deepen secondary school students' understanding and philosophical thinking skills.

Muhammad Mujtaba Mitra Zuana is a lecturer at IKHAC, Pacet Mojokerto, Indonesia. He earned both his undergraduate (2012) and graduate (2016) degrees at the State University of Surabaya (Unesa). Currently, he is studying the management science doctoral programme at the State University of Malang. He has been actively presenting papers at both national and international conferences. He is a reviewer and editor of several journals in Indonesia.

Muhammad Zuhdi, Ph.D., is a senior lecturer at the Faculty of Education, UIN Syarif Hidayatullah Jakarta. He obtained his Ph.D. from the Faculty of Education, McGill University Montreal. His research interests are curriculum, Islamic education and multicultural education. In addition to teaching and writing, Dr Zuhdi is serving as the editor-in-chief of *Tarbiya: Journal of Education in Muslim Society* (http://journal.uinjkt.ac.id/index.php/tarbiya) and a member of the Technical Advisory Committee of UNESCO's Project "Promoting Intercultural Dialogue and A Culture of Peace in Southeast Asia through Shared Histories" 2015. Dr Zuhdi received 'the Australian Alumni Award for Excellence in Education' in 2011.

Foreword

Seeking a modern balance between teacher instruction and student-centred learning is a core theme in this book. This is something that once existed in the history of Islam but has been overshadowed by much mutual misunderstanding. This book builds bridges, and to this end challenges, and solutions are presented across content knowledge, professional development and curriculum reform.

Examples abound in this book, and here are just a few: understanding how it is possible to introduce an environmental curriculum in Islamic schools and aspire to custodianship, rather than ownership of nature; the Islamic interest in the holistic flourishing of the student emphasises inquiry, curiosity and care and can usefully be used in teaching curriculum subjects that traditionally place an emphasis on knowledge content and reproduction of knowledge through memorisation; and introducing the critical thinking of the Socratic method to teachers makes it possible to generate shared discussions where insights from the Prophet are important to not only know about but also used to understand issues new and old, such as organ donation.

It is noted by the authors that some of the resources available to progress the bridging between teacher and student-centredness do not always contain examples and references to Islamic values and ways of living. When English is taught as a curriculum subject in Islamic settings, it does tend to highlight the norms of the Anglo-Saxon world.

With professional and curriculum development in mind, the contributions make a number of well-placed arguments. Of these, the following is central: while the continual development of the character of the teacher is important, developing pedagogy, digital understanding and assessment skills is identified as crucial and not always addressed at an individual or school level. An intriguing chapter on multiple intelligences demonstrates once again the bridge between secular and religious schooling and how this sets up children for the skills required in an increasingly complex world.

This is a book about what Islamic education adds to global education, not by ignoring 21st-century skills and student-centredness. On the contrary, we learn how they can be bridged to enrich the overall educational experience of all.

Foreword xxi

This is an elegant book that builds a bridge between Islamic teacher practice and 21st-century skills. Islamic material and educational practices can engage with COVID-19, sustainability and the presence of digital learning. Teacher-centredness can combine with the care of student learning and *Tarbyah*—the holistic flourishing of the student in an ever-changing global world.

Professor Stephen Dobson,
Victoria University of Wellington, New Zealand

Preface

Today's educational world has highly emphasised teacher instructional skills, competencies and professional development. In pursuance of 21st-century learning, schools around the globe face mounting pressures to improve teaching for better-quality learning outcomes. The public, especially parents, rely on teachers and believe that their children deserve to have teachers with 21st-century needed skills to reach out to all students without leaving anyone behind. Developed and some developing countries have taken effective measures through policies and robust training for teachers to support teaching and safeguard 21st-century learning in classrooms to respond to these needs.

Against this background, one concern is whether the Muslim world and Islamic schools "will rise with this tide" or follow a different path. Hence, knowing whether the measures that schools in Islamic countries have put together to achieve teaching excellence and ensure students coming from their schools are on par with the global students in terms of skills, knowledge and contributions to their societies is essential to know. To date, however, very little is known about Muslim teacher training or professional development. These subjects have yet to be put forward by any book or research on training or the level of training that Islamic schools in Islamic countries provide for their teachers to enhance 21st-century teaching skills. This scarcity has led me to think of ways to contribute to Islamic teachers' development and teaching.

With the overwhelming global problems facing Islamic schools and teachers, this book is necessary to address these issues from global perspectives with global solutions. This book discusses and tabulates the skills that Muslims or traditional Islamic teachers should possess. Islamic schools had been criticised for failing to modernise the methods of teaching and curriculum to withstand 21st-century challenges and respond to current needs. The book advocates the revamp of the *madrasa* system and a review of the Islamic curriculum and pedagogy across Muslim countries for Islamic schools to remain relevant and responsive to the demands of globalisation. Quintessentially, it discusses the adaptation of Islamic schools to modern teaching methods and the infusion of the latest instructional technology in the classroom to enrich teaching. Teacher quality is paramount for student achievement.

Preface xxiii

Moreover, this book emphasises training needs for Islamic teachers to adapt and adopt the new curricula to their students' learning needs. Last but not least, the book discusses Islamic education, knowledge and secularisation, and the adaptation and integration of the scientific method in teaching consistent with Islamic values to support modern teaching in Islamic schools for teachers' pedagogical practices. The book is divided into three parts. Prominent authors from around the world shared their knowledge and skills by contributing chapters to this book. The chapters provide insights, methods, approaches, perspectives, strategies and findings for Islamic teachers seeking to improve their teaching repertoire.

Part 1 of this book talks about content knowledge, pedagogy and teaching methods.

Chapter 1, "Sound Pedagogies and Mis-pedagogies in Teaching Islam: Learning from Canadian Muslim Educators" by Claire Alkouatli, provides contexts for pedagogies in teaching Islam in a minority Muslim context. Additionally, the author juxtaposes mis-pedagogies with sound pedagogies.

Chapter 2, "Are Contemporary Islamic Education and Their Pedagogical Approaches Fit for Purpose? A Critique and Way Forward" by Yahia Baiza, poses questions through analysis and exploration concerning whether contemporary Islamic education and pedagogies are fit for the purpose and whether they meet the needs of students and expectations of parents and societies in the 21st century. The author also looks at the dynamism of Islamic education and whether current Islamic education models serve the current and future needs of students.

Chapter 3, "Environmental Education and Indonesia's Traditional Islamic Boarding Schools: Curricular and Pedagogical Innovation in the Green Pesantren Initiative" by Florian Pohl and Ahmad Afnan Anshori, discusses the challenges of introducing environment education in Islamic schools in a societal context where state and local government leadership is sorely lacking and teacher training for environmental education is inadequate.

Chapter 4, "Developing an Islamic Teacher: Islamic Cultural Contents in an ELT Textbook in a Muslim High School in Southern Thailand" by Yusop Boonsuk and Eric A. Ambele, discusses ELT in Islamic schools and how choosing English language textbooks by Islamic teachers could integrate an Islamic learner" cultural contents and global contents. As a result, learners will not only be exposed to global foreign cultures but also their own local Thai Islamic cultures.

Chapter 5, "Islamic Instruction as a Student-Centred Approach" by Samina Malik and Nabi Bux Jumani, discusses contemporary instructional strategies for Islamic teachers that could enable them to meet 21st-century challenges and help their learners cope with this changing world.

Chapter 6, "Philosophical Inquiry as a Method for Teaching Islamic Education" by Wan Mazwati Wan Yusoff, Juhasni Adila Juperi and Abdul Shakour Preece, presents COPI as a method for teaching Islamic studies, which is not only effective in stimulating students' critical, creative and xxiv *Preface*

caring thinking but also promotes collaboration and verbal communication, engagement and self-confidence.

Chapter 7, "Technology Infusion in the Design of an Impactful Islamic Education Learning Experience" by Rosemaliza Binti Mohd Kamalludeen, addresses the fundamentals of instructional design, including constructive alignment when designing lessons that incorporate technology to ensure learning outcomes are achieved in a transformative approach to Islamic education. The chapter also shares relevant instructional design models that could guide Islamic education teachers in creating lessons that include the use of technology.

Part 2 of this book presents chapters on professional development, responsibility and lifelong learning.

Chapter 8, "Measures of Physiognomies in Fostering Islamic Teachers' Professionalism in Selected Al-Majiri Integrated Model Schools (AIMS) in Sokoto State, Nigeria" by Ahmad Tijani Surajudeen, investigates the conceptualised measures of physiognomies in connection with teachers' professionalism in selected AIMS in Sokoto State, Nigeria.

Chapter 9, "Enhancing Professionalism in Teaching Islamic studies through the Employment of Adequate Instructional Resources" by Jamiu Abdur-Rafiu, U. A. Ajidagba, and Aliyu Yunus, discusses the importance of instructional resources in teaching and learning of Islamic studies while focussing on the presentation of the definitions of the themes. The chapter also elucidates the concepts and analyses the principles guiding the selection and utilisation of instructional resources in teaching Islamic studies.

Chapter 10, "Improving Islamic Self-Motivation for Professional Development (Study in Islamic Boarding School)" by Muhammad Anas Ma'arif, Muhammad Mujtaba Mitra Zuana and Akhmad Sirojuddin, describes and analyses how to improve teacher professionalism in learning through self-motivation using an empirical approach.

Chapter 11, "Islamic Teacher Professionalism: The Role of Family, Society and Teacher Professionalisation" by Abulfazl Ghaffari and Dina Yousefi, uses a descriptive-analytic approach to specifically examine the professionalisation of Islamic education from the perspective of soul generation, which forms the theoretical background. The chapter also introduces the professionalisation of Islamic teaching by using the Qur'an for the principles and techniques.

Chapter 12, "Teachers' Roles in Making Multiple Intelligences Work in Indonesia's Muslim School" by Muhammad Zuhdi and Erba Rozalina Yulianti, describes teachers' roles in making multiple intelligences work in Muslim schools and investigates how Muslim schools implement the theory into practice. In addition, the chapter discusses how schools prepare their teachers to apply the theory in serving their students successfully.

Chapter 13, "Lifelong Learning among Islamic Studies Teachers: A Path for Teachers' Professionalism" by Merah Souad and Tahraoui Ramdane, explains the concept of lifelong learning in Islamic studies and its importance in the 21st century's educational attainment and the importance of lifelong learning for the professional development of Muslim teachers.

Preface xxv

Part 3 of this book comprises chapters on Islamic curriculum reform, assessment and Islamisation of knowledge.

Chapter 14, "Research-Based Reform of Madrasah Curriculum in Bosnia and Herzegovina and Its Implications for Fostering Teachers' Professional Development" by Amina Isanović Hadžiomerović and Dina Sijamhodžić-Nadarević, describes a research-based approach to educational reform implemented in a project designed to reform the curriculum of *madrasahs* in Bosnia and Herzegovina initiated in 2017 while empirically analysing the interpretations of the ongoing processes and participants' reflections.

Chapter 15, "Arabic Teaching at Australian Islamic Schools: Working with Student Diversity and Curriculum Challenges" by Nadia Selim, provides some teaching approaches for Arabic teachers to deal with diversity in their Arabic classes. Eventually, the chapter proposes a framework to improve their teaching and learning.

Chapter 16, "Islamisation of Knowledge: A Critical Integrated Approach" by Alhagi Manta Drammeh, highlights the centrality of Islamisation regarding the interface between reason and revelation, emphasising the need to embed the urgency of critical thinking into teaching and learning processes.

Chapter 17, "Maktab Teachers and Behaviour Education: Ruminations from a Teacher Education Programme in the UK" by Imran Mogra, discusses the development of Muslim teachers in the Maktab education sector of the United Kingdom. The chapter also presents the history of the Maktab and highlights its main salient features in the United Kingdom while discussing its key terms and celebrating some of its main contributions.

Chapter 18, "Islamic Religious Education (IRE) Teachers in the Netherlands: From Tradition-Based to Modern Teaching" by Ina ter Avest, discusses the adapted teaching materials for sex education in IRE. Moreover, the chapter articulates the differences between Islamic and secular-Western attitudes in the Netherlands towards sexuality and inadequate training for Islamic teachers in the Netherlands.

Chapter 19, "The Role of Supplementary Schools Education in Shaping the Islamic Identity of Muslim Youths in Europe" by Mohammad Mesbahi, discusses two major issues by first highlighting the identity crises within the Muslim community in Europe and then reviewing the importance of supplementary schools for preserving Islamic identity by addressing the issue of professional development within such institutions.

Chapter 20, "Crafting a Strategy to Assess the Learning of Islamic Studies in Elementary Schools" by Tahraoui Ramdane and Merah Souad, provides strategies for assessing and evaluating Islamic studies subjects at the elementary level and explains the necessity of tailoring different assessment and evaluation tools for the different segments of school subjects. In addition, the chapter highlights the uniqueness of the evaluation and assessment's aims of the Islamic studies subjects.

Due to the international backgrounds of the authors and their diversity, this book spans a range of areas that are of crucial importance to Islamic education and the professional development of teachers, such as teaching methods, curriculum, professional training, teacher knowledge, skills development, teacher empowerment, modernity and the improvement of pedagogical practices. The book equips teachers with the necessary knowledge and skills to handle today's pressing issues and solve modern-day problems. For these reasons, this volume will be of interest to Islamic teachers, Islamic school management, practitioners and policymakers who work in international and local settings.

Ismail Hussein Amzat (Ph.D.)

Acknowledgements

As the editor, I owe immense gratitude to the chapter authors of this book for their scholarly contributions; this book would not have been possible without your remarkable chapters. Thank you for your dedication and commitment to write the chapters, especially in the middle of the COVID-19 pandemic. I appreciate the patience and the trust that you have had in me. I am indebted to Routledge in Singapore for your trust and understanding. I thank Katie Peace for her coordination and support during the process, as well as the production team and graphic designers. My appreciation also goes to my Kulliyyah (Faculty) of Education and the Department of Social Foundation and Educational Leadership, IIUM, for academic support. I thank the endorsers of this book for your wonderful blurbs and Stephen Dobson for your remarkable foreword.

Last but not least, I would like to express my deep sadness and condolence on the loss of an author and a colleague, Assist. Prof. Dr Rosemaliza Binti Mohd Kamalludeen, who participated a chapter in this book titled "Technology Infusion in the Design of an Impactful Islamic Education Learning Experience". You will always be remembered and your academic works and contributions live on. May Allah forgive your sins and your soul.

Ismail Hussein Amzat (Ph.D.)

Part 1

Content Knowledge, Pedagogy and Teaching Methods

1 Sound Pedagogies and Mis-pedagogies in Teaching Islam
Learning from Canadian Muslim Educators

Claire Alkouatli

Introduction: New Pedagogies for Deep Learning

Imagine a child who bounds out of bed in the morning and rushes excitedly to get ready for a class that she loves. Now imagine a child who drags her feet and would rather go anywhere else than the class she dreads. The emotional valence differs between these two children and the degree to which they are primed to learn. As educators, the methods we use in the learning environments we create—*pedagogies*—are the primary means of engaging learners. Infused with principles and expressed in practices, pedagogies are mechanisms of teaching, learning and developing (Daniels, 2016), and differences in pedagogic quality may reflect differences in the efficacy of a learning environment and degrees of learner transformation. For the 21st century, 'new pedagogies' have been identified as learning partnerships between and among students and teachers, aiming towards *deep learning* as creating and doing, empowered by human creativity, inquiry, and purpose (Fullan & Langworthy, 2014). In Muslim educational communities, what are educators' pedagogies in teaching Islam? Do they promote deep learning for 21st-century learners? These questions frame the focus of this chapter. In interviews with Canadian Muslim educators, some potentially effective pedagogies were identified, along with some less-effective ones. In the next few paragraphs, I provide some context on pedagogies in teaching Islam, a brief review of recent literature and a description of the methodology foundational to this chapter. Sections 2 and 3 overview mis-pedagogies, which the educators recommended avoiding, and sound pedagogies, respectively. Section 4 provides some implications, recommendations and concluding thoughts.

Context: Islamic Pedagogy

One could argue that Islam, as a spiritually oriented way of life, has endured over successive generations through 'deep learning.' Accounts of the earliest sites of Islamic education describe situated, relational and participatory learning (Mogra, 2010; Nasr, 2012; Rufai, 2010), contemplation (Sahin, 2014) and inquiry (Ramadan, 2007). Muhammad's[1] pedagogies seem to

DOI: 10.4324/9781003193432-2

4   *Claire Alkouatli*

have been based on dynamic, dialogic relationships (Abu Ghuddah, 2017), where he worked with each of his companions' individual characteristics, asking questions and opinions, in nurturing holistic growth (Ramadan, 2007). Despite descriptions of holistic pedagogies, some question whether and how effective pedagogies are being implemented today (Al-Sadan, 1997; Sahin, 2014).

Conceptual explorations of pedagogy include Ajem and Memon's (2011) principles of Islamic pedagogy, Nasr's (2012) reflections on Islamic pedagogy in light of the Islamic tradition and Waghid's (2011) pedagogical framings. Recent empirical studies include educators' understandings of pedagogies after finishing an Islamic teacher education programme (Memon, Chown & Alkouatli, 2020), mosque-school educators' perspectives and practices (Alkouatli & Vadeboncoeur, 2018), youth identity formation in the United Kingdom and Kuwait (Sahin, 2014) and pedagogies at a weekend madrasa in Singapore (Rustham, Arifin & Abd Rashid, 2012). Studies on specific pedagogies include dialogic halaqah as a transformative pedagogy (Ahmed, 2019) and memorisation with and without understanding (Boyle, 2006; Gent & Muhammad, 2019). This chapter builds upon existing literature to offer some distinct pedagogical approaches to teaching Islam in the minority-Muslim (Canadian) context.

Methodology

This chapter features data from an interpretive study that engaged 35 Canadian Sunni Muslim educators in semi-structured interviews and halaqat circles (Ahmed, 2019) inquiring into what pedagogies they described using to teach Islam to Canadian children and youth. These educators taught in Islamic elementary schools, mosque/weekend schools and on a freelance basis. All people and place names are pseudonyms. Approximately 30 hours of audio-recorded talk was transcribed and thematically analysed (Braun & Clarke, 2006) to construct three overarching themes, each articulating a different angle of educators' pedagogies (see Alkouatli, forthcoming). Two sub-themes are described here: *sound pedagogies* and *mis-pedagogies*. While the educators' described their pedagogies specifically in relation to Canadian culture, they themselves hailed from 17 different countries and, as such, their pedagogies may be relevant to educators in a heterogeneous ummah, in a global, technological world.

Canadian Muslim Educators' Pedagogies

Sound pedagogies and mis-pedagogies were part of a larger theme that characterised pedagogical change over *time*: "New methods have been developed" (Yassine), over *place*: "The way how I *learned* Islam [back home] is not like how I'm *teaching* Islam now [in Canada]" (Hana) and over diversities of students' "attitudes, backgrounds, and life circumstances" (Jina). In light of changing contexts, sound pedagogies can and must, be engaging to children in a particular time and place. Full-time schoolteacher Asifa described, "At this time—in this era and generation—creativity is very important. You can have it be *boring*; you have to *attract* them to the religion!" Ineffective pedagogies, referred to here as mis-pedagogies, included those that faltered at the intersection between the complex, esoteric (*ghaybiat*) nature of Islamic material and an age of materialism, reason and secular epistemic hegemony (Alkouatli, 2020). Fatima asserted that educators cannot answer children's questions by simply stating,

> This is what's written in our Qur'an; this is what's written in our Sunnah—and that's it. If you do *this*, you go to *Jennah* [heaven]. If you do *that*, you go to *Nar* [fire]. We cannot tell them that!

Instead, Fatima described helping young Muslims inquire, reason and construct a 'why' relevant to their own lives: "They are living in a reasonable world. What if this *why* is not shaped well? They have to be mentally and emotionally satisfied with the answer." As such, educators must employ nuanced pedagogies to help a tech-savvy generation of self-learners make sense of Islam relevant to their lives, here and now.

'Connecting Islam to Negative Feelings' and Other Mis-pedagogies

Mis-pedagogies might be premised on good intentions, but the educators asserted that they were not methodologically effective. They involved ways of engaging with the primary sources, teachers' methods and pedagogies that equivocate, being more effective or less effective depending on how they are employed. Overarchingly, Halima critiqued many pedagogies as "connecting the Islamic study with the negative feelings of the child."

Teaching Islam as Ancient, Irrelevant, Negative and Difficult

Many educators critiqued the ways in which Islam in general, and the Qur'an and Sunnah in particular, were presented to children. Abid described, "Some people teach Qur'an as if it's something that is very old, outdated, or not for this era! That's not true!" Fatima recounted that people suggest Islam is *history*, not meant for now. Jina described that some contemporary Arabic media perpetuate an antiquated image of Islam: "Some sheikhs come up with a *fatwa* [legal ruling]—a very, very old fatwa—and start arguing about it! *My* mind does not accept such fatwas. So how would students here [in Canada] recognize them?" Jina described that even having been raised in a Muslim country (Morocco), she herself could not accept outdated rulings, so how could a young Canadian Muslim?

Compounding the problem of ancient irrelevance, Halima described the problem of negativity, which she described as happening all over the world: "This is where our problem lies: we do not remember the *deen* [Islam] except when a negative thing comes up!" Halima emphasised that neither student

6 Claire Alkouatli

nor teacher gets much out of negative learning, which may, in fact, push children away. Some teachers threaten: "'He *needs* to memorize!' And if he doesn't memorize—what? He will have punishment or something?" Halima lamented that this type of learning is not only painful in this life, but teachers are also threatening children that the next life will be painful, prompting Halima to query, "So what are we giving the child? There is no desire for the child to look forward to the religion!" Instead, she encouraged teachers to connect Islam to *positive* emotions and *taqwa* (God-consciousness) "to create the elements for them to connect and reflect *all* time—not only when they're doing something wrong."

Educators raised the problems of technicality and difficulty. Abid described that while correct recitation of the Qur'an is important, practical use is more important than theory:

> Teach them proper *tajwid* [pronunciation] without focusing on the *theory* but on the *practice*. [...] I just tell them to repeat the verses exactly like I am saying them. Then, when they say it later, they will know that what they are doing is called *tajwid*. If you give them too much theory of tajwid, chances are they won't be interested.

As such, proper pronunciation, tajwid, comes by engaging with it. Fatima expressed a similar concept in terms of Islamic studies:

> Can you imagine a child of five years and you tell him *aqidah* [creed]? Like, *what*? [...] "What's aqidah? Why should I learn about aqidah? I'm in Canada. I want to play! I want to draw! I want to listen to music! I want to have fun!"

In expressing the point that educators must not present Islamic material as technical and difficult, Fatima simultaneously underlined the Canadian cultural relevance of play and active learning. "Giving the child those names from the very beginning will give him that message that Islam something complicated, very hard, and boring. [...] He will pretend that he is listening. But he is not listening." Instead, Fatima advised, "So teach them everything that you want. Plant the seeds first. And then when they are ready, by the age of 11 or 12, 'Yes, this is Islam. This is aqidah!'" Here, the two educators emphasised a similar point: engage learners with the technically correct aspects *in practice*; later, they can study the theory behind those aspects.

Ineffective Methods: Skills, Stuffing and Forcing

A second major issue involved teacher methods. "What are the ingredients that we are actually making our lessons out of? Our *way* is very important" (Rasha). A challenge in Canadian Islamic schools is that "[t]hey hire anybody who speaks Arabic—without any [pedagogic] skills" (Halima). A related mis-pedagogy involved *informational stuffing*, which Faris described as an inter-generational problem, whereby parents were worried their children were losing Islam: "And they want to just *stuff* them with it and hope that they will somehow hold onto it. But this is not organic!" Instead, Faris identified that stuffing may actually increase a young person's sense of disconnection with Islam. "And that is what our Islamic education is doing, as of now, in most settings." Here, while the educational intention may be to have young Muslims learn and love Islam, the pedagogy of stuffing may have the opposite effect.

Many educators pointed out the widespread mis-pedagogy of teaching by *force* rather than by *choice*: "I have seen so many teachers, they teach by force and they do it wrong!" (Hana). Layla described force as liable to "mess up" children's formative early years: "'Go make *wudu* [ablution] and pray!' Okay, he would go make wudu and pray—but he is doing yoga, he is not praying! Prayer has to come from the heart." Instead, she presented an alternative way: *inviting* young people to participate in the ritual practices and *encouraging* them to participate when they are ready.

> Let's say they are 20 and now they *want* to pray because now the religion hits the heart, it is okay, because Allah (﷽) can *forgive* those [earlier] years. But if we mess up those years by forcing them, I think they will never reach the time where they will *love* it.

In other words, choice, agency and love—not force—will move a young person towards loving prayers as essential ways of communicating with God: "I think *that* is what Allah (﷽) wants," Layla said.

Equivocal Pedagogies: False Choice and Rewards

Beyond ineffective pedagogies, there was a category of *equivocal pedagogies* or pedagogies of widely differing value dependent on how they were used. While many of the educators mentioned the importance of choice, an insidious type of choice—*false choice*—was an equivocal pedagogy characterised by internal contradiction whereby the educators framed something as a choice, but it was not a free, authentic choice because it was laced with coercion. Hana described saying to the students, "You have the right to *choose*—even Allah gave you the right to choose [between] the correct way and the wrong way!" This begins well and echoes the literature whereby Sahin (2017) described inherent agency in our human nature (*fitra*), whereby "the Qur'an assigns a crucial role to human agency to accept a moral responsibility for looking after and caring for oneself" (p. 133). But then Hana followed up her emphasis on choice with more coercive questions:

> "What do you think, is getting to *Jannah* [heaven] much better or going to *Jahannam* [hell]?" You have to show them these two ways: "When you get in Jahannam, it is fire; you get burned. How do you feel? Is it

8 *Claire Alkouatli*

pain?" "Yeah, it is pain." "Okay, when you go to Jannah, whatever you wish for, you find it. Is that not nice?" They say, "Yeah, nice!"

This dialogue begs two questions: who would choose burning pain over something nice? And what emotions would this speech evoke in the child? Likewise, Layla described telling her students,

> Look, you are children now; nobody is forcing you to pray, not even Allah (☀). But if you pray at this age, you are guaranteeing your parents Jannah. Do you want to see your parents happy in Jannah? Because they will get Jannah just because of you!

What child would not want to make their parents happy? And is sending your parents to heaven versus not sending your parents to heaven a fair choice to offer a child? Layla summarised by equivocating, "Even though they are not making a choice, it should be a choice."

A contested and equivocal pedagogy was whether or not to give children rewards. Hala spoke about giving her students chocolates, small toys or balloons so that they would enjoy attending school. Dalia mentioned telling the students, "This is prayer time. We have to respect Allah. And if you pray in a good way, I will give you a gift!" She referred to this as *forcing* the children "in a good way." Halima, on the other hand, outright rejected the idea of rewarding children, saying,

> I am totally against rewards; I don't believe in it because it will never show anything and soon they will start hating coming to school because they're not as good in some areas as others, while they have their skills in different areas!

She elaborated that rewarding children diminished the fact that each child has something to contribute and each child has something to work on. Offering a common, instrumental perspective, Yassine linked earthly rewards to divine ones: "Allah gives us reward for everything that we will do. And so, of course, we should reward our children in the school when they do good" So, I asked Yassine, "But sometimes Allah will give us something *very* difficult that we have to deal with. You only realize later that it *was* the reward, because it didn't taste like chocolate or anything!" Yassine's reply revealed a perspective derived from the Qur'an:

> Allah tells us: "I will give you challenges and hardships in this world." So, once you are ready for this challenge, whatever trouble, whatever hardship, comes your way, then it is easy for you! But if you think: "I will have all the luxuries and everything!" when any trouble comes to you, then you get depressed.

Here, Yassine described a deeper mindset, whereby seeing challenges as connection points to God may make them easier to deal with. Yusr offered that Muslims have endured hardships throughout history—and, on a longer historical timeline, previous prophets too—yet they were always supported in the end. Marya concurred, "No matter what happens, we cannot lose hope. Life will get better because that's what Allah said!" Within an Islamic frame, then, rewarding children was both equivocal and complex: educators acknowledged that reward-giving may be a divine pedagogy, sometimes coming in the form of challenges. Educators might help children develop an Islamic resilience perspective, whereby hardships are part of life and divine challenges to be endured with patience, towards self-transformation as the reward itself.

"I Don't Want You Just Writing a Test" and Other Sound Pedagogies

If mis-pedagogies hindered the educators' efforts in making Islam exciting, here and now, sound pedagogies aimed for the opposite. Asifa's quote in this title referred to her assertion that pedagogies of Islamic education can, and must, transcend the ordinary scholastic towards being active, attractive and creative. Hamza described getting Islamic education out of the classroom and into the outdoors: "We don't want to teach Islam as any other subject in school. Islam is not a *set of information*; a *subject* to be learned, like math and history." Instead, Islam is best taught through living it, along with other people who live it well. In this section, educators share sound, engaging, tried-and-true pedagogical approaches.

Educator Responsiveness to Learner Uniqueness

Educators described forging relationships with students by responding to their concerns and passions, in interaction with the Canadian cultural context. Layla detailed keeping up with trends, new music and living the contemporary culture, along with the young learners around her:

> I always listen to what they say; to what they want to do. [...] When the kids want to talk to me about something, I don't block them! I want to show them, especially here in Canada, that you can be a Canadian—do whatever a Canadian will do—just your faith is different.

Marya described encouraging children to discuss topics of interest to them: "When they talk about things *they* know, then they will learn better." Jina described working on interpersonal skills: "Choosing topics that are relevant to their everyday life—this is very, very important—topics that they need to know about, helping them improve their interpersonal skills; how to be self-confident." She emphasised staying close to the learners as they grow and understanding their concerns. Attending to the child's interests includes recognising the uniqueness of each one, as Fatima said, "Each child develops in his or her own way. So, I have to know what this child is interested in. And

10 *Claire Alkouatli*

from that entrance, I can teach him whatever." She elaborated an emergent approach:

> Let's say a child is so interested in music. Why can't I teach him what I want to teach him about Islam through music? I cannot go and tell him, "Music is haram! No, put your music and instruments away! Allah is the greatest. You have to make wudu; you have to pray five times a day, you have to listen to your parents." Is this going to make him listen? No way! But if I say, "Okay, how about singing songs—Islamic songs—while playing your best instrument? [...] Instead of five little *ducks*, five little *prayers*!" [...] He can receive the information through the words and music!

Here, Fatima described engaging children in Islamic content using pedagogies revolving around the child's own interests. Working with individual interest and talent was reported in descriptions of Muhammad's pedagogy (Ramadan, 2007; Sahin, 2014), and thus educator responsiveness to learner uniqueness may be considered intrinsic to an *Islamic* pedagogy, in interaction with a learner's local context.

Open Dialogue

Educators described including in the day's lesson time for open, context-related dialogue in making sense of Islamic material together. Hamza invited the students to decide the day's lesson topic and then engage in discussion: "Students bring their own topics and they share it with the class, I always try to make sure everyone in class gets heard." He pointed out an aspect of Qur'anic pedagogy, whereby Allah talks to us in the Qur'an in the "form of a discussion." This point echoes Sahin's (2014) description of the pedagogic character of the Qur'an, expressing its central message through key narratives formed out of a myriad of dialogues, which "nurtures human spiritual development" (p. 16). Nour identified a pedagogic function of free time as being time to make connections between content and life. Conducting group dialogue on Islamic topics of interest to learners has been examined as pedagogy by Ahmed (2019) in a British educational context, whereby, "Dialogic halaqah can enable young Muslims to harness and embrace their double-consciousness and use their Islamic worldview to carve out personalised conceptualisations of their faith that have meaning for their lifeworlds" (p. 657).

Discovery Learning

Discovering alone, in small groups and in relationship with a teacher are contemporary pedagogical approaches aimed at meaning making. When teaching social etiquette practices, Sideen had the children take home a logbook to record their actions, as well as other people's *re*actions: "Try to read what the other person's body language is, and record it. And then tell me, 'What did you feel? How did they feel?'" In class, they would explore principles in imagined situations and role-playing: "They are coming up with the ideas [...], I think it sticks a lot better than me *instructing* them to do this or do that."

One of Faris' approaches to studying the Qur'an involved the students searching for key points in the verses: "Sometimes I let *them* identify the take home message for themselves. Other times, after some discussion, I would specify, this is what I want you to note down." Similarly, one of Abid's pedagogical approaches to the Qur'an was a type of thematic treasure hunt, whereby together they would read a surah, discuss its major themes and then Abid would invite the children to find echoes of the themes themselves:

> Surah Al Nahl. One of the major themes of this surah is the *na'ma*; the favors of Allah (☀) and His blessings. "I want you to find this blessing." And I give them time. [...] We use the English translation and also the Arabic. And everyone finds something! Because there are so many blessings in there!

While many of the educators emphasised an active process of meaning making, Nour said that meaning and reason within Islamic teachings cannot always be taught directly: students "must learn and discover by themselves."

Bringing Islam Alive Here and Now

Diametrically addressing the problems of teaching Islam as if it were ancient, irrelevant, negative and difficult was to make it timely, relevant, positive and easy. Marya identified the ancientness of the Qur'an as highlighting its miraculous nature: "The miracle of Qur'an is that it is for every time, place, and people." A source of wisdom to be applied here and now, many of the educators described, "Allah is not giving us these stories as just bedtime stories" (Sharifa). "Don't take the story as a story [...] No! There is always a connection in real life" (Huda). An educator's responsibility is to help young people make meaning of Islamic stories relevant to here and now. Fatima related Islam to feeding birds outside—"Islam teaches us how to be merciful with animals"—as part of a greater morality:

> *This is Islam.* You don't teach Islam that was thousands of years ago [...] that Islam is like space: something far beyond, something that we're not reaching, something that is not among us on earth. No—we live with it!

Part of helping learners make real-life connections is seeing the Islamic in the seemingly non-Islamic, and Saba described the importance of adults helping children critically discern. She gave an example of Muslim children

12   Claire Alkouatli

watching a mainstream movie along with non-Muslim peers and later analysing it Islamically:

> You're still going to let them watch because other kids are watching. But you're going to give them the *principles* of Islam through this movie: how they should be doing things, how they should be careful, how they should react to it, how *good* it is—in some parts—and how close it is to Islam in those parts. Always connect things to Islam.

Here, Saba highlighted cultivating Islamic analysis, discerning Islamic principles and appreciation of media in general. Thinking together with children is a sound pedagogy, as described by Cam (1995): "If we want children to learn how to think for themselves, we should engage them in thinking together" (p. 17).

Implications, Recommendations and Conclusions

Contemporary Muslim educators are charged with a precious endeavour: educating faithful young Muslims who are global citizens and exemplary leaders, ushering humanity forward, as Nasr (2012) described as our responsibility "in light of our being God's vicegerents" (p. 13). Key to this endeavour are pedagogies infused with Islamic principles, enacted through Islamic practices, in dynamic interaction with a prevailing cultural moment, which hold significant potential for cognitive, social-emotional and spiritual development. This is an area for further research. The educators in this study provided contextually relevant suggestions for pedagogies towards deep learning, empowered by individual and group creativity and intentional Islamic purpose. They illustrated that cultural context matters in teaching Islam. Most were highly mindful of the contemporary Canadian context while, simultaneously, their diverse cultures of origin came to bear on their pedagogies.

A first implication is that approaches to teaching Islam must be simultaneously local *and* global, whereby educators study the immediate cultural context in light of the international Muslim ummah to extract principles and practices from both to inform their pedagogies. A second implication is that educators play vital roles in helping young Muslims practically and conceptually integrate the differing worlds in which they live. From here, there are three overarching pedagogical recommendations for Muslim educators (see Table 1.1).

1. Critically analyse the multiple cultural contexts young Muslims inhabit, together with the learners themselves, while centring Islamic principles, practices and pedagogies (described in Alkouatli, forthcoming). Make your pedagogies relevant to the cultures of public schools, after-school activities, homes, neighbourhoods, countries and communities

Sound Pedagogies and Mis-pedagogies 13

Table 1.1 Pedagogical recommendations for educators and school administrators

Pedagogic Approach	*Encourage Sound Pedagogies*	*Notice Mis-pedagogies*	*Instead...*
1. Critically + creatively analyse cultural contexts in light of Islamic principles.	Centre Islamic principles + practices while employing appropriate dominant-culture pedagogies.	Avoid pedagogic approaches irrelevant to contemporary context + to transformative Islamic principles.	Interrogate your own pedagogical practices: why do you use certain ones? Engage learners in transformative pedagogies, no matter their source.
	Explore the wider world within Islamic content; explore Islamic content within the wider world.	Avoid presenting Islam as if it is outdated and difficult.	Highlight contemporary relevance of Islamic principles + practices towards helping learners integrate world views.
		Avoid connecting Islam to negative feelings.	Connect Islamic principles and practices with positive emotions, like discovery, joy, belonging.
2. Engage in active pedagogies that centre the learner/ educator/ contexts.	Engage learners in dialogue, discovery + inquiry to make deeper meaning. Support learners in conducting research + discovering for themselves.	Avoid 'stuffing' learners with information.	Invite learners to explore + discuss material together in meaning making with conscious intentionality.
3. Prepare young Muslims for responsibility + leadership.	Provide chances to make decisions for themselves. Invite learners to participate + lead + engage in public speaking.	Avoid forcing learners or giving them false choices. Be aware of pedagogies that equivocate (like rewards).	Provide learners with real, authentic choices as part of their *iktilaf* (divine responsibility). Constructively reorient these pedagogies to highlight their deeper purposes + potentials.

14 Claire Alkouatli

of origin. For example, many of these educators drew pedagogies from the dominant Canadian culture to teach Islam, like play and independent research. Sites of Islamic education need to be places where young Muslims hone important life skills *through* engagement with Islamic material.

2. Engage in active pedagogies that centre both the learners' and the educator's interests. Build time within the school day for children to lead and to dialogue with other learners on Islamic topics meaningful to them to develop self- and social awareness and expressive abilities. If educators learn about new trends, video games, pop culture, black holes, vast space and other topics in which the students are interested, they can use these topics as springboards for exploring Islamic content. Faris described how he was teaching a group of youth in a mosque school a Qur'anic verse on forgiveness when suddenly a boy got up and started to draw a diagram on the whiteboard. The boy was joined by a couple more boys and, together, they conceptually mapped "forgiveness" using mathematical equations derived from their public-school learning (see Figure 1.1). Faris supported what was a learner-led moment of meaning making. In helping young Muslims make sense of Islamic material in meaningful ways, our pedagogic approaches must be dynamically related to learners' interests.

3. The two previous recommendations—helping young Muslims develop analytic skills, vision, self-reflection/expression and Islamic reasoning—are foundational for a third: preparing young Muslims for responsibility and leadership in the larger society. Providing chances for boys and

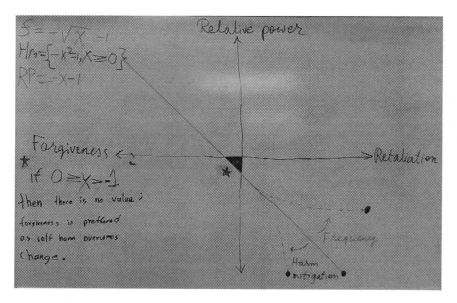

Figure 1.1 An example of students making meaning of Islamic concepts.

girls to make real decisions; to engage in research, dialogue and public speaking; and to lead others (including in acts of worship) are chances to practice living Islam in a complicated world. Yet, active and analytic learning for responsibility and leadership is not just leaving young people to discover for themselves, bereft of guidance. The educator's role is key. Faris explained how he would facilitate some independent exploration of the Qur'an, in addition to highlighting key verses that he wanted his students to know and remember: "I want you to memorize these words. These are beautiful and these are important." Adult guidance of the youngest members of our community is vitally important.

As this chapter has demonstrated, critical, reflective and creative pedagogies aim towards self-reflection, refinement and transformation. Moreover, they are rooted in Islamic pedagogical history: "The critical/reflective educational heritage of Islam shaping its devotional spirituality needs to be reclaimed so that young Muslims have a better chance to develop proper Islamic literacy, mature faith formation and engage creatively with the world around them" (Sahin, 2018, p. 4). Every Muslim learner and educator is situated in a particular cultural place and time, yet we all engage with the world through the internet, social media, globalisation, 'international' school curricula and travel. We live in multiple worlds and multiple *world views*. Helping young people employ an Islamic conceptual framework to analyse the best ideas, principles and practices of each of these worlds, and apply them towards larger social contribution, is an intrinsic quality of successful Muslim communities over time and an enduring legacy for Muslim educators.

Note

1 The words *peace and blessings be upon him*, uttered after Muhammad's name, are indicated by these Arabic words: ﷺ. Similarly, after the word Allah, ﷻ denotes most glorified, most high.

References

Abu Ghuddah, A.F. (2017). *Prophet Muhammad: The teacher. An insight into his teaching methods* (trans. M. Z. Abu Ghuddah). UK: Awakening Publications.

Ahmed, F. (2019). The potential of halaqah to be a transformative Islamic dialogic pedagogy. In N. Mercer, R. Wegerif & L. Major (Eds.). *The Routledge international handbook of research on dialogic education* (pp. 647–659). New York, NY: Routledge.

Ajem, R. & Memon, N. (2011). *Principles of Islamic pedagogy, a teacher's manual.* Islamic Teacher Education Program. Canada: Razi Group.

Alkouatli, C. (forthcoming). Muslim educators' pedagogies: Tools for self and social transformation. Harvard Educational Review

Alkouatli, C. (2020). An Islamic pedagogic instance in Canadian context: Towards epistemic multicentrism. In A. Abdi (Ed.). *Critical theorizations of education* (pp. 197–211). Leiden, the Netherlands: Brill Publishers.

16 *Claire Alkouatli*

Alkouatli, C. & Vadeboncoeur, J. A. (2018). Potential reproduction and renewal in a weekend mosque school in Canada: Educators' perspectives of learning and development. *Learning, Culture and Social Interaction, 19*: 29–39.

Al-Sadan, I.A. (1997). *An investigative study of the present professional preparation for teachers in primary schools in Saudi Arabia, with especial reference to Islamic and Arabic subjects* (Doctoral dissertation). Retrieved from University of Hull Digital Repository, https://hydra.hull.ac.uk/resources/hull:8001 on 22 October 2015.

Boyle, H. (2006). Memorization and learning in Islamic schools. *Comparative Education Review, 50*(3), 478–495.

Braun, V. & Clarke, V. (2006). Using thematic analysis in psychology. *Qualitative Research in Psychology, 3*(2), 77–101.

Cam, P. (1995). *Thinking together: Philosophical inquiry for the classroom.* Alexandria, NSW: Hale & Iremonger.

Daniels, H. (2016). *Vygotsky and pedagogy* (1st ed.). New York: Routledge.

Fullan, M. & Langworthy, M. (2014). *A rich seam: How new pedagogies find deep learning.* London: Pearson.

Gent, B. & Muhammad, A. (2019). Memorising and reciting a text without understanding its meaning: A multi-faceted consideration of this practice with particular reference to the Qur'an. *Religions, 10*(7), 425.

Memon, N.A., Chown, D. & Alkouatli, C. (2020). Descriptions and enactments of Islamic pedagogy: Reflections of alumni from an Islamic teacher education programme. *Pedagogy, Culture & Society, 29*(4): 631–649.

Mogra, I. (2010). Teachers and teaching: A contemporary Muslim understanding. *Religious Education, 105*(3), 317–329.

Nasr, S.H. (2012). Islamic pedagogy: An interview. *Islam & Science, 10*(1), 7–24.

Ramadan, T. (2007). *In the footsteps of the Prophet: Lessons from the life of Muhammad.* Oxford; New York, NY: Oxford University Press.

Rufai, S.A. (2010). Reviving contemporary Muslim education through Islamic-based teachings and evaluation methods. *Journal of Islam in Asia, 7*(2), 187–214.

Rustham, N., Arifin, M. & Abd Rashid, A. (2012). Teaching methodologies in a weekend madrasah: A study at Jamiyah Education Centre, Singapore. *International Journal of Arts and Commerce, 1*(2), 148–169.

Sahin, A. (2014). *New directions in Islamic education: Pedagogy and identity formation.* Leicestershire, UK: Kube.

Sahin, A. (2017). Education as compassionate transformation: The ethical heart of Islamic pedagogy. In P. Gibbs & O. Gibbs (Eds.). *Pedagogy of compassion at the heart of higher education* (pp. 127–137). Cham: Springer.

Sahin, A. (2018). Critical issues in Islamic education studies: Rethinking Islamic and western liberal secular values of education. *Religions, 9*(11), 335.

Waghid, Y. (2011). *Conceptions of Islamic education: Pedagogical framings.* New York, NY: Peter Lang.

2 Are Contemporary Islamic Education and Their Pedagogical Approaches Fit for Purpose? A Critique and Way Forward

Yahia Baiza

Introduction

All education systems evolve in their respective historical contexts which are, in turn, defined and influenced by socio-political, cultural and ideological factors and positions. So is the case with contemporary Islamic education and pedagogical approach. In Muslim societies, religion has always been a dominating force that influences almost all aspects of life. The centrality of God's presence and His words (the Qurʾan) and the Prophet Muhammad's *Sunna*, mainly studied through his *hadith*, have served as the main source of guidance and motivation for the pursuit of knowledge and education throughout Muslim history. It was a customary tradition for students to travel long and short distances to attend the educational circles of scholars and acquire knowledge and expertise in the fields of their interests. Due to the dearth of pens, paper and printed books, the teaching method was primarily based on oral instruction for which students had to rely on the power of their memory. Additional methods of learning included argumentative discussions (*munazara*) between students, as well as scholars themselves. Students were naturally required to learn teachers' lectures by heart and internalise them by rote learning so they could reproduce them at any time, particularly in the absence of their masters, with utmost accuracy as far as humanly possible. Therefore, oral instruction, memorisation by heart and teacher-centred pedagogical approach become the dominant teaching and learning methods and a key feature of Muslim education.

The situation, however, has significantly changed in the modern era. The printing press in the industrial era, and the advancement of modern communication and information technology and the invention of the Internet in recent decades have revolutionised the state of education, particularly access to and the dissemination of information and knowledge. These advancements have also led to the rise of a plethora of teaching and learning theories, approaches and models, resulting from discoveries in linguistic studies, psychology, sociology, economy and modern communication technology. Currently, there is a wide range of teaching and learning theories and approaches, which have shifted the focus of teaching and learning from teacher to student, from content to process, from rote learning to critical

DOI: 10.4324/9781003193432-3

18   *Yahia Baiza*

thinking and from accurate reproduction to knowledge management. These developments have changed the role of teachers from dictators of knowledge to guides, planners and facilitators, whereas students' roles have changed from passive recipients of knowledge to active explorers and critical thinkers.

Contemporary Muslim communities are making every effort to create modern and vibrant educational institutions that could energise the rise of new Islamic civilisations and cultures. To achieve this goal, they often link their current efforts with the civilisations and intellectual traditions of the past on the one hand and to adapt the new scientific achievements to the needs of their societies and indigenous cultures and Islamic traditions on the other. Within this hybrid framework, the development of an overarching concept and approach for education and teaching is of paramount importance. To answer the overarching question of whether contemporary Islamic education and pedagogy are fit for purpose, being posed earlier, it is important to develop an in-depth understanding of the history of Muslim intellectual traditions, especially the historicity of education, and teaching and learning methods, which provide the foundation and guiding principles for the contemporary debates and efforts in developing a modern and vibrant Islamic education and pedagogy. This investigation goes deep beyond the outward appearance of the history of Muslim intellectual traditions and institutions of learning and gives importance to the inward reality that matters most.

Muslim Traditions of Learning: Their Historicity and Internal Dynamism

In traditional Islamic education, pedagogical approaches revolve around the concept and nature of knowledge. Muslims associate the nature and origin of knowledge (*ʿilm* in Arabic) to God. They believe that God is the absolute source of knowledge, which is mediated to people through God's prophets. To prove this view, Muslims often refer to the Qurʾanic verses. In one of such verses, the Qurʾan states, "And He [Allah] taught Adam all the names, then showed them to the angels, saying: Inform Me of the names of these, if you are truthful" (Qurʾan, 2: 31). This verse introduces God as the teacher of Adam. In their interpretation of the verse, Muslims believe that God taught Adam the names and meaning of all things on Earth which the angels did not know. Also, Muslims believe that the concepts of knowledge and education—i.e., reading, writing and teaching—are present in the very first verses of the Qurʾan. In the year 610 CE, while the Prophet was in a state of meditation in a cave on Mount Hira, known as the Cave of Hira, Angel Gabriel visited the Prophet and revealed to him the first verses of what later came to be termed the 'Qurʾan.' In these verses, God commanded Muhammad son of Abdullah (the full name of the Prophet Muhammad before his designation as the Prophet of God) to "[r]ead in the name of your Lord.... Who taught [man to write] by the pen. Taught man what he knew not" (Qurʾan, 96: 1–5). These verses led Muslims to believe that knowledge is a creation and a bounteous act of God. Muslims also refer to the Prophet as the first teacher in Islam and the Prophet's Mosque (Masjid Rasul Allah) as the first Muslim institution of learning (Baiza, 2018b: 5). These events marked the beginning of a new tradition of learning, inspired by divine revelation, the Qur'an and the Prophet's manner of living. The Qur'an and the *Sunna* have become the two most important sources of knowledge and central pillars of education for Muslims. Muslims developed an organised system of learning, from elementary to higher degrees of learning, centuries after the death of the Prophet (d. 632 AD). Therefore, it is important to explore and develop a deeper understanding of how Muslims' traditions of learning and teaching evolved throughout history.

A series of major intellectual developments in the second half of the 2nd century after the *hijra* marked a significant change in Muslims' intellectual and educational traditions of learning. This phase is generally characterised by a rigorous process of translation of intellectual and scientific texts from other civilisations, cultures and languages into Arabic. Yahia Baiza writes that the Barmak family, Khalid Barmaki and his son Yahya Barmaki, from the northern province of Balkh in modern-day Afghanistan, played a leading role in establishing a translation centre (*Dar al-Tarjumah*) in the early ʿAbbasid caliphate (Baiza, 2018a: 85–86). Caliph Harun al-Rashid (r. 169–193/786–809) appointed Yahya Barmaki as his vizier. Under Yahya's supervision, scientific works were translated from Greek, Syriac, Hindi and Persian and other languages into Arabic. Yahya himself is believed to have written a book on astronomy and translated a book of medicine from Hindi into Arabic. Yahya's son, Moosa, was also engaged in translation works (Ghubar, 1957: 87–88). Soon after, Harun al-Rashid approved the establishment of *Dar al-Tarjumah* and Bayt al-Hikmah (House of Wisdom), also known as *Khazanat al-Hikmah* (Treasury of Wisdom). The translation works reached the height of their fame under Caliph al-Maʾmun (r. 197–218/813–833; Baiza, 2018a: 86).

Not far from Baghdad, the Fatimids, a Shiʿi Ismaili caliphate, developed parallel institutions of learning, magnificent libraries and research centres. The Fatimid al-Azhar Congregation Mosque (*Masjid Jamiʿ*), built during the years of 359/970 and 361/972, marked the first institution of higher learning (Kasa'i, 2008). The Fatimids also built libraries, with more than a million books, which were the richest in the world. According to al-Mawrizi's account, the Fatimid's Khazana al-Kutub alone held 601,000 books, among which there were 1,200 volumes of *Taʾrikh Tabari* (1998: 408–409). Retrospectively, the Fatimid's *Jamiʿ al-Azhar*, which is recognised to be the first university in the world, and the Fatimid libraries, with a culture of intellectual pluralism, attracted scientists and scholars from all fields and places. The translated texts, the development of libraries, research centres and institutions of higher learning provided sufficient intellectual and educational materials for Muslim intellectuals and researchers to contribute original research on various fields of knowledge of the time, from physics to metaphysics and philosophy, and develop their specific method of teaching and transmission of knowledge.

20 *Yahia Baiza*

The overall teaching and learning format was based on a direct one-to-one relationship between the master/teacher (*'alim*) and the disciple/learner (*talib*). The location of education varied from caliphal palaces, private homes and bookshops to mosques and *madrasa*s. The master would begin his session with a plenary lecture and continue with individual tutorials. The plenary session was held in the form of *halqa* (circle), session (*majlis*) and *zawiya* (corner), as scholars/teachers were sitting (*jalasa*) on the floor while their students were sitting in front of them in a circle (*halqa*) (Baiza, 2015: 190–91; Baiza, 2018a: 83). In large congregation mosques, many scholars were holding simultaneous teaching circles in different corners of the mosque. After receiving general instructions, students were free to work on the themes of the lectures on their own or with their peers. Their primary aim was to understand, memorise and internalised the lectures and their themes. Then, each student would present his learning to the master, who would either approve or give further instruction and clarification. The curriculum was not limited by the number of subjects and time. Rather, students' aptitudes, abilities and interests would dictate the content of the curriculum and the pace of the teaching and learning process. The process would continue until students mastered the entire subject/book and the scholar would transmit his knowledge to them. The institutions of higher learning, mainly in the form of the *madrasa* education system, with a fixed curriculum, textbooks, paid teachers and scholarships for students flourished in the 5th/11th century, when Nizam al-Mulk (d. 1092), the Seljuqid *vizier*, built a series of *madrasa*s in Baghdad, Persia and Khurasan, which came to be known as *Nizamiyya*, named after Nizam al-Mulk. However, outside the Nizamiyya system, Muslim education and teaching followed the traditional informal pattern.

The Inward Dynamism of Islamic Education and Intellectual Tradition

The inner dynamism of Muslim educational and intellectual traditions demonstrates a continuous tension between different groups of scholars. Even though Muslims regard the Qur'an and the Prophet's *Sunna* as the two main sources of knowledge, sectarian, theological and ideological views of knowledge have had disastrous impacts on education. In exploring and analysing the internal dynamism of Muslims' educational and intellectual traditions, it is important to understand the *'ulema*'s quest for, and will to monopolise, knowledge and use it as an instrument of power to control society and social relationships between people of different religious denominations. Therefore, an understanding of the discourse between knowledge and power is crucial in understanding the internal dynamism of Muslim educational and intellectual traditions.

The *'ulema*'s quest for knowledge and will to power marked a new beginning in the history of religion and polity. The conservative *'ulema*, by claiming to be the successors and heirs of the Prophet's religious authority, appropriated to themselves the role of bearers of "correct" knowledge. The rivalry was widespread, even though it was often understood to be limited to the level of traditionalists versus rationalists. As a typical example, the Qur²anic commentators and interpreters regarded *tafsīr* (the science of Qur²anic exegesis) as the foundation of religion and the highest discipline in the class of transmitted sciences. They viewed their work as the 'queen' of all sciences because it dealt with the knowledge of the Qur²an and *hadith*. On the contrary, jurisconsults (*fuqaha*) viewed their field as the noblest and the queen of all scholarly works because it dealt with the Qur²an, *hadith*, as well as the *shari²ah*, believing that they alone were capable of showing people 'the correct path.' Such self-centred rivalry permeated the spirit of the 5th/11th century (Saleh, 2004: 78–79). To firmly secure their position at the caliphal court and society, the elite class of *ʿulema* needed the support of the caliph.

The *ʿulema*-caliph alliance changed the inclusive spirit of knowledge and education. After establishing an alliance with the ʿAbbasid caliphate, the elite class of Sunni traditionalist *ʿulema* established themselves to the rank of lawmakers. The history of this change dates back to a conflictual situation that emerged between the Muʿtazilite rationalist school and the traditionalist *ʿulema*, especially *ahl-e hadith*, led by Ahmad ibn Hanbal. The Muʿatazilite's argued that the Qur²an is God's created words (*muhadath*) and human rational thinking can investigate, discover and understand the meanings of the divine revelations. By contrast, the Hanbalite and their supporters held a view that the Qur²an is eternal (*qadim*) and hence uncreated and cannot become subject to human rational inquiry. The notion of the createdness and uncreatedness of the Qur²an soon became the doctrinal symbol and a major point of contention between rationalists and traditionalists. To resolve the situation, the ʿAbbasid caliph al-Ma²mun (r. 193–198/809–813) ordered an investigation, known as *mihnah* (inquisition) in 218/833.

The inquisition not only unleashed a series of fierce debates between the two camps but also allowed the conservative *ʿulema* to use violence to suppress the Muʿtazilite and other rationalist schools. After the premature death of Caliph al-Ma²mun, who favoured the Muʿatazilite rationalist view and was keen to somewhat formalise it as the official doctrine of the caliphate, the Muʿtazilite soon became isolated and the Hanbalite group gained the upper hand. Years later, when al-Mutwakkil (r. 232–247/ 847–861) ascended to the throne of the caliphate, he needed the *ʿulema*'s support to bless him with religious legitimacy. Equally, the *ʿulema* was eager to side with the new caliph to suppress the rival Muʿtazilite camp. However, the alliance divided the caliphal power and authority. The *ʿulema* established themselves as the sole authority and lawmakers in all matters of religion, whereas the caliph's power and authority became limited to temporal affairs. Accordingly, the caliph would make every effort to keep the land safe for the *ʿulema* to oversee the implementation of the *shari²ah* and other religious affairs in society. In return, the *ʿulema* would bless the caliph and legitimise his temporal authority. This political alliance was not a good omen for religion and education, as it politicised both religion and knowledge.

22   Yahia Baiza

The unfolding situation had serious consequences, not only for the Muʿta-zilite and rationalists but, more importantly, also for the long-term future of education and intellectual traditions across Muslim societies. The ʿAbbasid caliph al-Qadir bi'llah (r. 380–422/991–1031) escalated the matter further by launching a new project, claiming to restore Sunni Islam. He staged a full-scale war against the rationalists and denounced the Shiʿi interpretation of Islam. In 408/1017, he publically denounced Muʿatazilite and Shiʿi Islam throughout the Abbasid territories. A year later, he wrote three epistles, col-lectively known as *al-Iʿtiqad al-Qadiri* (the Qadirite Creed), which were read out in the caliphal palace (*Dar al-Khilafah*) and in all small and con-gregational mosques. Abu al-Faraj ibn al-Jawzi (d. 597/1200) states that al-Qadir's decree declared,

> The word of God is uncreated (*kalam Allah Taʿala ghayr-e makhluq*) ... and anyone who maintains that it is created is an infidel (*kafir*) and so the shedding of his blood is permissible (*halal al-dam*) ... and this is the view of the People of *Ahl al-Sunna*h and *al-Jamaʿah*.
>
> (ibn al-Jawzi, 1992: 280–281)

The Qadirite Creed and the traditionalists' anti-rationalist position left long-term negative consequences on the Sunni educational institutions and traditions of learning. The new policies forbade argumentative debates (*jidal*) and discussions (*munazirah*) and ordered emulation (*taqlid*) instead (Al-Masʿūdī, 2005, Vol. 5: 253–254). The consequences of the emerging situation were directly felt across the institutions of higher learning and the practice of *ijtihad*, as independent and critical reasoning in matters of juris-prudence. In Sunni Islam, for instance, jurists are only allowed to reason and conduct their *ijtihad* or personal critical thinking within their respective school of jurisprudence or, at best, within the four Sunni schools of *fiqh*. They are not allowed to question the credibility of, let alone to reform, any aspect of the views of the four grand jurists—namely, Abu Hanifah, Malik, Shafiʿ, and Ahmad ibn Hanbal—even though many Sunni jurists are aware of the fact that many issues within each of these schools of *fiqh* are questionable and simply unacceptable, especially in present time. To prevent questioning the works of the four grand jurists, a widespread belief has been developed, saying that grand jurists of the yore knew everything in the best possible way, and there is no need for rethinking what they have already thought out for the community of believers.

The *ulema*-caliphate alliance kept the orthodoxy beyond the realm of sus-picion and criticism, whereas all other branches of Islam and non-Islamic faiths had to be criticised. The *ulema* made sure that blind and uncritical acceptance of other religious traditions are condemned with harsh criticism. As a result, Shiʿi and Sufi schools, as well as philosophers, were criticised and portrayed in the worst possible negative picture. For instance, feeling of hostility towards the Fatimid Shiʿi Ismaili was the key motivation for Salah al-Din Ayubi (d. 1193) to destroy the Fatimid research centres and libraries,

Are Contemporary Islamic Education   23

with an estimated one million books of all kinds of sciences of the time. It is reported that he sold the books for ten years and, at the same time, he threw books into the Nile and into a great heap, which was covered with sand so that a regular "hill of books" was formed (Pedersen, Makdisi, Rahman, & Hillenbrand, 2012). The destruction of such a centre of education and excellence does not lead to a positive impression and legacy for Islamic education. Rather, the ʿAbbasids and the Sunni orthodox ʿulema viewed the destruction of the Fatimid libraries and research centres as a triumph of Sunni Islam. Since then, Cairo has never managed to reach the excellence of the Fatimid era.

Regardless of how many contributions Muslim philosophers and scientists have made in the various fields of rational sciences, from philosophy and astronomy to medicine and mathematics, as Gustav Edmund von Grunebaum states, they did not become part of the fundamental needs and necessities of Muslim civilisations. Worldly knowledge had to conform to selective principles applied by the ʿulema (Reetz, 2010: 109). The ʿulema and the caliphs appreciated only these sciences as much as they could serve the needs of religion and the caliphate. Astronomy and mathematics were good as far as they could determine the direction of the prayer (*qibla*; von Grunebaum, 1955: 221) and predict military victory on the battlefields. The rulers appreciated physicians for the treatment of their illnesses and not for institutionalising their medical knowledge. If any field of rational sciences found favourable treatment, it was in exceptional situations when the ʿulema and temporal rulers were ready to go beyond and against the established strains of orthodoxy (von Grunebaum, 1955: 221). Situations of this kind were not the norm but exceptional moments.

The suppression of rationalism and the promotion of *taqlid* led to the gradual decline of *tahqiq* (the verification of (scientific) proposition by evidential ground). This, in turn, caused a major blow to the quality of teaching and learning. The promotion of *taqlid* opened the space for writing commentaries on the previous original works. It is no surprise that the shift of the spotlight on commentaries pushed original works to the margins. The new generation of 'scholars' began to display their skills in the 'expansion' and 'contraction' of previous commentaries. Therefore, a culture of writing commentary upon commentary upon commentary became a new field of scholarship. As the genre of commentary gained firm root among Muslim scholars, the commentary itself was considered to be a form of *tahqiq* and a new 'scientific' genre. As a result, rationalism and logic began to serve the culture of commentary and the expansion of grand legal works and their commentaries instead of introducing original ideas and expanding the boundaries of existing and new fields of knowledge. Rationalism and logic in the form of philosophy and independent critical thinking and reasoning were not included in the *madrasa* curriculum. However, students could acquire lessons in philosophy independently outside the *madrasa* system.

The prevailing attitude arrested the advancement of knowledge and education across Muslim societies. Being driven away from original research and

24 *Yahia Baiza*

critical thinking, substantial and lasting damages were inflicted to all aspects of education, from curriculum design, production of textbooks to methods of teaching and learning. Muslims realised the rise of new fields of knowledge in the outside world and stagnation inside their own institutions of learning when European empires began their sweeping waves of colonisation of the Muslim countries in the 19th and 20th centuries. Unlike the early period of Islam, when Muslims were actively searching for new sources of knowledge and were keen to appropriate them into their own religious patterns of thought, as Iqbal Muzafar puts it, Muslims in modern time were neither actively seeking new knowledge nor were able to appropriate it into their own matrix (2002: 213). The result was a new enigma, a total perplexity, not knowing what to do and how to respond to European supremacy.

In the modern era, Muslims faced two major questions: why have we come to this point, and what can we do about it? Much of the responses came from the reformists and within the broader framework set by the colonial empires. Muslim societies witnessed the rise of religious and secular reform groups, each with moderate and extremist subgroups. The moderate reformists argued for adopting the European model of education as the second-best alternative until new home-grown and dynamic systems of education could be developed. Sir Syed Ahmed Khan (d. 1898) and Muhammad Iqbal (d. 1938) in India; Sayyid Jamal al-Din al-Afghani (d. 1897) in Afghanistan, India and Egypt; and Muhammad ʿAbduh (d. 1905) and Rashid Rida (d. 1935) in Egypt promoted this line of thinking. Sir Syed established the Aligarh College in India based on the British educational model. Similar reform movements emerged in Turkey (Tanzimat and Young Turk Movement), Central Asia (Young Bukharan and Jadidi) and Afghanistan (Young Afghans). These groups called for the reform of jurisprudential schools of thought, as well as the adoption of the European educational, scientific, economic and political systems to the benefit of Muslim societies. The modernists tried to give a measured response but they had little familiarity with the philosophical and historical underpinnings of European modernity and its secular approach to all aspects of life.

Contrary to moderate reformists, extremist and radical religious groups called for a total rejection of everything that is European, under the pretext of being 'non-Islamic' from the orthodoxy's viewpoint. For instance, Mawlana Abu'l Hasan ʿAli Nadwi (d. 1999), a graduate of Darul Uloom of Nadwat al-ʿUlama in Lucknow, India, regarded Western secularism as an evil. He proposed the dissemination of the Islamic *daʿwa* and propagation of Islamic ethical norms as the only means to combat and defeat this evil (Husain & Ashraft, 1979: 21). The Salafists in Egypt, the Wahabis in Saudi Arabia and Deobandis and Nadwat al-ʿUlama in India pioneered this trend. By initiating a regressive trend, they argued for a return to the early period of Islam. However, despite their resistance, they could not escape the influence of the European modernity and education system. Although following a strictly conservative interpretation of Islam, Darul Uloom Deoband (founded in 1866) adopted the *Dars-e Nizami* curriculum and rejected the inclusion of modern subjects in social sciences, humanities and natural sciences, which could not resist the liberal education system forever. At least, in terms of management, administrative system, examination and awarding of degrees, Darul Uloom Deoband preferred the European administrative model instead to the medieval Muslim tradition of education and the certification of the teaching licence (*ijaza*). Eventually, Dar al-Uloom also established a department of computers in 1996 and English language and literature in 2002 for specialised courses (Ansari, 2016: 105; Reetz, 2010: 117).

Contemporary Islamic Education and Pedagogy

The early modernists' efforts inculcated a new consciousness and awakening across the Muslim countries, most of which gained their independence soon after the Second World War (1939–1945). National independence opened a new chapter, above all, in the field of education and the advancement of modern sciences and technology. The first major step towards this direction was taken in 1977 when King Abdul Aziz University organised the First World Congress on Muslim Education, which brought over 300 Muslim educationists together in Mecca. The participants gave high importance to reconnecting with the pre-colonised identities, as well as making use of modern sciences and technologies. To do so, the gathering introduced a series of new concepts, ideas and action plans that could lead to tangible results with promising impacts on education and Muslim societies, as well as bringing the conservative *ulema* on their side.

The idea of redefining the Islamic concept of education was a major objective of the conference. The conference secretary, Syed Ali Ashraf, stated that the conference seeks to redefine the Islamic concept of education from an Islamic standard viewpoint (Iqbal, 1978: 123). Ismaili Raji al-Faruqi proposed the idea of Islamizing modern social sciences, as a new vision for new Islamic education. A key task in developing and delivering the redefined Islamic education was the development of mechanisms that would not only realise the methods into practice but would also look into how to reconcile orthodoxy with modern scientific developments and draft Islamic education modules from preschool to university levels. On women's education, the conference delegates considered the current co-education system across all levels and many Muslim countries as a Western influence that leads to family fragmentation, delinquency and perversion. Congress recommended an end to this practice and the development of single-sex education instead (Iqbal, 1978: 123).

The concept of Islamisation of knowledge emerged as an ideological and developmental project. Its key protagonists—namely, al-Faruqi, Naquib al-Attas and Sayyed Hossein Nasr—played a leading role in furthering it. Al-Faruqi also played a leading role in the establishment of the International Institute of Islamic Thought in the United States and a network of International Islamic Universities in South Asia, the Far East and several African countries. In a nutshell, as expressed in the works of the named

26 Yahia Baiza

scholars, knowledge in Islam is based on the principle of the unity of God (*tawhid*) and a unified paradigm of knowledge (al-Faruqi, 1981). In Islam, as Seyyed Hussein Nasr says, there is an inseparable link between the sciences of nature and religion (1998: 94). However, Western modernity and its secular approach to all aspects of life have corrupted knowledge by removing its divinity and reducing it to a simple human rational level. As a result of this corruption, Nasr states that although science is legitimate in itself, its role, function and application have not only become illegitimate but also dangerous. This is because modern science lacks a higher form of, metaphysical, knowledge (1998: 14). Similarly, Syed Muhammad al-Naquib al-Attas states that confusion and error in modern knowledge and approaches to education are the primary causes that have led Muslims to an educational and intellectual state of stagnation. As a result, there is a leadership crisis and corruption in Muslim societies (Al-Attas, 1991: 2–3). Nasr adds to this and criticises Muslims for uncritically adopting Western science and education, whereas al-Attas consider the spread of Western secularism, secular education and values from preschool to tertiary levels as serious challenges for Muslims (1991: 46). To remedy modern science, Nasr argues for a spiritual and gnostic approach, stressing the revival of the metaphysical knowledge about nature (1998: 14). Al-Attas approaches the crisis through a tawhidic educational concept and proposes good moral criteria, based on the principle of *tawhid*, in addition to attaining good results in scientific subjects, as an essential part of university education and degree (1991: 46). The ultimate objective of this line of thinking, i.e. Islamisation of knowledge and sciences, is to educate students in a manner and means that would direct them toward the realisation and fulfilment of the twin roles that God has ordained for humanity, i.e. becoming the true servants and vicegerents of God on Earth.

The Islamisation of knowledge project is an apologetic and a reaction rather than a well-thought-out and systematic response to the Western liberal education system. In his criticism of Islamisation of knowledge and its supporters, Seyyed Vali Reza Nasr states that it has been developed in the spirit of political discourse rather than a level-headed academic undertaking, championed by self-styled thinkers who are not specialists in the field. This is why Islamisation of knowledge has been narrowed down to the assorted teaching of the *shariʿah* on a variety of topics. Instead of contributing to knowledge, it has created an enervating disjuncture between faith and knowledge in Islam (1991: 387). A major problem with the Islamisation of knowledge project is that the proposed responses are simplistic, black and white and divisive. Undoubtedly, the Western liberal education system has many gaps, mainly because it is based on a concept of modernity that is the backbone of secularism, which has pushed religion and spiritual morality out of the system. However, a black-and-white response cannot be a solution to the challenge of modernity and the liberal education system. At its best, Islamisation of knowledge and education overlooks the rich mosaic of Muslim cultures and affiliations to various interpretations of Islam, not to speak of religious plurality in Muslim majority countries, and the minority position of Muslims in Muslim minority countries on the other. Also, Islamisation of knowledge is completely ignorant of the internal dynamism of Islamic education and intellectual tradition, especially the factors that led to the stagnation of intellectual thought and the promotion of *taqlid* instead of *tahqiq*, as they were discussed in the previous section. Hence, the Islamisation of knowledge raises more questions than answers.

The Way Forward, Recommendations and Conclusion

This chapter has investigated Islamic education and pedagogy from historical and contemporary perspectives. To avoid the construction of a romantic account of the history of Islamic education and its teaching and learning methods, as well as to prevent a criticism detached from the historical and contemporary realities, it was important to conduct a credible examination of the historicity of Islamic education and the traditions of teaching and learning. Therefore, this investigation had to go deep beyond the outward, smooth and linear appearance of the history of Muslim intellectual traditions and institutions of learning, and to give importance to the inward dynamism and reality that matters most. This study concludes that the traditional *madrasa* and *madrasa*-style Islamic education, as well as modern Islamic education, are not fit for purpose.

This study proposes the concept of 'bio-rational pluralist education' within the broader framework of pluralism as a way forward for Muslim education and pedagogy. As this author has already explained elsewhere, the proposed concept and approach to education treat students as "living rational (bio-rational) beings, with diverse backgrounds and needs (pluralist), and as the true objects of education" (Baiza, 2018c: 11). Despite the diversity of philosophical and conceptual underpinnings across education systems and models, they all agree on one common purpose: to equip young learners with the knowledge, skills and intellectual tools that would enable them to realise what it means to be a human being, regardless of racial, religious, cultural, linguistic and other exterior differences. The realisation of this objective is only possible within the framework of pluralism and the proposed concept of 'bio-rational pluralist education.' The management of students' diverse backgrounds and needs requires a thorough understanding of, and engagement with, religious, cultural, ethnic and racial and linguistic elements in society. The proposed concept and educational approach places students in the centre of the education system and focusses on their educational, intellectual and social needs. Students ought to be the ultimate objective of any education system; otherwise, education turns into a missionary and political tool and loses its education and intellectual character.

Socially, diversity is a given situation. Every society has its cultural, religious, linguistic and ethnic diversity. Gender diversity is the least form of diversity. Hence, diversity is a given and pre-existing phenomenon into which every human being is born. On the contrary, pluralism is not given but an intentional effort that inherently requires tolerance and mutual acceptance at its basic level. Pluralism is not a philosophical text but a living, dynamic and vibrant process that requires constant engagement through constructive dialogue. Dialogue is the most effective tool that transforms diversity into pluralism, the conscious and purposeful management of diversity. Hence, it is important to note that pluralism is not relativism nor the loss or assimilation of one group's identity and heritage to the other. The Qur'an engages with contemporary Abrahamic and non-Abrahamic discourses (Baiza, 2018c, 12) and encourages Muslims to engage in dialogue with people of other nations (*shuʿub*) tribes (*qabaʾil*). The Qur'an says, "O you men! Surely We have created you from a male and a female, and made you nations and tribes that you may know each other" (Qur'an, 49: 13).

The existing traditional and modern Islamic education treats Islam as a 'single text' and not as a lived religion with multiple interpretations. Muslims follow a plurality of interpretations, including the interpretations of the *shariʿah*. The history of Muslim civilisations and the historicity of Muslim intellectual and educational traditions also demonstrate that Muslim societies have developed many different civilisational, intellectual and educational traditions. There has never been a single point of reference to any matter of life, from polity to education, in the past or today. Ignoring the diversity and lived reality of diversity in both Muslim majority and Muslim minority countries remains a major problem in traditional and modern systems of Islamic education.

Modern Islamic education and pedagogy raise more questions than answers. At the higher abstract level, the traditional and modern Islamic education and pedagogy oppose the Western liberal education system and its values, while the education systems of almost all Muslim countries either follow or are heavily influenced by the Western education models in one way or another. However, a black-and-white description of Islamic education, producing 'good men' that obey God and His will for humanity, whereas the Western education system produces 'good citizens' that obey the secular state, are problematic. The irreconcilable nature and content of contemporary Islamic education lead to the creation of a parallel instead of a pluralist and inclusive society. The current Islamic education system divides society between 'good' and 'evil' at worse, and 'good people' and 'good citizen' at best. It deliberately ignores that minorities in Muslim majority countries are 'good people' and 'loyal' to their society and country, though they may not necessarily follow the core religious tenets of the mainstream and dominant Islamic education. The problem is even more acute in Muslim minority countries, where they are expected and required to follow the national curriculum and participate in core educational activities that are developed around secular values or values of non-Islamic belief systems. Currently, the ideological positions of the traditional and modern systems of Islamic education do not help students as to how to treat diversity. Rather, it promotes alienation and disintegration. However, the concept of 'bio-rational pluralist education' brings learners from diverse backgrounds together, without imposing any kind of religious tenets and ideology. The proposed concept accommodates the diverse needs of students in Muslim majority and Muslim minority contexts. Also, it focusses on the educational and scientific needs of students, without dividing knowledge and sciences into 'Islamic' and 'non-Islamic.'

On teacher education, this study specifically recommends a pluralist teacher education model. Pluralist teacher education does not focus on the teacher's gender, religion and cultural background as the primary criteria for recruitment and teaching. Rather it focuses on merit, which encompasses the knowledge base and experience of a teacher. The pluralist teacher education concept does not segregate nor discriminate against students and teachers based on gender, religion and other social backgrounds.

Also, the pluralist teacher education model ensures an inclusive and balanced student-teacher-centred education, as opposed to an exclusively liberal student-centred approach, or traditional Muslim teacher-and-textbook-centred education. The relationship between student and teacher ought to be purposeful, reasonable and balanced. As they both are interrelated, the over-estimation of one over the other will lead to unnatural and educationally counterproductive results.

This model asserts that being a teacher *per se* is not enough to be at the centre of education, as being a student *per se* is not a satisfactory criterion for a student-centred approach. Equally, having a teacher education certificate is not by itself a satisfactory criterion for unquestionable authority, as being enrolled in a school programme as a student is not a satisfactory reason for attracting the spotlight. Also, a teacher is not an authoritative figure nor does she/he have all-around knowledge. A teacher is a person who teaches her/his acquired knowledge, while she/he continuously acquires new knowledge and skills. She/he is in a perpetual state of the teaching and learning process. However, the teacher's position as the transmitter of knowledge must be respected in the classroom and the school environment, so shall be the student's agency.

Bibliography

Al-Attas, Syed M. al-Naquib (1991) "Introduction," in Muhammad Naquib Al-Attas (ed.) *The concept of education in Islam: A framework for an Islamic philosophy of education.* Kuala Lumpur: International Institute of Islamic Thought and Civilization.

Al-Faruqi, Ismail Raji (1977) "Islamizing the Social Sciences." Paper presented at *the First World Conference on Muslim Education*, 31 March–8 April, Mecca.

Al-Faruqi, Ismail Raji (1981) *The Hijrah: The necessity of its Iqamat or Vergegenwartigung.* Kuala Lumpur: Muslim Youth Movement of Malaysia.

Al-Marīzī, Aḥmad b. ʿAlī (1998) *Kitāb al-mawāʿiz wa al-iʿtibār bi-dhikr al-khiṭaṭ wa-al-āthār, al-maʿrūf bil-khiṭaṭ al-Maqrīziyah.* Bairut: Dār al-Kutub al-ʿIlmiyyah.

Al-Masʿūdī, A. (2005) *Murūj al-dhahab wa maʿādin al-jawhar* (Meadows of gold and essence minerals). Vol. 3. Beirut: Al-Maktabah al-Asriyyah.

Ansari, Mohammad Asjad (2016) "Modern education in madrasas: A perspective study of Dar al-Uloom Deoband," in *Asia Pacific Journal of Research*, Vol. 1, No. 44, pp. 101–108.

30　*Yahia Baiza*

Baiza, Yahia (2015) "Les *madrasa*" (fiche No. 82, pp. 190–191), in M. Sebti and D. de Smet (eds.) *100 Fiches pour Comprendre l'islam* [100 Sheets to Understand Islam]. Paris: Bréal.

Baiza, Yahia (2018a) "Islamic education and development of educational traditions and institutions," in Holger Daun and Reza Arjmand (eds.) *Handbook of Islamic education*. Cham: Springer. pp. 77–97.

Baiza, Yahia (2018b) "The learned class ('Ulamāʾ) and education," in Holger Daun and Reza Arjmand (eds.) *Handbook of Islamic education*. Cham: Springer. pp. 113–133.

Baiza, Yahia (2018c) "Navigating education in troubled time: A critical pluralist discourse," in *OXSCIE 2018: Uncertainty, society and education*. Oxford: 2nd Oxford Symposium for Comparative and International Education.

Ghubar, Ghulam Muhammad (1957) "Ẓuhūr wa nufūdh-e Islam wa ʿArab dar Afghanistan, az 22 tā 205 hijrī" (The Rise and influence of Islam and the Arabs in Afghanistan, from 22 to 205 *hijrī*), in Ghulam Muhammad Ghubar (ed.) *Tāʾrīkh-e Afghanistan*. Vol. 3. Kabul: Maṭbūʿah-e Dawlatī. pp. 1–112.

von Grunebaum, Gustav Edmund (1955) *Islam: Essays in the nature and growth of a cultural tradition*. Abingdon: Routledge.

Husain, Syed Sajjad and Ashraft, Syed Ali (1979) *Crisis in Muslim education*. Jeddah: Hodder and Stoughton.

Ibn al-Jawzi (1992) in M. A. Atta (ed.) *al-Muntazim fi tāʾrīkh al-Muluk waʾl amam*. Vol. 15. Beirut: Dar al-Kutub al-ʿIlmiyyah.

Iqbal, Muhammad (1978) "First world congress on Muslim education and its possible implications for British Muslims," in *Learning for Living*, Vol. 17, No. 3, pp. 123–125.

Iqbal, Muzaffar (2002) *Islam and science*. Hampshire: Ashgate.

Kasa'i, Nurollah (2008) "Al-Azhar" Tr. Suheyl Umar, in Wilfred Madelung and Farhad Daftary (Editors-in-Chief) *Encyclopaedia Islamica*. Accessed February 4 2020. https://referenceworks-brillonline-com.iij.idm.oclc.org/entries/encyclopaedia-islamica/*-COM_0324.

Nasr, Seyyed Vali Reza (1991) "Islamization of knowledge: A critical review," in *Islamic Studies*, Vol. 30, No. 3, pp. 387–400.

Nasr, Seyyed Hussein (1998) *Man and nature: The spiritual crisis of modern man*. London: Unwin Hyman Limited.

Pedersen, Johannes, Makdisi, Goerge, Rahman, Munibur, and Hillenbrand, R. (2012) "Madrasa," in Bearman, P. Bianquis, T., Bosworth, C. E., Van Donzel, E., and Heinrichs, W. P. (Editors-in-Chief) *Encyclopaedia of Islam*, Second Edition. Accessed February 4 2021. https://referenceworks-brillonline-com.iij.idm.oclc.org/entries/encyclopaedia-of-islam-2/*-COM_0610

Reetz, Dietrich (2010) "From madrasa to university – The challenges and formats of Islamic education," in Akbar S. Ahmed and Tamara Sonn (Eds) *The sage handbook of Islamic studies*. London: Sage. pp. 106–139.

Saleh, Walid Ahmad (2004) *The formation of classical Tafsir formation: The Qurʾan commentary of al-Thalabi*. Leiden: Brill.

3 Environmental Education and Indonesia's Traditional Islamic Boarding Schools

Curricular and Pedagogical Innovation in the Green Pesantren Initiative

Ahmad Afnan Anshori and Florian Pohl

Introduction

An archipelago with one of the world's most diverse ecosystems, Indonesia is critically affected by environmental destruction. A sharp rise in population numbers exacerbates severe environmental problems that stem from exploiting the country's natural resources. Deforestation practices deplete carbon storage, cause high emissions and add to the persistently high level of air pollution. As a result, the country has become one of the world's largest emitters of greenhouse gases. It is also a major marine polluter with single-use plastics (Jambeck et al., 2015). Damages are not only environmental but also socio-economic. Roughly a third of the nation's population and close to two-thirds of the country's rural poor depend on ecosystem services for their living. Thus, it is not an exaggeration to say that ecological challenges are critical to Indonesia's national stability and the global system. Nevertheless, as in other parts of the Global South, attention to responsible stewardship and sustainable consumption remains weak in Indonesia, where, as a recent report by the World Bank found, "environmental values are not deeply embedded in society" (World Bank, 2014).

Presenting notable curricular, pedagogical and 'green' initiatives in Indonesian *pesantren*, the country's traditional Islamic boarding schools, this chapter proceeds from the assumption that education in general and Islamic schools specifically have a critical role in raising public awareness of environmental problems. More specifically, the chapter has three key objectives. First, we review some of the challenges with introducing environmental education in Islamic schools in a societal context where state and local government leadership is sorely lacking. We then discuss the example of the *Pesantren Hijau* or Green Pesantren programme initiated by the Institute for Disaster Response and Climate Change (Lembaga Penanggulangan Bencana dan Perubahan Iklim [LPBI]), which is part of the organisational structure of Nahdlatul Ulama, Indonesia's largest Muslim mass organisation. Here we are looking in more detail at one especially prominent green *pesantren* in the programme, Pesantren Annuqayah in East Java, to illustrate its holistic curriculum, innovative pedagogy and community engagement efforts. Finally,

DOI: 10.4324/9781003193432-4

32 *Ahmad Afnan Anshori and Florian Pohl*

we reflect on the broader takeaways for a culturally relevant environmental education in Islamic schools beyond Indonesia by paying specific attention to connections and dissonances with the dominant discourse on environmental education cultivated in the Global North.

The Challenges of Environmental Education

In its broadest sense, environmental education refers to educational practices that aim at fostering environmentally responsible citizens. The term goes back to the Tbilisi Declaration of 1977 that followed the first intergovernmental conference on environmental education organised by the United Nations Education, Scientific and Cultural Organization (UNESCO). The Declaration affirmed that environmental education aims at

> making individuals and communities understand the complex nature of the natural and the built environments resulting from the interaction of their biological, physical, social, economic, and cultural aspects, and acquire the knowledge, values, attitudes, and practical skills to participate effectively in anticipating and solving environmental problems, and in the management of the quality of the environment.
>
> (UNESCO, 1977, p. 25)

With its interdisciplinary ethos that emphasises the connections between the social and the natural worlds and a broad learning concept that includes students' emotional, technical and political capacities, the Tibilisi Declaration captures many salient features characteristic of alternative models that have emerged in the past decades. These include innovative approaches such as education for sustainable development or education for sustainability (e.g., Berryman & Sauvé, 2016). The reader should understand the chapter's preference for using the term environmental education in this broader sense as referring to a wide variety of educational initiatives that seek to promote environmental awareness and pro-environment action.

Raising students' environmental sensibilities that affect how they behave daily is a tall order for schools. As Kollmuss and Agyeman's famous study about barriers to pro-environmental behaviour has demonstrated, awareness is not a sufficient condition for acting pro-environmentally (Kollmuss & Agyeman, 2002). A key reason is that trade-offs between present gains and future losses mitigate against effective mobilisation on behalf of the environment. Moreover, paralleling the perceived distance in time, the spatial remove from which most people experience natural disasters further intensifies how people undervalue environmental hazards. Further complicating the situation is that even when clear data is available about dangers from ecological destruction, the information is rarely coupled with actionable information about how individuals and groups should respond to it in their daily lives. Although these challenges are formidable for any education system, Islamic schools frequently face additional obstacles in implementing effective environmental education.

Many Muslim-majority states still lack leadership on the level of state and local governments to prioritise sustainability issues in the official curriculum and to include environmental education in teacher training programmes. The results are an under-prepared teaching staff that misses sufficient knowledge and pedagogical skills and has few incentives to invest in environmental education. Continued reliance on rote learning and teaching to standardised national exams marks much of students' schooling experience. That an increasing number of Islamic schools follow official state curricula compounds the situation. To maintain the Islamic character of their education, these schools add on Islamic subjects and activities for their students, thereby leaving little space in an already crowded curriculum for a new field such as environmental education.

Indonesian Muslim Leadership in Environmental Education: The Green Pesantren Initiative

The severe environmental problems Indonesia is facing, on the whole, have failed to elicit a concerted response on the political level. There has been little discernible political will or bureaucratic competence to curb environmental exploitation and promote a public discourse on sustainability and environmental stewardship. Despite a mushrooming of new political parties following the democratic transition of 1998, the country has only recently seen the emergence of a 'green party' that seeks to compete in future national elections, and few of the established political parties include ecological issues in their party platform. The field of education reflects these shortcomings. A recent analysis finds that the current national curriculum affords environmental education little weight, mostly fails to alert students to the connections between economic development and environmental exploitation, and rarely considers human agency and responsibility concerning environmental destruction (Parker & Prabawa-Sear, 2020). The lack of political leadership has done little to strengthen environmental consciousness in Indonesia. Missing ecological concern in the sphere of government means that the promotion of environmental issues in Indonesia largely has been in the hands of universities and non-governmental organisations (NGOs), which have constituted the backbone of an emerging green movement (van der Laarse, 2016). This movement also includes Muhammadiyah and Nahdlatul Ulama, the country's two largest Muslim mass organisations. Both organisations have been instructive over the years in advancing a new environmental discourse by scaling up Islamic legal principles to mobilise the country's Muslim population towards pro-environmental behaviour (Gade, 2015). They also have developed their organisational infrastructure to respond to the environmental crisis. Nahdlatul Ulama's Institute for Disaster Response and Climate Change (LPBI) is noteworthy because it has been unlike many environmental NGOs in Indonesia actively involved in environmental education. One of its most recent efforts is the Green Pesantren or Pesantren Hijau initiative within the nationwide network of Islamic boarding schools culturally affiliated with the traditionalist leaning NU.

34 *Ahmad Afnan Anshori and Florian Pohl*

The *pesantren* are Indonesia's traditional boarding schools where students live and study under a religious scholar or *kiai*. They express a traditionalist orientation in their commitment to maintaining the canon of classical scholarship in the Islamic sciences (Dhofier, 1999). Historically informal and independent organisations, many *pesantren* have become increasingly integrated into the national education system since the 1970s by incorporating formal schools that teach a government-accredited curriculum. Despite these adaptations, *pesantren* have retained traditional characteristics such as boarding facilities often managed independently by students and pronounced community orientation. Moreover, most *pesantren* are in communities dependent on ecosystem services and particularly vulnerable to becoming victims of environmental damage. In addition to the charismatic authority the *kiai* commands in society, these characteristics explain the *pesantren* tradition's significant role in promoting environmental awareness beyond the student body in the community.

Dating to 2015, LPBI's Pesantren Hijau initiative aims at making Indonesia's boarding schools environmentally friendly institutions that instil environmental consciousness in their students and a commitment to pro-environment behaviour and drive the implementation of 'green' practices in their local communities. A first challenge LPBI had to consider was that the general lack of attention to environmental issues in Indonesian society also affects the low level of environmental awareness among *pesantren* teachers and students. Therefore, to increase motivation to participate in its initiative, LPBI specifically targets *pesantren* in communities that have felt the impact of environmental degradation. It gears its educational efforts to the specific problems these *pesantren* face, such as waste and water management, renewable energies and reforestation. A prominent school in the network of green *pesantren* that has developed a comprehensive environmental education programme is Pesantren Annuqayah in Sumenep, East Java.

Environmental Education in Practice: Pesantren Annuqayah, Sumenep

Pesantren Annuqayah is widely known in the green *pesantren* network for having begun integrating its environmental education initiatives into the school's official curriculum. Located in the District of Sumenep on the Eastern Javanese island of Madura, Annuqayah is one of the region's oldest *pesantren*. Since its foundation in 1887, it has grown into a large educational institution that serves more than 6,000 students with multiple schools across all grade levels, including formal schools that teach the government-accredited curriculum alongside additional Islamic subjects. Its rural location and deep connection to the surrounding community's needs have contributed to the school's long history of green practices. The school's reforestation efforts on the barren, mountainous slopes surrounding its campus garnered national attention in 1981 when Annuqayah received the Kalpataru Award for its conservation efforts from the government. However, its initiative to integrate environmental education more fully into the school's curriculum is of more recent origin. It dates to 2008 when a delegation of school administrators and educators participated in an international conference on environmental education and returned with the idea to address plastic waste with Annuqayah students. The commemoration of Earth Day in April 2008 offered the first opportunity to involve students in organised action on the issue.

About 50 students volunteered on Earth Day to pick up plastic trash in and around campus. Recruitment materials for the event spelled out some basic facts about the dangers of single-use plastic. The event itself included brief presentations and discussions of initiatives to reduce and recycle plastic waste. The event inspired students to form a group calling itself "Cool Collectors of Trash" (Pemulung Sampah Gaul or PSG) that would continue and broaden the school's campaign against plastic waste with the help of several faculty advisors. In addition to picking up trash, PSG members made community outreach a central element of their organisational profile: they campaigned on and off campus for separating waste and succeeded in having recycling bins installed campus-wide, started a waste bank that collects and recycles solid waste and lobbied the school's cafeteria and several food vendors in the community to use environmental-friendly alternatives to single-use plastic.

Creating waste banks (*bank sampah*) has become a standard practice for many *pesantren* to address solid waste problems in their communities. Frequently run by a supervisory board of *pesantren* staff, students and residents, waste banks receive solid waste from the school and local households. The waste bank uses organic waste to produce compost. Likewise, it sells inorganic waste to waste collectors or turns the inorganic materials into craft or building products that can be sold. Proceeds gained from the activities of the waste bank usually serve the school and its surrounding community. Moreover, in some instances, waste banks also allow students and local households to maintain individual accounts. The accounts get credited with the monetary value of the waste brought to the bank, and a person can withdraw funds as they would with a standard bank account.

PSG's successful outreach efforts have earned them invitations to present their initiatives to other communities and schools in the Sumenep area. The opportunity to broaden PSG's educational impact at Annuqayah occurred when the faculty advisor encouraged the group to participate in the 2009 Social Climate Challenge, a competition organised by the British Council in Indonesia. PSG registered three teams. Consistent with PSG's previous work, one team focussed on the plastic waste problem, whereas two new projects tackled local food and organic fertiliser issues. The two new projects attracted more students to PSG and drew in additional teachers who served as advisors to the different projects.

The next step towards anchoring environmental education more centrally in the school's instructional programme came in 2011 with the first 'environmental training camp.' Conceived as a multi-day extra-curricular

36 *Ahmad Afnan Anshori and Florian Pohl*

programme during school holidays, the training was open to students outside of PSG. It aimed at building students' environmental awareness and their creative, organisational and leadership capacities to tackle environmental issues in the local community. The academic portion of the training took place on Annuqayah's campus. Still, a large part of the programme was dedicated to project-oriented fieldwork in the community where students visited, observed and spoke with individuals and groups off campus. For one of the initial projects, students visited a local landfill in Sumenep to observe the daily intake of solid waste, learn from locals about the impact of the landfill on their community and interview scavengers who make a living searching the landfill for materials to sell. Another year, camp participants visited the group Laskar Hijau, an environmental non-profit on the East Javanese mainland engaged in an ambitious reforestation project of Mount Lemongan. Illegal logging in the early 2000s has caused a water crisis for communities around the mountain who depend on collecting water runoff in lakes to irrigate rice fields and other crops. As a result, students met with A'ak Abdullah Al-Kudus, a nationally renowned environmental activist and Laskar Hijau's director, for fieldwork. Known by his honorific Gus A'ak, he introduced students to the logistics of organising successful ecological campaigns. The final step of the training camp saw participants designing environmental projects in the local community, many of which have continued to live on in the work of PSG during subsequent school years.

In 2014, Environmental Education or *Pendidikan Lingkungan Hidup* (PLH) became a required curricular subject at Annuqayah's Senior High School (SMA 3). The subject gives students dedicated time to critically consider the complexities of environmental issues, explore the role human beings play in causing environmental destruction and take steps towards involving themselves in creating solutions to the crisis. In searching for a suitable curriculum model, the programme director and primary instructor for PLH at Annuqayah, Kiai M. Mushthafa, was dissatisfied with the few curriculum materials he found in government textbooks. These materials paid inadequate attention to human contributions to the environmental crisis and frequently focussed exclusively on individual behaviours rather than critically examining specific environmental issues' complex social, economic and political dimensions. Instead, Mushthafa pursued a vision for PLH that focussed on three key elements: complex knowledge of ecological issues, especially those of local relevance; human moral accountability for the environment; and involvement in pro-environment social action.

To help students engage critically with the complexities of environmental issues, Mushthafa designed a new textbook for use in PLH courses at Annuqayah. The book is a reader with materials from journals, magazines and newspapers. It relies heavily on articles from the Indonesian edition of *National Geographic Magazine* and includes long-form pieces from national and local newspapers. Topics of selected papers range from international cases such as coal mining in the United States and rising sea levels in Bangladesh to ones closer to home. Waste management, forest conservation, endangered species, renewable energy and the environmental movement feature in articles that anchor the issues in specific national and local contexts. While pieces from *National Geographic* include scientific theory and data, the reader overall pays attention to broader social, economic and political dimensions in the environmental issues it presents. The role of material development is linked explicitly with the destruction of the planet, and connections between the economy, society and the environment take centre stage in most articles. Despite the creative energies that went into developing textbook materials, the defining characteristic of PLH at Annuqayah remains its project-based pedagogical approach.

At the heart of the learning experience in PLH at Annuqayah are activities that take students out of the classroom and into the field to examine complex, real-world environmental issues in the local community around the school. Continuing the tradition of the earlier extra-curricular environmental training camps, students gain relevant ecological knowledge while seeking to understand specific problems and develop skills in designing public products that educate others on the issue and advocate for ways to bring about involvement and change.

Ramifications of the Pesantren Case for Environmental Education in Islamic Schools

On the most fundamental level, a key takeaway of the Green Pesantren initiative is that Islamic schools can and often do succeed in teaching students to think and act in pro-environmental ways. What is more, some of them are among the most progressive and forward-looking educational institutions in their communities. Given the urgent need for environmentally responsible citizens globally and the still persistently low levels of environmental awareness in majority-Muslim countries locally, this successful record should serve as encouragement and imperative for Muslim educators everywhere to elevate environmental education to a position of prominence in their schools. Beyond the programmatic objective of making environmental education a principal goal of Islamic education, this section highlights several specific dimensions of environmental education applicable to Islamic schools outside of the Indonesian *pesantren* tradition, such as a comprehensive, whole-school approach to environmental education, Islamically derived environmental ethos, green relations with the community, curricular and pedagogical innovation and leadership in teacher training.

Whole-School Approach

A characteristic of Pesantren Annuqayah's educational model is that it places the promotion of environmentally friendly habits and sensibilities at the centre of the school's educational mission. A result is a comprehensive approach to environmental education that touches on all aspects of a student's learning experience and extends the school's pro-environmental activities into

38 *Ahmad Afnan Anshori and Florian Pohl*

the local community. For example, Annuqayah's zero-plastic initiative shows how the school consistently promotes pro-environmental knowledge, attitudes and behaviour across all aspects of school life: zero-plastic policies apply across campus, including student housing and dining facilities, to complement the curricular and co-curricular projects that address the environmental impact of single-use plastic.

What is significant is that these policies have buy-in from all members of the school community. For example, students, staff and the school's top administrators refrain from using single-use plastic and commit to responsible waste-management practices. "We all practice what we preach," says programme director Mushthafa. The insistence that the school provides opportunities for students to apply what they learn practically in their school community is reminiscent of the "Just Community" model for moral education popularised by Lawrence Kohlberg. Kohlberg stressed the ethos of a school as a salient factor in moral education whereby students, teachers and administrators can apply the abstract moral ideals to the more tangible interactions and procedures relevant to the everyday affairs of the school (Kohlberg, 1985). The emphasis on the significance of community to motivate lasting behavioural change has recently been affirmed outside of educational theory. Observing that knowledge and attitudes are poor predictors of behaviour, social psychologists remind us that behaviour is intimately connected to identity and thus shaped by living in social and moral communities (Gatersleben, Murtagh, & Abrahamse, 2014). In other words, for individuals to change their behaviour, that change must happen on the communal level.

Islamic Environmental Ethos

Islamic schools constitute communities for which Islamic traditions provide an effective form of symbolic meaning. By embedding environmental education in an Islamic framework recognised by community members as an essential part of their identity, Islamic schools increase the social legitimacy of their educational programmes and the motivation to act in pro-environmental ways. At Pesantren Annuqayah, the responsibility for articulating such an Islamic environmental ethos falls to the school's leadership. Kiai M. Faizi, one of the senior members of the school's leadership team, leads by example in his refusal of single-use plastics. He also takes on a highly public role in presenting an Islamic rationale for his pro-environmental stance. The author of several books on environmentalism, Faizi draws on Islamic principles such as balance (*mizan*), justice (*'adl*) and stewardship (*khalifa*) to illustrate that care for the environment is not only compatible with but also required in Islam.

Faizi's Islamic rationale differs significantly from prevalent Islamic interpretations of human beings' role in God's creation. He departs from a strongly anthropocentric perspective of human beings as masters over creation and from an instrumental view of nature open to human exploitation—a view shared with dominant interpretive strands in other biblical traditions

Environmental Education and Indonesia's 39

such as Christianity and Judaism. Instead, Faizi emphasises that the role of human beings as stewards (*khalifa*) makes it incumbent upon them to look after and protect the environment. His views are an evocative example of the polyphonic interpretive possibilities of Islamic traditions and the specific ways Muslims can scale up normative Islamic principles to address ecological challenges.

Over the past decades, Muslim scholars have articulated Islamic ethical principles that can be used to teach environmental responsibility (e.g., Ahmad, 2005; Bharuddin, 2009; Dien, 2000; Foltz, Denny, & Baharuddin, 2003; Khalid & O'Brien, 1992; Parvaiz, 2009; Saniotis, 2012). The work of these scholars and educators offers what Michael Walzer calls "thick" motivations for pro-environmental action that are grounded in the cultural specifics, complexities and nuances of Islamic ethical traditions (Walzer, 1994). Moreover, given the significant public position Islamic schools frequently inhabit within their communities, this intellectual work also influences the broader public's pro-environmental beliefs, attitudes and actions.

Community Engagement

Recognising the vital link between behaviour and social identity that derives from one's membership in larger social communities impacts how Islamic schools engage with their local communities. Acknowledging that its pro-environmental mission cannot stop at the campus walls, Pesantren Annuqayah extends its sustainability activities into the local community. Through its Community Service Bureau (*Biro Pengabdian Masyarakat* or BPM), Pesantren Annuqayah manages environmental outreach. Next to the waste bank mentioned previously, BPM carries out ecological activities to reduce plastic waste, advance reforestation and promote local agricultural products. Equally significant for its green advocacy in the community are the school's economic relations. Hiring food vendors, contractors and service providers that prioritise green business practices sends a strong signal about the importance of environmental sustainability. Incentivising broader community segments towards sustainable practices takes seriously Islamic schools' leadership role as influential public institutions in their communities.

Student involvement in community relations also offers valuable learning experiences that demonstrate to students how their pro-environmental efforts are not academic but make a difference in the real world. However, a justified point of critique of environmental studies programmes that focus exclusively on extra-curricular sustainability work in the community is that such exercises can degenerate into a form of environmental volunteerism or, worse, unpaid environmental labour. This happens when students engage in sustainability work without a nuanced understanding of the causes and consequences of environmental destruction their efforts seek to solve. What is required instead is that these community practices be incorporated into a holistic environmental education programme so that the knowledge and skills students gain in their academic work inform their environmental activities (Tanu & Parker, 2018). On this curricular dimension of environmental education, Pesantren Annuqayah offers another critical takeaway for Islamic schools in and beyond Indonesia. By anchoring environmental education in the school's formal curriculum, Annuqayah enhances the visibility and value of environmental education in the hierarchy of the school's educational objectives.

Curricular and Pedagogical Innovation

Like other Islamic schools, formal education has become a central feature of Annuqayah's educational mission. Therefore, the *pesantren* leadership decided that the school's environmental vision needed to find material expression in the formal curriculum. As PLH, environmental education has been part of the formal curriculum at Pesantren Annuqayah since 2014. The increased visibility PLH enjoys due to its inclusion in the school's formal curriculum ensures that environmental education at Annuqayah is not treated as an academic afterthought but is central to its overall educational mission.

Although the new subject of PLH has increased the prestige of environmental education in the school's hierarchy of learning activities, it also was a stand-alone subject lacking any direct curricular connections with other subjects. For PLH to become a motor for cross-curricular development in environmental education, it had to be conceptualised cross-disciplinary. Consequently, students of PLH learn the science underlying environmental problems, consider their social, economic and moral dimensions and take concrete steps towards addressing and solving these issues. Such a broad set of transformative learning goals, which emphasises engaging students in identifying and addressing environmental problems, also places new demands on the 'how' of teaching. Central is the need for innovative pedagogical approaches in environmental education that equip students with higher-order cognitive skills (HOCS) to examine and competently address environmental problems in their lives.

Different from traditional ways of teaching that rely on rote learning, information recall and the comprehension of abstract facts, a forward-looking use of active learning and student-centred approaches characterises environmental education at Annuqayah. These methods engage students in hands-on discovery and collaborative problem-solving. The PLH curriculum incorporates aspects of high-impact pedagogies from experiential to outdoor, place-based, project-based, team-based and eco-justice learning. These pedagogies are 21st-century learning strategies in and beyond environmental education (e.g., Braun & Dierkes, 2017; Buck Institute for Education, n.d.; Foster & Linney, 2007; Gruenewald & Smith, 2007; Itin, 1999; Martusewicz, Edmundson, & Lupinacci, 2011). What unites these approaches is their emphasis on helping students develop HOCS relevant to solving the complex problems for global sustainability. These skills include "various overlapping and interwoven forms of cognitive capabilities, such as critical thinking, system thinking, question-asking, evaluative thinking, decision making, problem solving, and most importantly, transfer" (Zoller & Nahum, 2011, p. 209). With its self-consciously trans-disciplinary orientation and focus on HOCS, PLH at Annuqayah catalyses connections to other fields and disciplines that can be formalised in the curriculum over time.

Against the approach favoured in some of the literature on environmental education that incorporates sustainability teaching into all subjects and educational activities across a school's curriculum (UNESCO, 2006), Annuqayah's decision for PLH as a stand-alone subject should be understood as a strategic choice. In other words, the decision to anchor environmental education as a distinct subject in the formal curriculum does not replace more far-reaching goals for the curriculum. Instead, it constitutes a strategic first step in this direction. One of the reasons for the approach is that few teachers currently have the necessary expertise or training to relate environmental issues to their classes.

Teacher Training

Inadequate teacher training concerning environmental knowledge and pedagogy remains one of the most significant challenges for incorporating environmental education across the curriculum, including in the education systems of countries in the Global North. (For an insightful discussion of shortcomings in the US national education system, see McKeown-Ice [2000]). In Indonesia, as in other education systems of the Global South, the challenges are exacerbated by the lack of governmental leadership. In the absence of state-centric solutions to adequate teacher training, Annuqayah is collaborating with the growing number of organisations in the non-state sector for which environmental education has become a priority. For example, to improve the quality of environmental education throughout the school, the school sent several teachers to attend training in sustainability education organised by the British Council and other environmental NGOs.

Equally crucial to the success of environmental education initiatives is cultivating Islamic leadership in the environmental space. The Green Pesantren initiative, of which Pesantren Annuqayah is a prominent part, is an example of Islamic educational leadership. Nahdlatul Ulama's Disaster Management and Climate Change Institution, which facilitates the initiative, understands its role as a clearinghouse for information about best practices. Over the past years, LPBI has issued several publications, including guidelines for best practices, a collection of environmental-themed sermons by influential Islamic scholars and a guidebook on the core principles of the programme replete with detailed descriptions of noteworthy initiatives in some of its participating schools (Malik & Nafi', 2019). On top of these activities, LPBI has expanded its educational offerings by developing hands-on training programmes for *pesantren* teachers and students. These programmes combine academic modules on climate change and other environmental issues with skill-building in environmental management practices. What is essential is the active-participatory approach taken by LPBI: the training programmes take place on location in the *pesantren* so that participants can apply their environmental learning to the specific needs of their school community. For instance, participants learn to identify different types of waste their school produces and how to calculate the overall waste volume; they receive hands-on instruction in environmental-friendly management practices, such as recycling, composting and organic farming; and they draft proposals for how to implement some of the most relevant methods through specific programme initiatives and extra-curricular activities in their school.

In the absence of state leadership on environmental education, including adequate teacher training, Islamic leadership in the environmental sphere, alongside other non-state actors such as environmental NGOs, can enhance the public prominence of environmental issues. This leadership, in turn, serves to put pressure on regional and state leaders and institutions to elevate sustainability and environmental education throughout the national education systems.

Conclusions

The relative success of the Green Pesantren initiative is especially noteworthy considering that much of the literature on environmental education is preoccupied with the education systems of countries in the Global North (Gough, 2014). Islamic counterparts are rarely drawn into the conversation. Against such systematic privileging of non-Islamic perspectives, the example of Pesantren Annuqayah underscores that Islamic schools frequently exhibit features that make them promising sites for producing environmentally conscious citizens: like many Islamic schools, Annuqayah operates in an underserved community disproportionately affected by environmental destruction and for which, as a result, environmentalism is immediately relevant. Moreover, the religious framing of education pays attention to social, emotional and moral dimensions in the learning process. Against the suspicion of religious approaches to environmental education in some of the scholarship on environmental education coming from the Global North, Annuqayah's example demonstrates that the involvement of religion can and often does have positive effects by increasing the social and cultural legitimacy of pro-environment attitudes and behaviour among population segments for which Islamic traditions remain a significant source of identification. Coupled with the community orientation present in many Islamic schools, Annuqayah offers a culturally relevant and thus credible example of environmental stewardship for its students and the wider public. The contexts in which an Islamic school such as Pesantren Annuqayah develops and carries out its environmental education programmes is not always identical to those that frequently dominate the educational literature. However, it is also not entirely different. There is much to gain for those committed to environmental education from intentionally engaging with each other's approaches across traditions, religious and otherwise.

Bibliography

Ahmad, A. (2005). Islam and environmental law. In B. Taylor & J. Kaplan (Eds.), *Encyclopedia of religion and nature* (Vol. 1, pp. 885–887). New York: Continuum.

Berryman, T., & Sauvé, L. (2016). Ruling relationships in sustainable development and education for sustainable development. *The Journal of Environmental Education, 47*(2), 104–117.

Bharuddin, A. (2009). Religious studies, theology and sustainable development: An Islamic perspective. In C. D. Pater & I. Dankelman (Eds.), *Religion and sustainable development opportunities and challenges for higher education* (Vol. 46, pp. 129–150). Berlin: Lit.

Braun, T., & Dierkes, P. (2017). Connecting students to nature: How intensity of nature experience and students age influence the success of outdoor education programs. *Environmental Education Research, 23*(7), 937–949.

Buck Institute for Education. (n.d.). PBLWorks. Retrieved from https://www.pblworks.org.

Dhofier, Z. (1999). *The pesantren tradition: The role of the kyai in the maintenance of traditional Islam in Java.* Tempe, Ariz.: Monograph Series Press, Program for Southeast Asian Studies, Arizona State University.

Dien, M. I. (2000). *The environmental dimensions of Islam.* Cambridge, UK: Lutterworth Press.

Foltz, R. C., Denny, F. M., & Baharuddin, A. (Eds.). (2003). *Islam and ecology: A bestowed trust.* Cambridge, USA: Harvard University Press.

Foster, A., & Linney, G. (2007). *Reconnecting children through outdoor education: A research summary.* Toronto: The Council of Outdoor Educators.

Gade, A. M. (2015). Islamic law and the environment in Indonesia: Fatwa and Da'wa. *Worldviews, 19*(2), 161–183.

Gatersleben, B., Murtagh, N., & Abrahamse, W. (2014). Values, identity and pro-environmental behaviour. *Contemporary Social Science, 9*(4), 374–392.

Gough, N. (2014). Globalization and curriculum inquiry: Performing transnational imaginaries. In N. P. Stromquist & K. Monkman (Eds.), *Globalization and education: Integration and contestation across cultures* (pp. 87–101). Lanham: R & L Education.

Gruenewald, D. A., & Smith, G. A. (2007). *Place-based education in the global age* New York: Lawrence Erlbaum Associates.

Itin, G. M. (1999). Reasserting the philosophy of experiential education as a vehicle for change in the 21st century. *Journal of Experiential Education, 22*(2), 91–98.

Jambeck, J. R., Geyer, R., Wilcox, C., Siegler, T. R., Perryman, M., Andrady, A., & Law, K. L. (2015). Plastic waste inputs from land into the ocean. *Science, 347*(6223), 768–771.

Khalid, F. M., & O'Brien, J. (1992). *Islam and ecology.* London: Cassell.

Kohlberg, L. (1985). The just community approach to moral education in theory and practice. In W. Berkowitz & F. Oser (Eds.), *Moral education: Theory and practice* (pp. 27–88). Hillsdale, NJ: Erlbaum.

Kollmuss, A., & Agyeman, J. (2002). Mind the gap: Why do people act environmentally and what are the barriers to pro-environmental behavior? *Environmental Education Research, 8*(3), 239–260.

van der Laarse, M. C. (2016). *Environmentalism in Indonesia today.* (Master's degree in Asian studies). Leiden University.

Malik, I., & Nafi', M. Z. (Eds.). (2019). *Menuju pesantren hijau [Towards green pesantren]*. Jakarta: Lembaga Penanggulangan Bencana dan Perubahan Iklim Nahdlatul Ulama.

Martusewicz, R., Edmundson, J., & Lupinacci, J. (2011). *Ecojustice education: Towards diverse, democratic and sustainable communities*. New York: Routledge.

McKeown-Ice, R. (2000). Environmental education in the United States: A survey of pre-service teacher education programs. *The Journal of Environmental Education*, *32*(1), 4–11.

Parker, L., & Prabawa-Sear, K. (2020). *Environmental education in Indonesia: Creating responsible citizens in the global south?* New York: Routledge.

Parvaiz, A. (2009). Reorienting Islamic theology towards environmental consciousness & sustainability — A model for incorporating environmental education in Islamic education. In C. D. Pater & I. Dankelman (Eds.), *Religion and sustainable development opportunities and challenges for higher education* (Vol. 46, pp. 151–158). Berlin: Lit.

Saniotis, A. (2012). Muslims and ecology: Fostering Islamic environmental ethics. *Contemporary Islam*, *6*, 155–171.

Tanu, D., & Parker, L. (2018). Fun, "family," and friends: Developing pro-environmental behaviour among high school students in Indonesia. *Indonesia and the Malay World*, *46*, 303–324.

UNESCO. (1977). *Intergovernmental Conference on Environmental Education Final Report*. Retrieved from Tbilisi, USSR: http://www.gdrc.org/uem/ee/tbilisi.html

UNESCO. (2006). *Framework for the UNDESD International Implementation Scheme*. Retrieved from Paris: http://unesdoc.unesco.org/images/0014/001486/148650e.pdf.

Walzer, M. (1994). *Thick and thin: Moral argument at home and abroad*. Notre Dame: University of Notre Dame Press.

World Bank. (2014). *World Bank and environment in Indonesia*. Retrieved from www.worldbank.org/en/country/indonesia/brief/world-bank-and-environment-in-indonesia

Zoller, U., & Nahum, T. L. (2011). From teaching to KNOW to learning to THINK in science education. In B. J. Fraser, K. G. Tobin, & C. J. McRobbie (Eds.), *Second international handbook of science education* (pp. 209–229). Dordrecht, The Netherlands: Springer.

4 Developing an Islamic Teacher

Islamic Cultural Contents in an ELT Textbook in a Muslim High School in Southern Thailand

Yusop Boonsuk and Eric A. Ambele

Introduction

Nowadays, English is considered a global language with global ownership. It is now utilised by diverse ethnicities with different mother tongues and cultures, leading to multiple varieties of Englishes across geographic territories as a communication bridge for multilingual and multicultural communities (Ambele & Boonsuk, 2020). Thus, conventional frameworks in English language teaching (ELT) need to be reconceptualised, and their goals in non-native contexts reprioritised. Adherence to only Standard English (e.g., the United Kingdom and the United States) cultural representations in ELT textbooks in non-native contexts are now being questioned. Approaches that address communication success in cross-cultural settings and new linguistic landscapes are now receiving prioritised attention (Galloway & Rose, 2015). The transformed and diversified sociolinguistic landscape of English makes the language less attached to any specific English varieties or ethnic groups. Consequently, the language functions and scopes beyond geographical, social and ethnic boundaries.

Private Islamic schools or schools that offer secular-Islamic education are regarded as educational institutions with a long history in The Association of Southeast Asian Nations (ASEAN) (Margono, 2012). They are popular and play an essential role in education management and development among Asian countries—e.g., Malaysia, Indonesia, Brunei and Singapore. To effectively keep learners updated with the constant global dynamics of the 21st century, many educational institutions, including private Islamic schools, are taking proactive approaches, strategising administrative policies, and modifying pedagogical management to support social evolution and emerging economic-development requirements of their respective nations to match global needs. Since English is a global language and a medium for international, multilingual and multicultural communication among people with diverse mother tongues and cultures in and out of Asian contexts (Baker, 2015; Kirkpatrick, 2014), English proficiency has undeniably become a crucial life skill for a quality 21st-century global citizenship. Hence, one of the critical visions or strategies that many educational institutions around the world incorporate into their management plans is the development of learners'

DOI: 10.4324/9781003193432-5

English language skills, which is designed to prepare them for future domestic and international communicative encounters.

In the context of Thai private Islamic schools, achieving this goal in this unique setting is found challenging for Thai ELT practitioners. The constraint includes the integration of religious and general knowledge in the education of learners who have been raised with a strong tie to the Islamic way of life. This phenomenon is unique because, compared with the majority of non-Muslim throughout Thailand, these learners speak different dialects—e.g., local Melayu—observe Islamic norms, conduct Islamic practices and rites, maintain simple living routines and dress in colours within the Islamic-approved codes. As such, Islam plays an extremely crucial role in leading the ways these local learners live their lives. Unorthodox practices that go against religious codes are socially sectioned. Unlike other regions of Thailand that only administer general education, the educational models that work with the Islamic majority in the three southern border provinces are the ones that respect their Islamic identities and ways of life.

Furthermore, after thoroughly examining the ELT pedagogies currently employed in most of the educational institutions in Thailand, including Islamic schools, it was found that the teaching models and textbook cultural contents do not address the needs for preparing learners for real-life English encounters nor does it respond to the changes of the emerging sociolinguistic landscapes where English users no longer rely on the formerly mainstream English varieties, cultures, ethnicities and nations (e.g., the United Kingdom and the United States). Instead, English deserves its rightful global ownership for being a language of the world that is used by speakers from diverse linguistic backgrounds. Specifically, Thailand's ELT still primarily focusses on English as a foreign language (EFL) pedagogies with the ultimate purpose of pressuring learners to adopt native English norms (Ambele & Boonsuk, 2020, Jindapitak, 2019; Tarrayo et al., 2020). This phenomenon indicates that Western norms, cultures, values, ideologies, and perceptions still dominate most ELT industries in the world, and only the two English-speaking countries—i.e., the United States and the United Kingdom—are being held as standards in English language learning in Thai ELT contexts. Consequently, local non-native English learners (such as Thai Muslims) do not receive adequate opportunities to learn about their cultural beliefs and practices in English.

Conservative EFL ideologies are the main reason behind this trajectory in Thailand, as some teachers tend to discriminate against other 'non-standard' English varieties. However, with the increasing need to prepare Islamic teachers to teach English to Thai Muslims students, teachers need to be aware of the changing roles of English and pedagogically pay attention to and integrate the learners' sociocultural realities in their teaching of English. They should reconceptualise new objectives that address language pluricentricity and avoid idealisation of native English speakers (NES) to ensure that Thai Muslim learners are equipped with desirable competencies to handle the current diversity and fluidity inherent in the use of English. This means that Thai Islamic teachers should teach English with cultural and contextual flexibilities where NES norms are only used as references and not as the ELT goal. By so doing, ELT classrooms would potentially be a more powerful route towards English acquisition, as learners will be equipped to communicate with linguistic conventions that exist in multilingual and multicultural contexts (Byram et al., 2017).

To bridge this gap in ELT in Thailand and respond to learners' real-world English communication needs for private Islamic schools in Thailand, this study aims to analyse an ELT textbook used in a large, private Islamic school in Southern Thailand in order to identify consistencies of embedded language and cultural contents with the Islamic cultures and values which learners primarily believe in. The following research question was developed to achieve this aim:

> What cultural contents are reflected in an ELT textbook for Muslim learners in Southern Thailand, and are the contents a depiction of the learners' or foreign culture?

Private Islamic Schools in Asia

Private Islam schools were recognised as 'Pondoks,' some of the oldest education institutions in Southeast Asia with religious and educational roles for Muslims. Today, several categories of Islamic schools have emerged, such as private Islamic schools, Pondok Madrasah institutes, Tadika institutes for Quran education and mosque centres for Islamic studies. Tan (2014) estimated that different types of Islamic schools, including the aforementioned, constitute up to 60,000 institutions in ASEAN. Approximately 50,000 of them are in Indonesia. These institutions employ different administrative strategies and go by different names. For instance, in Java and Kalimantan, they are known as Pasantren and Pondok. At the same time, they are called Surau in West Sumatra and Dayah in Aceh. Thailand's southern provinces of Narathiwat, Yala and Pattani are prominent with private Islamic schools. The school's primary objectives were to transfer Islamic teachings and cultivate Muslim children on goodness, knowledge with moral balance and correct religious practices. The first major milestone which converted Pondok institutes into today's private Islamic schools was marked in 1961 when the state required these institutes to be officially registered. Subsequently, from 1965 to 1968, they were officially converted to public (civil) Islamic schools. Furthermore, in 1983, the state made another attempt to rename them as private Islamic schools in compliance with the Private School Act 1983. At present, private Islamic schools in Thailand are authorised to use the Basic Education Curriculum 2008 (2017 Revision), the same Thai public schools, as a mechanism to drive education.

Despite the abundance of private Islamic schools in ASEAN, their adaptation for social progression and responsiveness to modern national economic-development needs remain questionable. Doubts have been constantly raised regarding their positions, approaches and adaptation actions, especially when there is a need to integrate Islamic knowledge into secular education known to be mainly based on Westernised educational paradigms that significantly contradict Islamic ideologies (Rabasa, 2005; al-Otaibi & Rashid, 1997). These constraints present challenges to educational stakeholders, especially teachers and administrators, in managing, designing and planning educational systems, especially when integrating Islamic teachings with ever-changing secular knowledge (Abu Sulayman, 1989). To prepare learners for changes within the global society and address Thailand's needs as a developing country, Parallel Education (also known as Dualism Education) was chosen. This education system is used to administer two educational subsystems that do not share philosophical foundations or educational goals, such as traditional versus modern systems. In this case, the traditional system refers to religious education, which aims to educate learners on Islamic beliefs, faith and life journeys following Allah. In contrast, the modern system refers to secular disciplines with Western philosophy, which separates religion from politics. This education system only recognises scientific knowledge derived from scientifically tested hypotheses (Narongraksakhet, 2009; Wae-u-seng et al., 2009). Nonetheless, although private Islamic schools in Southern Thailand have been providing education for decades, learners' academic achievements and quality in many fields have not been satisfactory. In fact, they have been relatively lower compared to those of other regions. This notion is especially true with English courses, the focus of this study. Evidently, learners' English proficiency was extremely low, considering results in other South-East Asian countries (Assalihee et al., 2019). Besides the lack of learning motivation and negative attitude towards English language learning, another valid problem includes conditions where teachers opt for teaching content with minimal association with learners' values and cultures. Failure to reflect their cultural values offers limited learning practicality. Embedded cultural messages within these ELT pedagogies convey distant, abstract and intangible values that do not link to Islamic values and identities, which are the foundation of learners' upbringing. As a result, they experience difficulties in applying English in everyday life (Assalihee et al., 2019; Jindapitak & Boonsuk, 2018). Further discussion on this is in the following section.

ELT Textbook and Cultural Reflection

It is undeniable that learning English as a language also involves embedded cultural knowledge, and textbooks are excellent tools to offer exposure to the cultural diversity that comes with the English language (Harper & Widodo, 2020; Widodo, 2018). Textbooks are a form of media that influence ideas and form beliefs of English language learners. Hence, it is crucial to understand how English language teachers and learners came across and believe in specific cultures (Dinh & Sharifian, 2017; McConachy, 2018; Sherlock, 2016). On this note, Cortazzi and Jin (1999) proposed that language learning textbooks influence learners with three cultural information categories:

(1) 'source culture materials,' which refers to contents with learners' culture; (2) 'target culture materials,' which refers to contents with native English cultures; and (3) 'international target culture materials,' which refers to contents with cultural diversity. Apparently, native English cultures are among the most necessary information in ELT textbooks.

English speakers in Thailand use English as a lingua franca, and textbooks remain one of the most vital ELT tools. However, ELT contents in use nationwide were found to influence native English idealisation, including excessive portrayals of native English linguistics, cultural and inner circle ethnic orientation. Furthermore, most cultural contents in Thailand's ELT textbooks present significant inclination towards native English varieties, such as those spoken in the UK and the United States. Specifically, texts, conversations, tasks and photos in most textbook chapters straightforwardly present influences of Western consumerism, such as lifestyles, modern living, tourism, entertainment, food, technology, communication, middle-class individuals, adolescents, wealthy figures and famous celebrities from target cultures (Syrbe & Rose, 2018; Widodo, 2018). As a result, ELT media widely implemented in several Thai educational institutions today, including private Islamic schools, continue to adhere to Western societies' standards and values regardless of learners' cultural differences and internal conflicts. Therefore, current ELT seems to serve as a mechanism for cultural assimilation where Western cultures are free to spread influences and local cultures are excluded or omitted in English language classrooms (McConachy, 2018; Syrbe, & Rose, 2018). This ongoing educational phenomenon is inconsistent with current linguistic landscapes, English diversity and pluricentricity. Hence, the conventional strategy of English language education fails to address English communication development.

To comply with the globalised world where English roles have shifted towards being a lingua franca, ELT educators in Thailand are recommended to acknowledge cultural diversity and not neglect learners' home cultures. Similarly, all Thai ELT stakeholders (e.g., teachers, policymakers and curriculum designers) are recommended to select ELT textbooks that use contents relevant to learners' home cultures and familiar elements. For instance, appropriate textbooks for Thai Muslim learners should be related to Islamic values and cultures and differences in being Muslim. In other words, these textbooks should be less about native English norms, linguistics, cultures, ways of life and aspiration and more about cultural, contextual and English diversity, especially local factors closely associated with target ELT learners (Baker, 2015; Kusumaningputri & Widodo, 2018; Widodo, 2018). By acknowledging learners' cultural roots and selecting ELT textbooks with identity awareness, they are expected to feel more motivated when studying English. Hence, relevant and meaningful content that is related to learners' background knowledge does not only supplement and drive language development and acquisition but also facilitates learners to use English as a tool to reflect on and express their cultural values and identities, as well as communicate them to other English-speaking interlocutors within different cultural spheres.

Research Methodology

Textbook Sample

The sampled textbook is *New World* authored by Manuel dos Santos and globally published in 2019 by McGraw Hill and domestically published in Thailand by Thai Wattana Panit Co., Ltd. The textbook was approved by the Ministry of Education as a Secondary 4 ELT textbook of the Basic Education Core Curriculum 2008, and it contains 12 chapters: "Schools Then and Now," "You Have to Do It!," "Do You Know Where It Is?," "They're the Ones!," "Great Expectations," "Can You Help Me?," "Satisfaction Guaranteed," "Have You Seen It Yet?," "For How, Long?," "What Would You Do?," "What's It Made Of?," and "It's Fresh, Isn't It?" The main chapter contents were designed to enhance the four English language skills, including listening, speaking, reading and writing. Each chapter presents content in section sequence beginning with New Language "reading and listening", followed by Pronunciation "speaking", Conversation "speaking", Listening, Grammar "writing", and Speaking and Reading.

Analytical Procedures

Since this study aims to analyse the relevancy for Muslim learners of the ELT textbook's cultural contents, cultural data were analysed by qualitative content analysis from texts and images within the textbook. The contents include conversations, passages, pictures, tasks and grammar. Such contents were categorised according to themes based on the sociolinguistic cultural content analysis rubric (Ramirez & Hall, 1990) and cultural sources of the contents based on (1) the learners' cultures, (2) native cultures and (3) other cultures. In all, the cultural contents in the textbook were reviewed across all 12 chapters. Qualitative criteria on "the uses of language involving different topics, the situations in which communication may occur, and communicative purposes as presented in the texts" were employed. Subsequently, the "top-down coding or deductive approach" was implemented (i.e., when codes were found relevant to the study, coding was employed with the predetermined codes) in conjunction with the "bottom-up coding or inductive approach" (i.e., extracting codes). These emerging codes were further reviewed to determine relationships, and themes were modified, sorted and classified. As several themes were expected to emerge, the relevant and interrelated ones were merged into a cluster, whereas those that were irrelevant were eventually discarded.

Finding and Discussion

In this section, the cultural content findings from the textbook analysis are presented. We carefully examined the textbook by reading through the entire book several times and taking qualitative notes on related themes to the research question. The arrangement of the contents in this book is so

Table 4.1 Cultural evaluation in the textbook

Content Types	Native Culture	Other Cultures	Learners' Culture
Task	31	6	2
Image	27	7	3
Passage	14	1	-
Grammar	2	1	-
Conversation	2	-	-
Total (N)	76	15	5
Total (%)	**79.16**	**15.62**	**5.20**

that it is easy to read with content that clearly identifies each section. To answer the research question, the Muslim learners' cultural contents and how (whether or not) they reflect Islamic beliefs and practices are discussed in this section in order to provide evidence for the textbook evaluations based on its cultural content (see Table 4.1). This cultural content was then evaluated for how it reflects (1) the learners' cultures, (2) native cultures and (3) other cultures. Regarding this current study, the *learners' cultures* refer to contents associated with the Islamic learners' cultural depiction in Thailand while *native contents* are those associated with native-speaking English cultures (e.g., the United Kingdom and the United States). In addition, the contents which do not contain cultural depictions of either the learners' Islamic background or native contents are categorised in the *other cultures* category. In other words, *other cultures* are referenced to other non-native Expanding Circle cultures like other Asian nations (excluding Thailand).

In line with the aim of the study, the cultural content evaluation focusses only on those contents that are related to the learners' Thai or Islamic backgrounds given that the learners are Thai Muslims in Thailand studying in an Islamic school. That is, cultural references to the people, places, pictures that make up the book content are examined. This portrayed a sociocultural view of what content is being associated with the learners' background, native background and other backgrounds, as well as *which* and *what* culture dominates the book (see Table 4.1 for overall evaluation). As it can be clearly seen from Table 4.1, native cultural contents were the most dominant content type (79.16%), followed by other cultures (15.62%), with the learners' Islamic and Thai contents least depicted (5.20%). In Table 4.2, to elaborate, the qualitative evaluation of the book contents is presented and further discussed.

Learners

Aspects of Thai culture and news references, especially those in the southern part of Thailand where the students study, were the least represented in the book. Depictions were instead made to other Asian cultures and lifestyles (e.g., Malaysia and Indonesia) which the learners, supposedly, could still

52 Yusop Boonsuk and Eric A. Ambele

Table 4.2 Evaluation of cultural contents

Textbook	Cultural Contents	Comments
	Learners	• Very few Thai learners' cultural contents in the book. Instances of learners' Thai cultures, peoples, activities and food are scarcely represented, only in the review sections of each chapter.
		• Learners' Islamic cultural depictions are completely absent from the book.
	Native	• Lots of the cultural content cultures are from the native countries like the United Kingdom and the United States, depicted as authentic materials and cultures for effective English learning.
New World		• Pop cultures, news and innovations, lifestyles and chores are over-referenced to the Western culture showing clear preference for UK- and US-centred contents.
	Others	• Many non-Thai and non-native contents were depicted in the book, usually cultural contents from other Asian countries like China and Malaysia. Global cultures across some Asian countries depicting people and places are presented as static.

relate with given that they are likely to have more interactions with these Asian Muslim neighbours than with other native interlocutors (Rabasa, 2005). Overall, the book contents seem to alienate the Islamic learners from the lessons by focussing on non-Islamic cultural contents and other non-Thai depictions. A glaring example of Thai cultural depiction in the book is a listening exercise on the "Grand Palace, Bangkok" (p. 76). The learners' own Islamic cultures were under-represented in the book with only two clear examples that might suggest familiarity to the Islamic students in this school: (1) the "Taj Mahal" (p. 60), a Muslim mausoleum built by a Mughal emperor to honour his dead wife, and (2) pictures of a sheep to check "general knowledge" (p. 54) and a woollen thread from sheep's wool (p. 80). Although these two examples are drawn from other contexts like India and Australia, respectively, the general concept of a sheep is quite familiar in Muslim communities, as a sheep is a common slaughtered animal during Islamic feasts.

Native

Global cultural reflections, particularly from Western countries seemingly dominated most of the activities in the book. In keeping with its international target market and showcasing the native English-speaking cultures,

New World uses a lot of native cultural depictions, showing clear preferences for Western cultures (e.g., "Silly laws around the world" (p. 13) with examples from Western countries). Also, pop-culture and news references were over-represented by the Western cultures (see "Rolling Stones" p. 27). This meant that the learners would require some background knowledge of the Western context to understand such lessons, and even so, it is very unlikely that the learners will use the vocabularies learnt from such lessons in their out-of-classroom interactions. Put differently, the Islamic learners, by this native dominated cultural representation, are alienated from what is culturally familiar to them.

Other

Next to the native culture that dominated the book is the culture of other Asian nations. Other cultural representations depicted a cross-section of many Asian countries and locations in their examples, for example, "silk production in China" (p. 81) and the "Petronas Tower, Kuala Lumpur" (p. 90). In addition to the fact that these are specifically tied to other ASEAN nations, many of the examples also reflect what the learners are likely to encounter in daily life (e.g., "It's fresh, isn't it?" (p. 86–87)). It can also be seen across the book that its global cultural contents cover examples from across different native and non-native countries, however, with fewer instances of Thai and Islamic depictions with regards to learning English. The Expanding Circle cultures were further reflected with images and depictions of black, white, Asian and Latino, which can be seen throughout the book (e.g., p. 2, 6, 26 and 34).

It can be seen from the findings that most of the cultural contents in the textbook did not reflect the learners' Muslim background nor Islamic practices and beliefs. Put differently, the learners' Muslim and/or Thai culture appeared the least in the *New World* textbook. Textbooks, it should be noted, are significant and practical tools for teaching, especially in a context where English is learnt as a second or foreign language like Thailand. According to Baker (2015), Thailand imports her English textbooks from Western countries, which can justify why most textbooks' cultural contents are Western dominated. Nevertheless, given today's global role of English use and usage across different cultural contexts, the inclusion of culturally diversified contents in the textbooks will make learners from different cultural backgrounds to be aware of differences in culture and become intercultural citizens. Thus, Islamic schools might need to select books that can suit Muslim learners' Islamic culture, as well as other foreign cultures. Research has shown that learners with deficiencies in diverse cultural exposure might be confronted with cross-cultural communication problems (Alptekin, 1993; Chutong, 2020). Such cross-cultural knowledge can increase learners' awareness of their own culture while learning. Thus, fitting learners' cultural content in their teaching materials would be an effective way to achieve this goal. The

Islamic teachers should therefore have the independence of selecting the cultural content and productively applying it in their teaching. Of course, the teachers will also need to explain the diversity of cultures in Thailand, Asia and other parts of the world to their Muslim learners. For instance, ethnic diversity and religious diversity should be taught in class in order to help the Thai Muslim learners to prepare and understand their own cultures vis-à-vis other cultures.

Conclusion and Implications

The results of this study suggest that language is actually a social construct, as opposed to an invented system, and that it is contextualised with respect to the speakers' local setting. Native cultural imperialism plays a role in the cultural contents of the textbook.

Given that the textbook under study in this Islamic school lacks sufficient Islamic cultural depictions and is largely dominated by Western and other cultural reflections (as discussed in the findings), we believe that the Islamic teachers, in their choice of English language textbooks for Islamic schools, should choose books that integrate the Islamic learner's cultural contents and global contents so that the learners will not only be exposed to foreign global cultures but also their own local Thai Islamic cultures. Such textbook selection and Islamic teachers' integration of such mixed cultural contents in their teaching would ultimately contribute to the teachers' professional development in raising their Islamic learners' awareness of their own local and Islamic culture (as language users) and in turn positively impact on how the teachers teach their own students (as Islamic language teachers).

As a pedagogical practice, teachers, in exposing their students in Islamic schools to English, should ensure that the ELT textbook contents in Islamic schools should be heavily replete with Islamic linguistics, cultural and ethnic contents. This should be evident in not only the curriculums, textbooks and pictures but also in how the teachers use these materials to teach their learners, prioritising learners' local Islamic cultural contents and integrating it with other cultures associated with Inner and Outer Circle nations. Also, the teachers' would be better exposed and equipped with Islamic cultural content-knowledge to be able to integrate into their teaching for the learners' to have a good English language learning experience of familiar and local cultural content. By this practice, the teachers' Islamic cultural knowledge would increase their confidence in teaching their students to be proud of their own local Islamic and Thai culture. The teachers would be able to accommodate their teaching styles and impact their teaching of mixed Islamic and global content with a positive attitude. In addition, curriculum designers through the Ministry of Education should consider the inclusion of local cultures in designing English textbooks before publishing for school use in Thailand. In this way, cultural contents that are relevant to the learners' Thai local context can find expression in the books.

Limitations

- Researcher's subjectivity in evaluating the cultural contents in the textbooks
- No data from the producers, teachers or learners on why certain contents are included, omitted or taught as the case may be

References

Abu Sulayman, A. H. (1989). *Islamization of knowledge*. Riyadh: International Islamic.

Al-Otaibi, M. M., & Rashid, H. M. (1997). The role of schools in Islamic society: Historical and contemporary perspectives. *American Journal of Islamic Social Sciences*, *14*(4), 1–18.

Alptekin, C. (1993). Target-language culture in EFL materials. *ELT Journal*, *47*(2), 136–143.

Ambele, E. A., & Boonsuk, Y. (2020). Voices of learners in Thai ELT classrooms: A wake up call towards teaching English as a lingua franca. *Asian Englishes*, *23*(2), 201–217. doi:10.1080/13488678.2020.1759248

Assalihee, M., Boonsuk, Y., Bakoh, N., & Sano, I. L. (2019). Reconceptualizing the 21st century English pedagogies for Islamic school teachers in ASEAN. *Journal of Nusantara Studies (JONUS)*, *4*(1), 401–421.

Baker, W. (2015). Culture and complexity through English as a lingua franca: Rethinking competences and pedagogy in ELT. *Journal of English as a Lingua Franca*, *4*(1), 9–30.

Byram, M., Golubeva, I., Han, H., & Wagner, M. (2017). *From principles to practice in education for intercultural citizenship*. Bristol: Multilingual Matters.

Chutong, C. (2020). Cultural content in English for tourism textbook for English major students: A case study of Suratthani Rajabhat University, Southern Thailand. *Journal of Humanities and Social Sciences, Suratthani Rajabhat University*, *12*(1), 128–155.

Cortazzi, M., & Jin, L. (1999). Cultural mirrors: Materials and methods in the EFL classroom. In E. Peterson and B. Coltrane (Ed.), *Culture in second language teaching* (pp. 196–219). Cambridge CUP.

Dinh, T. N., & Sharifian, F. (2017). Vietnamese cultural conceptualisations in the locally developed English textbook: A case study of 'Lunar New Year'/'Tet'. *Asian Englishes*, *19*(2), 148–159.

Galloway, N., & Rose, H. (2015). *Introducing Global Englishes*. Routledge.

Harper, J., & Widodo, H. P. (2020). Perceptual mismatches in the interpretation of task-based ELT materials: A micro-evaluation of a task-based English lesson. *Innovation in Language Learning and Teaching*, *14*(2), 114–132.

Jindapitak, N. (2019). English as an ASEAN lingua franca and the role of nativeness in English education in Thailand: Moving toward the ASEAN Economic Community (AEC). *English Today*, *35*(2), 36–41.

Jindapitak, N., & Boonsuk, Y. (2018). Authoritative discourse in a locally-published ELT textbook in Thailand. *Indonesian Journal of Applied Linguistics*, *8*(2), 265–277.

Kirkpatrick, A. (2014). The language (s) of HE: EMI and/or ELF and/or multilingualism? *The Asian Journal of Applied Linguistics*, *1*(1), 4–15.

Kusumaningputri, R., & Widodo, H. P. (2018). Promoting Indonesian university students' critical intercultural awareness in tertiary EAL classrooms: The use of digital photograph-mediated intercultural tasks. *System*, *72*, 49–61.

Margono, U. (2012). Islamic education in Indonesia and Malaysia (the existence and implementation until 20th century). *At-Ta'dib*, *7*(2), 363–378.

McConachy, T. (2018). Critically engaging with cultural representations in foreign language textbooks. *Intercultural Education*, *29*(1), 77–88.

Narongraksakhet, I. (2009). Sathaban kan sueksa islam nai phak tai khong Thai. *Islamic Educational Institution in Southern Thailand*.

Rabasa, A. (2005). Islamic education in Southeast Asia. *Current Trends in Islamist Ideology*, *2*, 97–108.

Ramirez, A. G., & Hall, J. K. (1990). Language and culture in secondary level Spanish textbooks. *The Modern Language Journal*, *74*(1), 48–65.

Sherlock, Z. (2016). Japan's textbook inequality: How cultural bias affects foreign language acquisition. *Power and Education*, *8*(1), 73–87.

Syrbe, M., & Rose, H. (2018). An evaluation of the global orientation of English textbooks in Germany. *Innovation in Language Learning and Teaching*, *12*(2), 152–163.

Tan, C. (2014). Rationality and autonomy from the Enlightenment and Islamic perspectives. *Journal of Beliefs & Values*, *35*(3), 327–339.

Tarrayo, V. N., Ulla, M. B., & Lekwilai, P. (2020). Does Thai English exist? Voices from English language teachers in two Thai universities. *Asian Englishes*, 1–14.

Wae-u-seng, N., Vanitsuppavong, P., Narongraksakhet, I., Yisunsong, A., & Baka, M. (2009). Educational management of Islamic private schools in three southern border provinces. *Songklanakarin: E-Journal of Social Science & Humanities*, *15*(5), 739–765.

Widodo, H. P. (2018). A critical micro-semiotic analysis of values depicted in the Indonesian Ministry of National Education-endorsed secondary school English textbook. In H. P. Widodo, M. R. Perfecto, L. Van Canh, & A. Buripakdi (Eds.), *Situating moral and cultural values In ELT materials: The Southeast Asian context* (pp. 131–152). Cham: Springer.

5 Islamic Instruction as a Student-Centred Approach

Samina Malik and Nabi Bux Jumani

Introduction

In any Islamic teacher training programme, three fundamental modules should be considered. Teachers should be recruited based on established qualifications. There should be a proper guided and structured system for teacher training and practice. Teachers must be instructed and motivated to know that they perform a very honourable job and that it is known as a prophetic task (Rahman, 2018). The Islamic concept of teacher training covers a broader horizon to improve the overall orientation of the contemporary concept of education, which generally focusses only on the materialistic aspects of life (Syahidin, 2017). This chapter particularly focusses on one of the main themes of this book—that is, enabling Islamic teachers to be equipped with the latest "content knowledge and pedagogy" for the 21st century. There is very little talk on the need for professional development of Islamic teachers throughout the world, especially in terms of improving their content knowledge and pedagogical skills (Mustaffa & Rashid, 2019). The Islamic teacher training institutes should put their efforts in this respect to enable future teachers to be active agents and ready to meet the demands of the 21st century.

Kasim and Abdurajak (2018) emphasised that innovation in Islamic instructional strategies that support traditional Islamic school teachers is needed to handle the challenges as a result of new demands of the 21st century which later contribute to the promotion of children's lifelong learning and comprehensive development. Islamic teachers need to be provided with extensive training and practice in new teaching methods and the latest instructional strategies, which will also contribute to their professional development (Nawi, Hamzah, Ren, & Tamuri, 2015). Such modern facilities and extensive knowledge of the latest instructional approaches and methodologies would help Islamic teachers to update their instructional skills and involve themselves in continuous professional development for lifelong learning (Reeve & Jang, 2006). The scope of this chapter includes Islamic instruction/teaching, instructional approaches in Islamic education like inductive and deductive, constructivist and student-centred teaching approaches.

DOI: 10.4324/9781003193432-6

Concept of Pedagogy in Islam

The concept of Islamic pedagogy is derived directly from the Holy Qur'an and is termed 'Tarbiyya.' The term 'Tarbiyya' is closely related to the term 'education,' and in the Arabic language, it is rooted in the word 'Rubbaa,' which means to educate, cultivate, discipline and constructively raise children. There is a basic difference between Taleem and Tarbiyya. Tarbiyya is a planned activity focussing on the holistic development of children (physical, psychological, emotional and intellectual), whereas Taleem is about getting general knowledge and information that could be gained in both structured and non-formal ways (Sabrin, 2012). The Islamic pedagogy emphasises individuals to be active parts of the educational process and apply learnt knowledge in their everyday lives. The Islamic pedagogy puts empathises on teacher training in a way that enables them to be caring and loving guardians to their students (Abidin, 2018). In Arabic, the term 'Rubban' is employed for the people who not only take care of their pupils but also accept responsibility for their welfare and comprehensive grooming.

Islamic teachers are encountering challenges in the fast-growing innovations in the field of technology. To cope with the challenges, Islamic teachers need to learn instructional strategies that would assist them in dealing with diversified students who belong to a multicultural background and achieve broad instructional objectives (Wekke & Lubis, 2011). The rapid changes in the fields of social, economic, political and technology require Islamic education to be transformed following new demands and meet the global and international challenges (Mohd-Aliff, Ezad, Adibah, & Mohd, 2013; Yaming & Yu-Liang, 2011). It is also important to note that the concept of pedagogy has been changed, and the Islamic perspective on instructional activities also promotes teachers to be facilitators and guiders instead of merely transmitting the subject content to students (Nawi & Ramlan, 2014). According to the Islamic pedagogy, teachers are expected to be mentors and role models for their students and contribute to their Tarbiyya.

Instructional Approaches in Islamic Education

In education, the term 'instructional approach' is defined as effective ways of teaching various subjects to achieve instructional objectives. There are many instructional approaches, such as inductive and deductive, student-centred and teacher-centred and the constructivist approach. The knowledge of instructional approaches as inductive, deductive, student-centre approaches, scaffolding, constructivism and the use of emerging technology guides Islamic teachers with practical implications in the new era of demands and globalisation. It could provide enriched pedagogical knowledge to future teachers that would greatly contribute to their professional development (Nawi & Ramlan, 2014). This supplement content can enable traditional Islamic teachers with a professional training platform for their lifelong learning and improve their instructional expertise in the field of handling the complex learning demands of learners.

1. Prophetic Instruction Approach

The prophetic instructional strategies are denoted with curiosity and inquiry-based instruction and reflect modern pedagogies, which are emphasised nowadays for the professional development of teachers to support the effective learning of students. These prophetic teaching strategies are higher-order thinking, deep knowledge, memorisation, deep understanding, substantive conversation, knowledge as problematic, research-based instruction and meta-language teaching methods. Instructional methods that have been reflected in the Holy Qur'an are the habituation method, exemplary method and method of advice that is called "Targhib and Tarhib"; the analogy and story method called "Amtsal"; and the dialogue method that is called "Hiwar" (Asyafah, 2014); these lecture and discussion methods are also widely applied in Islamic instructions.

It is, therefore, very important to explore what teaching approaches and methods have been suggested by various Islamic scholars. Al-Ghazali explained that the educators/teachers have to follow the principle of "child-centred" learning, which is more concerned with students than educators themselves (Kasim, 2014). Ghazali has recommended the following teaching principles, which are based on a student-centred learning approach and purely based on psychological principles, such as teachers and students should respect each other, lessons should be based on previous knowledge and experiences of students, simplifying the lessons moves from simple to complex, show affection, consider the abilities of students and avoid double standards.

Ibn Khaldun proposed the instructional method that is grounded in the child-centred approach and psychological principles—he suggested that a difficult lesson should not be given to beginners, and students must be given organised instructional material that leads them towards perfection. He further emphasised that the lesson should be according to the understanding level of students and must not be beyond their ability. According to al-Farabi's teaching philosophy, the key purpose of education is to enable students to achieve the highest status (Marifa) and try to explore things that are not known to them. For him, the increase in knowledge is a natural human desire which should be fulfilled by the teachers and the educational process. Ibn e Sina also emphasised child-centred education and follows their psychological needs and advises instructors to pay close attention to the "natural" intellectual capabilities of pupils and choose topics to be taught that match the pupils' mental capacity and level of education. At last, this chapter will elaborate on 'peer observation and feedback.' Peer observation involves individuals in observing each other's practices and learning from one another, focussing on learners' individual needs and the opportunities to both learn from others' practices and offer constructive feedback to peers.

2. Inductive and Deductive Approach

In the Islamic perspective, there are two main approaches—deductive and inductive approaches. The deductive approach usually starts with a more

60 Samina Malik and Nabi Bux Jumani

general topic, law, theory, or principle and leads towards more specific facts (Lubis et al., 2011), whereas the inductive approach is very investigative that involves various instructional strategies such as problem-based learning, inquiry-based lessons, project-based instruction, discovery methods and case-based studies (Rosyad, 2019). These inductive instructional methods inspire and motivate learners to critically think, develop objective and rational thinking and appreciate differences.

The inductive slant involves collecting, interpreting and using the data to generalise their conclusions as to construct a new type of knowledge. Whereas the deductive approach leads the application of laws, principles, formulas and rules to specific situations or phenomena. The application of these approaches enables teachers to achieve their broad instructional objectives more effectively and efficiently (Lubis et al., 2011). Therefore, Islamic teachers need to follow these approaches and create situations for complex and effective learning while emphasising the previous knowledge and experiences of students that could provide a significant basis for constructive instruction.

The Islamic instruction significantly follows the inductive approach and promotes the inquiry method, problem-based learning and discovery method. The teachers use an inductive method as an instructional strategy and lead information from factual situations to general theories. According to Pritchard (2014), for effective learning, using both inductive and deductive strategies as a scientific method perpetually involves both inductive and deductive perspectives (Rosyad, 2019). In the scientific method, teachers employ new observations and infer new theories and principles based on these observations and in the other way test pre-existing theories in the form of experimentations and deduce consequences to verify these theories and principles.

The inductive approach is used as an umbrella that involves a wide range of instructional strategies such as problem-based learning, inquiry-based learning, discovery learning, case studies and project learning. These are all methods that are learner-centred based and impose responsibility more on the shoulders of students than the teachers. Whereas the traditional instruction approaches are more teacher-centred and follow a deductive approach (Jafari, 2014), many studies supported the fact that students learn more effectively by employing new information and knowledge into the already existing mental structure (Kasim, 2014; Pritchard, 2014; Rahman, 2018). This leads to the concept that students construct their knowledge and reality based on available principles and is characterised as a constructivist approach (Rosyad, 2019). This approach promotes collaborative and cooperative learning among students by indulging them in more active learning—i.e., discussion, problem-solving, questioning and projects; much work is done in or out of the classroom in group forms.

3. Constructivism/Student-Centred Approach

In Islam, education is a very purposeful and conscious activity managed by teachers to ensure the comprehensive development of the learners' personalities. Islamic education covers every aspect of human education by focussing on the heart, mind and soul. It helps people to get prepared for accepting all good and evil, bitter and sweet of their society, and become productive members of the society (Abidin, 2018). In the Islamic perspective, student-centred learning demands a specific professional training programme for teachers emphasising certain innovative instructional methods which mainly emphasise what is going to be done and why is this done.

Reeve and Jang (2006) asserted that these instructional strategies will contribute to their professional growth and also help them to develop higher-order thinking, assist learners to be independent learners, activate their previous experience and knowledge by providing multiple representation content and also promote learners' sense of responsibility to control their learning processes. Abidin (2018) proposed that various Islamic teaching methods deliver content and instructional material in an effective way that facilitates learning, creativity and stimulates their desire to learn. These instructional methods also lead learners to be self-evaluators and solve their learning problems by providing a conducive learning environment (Ambrose et al., 2010). Effective learning always takes place where a teacher feels students are copartners and constructs learning activities based on what students think and what they know already.

Lubis et al. (2011) stressed that it is very significant to enable learners to value their religious teachings and follow them in their daily lives. This is also the spirit of Islamic education—students must be able to explore the world and learn social values to live together. To achieve the aforementioned objectives, the instructional strategies play a very significant role, and if teaching methods are not appropriate, it will be hard to meet all of the standards. The constructivist approach follows the content and learning experiences that are familiar to their learners so they can develop connections within the existing patterns of their knowledge to make the learning permanent (Abidin, 2018). This instructional approach enables teachers to create a strong instructional guide and learning experiences that help them in achieving their objectives more effectively and efficiently.

Various studies pointed out that many Islamic teachers don't follow modern instructional approaches like student-centred and constructivism, which causes the failure of their instructions efforts because they are unable to meet the challenges of the 21st century (Kasim & Abdurajak, 2018; Mustaffa & Rashid, 2019; Nawi & Ramlan, 2014). They stressed the need for Islamic education teachers' training regarding new instructional approaches and student-centred instructional strategies. It is emphasised that Islamic teachers must be provided with explicit and practical training programmes where they experience new instructional methods and constructive approaches of teaching that meet the international standards and modern teachers' competencies (Mushtaq, Mustafa, & Abdulghaffar, 2016). As it is the spiritual obligation of an Islamic teacher to be sincere and care for their students, the main concern should be for their Tarbiyya and lifelong learning.

In the 21st century, various challenges and issues have been faced by Islamic teachers, especially in managing their classrooms, transforming knowledge into action and searching for a suitable teaching approach (Kasim & Abdurajak, 2018). Kasim and Abdurajak (2018) emphasised that learning and teaching strategies need to be student-oriented, fun-based, collaborative and focussed on the thinking and soft skills development of learners, and Islamic teachers must be professionally trained in this regard. Hence, traditional Islamic education and instructional practices are still following old and outdated approaches towards the teaching-learning process (Jafari, 2014), whereas there is a dire need for changing the mindset of Islamic teachers by providing them with specific professional training and enabling them to use modern instructional methods (Nawi, Hamzah, Ren, & Tamuri, 2015), which assist them in empowering their students and preparing them for this new and challenging world.

4. Scaffolding Concept in Islamic Instruction

In Islamic teaching, the concept of scaffolding is significantly emphasised, and its proof is the gradual revelation of the Holy Qur'an over 23 years, as it is believed that human behaviour changes over time, and it could take many years to modify the attitudes and behaviours of people (Sabrin, 2012). Imam Ghazali is a well-recognised figure in Western literature as the most quoted theologist due to his Ahl Al-Kalaam. He proposed some important rules of conduct for Islamic teachers that are very much related to the current perspectives of modern educationists. He stressed that teachers should be very caring and loving towards their students, be sincere and honest in fulfilling their responsibilities, scaffold their students via building their instructional plans on the students' previous knowledge and experiences so that their interest in learning will be retained, privately pinpoint students' bad behaviour instead of highlighting them in front of their peers and practice on themselves whatever they advise to their students. It is also important for teachers to understand students' abilities and interests so that they can provide appropriate learning experiences rather than overwhelming the students (Rahman, 2018). Through the exploration of Islamic doctrines, we can observe the practical explanations of Prophet Muhammad in the form of His actions, such as upholding one's covenants, helping needy people, maintaining strong kinships, being fair and humble in one's deeds, so that other people can understand how to behave and practice certain principles of Islam.

5. Technology-Based Instruction

Many teachers in religious institutions generally use two techniques for teaching: memorisation and the textbook method (Jafari, 2014). It is assumed that religious subjects can only be taught by memorising the content and following the lecture methods and reading methods. Haynes (2009) observed that few Islamic teachers practice modern techniques, use technologies and infuse the inductive approaches, such as the demonstration method, discussion and problem-solving methods, especially in religious schools. There is a long list of modern approaches, methods and techniques which could be used in religious education like questioning, inquiry, collaborative and technology-based instructional strategies (Zedan, Yusoff, & Mohamed, 2015). This is very important for Islamic instructors to learn various innovative instructional strategies and technologies to fulfil their main objective of instruction as to promote students' self-learning, lifelong learning, creative and critical thinking.

One of the new instructional approaches is the use of Information and Communication Technologies (ICT) that is widely employed for effective and efficient instruction at all levels. The use of technology enables teachers to teach complex material/content in an interesting way that could be more understandable for students and enable them to apply the learnt information in their daily life. By using ICTs, teachers can achieve instructional goals and meet global challenges within a short time facing fewer difficulties (Lubis et al., 2011). Many technology-related instructional materials are available for teachers' help, such as Mustaffa and Rashid's (2019) suggested technology-based instructional materials, including worksheets, modules, pictures, videos, textbooks and CDs/DVDs, which are available in the form of computer-based programmes.

The primary characteristic of Islamic pedagogy is that it emphasises the holistic development of children and promotes strong relationships among students and teachers by developing apprenticeship relationships among both of these. Hence, the technology could provide a strong path for interactive and collaborative instructional opportunities for Islamic teachers (Amri, Tahir, & Ahmad, 2017). Wekke and Lubis (2011) highlighted that the age of technology is just the age of information that is rarely contributing to the modification of human behaviours and hearts. It is also emphasised that the excessive and careless use of technology could lead to some harm to humanity—e.g., by damaging the environment, destructive relationships due to excessive use of technology and a materialistic approach towards life. Therefore, a careful attitude needs to be developed among teachers to use technology and the latest instructional gadgets for constructive and positive behaviour development among students and bring about healthy social change (Wekke & Lubis, 2011). Sabrin (2012) also supported the importance of using technologies in Islamic instruction to broaden the students' knowledge and cultivate critical thinking among them, as without understanding, students would not be able to apply their knowledge in life.

6. Impact of Globalisation on Islamic Instruction

Globalisation has changed every field of life, particularly educational practices. It is very important to broaden the Islamic teachers' perspective on how globalisation is affecting the whole teaching-learning process. There are three main effects of globalisation on education: (1) transformation in the curriculum, (2) instructional styles and (3) digital practices in education. These all need to be considered due to rapidly changing societies, students' interests and job market demands (Nawi, Jamsari, Hamzah, Sulaiman, & Umar, 2012). These advancements in global practices opened the way for Islamic education to acclimate itself with new changes and get benefits from global practices to bring reforms to Islamic instructional practices. Islamic teachers have to be trained in a way that they can adopt modern instructional practices and implement new teaching-learning methods in schools for promoting quality education.

Few studies highlighted that Islamic teachers rarely use modern and global instructional strategies that could attract students' interests and attention (Ab Halim & Nik, 2010; Ahmad & Ab Halim, 2010). Teachers usually use lecture and direct methods for teaching Islamic concepts and adopt these instructional practices because they are easy to manage and do not involve much cost, time or effort. It is stressed that Islamic teachers' training institutions have to promote global perspectives about teaching and learning among teachers and change their ways of instruction to meet current challenges (Nawi, Jamsari, Hamzah, Sulaiman, & Umar, 2012). In the same perspective, many studies support the use of technologies and modern techniques to improve students' interests, understanding levels and assist teachers with making their teaching more attractive and easy (Ab Halim & Nik, 2010; Nawi, Jamsari, Hamzah, Sulaiman, & Umar, 2012). Islamic teachers especially should put forth a special effort to learn ICT and use technology to make their instructional practices more attractive and effective to achieve broader religious objectives.

Discussion and Conclusion

The Islamic education philosophy always accentuates the development of comprehensive a personality, attitude and world view which should be consistent with the knowledge and appreciation of the Qur'an and Sunnah (Mushtaq, Mustafa, & Abdulghaffar, 2016). The literature revealed that Islamic teachers are not prominently practicing the student-centred approach during their teachings; rather, they are more focussed on the content alone, which has a negative effect on students' learning (Nawi & Ramlan, 2014). The selection of appropriate instructional strategies is very significant, as they could improve students' achievement and enhance the quality of the educational process. Islamic teachers must be provided with essential knowledge and training about modern instructional strategies so that they can equip their students with the modern skills needed to meet global world challenges. In forthcoming paragraphs, some important student-centred instructional strategies are discussed.

There are many student-centred approaches which could be helpful for Islamic teachers to adopt for effective teaching of Islamic content, such as cooperative learning that involves small groups working to achieve common goals and complete set tasks; brainstorming in which learners are placed in a situation and encouraged to think reflectively and creatively; discussion, which is a student-centred approach that involves the presentation of an issue and students being asked to talk about it, listen and contribute carefully and try to go for a conclusion or solution of the issue; small group approach involves grouping the individuals on the basis of their characteristics and assigning them specific roles to accomplish a given task; presentation is another student-centred approach that mainly involves giving students individual or group assignments that have to be completed by following the given guidelines and set criteria; and panel/expert includes students working on a topic, which can include many voices on the single topic, and students can write or ask questions/comments on that topic.

Simulation is a computer-based instruction that involves technology to create a simulation of a real situation, and students are allowed to practice individually without the fear of failure. Role play is very useful instruction that allows the learners to create a particular role, plan it and experience it. Demonstrations are fun activities that involve students fully in certain tasks, and they have to demonstrate the given tasks, such as cooking or science activities. A project is one of the important student-centred approaches that stimulate students to learn what they could do in a particular workplace. Inquiry-based is another instructional strategy that involves learners in critical thinking and problem-solving skills, and students are put in a critical situation and asked to inquire about that situation and come up with certain solutions or answers.

The discovery method as a teaching strategy can be broader or narrow in scope and allows the learners to select a topic and explore it in detail. Jigsaw is also a new instructional strategy that allows students to work in groups; every student is assigned a different task and later all come and discuss their work with each other. Workshop as an instructional activity involves allowing students to plan and conduct a workshop on the selected theme and at the end provide detailed feedback about the results of their workshop. Competition is one of the important learner-centred instructional strategies that engage students in various competitions on the inter-/intra-school level, and problem-based learning indulges students in a particular problem and asks them to find out possible alternatives for a solution, select the best alternative and solve the problem.

This chapter provided enriched knowledge to its readers regarding the true concept of Islamic ideology related to instructional practices and teachers' professional development in line with the modern instructional approaches and student-centred instructional strategies. This deepening text could enable the readers to comprehend that Islamic instruction is not deviating from modern innovation in the teaching-learning process; hence, it has already offered and supported modern instructional practices and teachers' professional development since 1,400 years back.

This chapter discussed the need for Islamic teachers to transition from traditional strategies, approaches and methods to modern or contemporary ones. It also brought into focus the need for a revolution in teacher training

66 Samina Malik and Nabi Bux Jumani

modules so that Islamic students can be fitted for the 21st century. Moreover, it provided highlights of some modern instructional strategies which are driven from the prophetic instruction approach in Islam—e.g., higher-order thinking, deep knowledge, deep understanding, problem-based learning, understanding and memorisation, discussion method, research-based instruction (Asyafah, 2014). Furthermore, student-centred, project-based and problem-based teaching have been elaborated on and are also encouraged in the perspective of Islamic instructional strategies and should be the main focus of professional training programmes of Islamic teachers. At the end of this chapter, the teaching strategies related to students' active engagements in learning and the use of technology in instructional practices were discussed as some key considerations for the professional growth of Islamic teachers.

References

Ab Halim, T., & Nik, R. N. (2010). *Kaedah Pengajaran dan Pembelajaran Pendidikan Islam*. Bangi, Malaysia: Penerbit Universiti Kebangsaan.

Abidin, M. Z. (2018). Ulama in Indonesian urban society: A view of their role and position in the change of age. *Journal of Theologia, 28*(2), 235–254.

Ahmad, Y. K., & Ab Halim, T. (2010). Pedagogical content knowledge of teaching the faith: A case study of excellent teachers of Islamic Education. *Journal of Islamic & Arabic Education, 2*(2), 13–30.

Ambrose, S. A., Bridges, M. W., DiPietro, M., Lovett, M. C., & Norman, M. K. (2010). *How learning works: Seven research-based principles for smart teaching*. USA: John Wiley & Sons.

Amri, M., Tahir, S. Z., & Ahmad, S. (2017). The implementation of Islamic teaching in multiculturalism society: A case study at pesantren schools in Indonesia. *Asian Social Science, 13*(6), 125–132.

Asyafah, A. (2014). Research based instruction in the teaching of Islamic education. *SpringerPlus, 3*(1), 755.

Haynes, J. (2009). Conflict, conflict resolution and peace-building: The role of religion in Mozambique, Nigeria and Cambodia. *Commonwealth & Comparative Politics, 47*(1), 52–75.

Jafari, Z. (2014). A comparison of conventional lecture and team-based learning methods in terms of student learning and teaching satisfaction. *Medical Journal of the Islamic Republic of Iran, 28*(5). Retrieved from https://www.ncbi.nlm.nih.gov/pmc/articles/PMC4154282/

Kasim, T. S. (2014). Teaching paradigms: An analysis of traditional and student-centred approaches. *Journal of Usuluddin, 40*, 199–218.

Kasim, T. S., & Abdurajak, F. S. (2018). Issues and challenges in teaching and learning: An analysis of Islamic education novice teachers' practices. *International Journal of Education, Psychology and Counselling, 3*(12), 99–109.

Lubis, M. A., Yunus, M. M., Diao, M., Muhamad, T. A., Mustapha, R., & Ishak, N. M. (2011). The perception and method in teaching and learning Islamic education. *International Journal of Education Information Technologies, 1*(5), 69-78

Mohd-Aliff, M. N., Ezad, A. J., Adibah, S., & Mohd, I. H. (2013). Development and evaluation of ning social network for teaching training online surveillance. *Turkish Online Journal of Distance Education, 14*(1), 245–255.

Mushtaq, S., Mustafa, M. T., & Abdulghaffar. (2016). National Professional Standards for Teachers in Pakistan in light of teaching of the Holy Prophet (P.B.U.H). *Journal of Policy Research, 1*(4), 171–181.

Mustaffa, A., & Rashid, A. A. (2019). Teaching methodologies in Islamic education in 21st century; challenges and pespective. *6 th International Conference in Islamic Education: Rabbani Education 2018,* (pp. 608–614). Kota Bharu, Kelantan.

Nawi, A., Hamzah, M. I., Ren, C. C., & Tamuri, A. H. (2015). Adoption of mobile technology for teaching preparation in improving teaching quality of teachers. *International Journal of Instruction, 8*(2), 113–124.

Nawi, M. A., Jamsari, E. A., Hamzah, M. I., Sulaiman, A., & Umar, A. (2012). The impact of globalization on current Islamic education. *Australian Journal of Basic and Applied Sciences, 6*(8), 74–78.

Nawi, M. A., & Ramlan, Y. (2014). A study on the strategies and practice of teaching among trainee teachers during teaching training. *The Online Journal of Islamic Education, 2*(1), 1–6.

Pritchard, A. (2014). *Ways of learning: Learning theories and learning styles in the classroom* (3rd ed.). New York: Routledge.

Rahman, M. (2018). Education, teaching methods and techniques in the early years of Islam during the era of prophet Muhammad (SAW). *IJRDO-Journal of Business Management, 4*(2), 1–22.

Reeve, J., & Jang, H. (2006). What teachers say and do to support students' autonomy during a learning activity. *Journal of Educational Psychology, 98*(1), 209–218.

Rosyad, A. M. (2019). The implementation of inductive teaching and learning methods in Islamic education learning. *Risâlah, Jurnal Pendidikan dan Studi Islam, 6*(1), 63–79.

Sabrin, M. (2012). *The Arab Spring and education: The need for an Islamic pedagogy.* Amazon.com: KindleBooks.

Syahidin. (2017). The teacher education in Islamic views: A conceptual analysis to increase teacher and lecturer professionalism Islamic religious education in Indonesia. *International Journal of Recent Scientific Research, 8*(10), 20593–20596.

Wekke, I. S., & Lubis, M. A. (2011). Educational technology on teaching and learning of integrated Islamic education in Brunei Darussalam. *Ulumuna, 15*(1), 185–204.

Yaming, T., & Yu-Liang, T. (2011). Adoption of mobile technology for language learning: Teacher attitudes and challenges. *The Journal of the JALT CALL SIG, 7*(1), 3–18.

Zedan, A. M., Yusoff, M. Y., & Mohamed, M. (2015). An innovative teaching method in Islamic studies: The use of PowerPoint in University of Malaya as case study. *4th World Conference On Educational Technology Researches, WCETR 2014. 182,* pp. 543–549. Malaysia: Procedia—Social and Behavioral Sciences.

6 Philosophical Inquiry as a Method for Teaching Islamic Education

Wan Mazwati Wan Yusoff, Juhasni Adila Juperi and Abdul Shakour Preece

Introduction

Traditional Pedagogy

Islamic studies is one of the subjects that must be taken by Muslim students undergoing Islamic education. Within Islamic studies, subject students are exposed to topics like *aqīdah, fiqh*, Islamic history, *sīrah, akhlāq* and al-Qur'ān. The aim of Islamic education is to produce good Muslims who are well-balanced physically, psychologically, intellectually and spiritually. The noble aim of Islamic education can be achieved, if and only if, students are able to use their reflective thinking to deeply understand and develop a systematic Islamic world view that is manifested in right action. However, the reality of young Muslims today is that their knowledge of Islam is not manifested in good moral behaviour. Probably their understanding of Islamic faith is shallow—that is, at the level of memorisation of the elements of Islam without the use of reflection or higher-order thinking. The Qur'an exhorts Muslims to use their intellect to think; however, the prevalent teaching method used by Islamic education teachers does not stimulate thinking or deep understanding.

The sad reality is that Islamic studies is taught through indoctrination and rigid teaching methods (Ali Riaz, 2014; Tan & Ding 2014). Teachers employ lecture and rote learning, putting too much emphasis on memorisation of facts (Aderi, Noh, & Kasim, 2012; Rosnani, Suhailah, & Juhasni Adila, 2014). Such traditional pedagogy requires students to learn by memorising facts and information first, and only promoting discussion after students have 'mastered' the knowledge. They are discouraged from asking provocative questions, questions that could enhance their thinking skills. Thus, they become passive recipients of information. Consequently, discussion, dialogue and student involvement are almost non-existent in traditional classrooms (Zedan, Yusoff, & Mohamed, 2015; Norfadelah & Ahmad Tijani, 2015; Nursafra et al., 2016). The result of this is that students lose interest in learning Islamic studies (Wan Mazwati, Preece, & Lina Mursyidah, 2018). This mismatch between student motivation and teaching methods results in failure to achieve the goal of developing good moral character, based

DOI: 10.4324/9781003193432-7

on Islamic teachings. In contrast, 'community of philosophical inquiry' or 'COPI' method, employs a constructivist approach that co-opts students into the teaching-learning process, making the class more learner-centred and engaging.

The COPI method has been found to be effective in promoting higher-order thinking skills, including 'caring' thinking or ethical thinking, which, in turn, develops deeper understanding in students. Philosophical inquiry was the primary method used in 'Philosophy for Children' (P4C), a programme founded by Matthew Lipman (2003) in 1974 at the Institute for Advancement in Philosophy for Children at Montclair State University, New Jersey. In 2006, Professor Rosnani Hashim established the Centre for Philosophical Inquiry in Education, now known as the Centre for Teaching Thinking, at the Kulliyyah of Education in the International Islamic University Malaysia, after empirical evidence supported the effectiveness of COPI for encouraging reflection, engagement, self-confidence and communication skills among primary school children. Pupils at government and private Islamic schools were seen, almost for the first time, to share their opinions and listen to one another in a community of inquiry. Other studies employing COPI method for Islamic studies showed similar positive results in terms of student confidence, student understanding, thinking skills and language development (Juhasni Adila, 2010; Preece, 2012; Rosnani, Suhailah & Juhasni, 2014; Wan Mazwati & Lina Mursyidah, 2016; Nursafra et al., 2016; Wan Mazwati, Preece, & Lina Mursyidah, 2018; Rosnani & Hendon, 2020). We will now go on to discuss the fundamentals of COPI, their relevance to Islamic studies and how they contribute to teachers' professional development.

What Is COPI?

A 'community' in this context refers to a group of people who share a common interest or goal. COPI represents a group of individuals who collaborate, through Socratic dialogue, to inquire into philosophical problems in order to progress towards truth. Truth may be logical, metaphysical, epistemological, ethical, aesthetic, social or political in nature. In other words, students discuss philosophical problems and issues related to logic, faith, knowledge and values using procedures that are "disciplined by logic" (Lipman, 2003: 92).

How Is COPI Conducted?

COPI, as we have seen, is an avenue for learners to enhance their thinking skills, discuss moral issues, question assumptions or justify moral judgements by deliberating upon social issues. This is in stark contrast to students who are passive recipients of a lecture or '*derse*.' Due to the routinisation of conventional classrooms, students often become blasé and desensitised to familiar content, causing them to cease questioning, reflecting or appreciating the profound nature of what they are studying (Badri, 2018). In contrast,

COPI encourages students to be active learners who participate in dialogue. After exposing them to some philosophical content, students formulate their own questions, which they discuss, sharing personal experiences, views and even anecdotes. In this way, students achieve a shared understanding of the Islamic knowledge in question, under the guidance and facilitation of their teacher. At times, it can feel a bit like surfing a wave of conversation in a group! "It is an example of the value of shared experience" (Lipman, 2003: 93). Nevertheless, teachers need to remind students to be respectful of one another's opinions, especially during disagreements. After all, being considerate and thoughtful are all part of becoming a reasonable individual. As such, COPI provides a healthy environment for the development of students' soft skills and ethical thinking. An example of a controversial question for discussion might be, What is the place of gender roles in Islam? Through practising discussion in a community of inquiry, students hone their ability to make informed decisions—an important life skill. In addition, COPI contributes to the formation of a systematic world view since the content of COPI discussions covers the fundamentals of life.

Why Use COPI for Islamic Education Teachers' Professional Development?

For teaching and learning to be effective in the 21st century, Islamic education teachers need to be well-equipped with the skills necessary to engage learners, both cognitively and effectively. Ledward and Hirata (2011) claim we are living in a knowledge economy rather than an industrial economy; hence, routine skills are no longer essential. There is a wealth of information readily available to students online; therefore, learners need to be able to apply this knowledge to solve complex problems. In addition, nowadays, learners may be technologically more advanced than their teachers, thus Islamic education teachers need to keep half a step ahead of their students if they are to become role models for them. By embracing modernity and integrating this into the *tawhidic* world view of Islam, teachers make Islamic studies more appealing and relevant to the everyday experiences and environment of students.

Society is continually developing, and so the teaching methods of Islamic studies should advance too. Old-fashioned, dogmatic approaches will only demotivate students from learning. Teachers and students need to develop a 'critical disposition' because the issues and problems facing them in the modern world are becoming increasingly complex. If teachers and students can connect the original sources of Islam—i.e., *Qur'an* and *Sunnah*—to modern-day issues like organ donation, gay rights and feminism, etc., it will make Islamic studies more relevant and interesting. Failure to do so could result in Islamic education becoming like a dinosaur that seems irrelevant and archaic to learners. Faulkner and Latham (2016) claim that teachers need to have a 'growth' mindset rather than a 'fixed' one. Meaning that they are able to adapt to changes in education by developing new strategies. In other words, they can construct new knowledge and methods for futures, hitherto unknown yet filled with possibility.

The authors believe that COPI is a viable response to the current need for reform in Islamic education. This is in spite of the fact that it was originally intended by the P4C movement to develop the philosophical thinking of young American children. The authors maintain that Islamic education teachers can not only implement this approach to deepen the thinking of their students but also to improve their own thinking. Put another way, Islamic education teachers need to develop the disposition of questioning and reflecting upon the issues surrounding them if they are to play their role as facilitators of the advancement of students' philosophical inquiry and critical thinking skills (Loh, Hong, & Koh, 2018).

The findings of a study conducted by Baker and Fisher (2016) about the effects of P4C on teachers, showed that the implementation of P4C developed reflection and independence in them. The study also proposed COPI as a bridge for developing professional skills and dialogue, moving teachers from being just 'good' to 'outstanding.' These recommendations are in-line with the findings of an interview conducted by O'Riordan's (2015) with a teacher who states that the COPI process helped her recognise the importance of discussion and exploration in learning. Equally important was the ability of COPI to improve her autonomy and self-confidence as a teacher. In another study by Green, Condy and Chigona (2012), it was observed that COPI empowered pre-service teachers by developing their thinking skills and habits of mind in their personal lives, their professional lives and in the children they taught. All this indicates that COPI presents teachers with tangible and practical methods for introducing thinking skills to Islamic studies.

Based on the previous evidence, it is clear that the benefits of COPI extend not only to the students who experience it but also to the teachers who teach it. As a consequence, the authors advocate the use of COPI in Islamic education to enhance teachers' professionalism by increasing their confidence, honing their thinking skills, improving their discourse and developing in them a critical disposition for the benefit of the creativity and criticality of their students.

The COPI Session

A COPI session involves several stages. Firstly, the session begins with a teacher or facilitator sitting with students in a big circle or U-shaped formation. This is to promote interaction and face-to-face communication. In the first session, the facilitator will usually discuss the rules that students are supposed to follow. These rules include listening to others attentively, taking turns when speaking, respecting other's opinions, arguing with ideas and not the person who posited the ideas, asking questions, examining disagreements, deliberating others' ideas, interpreting and finding solutions, questioning others' claims and postulations, being open to criticism and identifying and creating relationships between ideas. For example, students

72 *Wan Mazwati Wan Yusoff et al.*

may discuss the question, "Can Muslims say 'Merry Christmas' to their non-Muslim friends?"

These procedures represent the process of inquiry and of excellent thinking, which is a multi-dimensional behaviour. Further examples of thinking behaviour are providing and demanding good reasons, looking for clarification, explaining the meaning of concepts, making sound conclusions, making hypotheses, listing counter-examples, identifying assumptions, detecting formal and informal fallacies and deducing logical consequences" (Sharp, 1993).

The basic steps of a COPI session are as follows:

Step 1: Present the stimulus material, in the case of stories, by asking students to read aloud a line at a time or a paragraph at a time until the end of the given text. The teacher may also ask students who are advanced readers to read silently. In the case of stimulus materials, such as pictures, images or videos, the students are asked to study the materials for a few minutes before proceeding to the next step.

Step 2: Give students time to voice out their first reflections or summarise the gist of the story or stimulus.

Step 3: Ask students to formulate philosophical questions based on the stimulus material. Questions asked by students should be written on the whiteboard with students' names beside them. This is done to raise their confidence and self-esteem. It also enables the facilitator to get back to the asker of the question for clarification if necessary. The number of questions asked will depend on the time available for the session.

Step 4: Ask students to read all the questions on the board and identify the main theme of each one. Write the themes up on the board so that the questions with the same theme can be discussed together. Allow students to choose the themes they would like to discuss, although, if the teacher is following a syllabus of philosophical themes, then he or she may choose the questions to be discussed. The teacher may cue students with questions of his or her own to get them started; however, the main purpose of COPI is to encourage philosophical discussion based on questions created by students themselves that were inspired by the stimulus material.

Step 5: Hold a whole-class discussion where students collaboratively explore and answer each other's questions. Remind students they are free to voice out their ideas and opinions but in accordance with the rules of COPI explained earlier. The teacher facilitates the discussion using Socratic questioning to get students clarifying meanings, justifying their responses, giving examples and counter-examples, detecting inconsistencies in arguments, building on others' ideas and synthesising relevant ideas presented in the discussion to come up with new innovative solutions to the questions posed.

Step 6: The COPI session ends with students reflecting upon the thinking that took place, making them more aware of their own thinking process,

Philosophical Inquiry as a Method 73

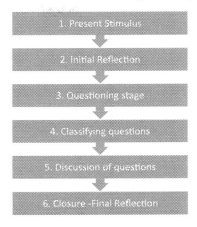

Figure 6.1 Summary of a COPI session.

the type of thinking skills they used, the flaws in their thinking and the lessons learned. The latter can be taken away for further reflection and sharing at home.

One of the beauties of Islamic educators using COPI is that Islamic studies comprises many philosophical concepts and issues, including beliefs, values, principles and rituals. These require understanding for them to be internalised over time. Otherwise, they may just be taught parrot-fashion without understanding or reflection (Figure 6.1).

Stimulus Material

A wide array of materials can be used as a stimulus for COPI. Anything that excites students' thinking and a sense of wonder such as philosophical novels, thinking stories, folktales, children's fiction, picture books, poetry, pictures, photos, artefacts, objects, drama, music, video clips and movies. For Islamic studies, we can add to this list factual narratives about the Prophets, stories from the Qur'an, hadith and Qur'anic verses. In short, anything that promotes higher-order thinking can be used as a stimulus for COPI. These stimuli range from specially written thinking stories to something as simple as an object like a pen, which could inspire us to ask the question, "Why did Allah Almighty use the word 'pen' in *Surah Al-Alaq?*"

COPI stimuli may be of various types; however, the founder of the P4C movement, Mathew Lipman, preferred stories. This is because narratives appeal to a wide variety of people, especially the young (Fisher, 1998). Stories based on real-life experiences can be organised in such a way that they appeal to the emotion and intellect of the reader and provide valuable lessons about the world around us. In addition, Islamic studies stimuli need to include elements necessary for the formation of a systematic Islamic world

74   *Wan Mazwati Wan Yusoff et al.*

view—i.e., thinking and reflecting on the signs of Allah in the universe and in the Qur'an. Another important element is Muslim characters engaging in thinking within the stories. This provides the reader with a good role model of thinking that they can emulate in their discussions. Last but not least, stimulus materials should include the problems and issues facing Islam and Muslims in the modern world. Most importantly, stimulus materials should spark students' curiosity, engendering within them a sense of wonder and excitement that will promote deep thinking about the equivocation of language or the incongruousness of human experience embedded in the materials.

Philosophical Questions

Generally speaking, there are three types of questions: simple questions that require straightforward thinking, questions not answered yet but which can be answered through empirical research and philosophical questions that require complex thinking. COPI addresses philosophical questions that require deep thinking. For example, in the case of Islamic education, one might ask, How do we know God exists? Are we free? Can we steal to help the poor? According to Cam (1995),

> [P]hilosophical questions are essentially contentious. They do not call for correct answers. They demand further investigation and admit different answers that may have one merit or another. They point to problems that cannot be solved by calculation, or consulting a book, or by remembering what the teacher has said. They require students to think for themselves.

As such, answering philosophical questions leads us to new insights, greater understanding and reasoned judgements. In this way, Islamic education students can apply their knowledge to both practical and hypothetical situations.

Discussion

COPI discussions progress by means of Socratic questioning. Socratic questioning consists of a series of questions that lead students towards higher-order thinking skills, such as demanding clarifying concepts, exploring assumptions, justifying arguments, providing evidence, determining the logic of consequences, considering different perspectives and questioning the question.

Other high similar skills promoted by philosophical discussion are critical questioning, clarifying meaning, giving and analysing justifications, probing and analysing assumptions, discovering new perspectives and explanations, testing ideas and evaluating the consequences of beliefs and actions. The emphasis of a philosophical discussion is not so much the end result, but rather the 'good thinking' process that one goes through.

During philosophical discussions, students discover new depths of understanding, as well as recognise the flaws in their own thinking. This enables them to self-correct and hopefully adopt a new perspective on life, their faith or on society. As an illustration, dilemmas between one's culture and one's faith may present conflicting viewpoints dressing, superstition and taboos, etc. In COPI, students strive to reach a consensus. This requires them to analyse and clarify problems, build on each other's ideas and synthesise different viewpoints. The goal of this is to arrive at 'innovative outcomes' not seen or thought of before by students.

If Islamic education teachers are looking for a way to promote creativity, then this is it. COPI allows students to express themselves and evaluate the ideas and opinions of others, and this leads them to question their own ideas and beliefs. This, in turn, will give them confidence when they face criticism or contentious ideologies in the future.

The Role of the Teacher

During COPI discussions, the teacher takes on the role of a facilitator, guiding students to connect the themes and questions under discussion to their lives. Through the example of the teacher, students gain alternative perspectives about common issues that broaden their horizons and, most importantly, provide them with a role model in the pursuit of meaning. It is therefore crucial for Islamic education teachers to demonstrate excellence in thinking and behaviour. According to Lipman (1991), the role of the teacher during philosophical discussions involves the following:

1. Eliciting the views and requesting clarification from students
2. Explaining and interpreting students' responses to confirm understanding
3. Pointing out inconsistencies in students' responses
4. Searching for the assumptions underlying students' claims
5. Identifying fallacies in students' reasoning
6. Asking students for justification

Inquiry Plan Samples

The following are examples of lesson plans that use COPI as a method of instruction. The lesson plans do not require teachers to prepare any special material ahead of time (except Sample 3, which requires a story). Teachers may use any material available in their Islamic studies textbooks as a stimulus for COPI. What is important is the way they use these stimuli and the kind of questions raised by students.

'Leading questions' are questions that the teacher considers crucial for guiding the inquiry process. Leading questions are more philosophical in nature, being concerned with the issues and concepts embedded in the text or stimulus. For this reason, teachers need to prepare leading questions ahead of time in case students, particularly at the early stages, are unable to formulate sufficiently complex questions for a meaningful inquiry.

76   *Wan Mazwati Wan Yusoff et al.*

Sample 1

Stimulus: picture of a child making du'ā (supplication)
Concept: du'ā (supplication)
Level: Upper primary and above
Leading questions:

- What is du'ā?
- Do animals pray/make du'ā?
- Do you have to be a Muslim for your du'ā to be accepted? What about the people of other religions?
- Are all the sayings of our parents considered as du'ā? What if parents say something bad about us?
- How is it that unbelievers, who seldom pray, may appear to be successful in the world?
- Can the du'ā of a thief or a sinner be accepted?

Sample 2

Stimulus: Qur'anic verse, Surah 'Āli Imrān, verse 110
Concepts: 'The best people' (*khaira ummah*), enjoining good and forbidding evil (*da'wah*)

> You are now the best people brought forth for (the guidance and reform of) mankind. You enjoin what is right and forbid what is wrong and believe in Allah. Had the People of the Book believed it were better for them. Some of them are believers but most of them are transgressors.

Level: Lower secondary and above
Leading questions:

- What is the meaning of the phrase 'the best people' (*khaira ummah*) in the Qur'anic verse? How can we define it?
- Are Muslims still 'the best people'? Does this verse apply to Muslims nowadays?
- If we Muslims are not 'the best people' anymore, what are the implications of this?
- How can we apply the concept of *khaira ummah* in our personal lives?
- Muhammad Abduh once said, "I went to the West and saw Islam but no Muslims. When I returned to the East, I saw Muslims but no Islam." How true is this?

Philosophical Inquiry as a Method 77

Sample 3

Stimulus: Thinking story "Garbage"

> Agam, a six-year-old boy, went home with a sad face. His father picked him up from school and along the way home noticed his son's unhappy expression. The father was worried and could not stop asking himself what had happened to his beloved son.
>
> "Agam," he said.
>
> "Yes, Daddy," answered the son.
>
> "I saw your sad face since I picked you up from the school. You didn't even talk to me while we've been in the car. Is there something bad that happened at school?"
>
> "Our teacher gave us an exercise to do in class with 5 questions to be answered. I could only answer 4 questions, so she gave me 80 for my total score. I am disappointed because actually, I did my best to answer all the questions correctly," explained the boy.
>
> "Don't worry, dear, you can try better next time," the father advised.
>
> "Yes, Daddy" replied the son.
>
> The father was curious about the questions because normally his son could answer all the questions given in school correctly. So he asked his son, "What was the question you couldn't answer?"
>
> The question was, "We should throw garbage into…?"
>
> "So, what was your answer?" the father asked.
>
> "The river…" answered the son innocently.

Concept: environment, social responsibility, cleanliness
Level: Upper primary and above
Leading questions:

- Why did Agam suggest dumping rubbish into the river?
- How can we care for our environment?
- How can we stop people from littering?
- Why do people drop litter?
- We Muslims believe that the world will come to an end; therefore, why do we bother taking care of the earth if it is going to end anyway?
- Is getting a high score in examinations the most important thing?
- How is cleanliness related to our faith *(īmān)*?

Conclusion

The world is changing at an ever-increasing pace with the proliferation of knowledge and information causing dramatic transformations in technology, society and education. Students are constantly being bombarded by social media and multimedia on a daily basis; therefore, to counteract this, Islamic studies teachers need to keep abreast of the changes or risk losing their students' attention. It is high time that Islamic studies teachers move out of their comfort zones and transform their teaching methods, making them more relevant to 21st-century teaching and learning. To achieve this, they need to supplement more traditional teaching strategies such as direct instruction and rote learning with more engaging, learner-centred methods like COPI, where students can participate in the learning process and construct their own meaning and understanding.

It may be challenging for Islamic studies teachers to change the way they do things since we often teach the way we were taught. Yet to be more effective, teachers must upgrade their knowledge and skills, particularly in the areas of discussion, questioning and higher-order thinking by adopting a less authoritative style of interaction, especially during COPI discussions. In COPI, students and teachers discuss on equal terms. Everyone's view is equally valid, and teachers should avoid shutting down students or supplying them with the 'right' answers, particularly when questions have no clear right or wrong answer. Instead, teachers need to be sensitive to students' ideas and opinions, withholding judgement and encouraging them to explain, justify and support their views with reasons and evidence. This will require listening on the part of teachers and students. Such changes may seem daunting, yet the rewards for the classroom will be many.

Teachers who have taught for long periods of time often get stuck in a rut, with the result that their classes become repetitive and boring. By adopting a new method such as COPI, it will help to make Islamic studies fresh and fun again, while utilising the same materials. Moreover, COPI helps teachers to develop their own critical thinking, questioning skills and pedagogy, and this will benefit them in their personal and professional lives, moving them from being mediocre to outstanding. By developing a growth mindset, teachers can enhance their skills of reflection, and this will make them more effective and independent as teachers. Lastly, by taking on the role of COPI facilitator, teachers shift their classroom from being teacher-centred to learner-centred.

Vis-à-vis the benefits for students, COPI provides them with a variety of different stimuli; thus making Islamic studies more interesting and engaging. Secondly, students get the opportunity to participate in meaningful discussions about issues of relevance to them. In so doing, they get the opportunity to share their views and opinions about real-life problems. This is not only good for developing their critical, creative and caring thinking, but it also boosts their self-confidence and improves their soft skills as they agree, disagree and communicate their ideas with other students. Lastly, the authors contend that COPI will help to deepen students' understanding of the Islamic studies content so that instead of simply memorising it parrot-fashion, they will internalise it and transfer it to their lives, hopefully applying it in the form of good action and good behaviour.

References

Aderi, M., Noh, C., & Kasim, A. Y. (2012). Teaching of Islamic doctrine and beliefs in school subject content knowledge and pedagogical considerations. *International Journal of Humanities and Social Science*, 2 (11), 258–264.

Badri, M. (2018). *Contemplation: An Islamic psychospiritual study (New edition)*. London: International Institute of Islamic Thought (IIIT).

Baker, G., & Fisher, A. (2016). Philosophy, pedagogy and personal identity: Listening to the teachers in PFC. *Analytic Teaching and Philosophical Praxis*, 37(1), 30–38.

Cam, P. (1995). *Thinking together: Philosophical inquiry for the classroom*. Sydney, Australia: Hale & Iremonger Pty. Ltd.

Faulkner, J., & Latham, G. (2016). Adventurous lives: Teacher qualities for 21st century learning. *Australian Journal of Teacher Education* (Online), 41(4), 137.

Fisher, R. (1998). Stories for thinking: Developing critical literacy through the use of narrative. *Analytic Teaching*, 18(1), 16–27.

Green, L., Condy, J., & Chigona, A. (2012). Developing the language of thinking within a classroom community of inquiry: Pre-service teachers' experiences. *South African Journal of Education*, 32(3), 319–330.

Juhasni Adila, J. (2010). *Philosophical inquiry in Islamic education and its effect in the development of questioning skills among secondary school students. Unpublished project paper submitted as a course requirement for the degree of master of education*, International Islamic University Malaysia, Kuala Lumpur.

Ledward, B. C., & Hirata, D. (2011). *An overview of 21st century skills. Summary of 21st century skills for students and teachers*. Pacific Policy Research Center. Kamehameha Schools. Research & Evaluation, Honolulu.

Lipman, M. (1991). *Thinking in education*. New York: Cambridge University Press.

Lipman, M. (2003). *Thinking in education* (2nd ed.). New York: Cambridge University Press.

Loh, J., Hong, H., & Koh, E. (2018). Transforming teaching through collaborative reflection: A Singaporean case study. *Malaysian Journal of ELT Research*, 13(1), 1–11.

Norfadelah & Ahmad Tijani. (2015). Islamic theoretical model for Islamic critical thinking in teaching and learning of Islamic education. *Gse E-journal of Education*, 3, 34–44.

Nursafra, M. Z., Mohd Isa, H., Khadijah, A. R., & Akbar, W. A. (2016). Ke arah guru Pendidikan Islam sebagai pemikir kritis. *Sains Humanika*, 8(3), 9–15.

O'Riordan, N. (2015). Implementing P4C in the primary classroom: Some fuzzy predictions. *Journal of Philosophy in Schools*, 2(2), 30–47.

Preece, A. S. (2012). *Benefitting Muslim learner's using philosophical inquiry*. [Conference presentation] The 21st MELTA International Conference, Kuala Lumpur.

Riaz, A. (2014). Madrassah education in Bangladesh: Contestations and accommodations. In Sa'eda Buang & Phyllis Ghim-Lian Chew (Eds.). *Muslim education in the 21st century*, pp. 12–35. New York: Routledge.

Rosnani, H., & Hendon, A. (2020). Teaching thinking through Qur'anic stories using the Hikmah pedagogy of philosophical inquiry. *IIUM Journal of Educational Studies*, 8(1), 89–111.

Rosnani, H., Suhailah, H., & Juhasni Adila, J. (2014). The Hikmah (Wisdom) Program: A philosophical inquiry for the teaching of Islamic education in Malaysia. In *Muslim education in the 21st century*, pp. 137–153. New York: Routledge.

Sharp, A. M. (1993). Peirce, feminism, and philosophy for children. *Analytic Teaching*, 14(1), 51–62.

Tan, C & Ding, K. (2014). The role, developments and challenges of Islamic Education in China. Dlm. Sa'eda Buang & Phyllis Ghim-Lian Chew. *Muslim Education in the 21st Century*, pp. 55–69. New York: Routledge.

Wan Mazwati, W. Y., & Lina Mursyidah, H. (2016). Philosophical inquiry method for enhancing higher order thinking in teaching Aqidah to form two students. In Tengku Sarina Aini Tengku Kasim, Asyraf Isyraqi Jamil, Ahmad Yussuf, Mohd Anuar Mamat, A. Bamba, & Abd Aziz Rekan (Eds.). *Pendidikan Islam dan Cabaran Globalisasi (Islamic Education and the Challenges of Globalization)*, pp. 303–331. Kuala Lumpur: Akademi Pendidikan Islam, Universiti Malaya.

Wan Mazwati, W. Y., Preece, A. S., & Lina Mursyidah, H. (2018). Students' experiences in teaching and learning Islamic education using philosophical inquiry method. *Journal of Education and Learning*, 12(2), 266–274.

Zedan, A. M., Yusoff, M. Y. Z. B. M., & Mohamed, M. R. B. (2015). An innovative teaching method in Islamic studies: The use of power point in University of Malaya as case study. *Procedia-Social Behavioral Sciences*, 182, 543–549.

7 Technology Infusion in the Design of an Impactful Islamic Education Learning Experience

Rosemaliza Binti Mohd Kamalludeen

More than 1.2 billion children worldwide were affected when schools faced closure during the first global outbreak of the COVID-19 pandemic since February 2020 (Li & Lalani, 2020). All institutions of learning were forced to rely on technology to keep formal learning alive. Despite having very little to no training on e-learning, many educators deep-dived into Web 2.0, building their online teaching skills rapidly, while barely surviving remote teaching and learning to ensure lessons continue. Parents became instant "frontliners" in ensuring their children engage in online learning, although faced with tremendous difficulties including (1) economic limitations (i.e., bearing additional internet subscription fees and purchasing devices), (2) a lack of teaching skills and (3) little to no understanding of content knowledge (Akmal & Ritonga, 2020).

Islamic education is no exception. Being predominantly delivered face-to-face, the teaching of Islamic studies needed to continue despite the pandemic. The *mu'alim* and *mu'alimah* had to adapt fast and embrace the usage of technology. Even before COVID-19, Islamic education teachers were in dire need to be equipped with qualifications and competencies that are in line with the demands of the Industrial Revolution (IR) 4.0 (Harto, 2018). Being technologically savvy not only constitutes the ability to use tools in the classroom but also to know when is the best time to use the right tool so that learning is maximised.

Therefore, this chapter will address the fundamentals of instructional design, including constructive alignment when designing lessons that incorporate technology to ensure learning outcomes are achieved in a transformative approach to Islamic education. Relevant instructional design models will be elaborated to guide Islamic education teachers in designing their lessons that include the use of technology.

Learning in the Era of IR 4.0

IR 4.0 happened when biological, physical and digital advancements became inseparable. In this era, information technology facilitates the spread of knowledge more conveniently than ever before. When a person

DOI: 10.4324/9781003193432-8

is curious about a particular topic, he or she will be able to access information about it in a fraction of a second just by tapping on their mobile devices. This technology is also used to spread the true (and unfortunately, untrue) messages of Islam across the globe, teaching the world community about Islam's doctrine of peace and love, promoting the sunnah of Prophet Muhammad S.A.W., as well as helping Islamic educational institutes teach Islamic values more effectively (Saifee, Sahikh, Sultan, Baloach, & Khalid, 2012). Saifee et al. added that new technologies of IR 4.0 would empower innovative pedagogies, where new virtual learning experiences are enhanced and encouraged.

Prior to COVID-19, the educational technology industry was already experiencing high-level growth and adoption with the global online learning market expected to reach USD$350 billion by the year 2025 (Li & Lalani, 2020). Responding to the demands of IR 4.0, teaching and learning actively incorporate new technologies like artificial intelligence, virtual reality, augmented reality, 3D printing and deep learning. COVID-19 further accelerated the growth of educational technology adoption; even laggards were forced to embrace it or perish.

Advocates of instructional technology promoted technology-infused pedagogies to ensure that learning is made relevant to today's generation of digital native learners. Student interactivity in lessons increases with the use of technology and improves the convenience and effectiveness of the transfer of knowledge processes (Raja & Nagasubramani, 2018). Learning with the aid of technology opens up opportunities for unconventional learning to happen, especially for digital natives. Integrating technology into teaching and learning has been researched comprehensively, with most outcomes suggesting the benefits far surpass disadvantages. It allows for active participation through interactive response applications like Mentimeter, Quizizz and Kahoot!; interacting with dynamic media content; collaborative learning regardless of location and time; immediate response to assignments through automated grading; and easy access to up-to-date content.

As a result of learning from the pandemic experiences, learning will never be the same. Technology and learning cannot be separated. However, for technology-infused lessons to be effective, proper planning must be done. Aimlessly bombarding students with fancy apps with the hope that learning is made more engaging could have adverse effects on engagement itself and also the achievement of learning outcomes. Students might get hyped, but they have no clue what the content is all about.

Acknowledging the importance of planning in technology infusion, I will focus on the fundamentals of instructional design to assist Islamic education teachers in planning their technology-infused classrooms to ensure that the delivery of Islamic education stays current and relevant for digital native learners. Based on the Technological, Pedagogical and Content Knowledge framework, *mu'alim* and *mu'alimah* of the digital age need to be equipped not only with pedagogical and content knowledge but also to fully understand how to use technology to teach (Mishra & Koehler, 2006).

Islamic Education and Educational Technology

For Islamic education, most scholars agree that there are three main objectives. First is *tarbyah*, which indicates Islamic education is for the purposes of nurturing and caring for the learner. Second is *ta'lim*, indicating the imparting of knowledge to the learners and third, *ta'dib*, which indicates the disciplining of the mind, body and soul (Hussain, 2004). Based on these three objectives, scholars agree that Islamic education intends to be transformative—that is, to explicitly observe significant holistic change in the learners, including cognitive, spiritual, physical and emotional. However, the current approach to Islamic education is seen as informative rather than transformative as the curriculum design mostly covers content delivery as opposed to holistic approaches to teaching. According to Hashim (2004), Islamic education has not been addressing the three objectives, and she calls for its reformation. She asserts, "An effective Islamic education program would help instill Islamic values, develop strong character, and more importantly, develop critical and wise minds" (pp. 136–137).

The teaching of Islamic education around the world differs in terms of curriculum and instruction. In Malaysia, for instance, Islamic education is embedded into the national curriculum, and it is made compulsory for Muslim students to learn the syllabus, as Islam is the official religion of the country. In Indonesia, religious education is made available to all students, including Islamic education in state-run schools (Setiawan, 2020). As for Qur'anic studies, Setiawan (2020) mentioned that most *tahfiz* or religious schools in Malaysia, Indonesia and Thailand approach the learning of the Qur'an through rote memorisation, and some schools require students to be able to recite the Qur'an in Arabic without any mistakes, although students are not well versed in the Arabic language.

While Islamic education has always been delivered through teacher-led face-to-face instruction, the current demands for e-learning force both educators and learners to embrace technology as one of the main avenues for learning. Therefore, it is imperative to highlight the importance of instructional or learning design knowledge in designing impactful Islamic education lessons while keeping abreast of the current trends in education by incorporating technology in its curriculum.

Constructive Alignment

From the perspectives of instructional design, learning objectives and learning outcomes determine how Islamic education should be delivered and assessed, which will ultimately measure the impact of the curriculum on learners. These three elements – learning outcomes, learning activities and assessment of learning must be aligned in order for the learners to successfully achieve the objectives of the lesson (Biggs, 1999). This alignment is called constructive alignment, a fundamental model developed by John Biggs to address the importance of meaningful learning (Figure 7.1).

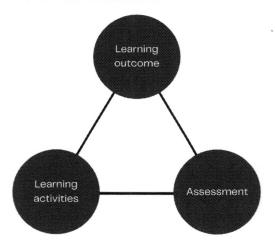

Figure 7.1 Constructive alignment by John Biggs.

According to Biggs, education is about "conceptual change" as opposed to merely the acquisition of information (p. 60). He further elaborates that conceptual change happens as follows:

(i) students are clear of the learning objective and where they will end up at the end of the lesson;
(ii) students are motivated and feel the need to achieve the learning objectives;
(iii) students focus on learning tasks freely or voluntarily, not because they are being monitored to do so; and
(iv) students are able to work collaboratively and engage in conversations with their peers and teachers.

Reflecting upon the four events that indicate the occurrence of conceptual change or transformative education, Islamic education teachers need to look into the alignment of intended learning outcomes with the way Islamic education is being taught and assessed. What is the actual intention of the curriculum – is it to simply 'inform' learners about Islam or is the curriculum meant to 'transform' the learners into better Muslims and members of the society?

Constructive alignment helps curriculum developers and teachers to reimagine and realign the primary purpose of delivering the curriculum. This is a fundamental part of instructional design, as a well-designed course or lesson always needs to begin with the right intention—i.e., intended learning outcomes.

Fundamentals of Instructional Design

Instructional design is generally defined as a systematic process of planning and developing learning programmes to help learners achieve learning goals and objectives. Reigeluth (1983) asserts that instructional design prescribes "optimal methods of instruction to bring about desired changes in student knowledge and skills" (p. 4). The starting point of instructional design is identifying what students should learn (Seel, Lehmann, Blumschein, & Podolskiy, 2017), which Gagné (1985) has classified into five main categories—namely, verbal information, intellectual skills, cognitive strategies, motor skills and attitudes.

Another term that is commonly used is learning design. According to Seel et al. (2017), scholars debate upon the appropriateness of both terminologies from the behaviourist-constructivist standpoint. Instructional design is arguably a more appropriate term describing teaching activities that help students improve their learning while learning design is focussed on learning activities, facilitated by the instructor, also aiming towards the improvement of student learning. Seel et al. concluded that both terms are actually two sides of the same coin. They both aim at systematically designing learning environments that enable students to achieve intended learning outcomes.

In short, instructional design or learning design are both regarded as tools in developing a learning environment that facilitates the achievement of intended learning outcomes. These tools are widely used to systematically design impactful learning programmes for various institutions, including formal schooling, tertiary education and workplace learning.

Instructional Design Process for Infusing Technology into Islamic Education

Infusing technology in teaching and learning must go through elaborate instructional design processes, as they must support learners in achieving learning outcomes. There are more than 40 instructional design models developed by scholars to guide curriculum designers in producing better learning plans to give students impactful learning experiences. The ADDIE model, for instance, holds the philosophy of intentional learning to be student-centred, innovative, authentic and inspirational (Branch, 2009). It is one of the most commonly referred to models and was originally developed for the US Air Force training programmes in 1975. 'ADDIE' stands for the five phases of instructional design – Analysis, Design, Development, Implementation and Evaluation. ADDIE became the basis of most instructional design models, as it is dynamic and adaptable depending upon the various needs of learners.

To assist Islamic education teachers in developing learning programmes that involve the usage of technology tools, I will discuss the ASSURE model that was developed by Smaldino (1996) based on the ADDIE model, aimed to assist teachers in developing lessons that integrate the usage of technology. Like ADDIE, ASSURE also got its name from the six steps that guide teachers throughout the instructional design process.

The ASSURE Model

ASSURE is an acronym for the steps in the instructional design process suggested by its founder, Smaldino (1996). The steps are (1) analyse learner characteristics; (2) state objectives; (3) select, modify or design materials; (4) utilise materials; (5) require learner response; and (6) evaluation. The step-by-step approach intends to effectively integrate technology into lessons so that learning outcomes can be achieved (Figure 7.2).

While the use of technology is essential in teaching and learning, it must be selected and used purposefully. Islamic education teachers may use this model as a guide to systematically incorporate technology into their lessons. The six steps in the ASSURE model are elaborated next.

1. Analyse Learner Characteristics
   Before planning instruction, Smaldino, Rowther and Russell (2014) recommend that teachers gain as much information as possible about their learners. This is to ensure that the lessons planned are suitable for learners in terms of their characteristics, needs and backgrounds with respect to the intended learning outcomes.

   The important information that teachers need to analyse about learners as recommended by Smaldino, Rowther and Russell (2014) are listed as follows:
   a) General Characteristics
      The generic information that is useful for teachers to have may be in the form of constant variables, such as gender and ethnicity, or those

Figure 7.2 The ASSURE instructional design model.

that vary, such as attitude and interest. Information such as the total number of students in class, age group, level (e.g., grade) and socio-economic status will assist teachers in selecting appropriate media to be used in the lessons. For Islamic studies, for instance, it is helpful for teachers to learn the family background of each student and also their religious practices so that the lessons can be made relevant and understood better by the learners.

Lessons can be better designed by gathering as much information as possible about the learners. To do this, teachers can use a survey form, or simply engage in casual conversations with their students. The better the rapport teachers have with students, the more information can be obtained.

b) Specific Entry Competencies
Students' prior knowledge is one of the most important elements that will help them grasp new concepts better (Smaldino, Rowther, & Russell, 2014). From a constructivist viewpoint, learners build understanding upon what they already know. Entry competencies information can be gathered via formal or informal means. Teachers may simply ask questions in the class or utilise assessment tools, such as quizzes and tests.

Having knowledge about students' entry competencies will help teachers decide how to navigate through the curriculum and emphasise concepts that are unfamiliar to the students. It is also important to note the depth of understanding that students have about a particular topic so that teachers do not miss out on the important points that students need to master. For instance, students might know how to recite Al-Fatihah fluently and understand the tafsir, but they need help on its tadabbur. Teachers can gauge student mastery of Al-Fatihah by simply asking students questions and observing their responses.

c) Learning Styles
According to Smaldino, Rowther and Russell (2014), learning styles refer to "psychological traits that determine how an individual perceives, interacts with, and responds emotionally to learning environments" (p. 54). These traits include multiple intelligences, perceptual preferences and strengths, information processing habits, motivation and physiological factors. Knowing how students learn best guides teachers in deciding upon the way content is being taught and also determines the selection of learning materials.

Digital natives generally prefer using technology tools to facilitate their learning rather than looking into books and other printed materials. Setiawan (2019) asserts Generation Z—i.e., the people who were born and grew up with technology—generally prefer interacting online. For instance, Nur Syafiqah (2020) in her dissertation found that undergraduate students who are learning the

88 *Rosemaliza Binti Mohd Kamalludeen*

Arabic language are inclined to use mobile applications as a desirable learning tool. Knowing this information should encourage Islamic education teachers to resource for digital materials to be used in their classes.

2. State Standards and Objectives

Smaldino et al. indicated that standards are descriptions of expected student performance outcomes that are established by authorities of education depending on the context of each country while learning objectives are statements of what the learners will achieve after they have gone through the particular lesson or learning session. From another perspective, Biggs (2003) defined learning outcomes as what we intend for the students to learn and be able to do after going through a particular lesson. Both terminologies point to the same critical element in instructional design, that is to identify the endgame of each lesson – the competencies that learners should master upon completion of the set of instruction, whether they are knowledge, skills or attitude. Therefore any approaches to teaching, including the technology that we use, must fulfil the purposes of achieving those learning outcomes.

Islamic education teachers must be clear of the intended learning outcomes that they want learners to achieve before deciding on any approaches or deciding on a particular technology tool to be used in class. For example, the learning outcome of a lesson is that learners are expected to perform the wudhu' according to the correct sequences— teachers might want to ask students to view a video demonstration and then ask the students to imitate the actions. It would not be suitable for teachers to ask learners to read notes posted on the learning management system and then answer questions on interactive tools like Quizziz or Mentimeter about wudhu' as the intended learning outcome for students to be able to perform the wudhu', in the correct sequence would not be realised. While interactive quiz tools are fun and exciting, when used inappropriately, they might not help learners achieve the intended learning outcomes.

3. Select Strategies, Technology, Media and Materials

After analysing learners and defining learning objectives, teachers may now begin to select suitable teaching strategies, technology tools and also learning materials for use in the classroom. Selecting teaching strategies involves deciding between teacher-centred or student-centred instruction (Smaldino, Rowther, & Russell, 2014) and would heavily depend on learning objectives as well as learner characteristics.

The ASSURE model suggests a list of selection criteria that teachers may refer to when selecting appropriate technology tools to be incorporated into lessons. It is suggested that the technology tools and learning materials are (1) aligned with learning outcomes, (2) equipped with accurate and current information, (3) using language that is age-appropriate, (4) able to spark student interest and engagement, (5) of quality

Technology Infusion in the Design 89

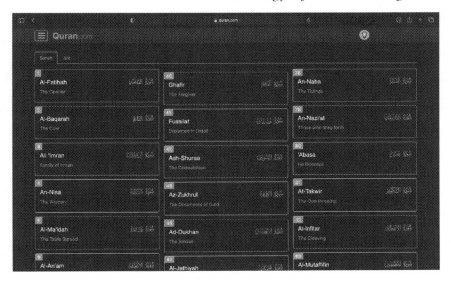

Figure 7.3 A screenshot of Quran.com.

in their technical specifications, (6) easy to use, (7) bias-free and (8) supplemented with user guidance and directions (Smaldino, Rowther, & Russell, 2014).

There are various versions of Qur'an applications online that can be used for Qur'anic studies. For example, Quran.com offers users the ability to quickly search specific chapters and verses just by clicking on its dropdown menu. Please refer to Figure 7.3. This is exciting for learners when learning about different verses that discuss one particular fiqh issue, as they can easily locate each verse within seconds.

Islamic education teachers may explore the web for various resources for teaching Islamic studies, or they may develop their own tools. One example of this is the "iCakna Solat" augmented reality tool by award-winning Ustaz Jazmi Amin that encourages students to perform the solat with proper actions and sequence. The video explaining this tool can be found on YouTube: https://www.youtube.com/watch?v=_E5uVwdEpao. The scannable QR code is as displayed in Figure 7.4.

Teachers may also modify existing resources that are found on the web. The Open Educational Resources (OER) movement allows materials to be modified by different users without having to worry about copyright restrictions. OER materials are meant to be shared, distributed, modified and developed for the purposes of education. More information on OER can be accessed from https://creativecommons.org/.

While creating new materials might seem far-fetched by some teachers due to technological challenges, there are content creation tools that are available on the web. For instance, puzzle builders can be customised to suit different needs. There is also a myriad of gamification tools available

Figure 7.4 Link to iCakna Solat YouTube video explanation.

such as Quizizz, Mentimeter and Quizlet. Teachers can take advantage of these user-friendly tools to build interactive quizzes, assessments and student-centred learning activities while responding to digital native preferences of learning through the use of technology.

One important aspect to pay attention to is technology must ease learning processes. Should the choice of a technology tool cause more complications, take longer time to achieve learning outcomes and inconvenience learners, then that particular tool might not be a suitable one. Therefore, teachers may experiment with different tools until they find one that is suitable for their needs.

4. Utilise Materials

This step involves planning and implementing technology usage in the learning environment. Smaldino, Rowther and Russell (2014) recommend the "5 Ps" process as follows:

a) Preview the Technology, Media and Materials

Teachers will be presented with various choices of tools and materials that can be integrated into lessons. Therefore, previewing and screening those choices is crucial to ensure the selected materials are aligned with the objectives of the lesson.

b) Prepare the Technology, Media and Materials

Once the materials are selected, modifying or arranging the materials is necessary based on the learning objectives and lesson flow. For example, should a video of Surah Al-Baqarah recitation be chosen to accompany discussions on riba', then teachers can bookmark and zoom in to verse 275. In another example, teachers may also overlay subtitles in videos that have narrations with slang that is not familiar to the students.

Technology Infusion in the Design   91

c) Prepare the Environment

The learning environment should be conducive to accommodate the usage of selected technology tools and materials. For example, when using interactive gamification tools like Quizizz and Quizlet, access to the internet must be reliable via Wi-Fi or mobile data, and students should be equipped with suitable devices. When using search engines for scavenger hunt activities for younger age groups, teachers must take extra precautions by ensuring firewalls are in place and access to improper websites is blocked.

d) Prepare the Learners

Learners must be made aware of the lesson objectives so that they will be able to relate the learning activities to what they are expected to achieve. They must also be taught how to use unfamiliar apps or devices before actual learning activities take place.

e) Provide the Learning Experience.

Once all preparations are in place, the lesson may now commence. Teachers may need to practice using new technology tools that are unfamiliar before implementing them in lessons.

5. Require Learner Participation

From a constructivist viewpoint, "learning is an active mental process built from relevant authentic experiences for which students receive informative feedback, a response that lets them know the degree to which they have achieved the objective and how to improve their performance" (Smaldino, Rowther, & Russell, 2014, p. 66). This simply means that learners must respond to learning activities for teachers to gauge their performance in terms of achieving the learning outcomes. With the use of technology, getting learners to actively respond is almost effortless through interactive applications like Mentimeter, Sli.do and Quizizz. Communication between teachers and learners is also more efficient and transparent through messaging applications like WhatsApp and Telegram.

For Islamic education teachers, learner participation can be easily done for various activities. For example, when learning to recite the Qur'an, learners may post their recitations on a video message board app called Flipgrid and then get their peers to listen and provide constructive responses, also via a video message. Another tool for student responses is Google Forms. Going back to basics, Google Forms can be used to create quizzes and assignments that require students to respond via selecting multiple choice answers or open-ended questions.

6. Evaluate and Revise

Teachers are encouraged to evaluate the effectiveness of each lesson, in terms of learning objectives achievement and student engagement to gauge whether the approaches, technology tools and learning materials are supporting the learning experience. Teachers may keep a record of reflection notes to be used as a reference for lessons that are successful and can be reused, or revisit lessons that did not go as planned for improvement. Student feedback is also valuable information to assess the effectiveness of technology tools and materials used in the classroom.

In terms of evaluating learner achievement, there are various tools that can be used to either replace or supplement traditional paper and pencil methods of assessment. Electronic portfolios, or e-portfolios, are highly recommended, as all student work can be stored as digital files. The e-portfolio can be in the form of repositories, like Google Drive, or a more presentable format, like a website.

Conclusion

Information technology and its rapid advancement have enabled learners to access any piece of knowledge without having to leave home (Saifee et al., 2012). This includes learners of Islamic education who are served with a cornucopia of learning resources in the forms of videos, massive open online courses or social media content. Non-Muslims all around the world are also free to access any content and learn more about Islam, the religion of peace. Therefore, it is imperative that Islamic education teachers take advantage of this powerful tool of the 21st century to propagate the messages of Islam. Teaching in a brick-and-mortar setting allows us to convey 'ilm to perhaps 30–40 students at one time. However, leveraging technology, the 'alim may now spread 'ilm to limitless numbers of learners as there is no boundary in the virtual world.

As Sahl bin Mu'adh bin Anas narrated from his father,

The Prophet said: "Whoever teaches some knowledge will have the reward of the one who acts upon it, without that detracting from his reward in the slightest." (Sunan Ibn Majah, Vol. 1, Book 1, Hadith 240)

Although Saifee et al. (2012) found in previous research that teachers are resistant to change, especially in technological advancements, there are those who welcome the changes and embrace them to the fullest. Lotfi et al. (2014) developed a serious game to teach children and new converts about solat, and it was received positively by learners. Therefore, with a myriad of research findings pointing to the benefits of incorporating technology in lessons, I resolutely encourage all Islamic education teachers to harness the power of technology in ensuring maximum engagement among digital native learners. When COVID-19 passes us by, the education landscape will definitely embrace the infusion of technology and take leaps ahead in its endeavour to make the world a better place. Islamic education must then not be left behind.

References

Akmal, R., & Ritonga, M. (2020). Pembelajaran pendidikan Agama Islam di masa Covid-19: Analisis terhadap problem serta solusi bagi orang tua. *Tarbawi: Jurnal Pendidikan Agama Islam*, 5(2), pp. 178–188.

Biggs, J. (2003). Aligning Teaching and Assessing to Course Objectives. *Teaching and Learning in Higher Education: New Trends and Innovations (Conference)*. University of Aveiro

Biggs, J. (1999). What the student does: Teaching for enhanced learning. *Higher Education Research & Development*, *18*(1), pp. 57–75. doi:10.1080/0729436990180105

Branch, R. M. (2009). *Instructional design: The ADDIE approach*. NY: Springer.

Gagné, E. D. (1985). *The cognitive psychology of school learning*. Boston, MA: Little, Brown and Company.

Harto, K. (2018). Tantangan Dosen PTKI di Era Indutsri 4.0. *Jurnal Tatsqif*, *16*(1), pp. 1–15. Retrieved from https://journal.uinmataram.ac.id/index.php/tatsqif/article/view/159/83

Hashim, R. (2004). Rethinking Islamic education in facing the challenges of the twenty-first century. *American Journal of Islamic Social Sciences*, *22*(4), pp. 133–147.

Hussain, A. (2004). Islamic education: Why is there a need for it? *Journal of Beliefs & Values*, *25*(3), pp. 317–323.

Ibrahim, A. A. (2015). Comparative analysis between system approach, Kemp, and ASSURE instructional design models. *International Journal of Education and Research*, *3*(12), pp. 261–270.

Li, C., & Lalani, F. (2020). The COVID-19 pandemic has changed education forever. This is how. *The World Economic Forum COVID Action Platform*. Retrieved from https://www.weforum.org/agenda/2020/04/coronavirus-education-global-covid19-online-digital-learning/

Lotfi, E., Amine, B., Fatiha, E., & Mohammed, B. (2014). Learning to pray, Islamic children's game. *2014 International Conference on Multimedia Computing and Systems (ICMCS)*. doi:10.1109/icmcs.2014.6911271

Mishra, P. & Koehler, M. J. (2006). Technological pedagogical content knowledge: A framework for teacher knowledge. *Teachers College Record*, *108*(6), pp. 1017–1054. Retrieved from http://114.red-88-12-10.staticip.rima-tde.net/mochila/didactica/mishra-koehler-tcr2006.pdf

Nur Syafiqah, H. (2020). *Mobile application for confinement services* [Final year project report] (Unpublished).

Raja, R. & Nagasubramani, P. C. (2018). Impact of modern technology in education. *Journal of Applied and Advanced Research*, *3*(1). doi:10.21839/jaar.2018.v3S1.165

Reigeluth, C. M. (1983). Instructional design: What is it and why is it? In C. M. Reigeluth (Ed.), *Instructional design theories and models: An overview of their current status*. Hillsdale, NJ: Lawrence Erlbaum Associates.

Saifee, A. R., Sahikh, Z. A., Sultan, S., Baloach, A. G., & Khalid, I. (2012). The role of mass media & information technology in Islamic education. *European Journal of Social Sciences*, *32*(3), pp. 380–390. Retrieved from http://www.europeanjournalofsocialsciences.com

Seel, N. M., Lehmann, T., Blumschein, P., & Podolskiy, O. A. (2017). *Instructional design for learning: Theoretical foundations*. Boston: Sense.

Setiawan, A. E. B. (2019). Self socialization process of Generation Z based on type online game at Smk Negeri 4 Kota Probolinggo. *Interaktif Journal ilmu-ilmu social*, *11*(2), 127–137.

Setiawan, A. R. (2020). Islamic education in Southeast Asia. doi:10.35542/osf.io/dnjqv

Smaldino, S., Rowther, D. L., & Russell, J. D. (2014). *Instructional technology and new media for learning*, 10th ed. Pearson: Essex.

Smaldino, S. (1996). *Effective techniques for distance education instruction. Proceedings of Annual Conference on Frontiers in Education*. Salt Lake City.

Part 2

Professional Development, Responsibility and Lifelong Learning

8 Measures of Physiognomies in Fostering Islamic Teachers' Professionalism in Selected Al-Majiri Integrated Model Schools (AIMS) in Sokoto State, Nigeria

Ahmad Tijani Surajudeen

Introduction

Nigeria is the nexus of the African continent because the country contributes immensely to all spheres of human endeavours, such as peacekeeping, inter-regional security, socio-economic, educational development, among others. The population of the country is over 200 million, with more than 500 ethnic groups speaking different languages, but Hausa, Yoruba and Igbo are the majority ethnic groups in the country. There are six geo-political Zones in Nigeria and 36 states in the country. Sokoto State is one of the states in the north-western geo-political zone of the country. Undoubtedly, the con-tributions of the traditional *madrasah* or *Al-Majiri* system in teaching of the Qur'an and other rudiments of Islamic knowledge in predominantly Muslim communities like northern Nigeria in general and Sokoto State in particular in the past cannot be underestimated (Ibrahim & Abdur-Rafiu, 2020).

However, the system has been fervently criticised for many reasons, among which are the system's rigidity in the contents/curricula, lack of proper ori-entation by most Islamic teachers and inadequate professionalism in teach-ers' careers (Ahmad & Awang Mat, 2011). More so, in an attempt to address multifarious challenges of traditional *madrasah* and *Al-Majiri* systems, the Federal Government of Nigeria initiated the idea of establishing *Al-Majiri* Integrated Model Schools (AIMS), as well as harmonising it with the Uni-versal Basic Education Programme under the Ministry of Education in Nige-ria in general and Sokoto State in particular (Ibrahim & Abdur-Rafiu, 2020; Isiaka, 2015; Ministerial Committee on *Madrasah*, 2010). Onwards, there are overwhelming studies on the *Al-Majiri* system in northern Nigeria, and most of the studies advocated for the incorporation of conventional subjects with Islamic subjects in the country (Abdulazeez & Musa, 2015; Ibrahim & Abdur-Rafiu, 2020; Isiaka, 2015).

Nonetheless, exploring the conceptualisation of measures of physiogno-mies in connection with teachers' professionalism in AIMS remains a gap to be filled in the existing body of knowledge, which is necessary especially towards its integration into mainstream education as the literature contends

DOI: 10.4324/9781003193432-10

(Ibrahim & Abdur-Rafiu, 2020; Yusha'u, Tsafe, Babangida, & Lawal, 2013). Indeed, the term 'professionalism' has no universally accepted definition, but it can be seen as the acquisition of professional dispositions that will enable teachers to discharge their responsibilities effectively and efficiently (Brown & Ferrill, 2009). Additionally, professional dispositions refer to knowledge, skills and competencies expected of teachers in discharging their responsibilities (Creasy, 2015). All the aforementioned components (i.e., knowledge, skill and competencies) are essential traits of teachers which must be cultivated in teacher education programmes. The vital traits of teachers in discharging their professional responsibilities are regarded as physiognomies.

Therefore, in this chapter, the conceptual background considers five common components as physiognomies of Islamic teachers—namely, personality, teacher-student relations, teachers' classroom management, involvement in school administration and developing professionally in connection with professionalism. *AIMS* has been growing in size; nonetheless, career professionalism or development of Islamic studies teachers receives less focus of attention among policymakers and school authorities, in recent times. Therefore, this chapter attempts to explore the physiognomies of Islamic teachers in order to improve their professional career development in selected AIMS in Sokoto State, Nigeria. Thus, this chapter attempts to answer the following research question: "How well do the measures of physiognomies predict professionalism of Islamic studies teachers in selected AIMS in Sokoto State Nigeria?" Thus, the subsequent subheading explains the overview of physiognomies.

Conceptual Overview of Physiognomies

The word 'physiognomy' is from two Greek words: 'physis,' which means 'nature,' and 'gnomon,' which refers to 'judge or interpreter.' In the ancient usage of the term 'physiognomy,' it was referred to as the relationship based on an individual's outward appearance and inner traits. Hence, physiognomic theory first appeared in the 15th century by Zopyrus who featured in a dialogue by Phaedo of Elis where Aristotle used to make a frequent reference to the theory in his "prior analytics" as literature contends (Grayson, 2005). Technically, physiognomy in this chapter refers to the assessment of the characters or personalities of teachers. The usage of the word 'physiognomy' is relevant in explaining the traits of teachers in AIMS in order to enhance their professional development. The justification for the use of the word 'physiognomies' in this chapter is that the Federal Government of Nigeria has been trying to improve the system of AIMS in the country, and the assessment of teachers' professional career development remains an essential part of the whole system.

Furthermore, there are many predictors in examining particular variables, but this study is limited to the significant predictors of physiognomies, which are (1) teachers' personalities, (2) teacher-student relations, (3) teachers' classroom management, (4) teachers' involvement in school administration,

(5) developing professionally and (6) teachers' professionalism. Each of these is explicated in the subsequent paragraphs.

First, a teacher's personality is important for getting into the minds of learners. The emotional stability of teachers is essential in handling teaching tasks effectively and efficiently. More importantly, as an integral part of teachers' personalities, literature contends that self-motivation is essential in discharging one's responsibilities (Brown & Ferrill, 2009). Thus, teachers' exemplary characters, which manifest in their interactions with students, should be internalised by the students in taking teachers as their role models. Also, the position by which Islam places teachers cannot be underrated, as explained by prominent Muslim scholars like Al-Ghāzālī (1058–1111 AH). More importantly, literature contends that teachers' receptiveness or approachability is important because they should not see themselves as arbiters of knowledge (Grady, Helbling, & Lubeck, 2008).

Second, teacher-student relations represent another factor explored in this research. Reiteratively, Islamic teachers have demanding and complex roles to play because they are not neural in moulding the characters and behaviours of the learners. Inferably, their responsibilities, unlike teachers of other subjects, go beyond 40- to 45-minute classroom teaching. They specifically combine both the cultivation of spirituality and inculcation of moral character. Indeed, the evaluation of a lesson should be practically based on the extent to which students were able to internalise especially certain elements of internal and external spirituality, as well as ethical behaviours in order to address negative perceptions, such as the dichotomy between Islamic and non-Islamic subjects ascribed with *Al-Majiri* system in the country (Oladosu, 2012; Omeni, 2015; Taiwo, 2013).

Third, classroom management skill refers to teaching effectiveness, teaching competence, teachers' abilities in planning, implementing and evaluating classroom instructions. This is why the literature contends that evaluation and assessment are core aspects of classroom activities (Danielson, 2013; Torrance, 2001). For instance, the exponent of the public school system in America, Horace Mann, contends, "Teaching is the most difficult of all Arts and profoundest of all Sciences" (US Department of Education, 2000). It is not doubtful to posit that this assertion is also relevant in explaining the roles and characteristics of Islamic teachers, either in traditional Islamic or conventional schools in Nigeria. In addition, studies assert that information and communication technologies are effective in the professional development of teacher training programmes in Nigeria (Olakunlehin, 2007; UNESCO, 2002; Wegerif, 2007). It is reiterated that in order to expand the space of learning, teachers are expected to engage the learners in the classroom activities (Wegerif, 2007).

Fourth, teachers' involvement in school administration is an important aspect in determining teachers' professionalism. The literature contends that active involvement in the implementation of school policies is very paramount in order to be supportive of the school leadership, especially towards the implementation of teaching and learning activities using effective strategies and techniques of teaching (Lubis et al., 2010; Sulaeman & Marlina, 2017). In addition, teachers are expected to display positive rapport with parents because they represent the image of the school. It is undoubtedly significant that the decision-making skills of teachers play active roles in the overall activities of the schools (Brown & Ferrill, 2009).

Fifth, the professional development of teachers of Islamic studies in AIMS is paramount, especially through their active participation in various seminars or workshops either within or outside the schools in order to foster their teaching effectiveness (Brown & Ferrill, 2009). Hence, any skill or information gathered from the seminars or conferences must be harmonised with the daily instructional activities taking place in the classroom setting (Torrance, 2001). The literature contends that teachers should not confine themselves to only their professional bodies; rather, they should attend programmes of other professional bodies in order to acquire the necessary professional qualities that will make them excel as teachers (US Department of Education, 2000). This can also be useful to teachers of AIMS.

Sixth, teachers' professionalism is dependent upon the aforementioned measures of physiognomies. Professionalism in teaching refers to the acquisition of essential skills, competence and character expected by teachers in discharging their responsibilities. Additionally, showcasing basic skills, competence, efficiency, proficiency, expertise, know-how, experience, effectiveness, among others (Brown & Ferrill, 2009), demonstrates integral elements in enhancing Islamic studies teachers' professionalism as part of teacher preparation programmes in the country.

The foregoing conceptualisation of factors of physiognomies in professionalising the career of Islamic teachers through the acquisition of up-to-date knowledge of the subject matter and required skills does not create an impression that teachers are the target of change, but they are the agents of change within the school.

Methodology

A quantitative, descriptive survey research design was used in this chapter. Different aspects were covered, which were as follows: population, sample and sampling, instrument (validity and reliability), data collection and analytic approach. Each of these is explained in the subsequent paragraphs.

First, concerning the population and sample, the population of the study was estimated as 1,500 teachers, according to the data drawn among Islamic/Arabic studies teachers in AIMS in Sokoto State Nigeria. While regarding the sample, the Raosoft sample size calculator was used to select the sample size of 306, which was drawn among teachers of Islamic studies in selected AIMS in Sokoto—namely, the Denge Shunni, Gagi and Wammakko areas of Sokoto State, Nigeria. The sampling technique employed in this study was convenient and simple random sampling.

Second, the instrument employed for data collection was a questionnaire adopted from the existing body of knowledge (Ashaaria et al., 2012; Brown

& Ferrill, 2009; Creasy, 2015; Lubis et al., 2010; Olakunlehin, 2007). The validity and reliability of the instrument were established. On one hand, concerning the validity, opinions of the experts in education were sought where necessary observations and corrections were incorporated into the final draft of the instrument. On the other hand, the reliability of the instrument was also established by reporting Cronbach's alpha for the internal consistency of the instrument. The following Likert scale was employed in the instrument (questionnaire)—namely, (1 = Strongly Disagree (SD), 2 = Disagree (D), 3 = Agree (A) and 4 = Strongly Agree (SA) in measuring the views of the respondents on the characteristics or physiognomies of Islamic/Arabic teachers while collecting data. Physiognomies are positioned as independent variables, and their measures are teachers' personalities, teacher-student relations, teachers' classroom management, teachers' involvement in school administration, developing professionally, while teachers' professionalism is considered a dependent variable. The analysis of data was done with the use of the Statistical Package for Social Sciences (SPSS; version 23.0). Six variables were explored in this research and six parameters were used in measuring each factor as embodied in the questionnaire. Based on the internal consistency of the instrument, the report of Cronbach's alpha for the internal consistency of the instrument is as follows: teachers' personalities (TPS) = .846, teacher-student relations (TSR) = .690, teachers' classroom management (TCM) = .635, teachers' involvement in school administration (ISA)= .693, developing professionally (TDP) = .747 and teachers' professionalism (TPF) = .914. All the items attained a degree of internal consistency. The aforementioned explication of excellence and goodness of the instrument is in accordance with the criteria of George and Mallery (2003). This inferably means that the internal consistency of the instrument demonstrated that the instrument measured what it was designed to measure.

Third, the data was collected via questionnaire among the teachers of AIMS through the help of three research assistants. In addition, pertaining to the data analysis, SPSS (version 23.0) was used, descriptive statistics were used for demographic information of the respondents and multiple regression analysis was employed to answer the research question where various assumptions were taken into consideration.

Results

This part presents the results of the study, which were subdivided into two major parts—namely, demographic information of the respondents and findings of the study. The majority of the respondents were male (224 or 73%) while 82 (27%) were female. Pertaining to the age of the respondents, the majority were between 26 and 30 years (100 or 33%), 97 or 32% of the sampled respondents were between 21 and 25 years, 45 or 15% of the respondents were between 31 and 35 years and 64 or 21% were 36 and above. Concerning the state of origin of the respondents, the majority (289 or 94%) were from Sokoto State, while only 17 (7%) were from other

102 *Ahmad Tijani Surajudeen*

states. In addition, based on the strata of the respondents, 293 (96%) were from urban areas, while just 13 (4%) were from rural areas. Apart from the presentation of the demographic data of the respondents, the subsequent sub-headings present the findings of the study based on the research question mentioned earlier.

Research Question: How well do the measures of physiognomies predict professionalism of Islamic studies teachers in selected AIMS in Sokoto State, Nigeria?

Standard multiple regression was used to determine how measures of physiognomies predict the professionalism of Islamic studies teachers in selected AIMS in Sokoto State. Various assumptions mentioned by Pallant (2011) were strictly observed while performing the analysis using multiple regression to determine how a set of variables (i.e., measures of physiognomies) predict professionalism of Islamic studies teachers in selected AIMS in Sokoto State, Nigeria. The correlation between a set of measures of physiognomies and teachers' professionalism was examined whereby the criterion of a threshold of .7 was used, as mentioned by Pallant (2011). The measures of physiognomies (teachers' personalities = .45, TSR =.66, teachers' classroom management = .57, teachers' classroom management = .59 and developing professionally = .63, respectively) correlate substantially with Islamic studies teachers' professionalism. It is because the values obtained for correlation were less than the required threshold of .7 that all the variables were retained.

Also, the assumption of collinearity diagnostics was checked via coefficients where tolerance and VIF were determined. On one hand, if the value obtained from tolerance is less than .10 while on the other hand, if the value of VIF is above 10, this is an indication of higher multiple correlations with other variables, which is the possibility of multicollinearity (Pallant, 2011). As a result, the values of tolerance in relation to the measures of physiognomies are teachers' personalities = .207, TSR = .170, teachers' classroom management = .389, ISA = .561 and developing professionally = .061, respectively. This is also supported by VIF, as the values obtained, as shown in the coefficients table (Table 8.1), of data output was less than .10. It was also a further indication that there was no violation of multicollinearity.

Furthermore, in order to determine how much of the variance in the dependent variable (i.e., teachers' professionalism) is being explained by the model which includes five other variables explored in this research,

Table 8.1 Model summary

Model	R	R-Squared	Adjusted R Square	Std. Error of the Estimate	R-Square dChange	Change Statistics				
						F Change	df1	df2	Sig. F Change	Durbin-Watson
1	.968[a]	.936	.935	5.55910	.936	880.401	5	300	.000	1.888

[a] Predictors: (Constant), TDP, ISA, TCM, TPS, TSR
[b] Dependent Variable: TPF

the value of R-squared was used to determine it. The value of R-squared obtained was 93.6% of the variance in teachers' professionalism in AIMS. This value could not be considered as an overestimation as a result of the fact that there was a sample of 306 used for the study. Similarly, even when adjusted R-squared was considered, the value (93.5%) was still almost the same as the value obtained from R-squared, which was a further justification for the appropriateness of the sample used for the study, as shown in Table 8.1, the model summary.

Onwards, the statistical significance of the result was further assessed using an analysis of variance (ANOVA) table of data output. The model of the study demonstrated statistical significance (Sig. = .000, which showed p < .0005). This means that the factors of physiognomies adequately and statistically predicted teachers' professionalism. However, the most predictive variables of physiognomies that contributed to teachers' professionalism, as included in the model, were determined using beta in standardised coefficients, as shown in the coefficients table (Table 8.2). In determining this, Pallant (2011) posits that the negative sign in the threshold of beta does not affect the interpretation of the standardised coefficients. The most predictive factor of teachers' professionalism was ISA because it has the largest coefficient of .65. This means that teachers' ISA at AIMS made a unique contribution to their professionalism or professional career development, especially when there was a control in variance explained by the variables contained in the model. However, there was a slightly lower beta value (−.14) in standardised coefficients for TSR, which was an indication that it made a less unique contribution to teachers' professionalism. Table 8.2 shows coefficients obtained from data output.

Nonetheless, there was the statistical significance of all measures of physiognomies on teachers' professionalism because the value obtained for Sig. = .000 was less than the required threshold of .05. This was a further unique contribution that measures of physiognomies adequately predicted teachers' professionalism in selected *AIMS* in Sokoto State, Nigeria. In addition, the normal probability plot (P-P) of the regression standardised residual was

Table 8.2 Coefficients

Model	Standardised Coefficients	T	Sig.	Collinearity Statistics	
	Beta			Tolerance	VIF
(Constant)		−6.011	.000		
TPS	−.316	−9.855	.000	.207	4.822
TSR	−.144	−4.078	.000	.170	5.880
TCM	.197	8.439	.000	.389	2.568
ISA	.654	33.623	.000	.561	1.782
TDP	.579	9.833	.000	.061	16.308

a Dependent Variable: TPF

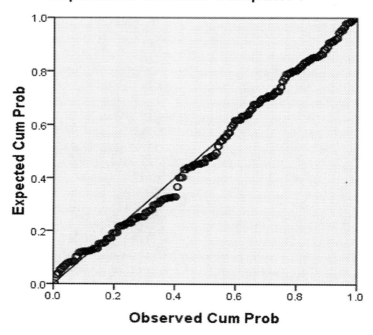

Figure 8.1 Normal probability plot (P-P) of the regression standardised residual.

determined. There were points lying straight on a diagonal line from the bottom left to the top right, which was an indication that there were no major deviations from normality, as shown in Figure 8.1, as literature such as Pallant (2011) posits.

Also, the scatterplot did not demonstrate outliers because the standardised residual, as shown in the scatterplot, was not more than 3.3 or less than −3.3, as shown in Figure 8.2, as the literature contends (Pallant, 2011).

Discussion of Major Findings

The prime aim of the government with regards to the initiative of *AIMS* in various parts of Nigeria in general and Sokoto State in particular was to harmonise between Islamic and Western systems in order to respond to the challenges of the dichotomy of knowledge as identified in the existing literature (Ahmad & Awang Mat, 2011). Notably, the study by Syah (2016) elucidates the challenges of Islamic education based on historical, political and sociocultural perspectives. Additionally, a number of studies have investigated the *Al-Majiri* system in the northern part of the country (AbdulAzeez & Musa, 2015; Ahmad & Awang Mat, 2011; Ibrahim & Abdur-Rafiu, 2020; Isiaka, 2015; Oladosu, 2012Taiwo, 2013). More specifically, Taiwo (2013) clamoured for the transformation of the *Al-Majiri*

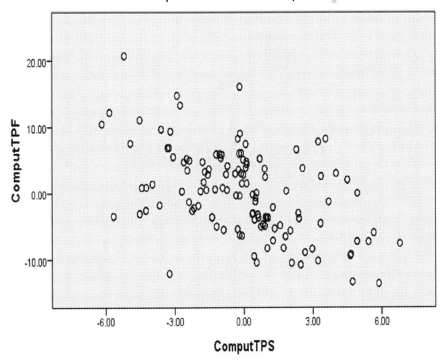

Figure 8.2 Scatterplot of the model.

system for national development. Nonetheless, in spite of various studies, the professionalism of teachers' careers as the gap that this present study bridged remains an important aspect in order to achieve the prime target of AIMS. Thus, the professional responsibilities of teachers played significant roles as investigated in this study.

Based on the overall findings of this study, the demographic backgrounds of the respondents demonstrated that the teachers of AIMS were qualified to respond to the instrument of the study investigating the professional development of their careers. Undoubtedly, the factors of physiognomies are conceptualised to explore the professional career development of teachers of AIMS in this study. There was a gap in the existing literature with respect to determining the most predictive factor of physiognomies in improving the professionalism of teachers. This study tried to bridge the gap in the existing body of knowledge by demonstrating the factor of teachers' physiognomies that mostly predicted their professionalism using standard multiple regression. There was a substantial correlation between factors of physiognomies and the professional careers of teachers in *AIMS*.

106 *Ahmad Tijani Surajudeen*

The findings showed that ISA by the teachers of AIMS was the most important factor that predicted their professional career development. The statistical significance has further confirmed that the factors of physiognomies can effectively foster teachers' professionalism in AIMS. There is no wonder that this finding is further affirmation of the previous studies that considered teachers as implementers of programmes and activities through effective strategies and techniques of teaching in the classroom setting (Brehm, 2006; Brown & Ferrill, 2009). More importantly, the integration of multimedia into classroom activities while teaching Islamic subjects in AIMS can further enhance learning and strengthen professionalism by the teachers as the literature contends (Sulaeman & Marlina, 2017; UNESCO, 2002). Nonetheless, there is a need to improve on TSR, as well as some other factors of physiognomies that were explored in this study. The overall findings are an indication of the modernisation of the traditional system, which is contrary to the finding of Ashaaria et al. (2012), who posited that Islamic schools cannot modernise their methods to suit the needs of the 21st century. This study also goes contrary to the agitation of Syah (2016) that there is inadequate professional career development and training towards improving teachers' skills for the maximisation of students' performance.

Conclusion

The chapter has demonstrated that five common factors of physiognomies are entrenched in improving teachers' professionalism, which requires a focus of attention in order to standardise AIMS in Sokoto State, Nigeria. The various conceptual hypothesised factors of physiognomies of Islamic studies teachers have been substantiated with the data collected from the teachers of AIMS in Sokoto State. The uniqueness of this chapter lies in the conceptualisation of various factors of physiognomies in fostering professionalism in discharging teachers' responsibilities. In spite of the foregoing, the limitations of this study are the restrictions of physiognomies to five common factors in connection with teachers' professionalism in the context of AIMS. There are other essential factors or measures of professionalism, but they were not exhausted in this study. Also, the study utilised only quantitative data analysis in exploring factors of physiognomies in improving the professionalism of teachers in AIMS in Sokoto State. In spite of the limitations, the uniqueness of the study reflects the contributions of the conceptualisation of five common factors in predicting teachers' professionalism, but most studies on the *Al-Majiri* system were theoretical in nature. Hence, this study makes a vital contribution to the existing literature by empirically exploring the measures of physiognomies in connection with teachers' career development in AIMS. Additionally, the chapter has substantial direction for further exploration of factors that could improve the professional career development of teachers in AIMS. It is hopeful that the findings of this study will be useful to many stakeholders, such as federal and state governments, policymakers, ministries of education, among others, that are concerned with addressing the problems of AIMS in the country by professionalising teachers' careers. The following recommendations are therefore made based on this study:

1. All the stakeholders, specifically the government, principals, teachers, students, philanthropists, non-governmental organisations, parents and many others, should collaborate in improving the system of AIMS in order to attain efficiency and effectiveness of the system for national development and nation-building in Nigeria.
2. There is a need to put more focus on seminars and workshops in order to enhance the professionalism of teachers in AIMS in Sokoto State in particular and Nigeria in general.
3. There is a need for funds by the government towards the provision of instructional materials, such as multimedia, in order for teachers to have efficient classroom management in the 21st century in the country.
4. An emphasis on teachers' professional career development can address the rigidity of the traditional system in predominant northern Nigeria, which the system of AIMS has been trying to bridge.
5. Future studies can also empirically explore the perception of students of AIMS with respect to the manifestation of professionalism in discharging teachers' responsibilities, especially by using mixed methods (i.e., quantitative and quantitative data).

References

Abdulazeez, B.S. & Musa, A. O. (2015). Situations of Al-Majiri System of education in contemporary Nigeria: Matters arising. *Ilorin Journal of Religious Studies (IJOURELS)*, 5(2), pp. 37–46.

Ahmad, T.S. & Awang Mat, M. Z. (2011). *Integration of Naqliyah and Aqliyah Knowledge: A framework for the transformation of Al-Majiri Madrasah education in Nigeria*. Malaysia ICIEL.

Ahmad, T. S. & Muhinat, B. B. (2020). ICT in fostering professionalism in teacher training in Nigeria: Implication for curriculum implementation in the 21st century. In *Integration of technology into teaching and learning in nigerian educational system in the 21st century*, edited by: S.A. Tijani, N.I. Tambuwal, A. Yusuf & A.A. Salawu, pp. 14–27.

Ashaaria, M. F., et al. (2012). An assessment of teaching and learning methodology in Islamic studies. *Procedia—Social and Behavioral Sciences*, 59, 618–626

Brehm, B., (2006). Instructional design and assessment. An interdisciplinary approach to introducing professionalism. *American Journal of Pharmaceutical Education*, 70(4), pp. 1–5.

Brown, D., & Ferrill, M.J. (2009). The taxonomy of professionalism: Reframing the academic pursuit of professional development. *American Journal of Pharmaceutical Education*, 83(4), pp. 1–10.

Creasy, K.L. (2015). Defining professionalism in teacher education programme. *Journal of Education and Social Policy*, 2(2), pp. 23–25.

Creswell, J.W. (2005). *Educational research: Planning, conducting and evaluating quantitative and qualitative research* (2nd ed.). London: United Kingdom.

Danielson, C. (2013). *The framework for teaching evaluation*. [Online] Retrieved from www.teachscape.com on 15 December 2020.

George, D., & Mallery, P. (2003). *SPSS for Windows step by step: A simple guide and reference. 11.0 update* (4th ed.). Boston: Allyn & Bacon.

Grady, M.P., Helbling, K.C., & Lubeck, D.R. (2008). *Teacher professionalism since A nation at risk. Phi Delta Kappan*, 89(603–604), p. 607.

Grayson, E. (2005). "Weird science, weirder unity: Phrenology and physiognomy in Edgar Allan Poe." *Mode*, 1, pp. 56–77.

Ibrahim, A.S. & Abdur-Rafiu, J. (2020). Relevance of integrated Al-Majiri education system in the implementation of universal basic education programme in Nigeria. In *Language, education and religion for national development, A Festschrift in Honour of Prof. A.G.A.S. Oladosu*, eds. M.M. Jimba, M.M. Adedimeji, M.A. Lawal & M.S. Abdullahi, University Ilorin, pp. 252–260.

Isiaka, T. O. (2015). A Pilot Study of the Challenges of Infusing Almajiri Educational System into the Universal Basic Education in Sokoto, Nigeria. *Journal of Education and Practice*, 6(16), pp. 10–16.

Lubis, M. A., et al. (2010). The effectiveness of strategies and techniques in teaching and learning Islamic education. Selected Topics in Education and Educational Technology. *9th WSEAS International Conference on Education and Educational Technology (EDU '10)*. Iwate Prefectural University, Japan.

Ministerial Committee on *Madrasah* Education (2010). *Framework for the Development of madrasah education in Nigeria and its integration into the UBE Scheme*. Submitted by the Technical Sub-Committee to the Ministerial Committee on Madrasah Education in Nigeria, pp. 1–84.

National Policy on Education (2013). (1977, revised 1998, 2005). Lagos: NERDC-Nigeria

Oladosu, A.G.A.S. (2012). Arabic and Islamic education in Nigeria: The case of Al-Majiri Schools. In *World academy of science, engineering and technology*, pp. 1820–1824.

Olakunlehin, F.K. (2007). Information and communication technologies in teacher training and professional development in Nigeria. *Turkish Online Journal of Distance Learning*, 1(1), pp. 133–142.

Omeni, A. (2015). The *Almajiri* in Northern Nigeria: Militancy, perceptions, challenges, and state policies. *African Conflict and Peacebuilding Review*, 5(2), pp. 128–142.

Pallant, J. (2011). *SPSS survival manual: A step by step guide to data analysis using SPSS for Windows (Version 10)*. Open University Press: Chicago, Illinois, USA.

Sulaeman, M. & Marlina, Y. (2017). The use of multimedia in teaching Dirasah Islamiyah course in higher education institutions in Indonesia. *Journal of Education and Practice*, 8(15), p. 2017.

Syah, M. N. (2016). Challenges of Islamic education in the Muslim world: A historical, political, and socio-cultural perspective. QIJIS: *Qudus International Journal of Islamic Studies*, 4(1),

Taiwo, F. J. (2013). Transforming the Almajiri education for the benefit of the Nigerian society. *Journal of Educational and Social Research*, 67.

Torrance, H. (2001). *Assessment for learning: developing formative assessment in the classroom. Education* 3–13, pp. 26–32.

US Department of Education. (2000). Does professional development change teaching practice? Results from a three-year study, *executive summary (report)*. Washington D.C.

Measures of Physiognomies 109

UBEC (2010). *Ministerial presentation to national economic council by national implementation committee on Almajiri'*, pp. 1–11. Abuja: Universal Basic Education Commission.

UNESCO (2002). *Information and communication technology in education–A curriculum for schools and programme for teacher development.* Paris: UNESCO.

Wegerif, R. (2007). *Dialogic, educational and technology: Expanding the space of learning.* New York: Springer-Verlag.

Yusha'u, M.A., Tsafe, A.K., Babangida, S.I. & Lawal, N.I. (2013). Problems and prospects of integrated almajiri education in northern Nigeria. *Scientific Journal of Pure and Applied Sciences*, 2pp. 125–134.

9 Enhancing Professionalism in Teaching Islamic Studies through Employment of Adequate Instructional Resources

Jamiu Abdur-Rafiu, U. A. Ajidagba and Yunus Aliyu

Introduction

Instructional resources (IR) constitute an integral aspect of instructional delivery. In the teaching of any given subject, a prospective teacher would require some aids that would be employed to facilitate his or her teaching. Thus, IR are referred to as teaching aids; these are materials and equipment that serve as vehicles which are channelled with ease to their destination. The instructional strategies usually employed by teachers—providing structured context, asking and responding to questions, arousing curiosity and giving information—have all been incorporated into programmes delivered by media ranging from books, charts and other visual materials to electronics, such as television projectors and computers.

Media can be defined as a unique presentation of modes which fulfil a unique psychological function or a combination of various elements, which results in a particular mode of communication. Educational media thus refers to all relevant materials utilised by a teacher during the instructional process to facilitate teaching and learning and for the purpose of making the contents of the instructions more practical and understandable (Ogbaji, 2017).

For effective instruction, there must be appropriate instructional media for a particular topic, which will provide a high degree of interest for both teachers and students. With the effective and appropriate use of instructional media, the students thought processes will develop and continue because this will bring students' interests into the lesson. By the use of these IR, the students' facility of learning will develop (Umar, 2010).

Islamic studies could be viewed as the totality of learning experiences which centre on the relationship between man and his Creator and between man and his fellow men. It is a medium for transforming and effecting national all-around development (Abdur-Rafiu, 2014). Islamic studies as a subject or course of study revolves around studying the principles and doctrines of the Islamic religion. It is a subject that is studied at all levels of education. However, every subject being taught at all levels has strategies, techniques and apparatuses suitable for its teaching.

DOI: 10.4324/9781003193432-11

In addition, Kumar (2012) was of the view that the effectiveness of an educational process is not improved merely by the introduction of technology into it but rather a function of human skills of employing the technology, as well as the hardware and software components of technology. Kumar (2012) described the teacher as a system with four broad functions, as illustrated in the following diagram.

1. **Planning:** This implies the establishment of objectives, preparation of units and schedule of training, etc.
2. **Organising:** It connotes the arrangement of the learning resources, utilisation of IR, etc.
3. **Leading:** It includes motivation, encouragement and provision of stimuli to the students in the teaching-learning process.
4. **Controlling:** It revolves around assessment, feedback and regulation so as to realise the objectives optimally.

The aforementioned functions of a teacher are, however, germane to teacher professionalism. Hence, to enhance professionalism in teaching, teachers need to be conversant in these functions. An Islamic studies teacher needs to be acquainted with the knowledge, uses and significance of IR. It actively assists the learners to apply more accurately what has been learnt. It is against this backdrop that this study was carried out to expound on the role of IR in teaching and learning Islamic studies with a view towards the enhancement of professionalism in the subject.

Methodology

An analytical method was employed. Information was sourced from textbooks, empirical field studies and electronic sources.

Review of Related Literature

Concept of and Importance of IR

IR as a concept revolve around materials needed in the teaching-learning situation for the purpose of facilitating the situation and achieving the instructional objectives. More so, the concept has attracted the interests of various educationists who have expounded on its essence and essentials.

Amuzu (2018) noted that IR include people, events, places or materials that are used to enhance learning, usually by simplifying a difficult situation or making uninteresting learning attractive for learning. It could be noted from the foregoing facts that the spectrum of personnel, materials and facilities that are designed, arranged, adopted and applied during the teaching-learning situation in order to make the teaching interesting to the learner and facilitate the realisation of teaching objectives are referred to as

IR. A professional teacher, therefore, needs to be conversant in the resources that are suitable for the subject matter he or she teaches.

Adoption of IR in teaching has a profound effect on the performance of the teacher and the achievement of the pupils. This could be corroborated with the findings of various empirical studies. For instance, Eny, Djamiah, Haryanto, and Baso (2013) developed a Model of Creating Instructional Materials Based on the School Curriculum for Indonesian Secondary Schools. Their findings showed that there was correlation between the usage of instructional materials and students' academic performance. The study revealed that both teachers and students subscribed to the fact that appropriate instructional materials are good enough to be used in the teaching and learning process.

They also stressed that instructional materials which are based on the curriculum and students' needs may increase students' learning outcomes and obtain the purpose of the school curriculum. Instructional materials are the basic tools upon which the quality of education being provided to the children in schools is determined. They help in not only simplifying learning but also in making learning practical, effective and understandable to the learners, as well as helping the students to maintain a flexible classroom environment (Onyia, 2013). Perhaps this might be why Eny, Djamiah, Haryanto, and Baso (2013) concluded that IR used by the teachers constitute significant factors that influence good learning outcomes.

Adelodun and Asiru (2015) examined the role played by IR in enhancing students' performance in the English language. Their findings showed that there is a significant relationship between the use of instructional materials and the performance of high-achieving students in the English language. They, however, recommended that teachers should always make use of IR because they arouse students' attention during the instructional process. IR enhance the memory level of the students. Adelodun and Asiru (2015) emphasised that the talk-and-chalk method alone cannot lead to a successful pedagogy, and as such, the teacher needs to apply instructional media so as to stimulate the teaching-learning process.

Bisiriyu (2016) investigated instructional materials as correlates of students' academic performance in senior secondary schools. He found that students taught with instructional materials performed better than those taught without instructional materials. He posited that for successful implementation of any educational programme, there is a need for the provision of adequate IR, as IR give room for the extension of the range of experience available to learners, thereby making the learning experience richer.

In her study, Alabere (2017) evaluated the use of instructional materials in teaching English language as a second language among secondary school students. The study revealed that the performance of the secondary school students taught with the use of teaching materials was better than those taught without the use of instructional materials. Koech (2017) also studied IR used in teaching and learning in public pre-schools in Kenya. His

Enhancing Professionalism in Teaching   113

main recommendation was that there is a need to use a variety of IR that are cheaply available within the school environment. Ogbaji (2017), while assessing teachers' perceptions of the utilisation of instructional materials in teaching social studies, found that teachers perceive instructional materials as necessary for effective teaching and learning.

The use of IR is especially important and relevant because some topics that appear abstract would be concretised through the use of instructional media. Adoption of IR makes the teacher arouse many senses in learners and brings them into complete involvement in the learning situation. A multiple approach through hearing, seeing, touching, smelling and tasting makes for a more complete understanding of the lesson (Amuzu, 2018).

Classifications of IR

IR have been categorised into various categories. However, the five categories that have been adopted in this work are presented as follows:

1. **Audio Media:** These are IR that mostly appeal to the sense of hearing. Examples of these IR are programmes or software such as audiotapes, records (long or short play), on-the-air broadcasts from radio boxes, telephonic and mobile systems of communication and audio CDs (Abolade, 2004). Practically, in the present time, most especially with the outbreak of the COVID-19 pandemic, many institutions of learning are closed, and most institutions resorted to e-learning. Thus, lessons and lectures are recorded in the form of audio for the consumption of learners. Audio channels clarify and supplement the visuals (Kumar, 2012).
2. **Visual Media:** Are teaching and learning devices that mostly appeal to the sense of seeing only. They can be sub-categorised into projected and non-projected visuals. The projected visuals require electricity for projection—e.g., films, slides, transparencies using their projectors. The non-projected ones do not need a light source—e.g., pictures, maps, globes, posters, realia and so on. Visuals contribute more to learning than audio channels (Kumar, 2012).
3. **Audio-Visual Media:** This refers to those instructional materials which provide the students with the opportunity of seeing and hearing at the same time. For example, educational television and closed-circuit television. Audio-visual aids improve the quality of the message; they impart audio and visual dimensions (Kumar, 2012).
4. **Community Resources:** These are human and non-human resources that are within the reach of both teachers and learners. Examples of community resources for Islamic studies include *masjid* (mosques), *madaris* (Qur'anic schools) and other historic places.
5. **Resource Persons:** These are professionals and experts in their various disciplines. These include chief imams, veteran Islamic teachers, renowned educationists, administrators, etc. A resource person can be

invited into the classroom to come and give a lecture on any topic that is related to what the teacher has taught or will teach to his/her students. A resource person can be from an immediate environment of the student. In that case, the resource person is called a community resource person. If he or she comes from afar, he or she is simply called a resource person.

Principles Guiding the Selection and Effective Utilisation of IR in the Islamic Studies Classroom

According to Umar (2010), before selecting resources for a classroom presentation, there are some factors that are to be considered, such as subject matter or topic, instructional objective, suitability, content accuracy, availability, size of the class, costs, teachers' capability and, lastly, operating facilities:

1. **Subject Matter or Topic:** The first thing for a teacher of religious education to do is to be familiar with the scheme of work from where the topic to be taught will be taken.
2. **Instructional Objective/ Objective Specification:** The first thing is to find an answer to the question, "What is it that one is trying to achieve?" What one set out to achieve should be considered. That is, what do you hope to achieve by using the media/medium?
3. **Suitability/Optimum Fit:** Is the information contained in the media appropriate to the age, ability and characters of learners? One needs to consider the interest of the learners. No one instructional material is best for all purposes and at all times to all learners. So, choose instructional materials that are appropriate to instructional tasks and that can benefit as many learners as possible
4. **Content Accuracy:** The teacher needs to consider whether the information contained therein is correct or not. The content must be authentic, valid and should contain current information or the latest ideas.
5. **Technical Quality:** That is, how accurate is the hardware that contains the information it is supposed to bear. For instance, a picture to be used should be clear and visible. Likewise, the electrically operated teaching materials such as slides, radios, videos and television should ensure technical accuracy so as to facilitate the realisation of the instructional objectives.
6. **Availability:** The case of purchasing, borrowing or producing educational media is of topmost consideration. It will be unreasonable to select the media that are not within your reach. It is of no use selecting materials that are not available in your school or environment for either purchasing or borrowing. The teaching aids to be used by the teacher must be readily available.
7. **Size of the Class:** The number of learners in a class will determine to an extent the type of media to be utilised. If the learners are large in number, then bold visuals or projectors are to be used.

8. **Cost:** One needs to consider the cost vis-à-vis the utilisation benefit. The teacher should also consider his or her purse or that of the school.
9. **Teacher's Capability:** The teacher should ensure that he or she is capable of manipulating effectively the material or equipment selected for teaching.
10. **Operating Facilities:** There is a need to ensure that the facilities for operating the selected media for classroom instruction are available and functional.
11. **Duration of the Lesson:** The time allocated to a particular subject also determines which aid a teacher will choose. If the time allocated to the subject is too small, it may not be advisable for the teacher to use teaching aids that will require a longer period.
12. **School Location/Environmental Conditions/Constraints:** The location of the school is another important factor which determines the selection of IR. The reason is that there are some teaching aids which require the use of electricity, and where electricity is not available, it may be difficult to use such teaching aids.
13. **Multi-media Presentation:** Wise and creative use of a variety of media at different levels of lesson development can be effective in achieving various instructional objectives. This allows for a variety of learners to be reached easily. However, too many instructional media that are not well coordinated and methodologically presented can create confusion in the classroom.
14. **Preparation and Preview:** It is important for the teacher to prepare himself/herself well in advance if the instructional media must be effectively utilised.
15. **Evaluation:** Instructional media needs to be evaluated in terms of suitability to the objectives, appeal to the learners, cost-effectiveness and learner-achievement level. After the presentation, the teacher needs to review if the materials have been used effectively (Adedeji, 2000).

Selected Islamic Studies Topics and the Relevant IR

It is pertinent to note the following points when preparing for instructional media, as suggested by Kumar (2012):

a. Simplified line drawings are more effective than shaded drawings and elaborate figures
b. A visual should be made to scale in order to aid visual perception of relative sizes
c. Colour, dramatic presentations, special effects and humour are good motivators to catch a learner's attention
d. Action should be shown the way the learner would see it if he or she were actually there and doing the job
e. Liberal use of titles, questions and other printed words can improve teaching effectiveness

116   Jamiu Abdur-Rafiu et al.

f. Printing and visual cueing direct the attention of the learner effectively
g. The audio channel with commentary and sound effects, etc., should be used as an interjection on the pictorial channel rather than in a continuous form parallel to it
h. Use of upper- and lower-case letters in running text and for cue points is better than writing all capitals
i. Text on a computer screen should be big enough to be legible from two metres away
j. Use boldface, easily readable type letters and colour

Once all the principles are considered before the Islamic studies teacher sets out for a lesson, it is not impossible that his/her lesson will be quite fruitful. Practical instances are however presented here.

Islamic studies in schools encompasses various branches and divisions. These are broadly categorised into the following:

a. The Qur'an
b. Hadith
c. Tahdhib (Moral Teachings)
d. Tawhid (Creeds)
e. Fiqh (Jurisprudence)
f. Mu'amalat (Human Transactions)
g. Tarikh (Historical Development of Islam)

Thus, the appropriate IR for topics in each of these branches are illustrated in Table 9.1:

Improvisation of Instructional Materials

To improvise means to substitute for the real thing. It involves using locally available materials as substitutes for the original or factory-made ones. Substitutes are made from available materials when the real equipment is not available or too costly. Improvisation requires a grateful and dynamic teacher to improvise a lot of things. For instance, a battery is suitably substituted for electricity. With a paper machine technique, many instructional materials can be improvised. A lot of materials are available in our environment for improvisation. Some of these production materials are old newspaper type, balloon, x-ray films tracing paper, cardboard and plywood, cardboard, etc.

The objectives of improvisation are as follows:

a. To make available materials that are not costly but effective
b. To produce durable materials that can stand the test of time
c. To ensure that learning is possible without the original instructional materials

Table 9.1 Branches and divisions of IR

Parts/Section/ Branch/Content	Objectives	Human and Material Resources for Teaching
QUR'AN	Students should be able to a. read Qur'anic surah correctly with Tajwid, b. recite the Surah from memory, c. render the translation of the Surah, d. deduce the lessons contained in the Surah and e. apply the lessons to daily life.	1. Resource persons—e.g., Hafiz (professional Qur'anic memoriser), Qari' (professional Qur'anic reciter) 2. Audio media—e.g., tape recorder, cassettes, recorded recitations 3. Visual media—e.g., cardboard containing texts, flashcards, projectors, CDs 4. Audio-visual media—e.g., video, television programmes, computers 5. Realia—e.g., copies of the Glorious Qur'an
Hadith	Students should be able to a. read Arabic text of a given Hadith, b. identify difficult words and give their correct pronunciations, c. memorise the Hadith, d. enumerate the lessons contained in the hadith and e. apply the lessons of the hadith to daily life.	1. Human resources—a specialist in the field of Hadith 2. Audio media e.g., tape recorder, cassettes, recorded ahadith 3. Visual media—e.g., plastic boards, cardboard, flashcards 4. Audio-visual media—e.g., video, television programmes, computers 5. Realia—e.g., hadith textbooks, etc.

(*Continued*)

Table 9.1 (Continued)

Parts/Section/ Branch/Content	*Objectives*	*Human and Material Resources for Teaching*
TAHDHIB (**Moral Teachings**)	Student should be able to a. identify the meaning of certain Qur'anic verses and b. identify the implications of those verses.	1. Human resources—e.g., people with characters worthy of emulation in the community 2. Audio media—e.g., tape recorder, cassettes, recorded Qur'anic and ahadith excerpts on morals 3. Visual media—e.g., charts, posters, containing hints on morals, still pictures 4. Audio-visual media—e.g., video, television programmes, computers, dramatisation of the events portraying morals, demonstrations, television/videos 5. Realia—e.g., textbooks on morals
TAWHID	Students should be able to a. state the existence of created things in which indicate the existence of the Creator and b. identify the indications of the existence of Allah and His attributes as the Creator in the light of Al-Qur'an 56.57–56.62, etc.	1. Human resources—e.g., specialists in the field of Tawhid 2. Audio media—e.g., tape recorder 3. Visual media—e.g., charts depicting some natural phenomenal (e.g., sun, moon, stars, rivers, mountains, rotation of the earth seasons) still pictures, film/film strips 4. Audio-visual media—e.g., video, television programmes, computers 5. Realia—e.g., textbooks on Tawhid
IBADAT (**Worship**)	Students should be able to a. recall what *Ibadah* is. b. describe what is a *rak'ah* in salat, c. identify how to amend salat and d. demonstrate how to replace such rak'ah.	1. Human resources—e.g., jurists 2. Audio media—e.g., tape recorder 3. Visual media—e.g., charts, still pictures, film/film strips, calendars, programmed instruction 4. Audio-visual media—e.g., video, television programmes, computers, demonstration 5. Realia—e.g., textbooks on *Fiqh*

MU'MALAT (**Human Transaction**)	Students should be able to a. explain what is meant by *Amanah* and b. quote the meaning of Q.5 V.1 and the hadith.	1. Human resources—e.g., jurists, scholars of Hadith, exegetes 2. Audio media—e.g., tape recorder 3. Visual media—e.g., Charts, still pictures, film/film strips, calendar etc. 4. Audio-visual media—e.g., video, television programmes, computers, demonstration 5. Realia—e.g., textbooks on *Fiqh*
TARIKH (**HISTORICAL DEVELOPMENT**)	a. Historical development of the life of the prophet and the leadership of the four orthodox caliphs b. The spread of Islam c. Contributions of Muslims to world civilisation	1. Resources persons historian—e.g., historians 2. Audio media—e.g., tape recorder 3. Visual media—e.g., charts, slides still pictures, film/film strips about battles of badr, uhud and some Islamic conquests, calendars 4. Audio-visual media—e.g., video, displays, drama/demonstration television programmes, computers, demonstrations 5. Realia—e.g., textbooks on *Fiqh*

120 *Jamiu Abdur-Rafiu et al.*

Importance of Improvisation

1. It will boost the ego or morale of the teacher and bring out the interesting skills in him or her.
2. It makes learning more realistic because it deals with things within the local environment. A resourceful teacher can use improvised materials to make teaching and learning more meaningful and remodel imported teaching aids to suit his or her local conditions.

Skills for Improvising IR

The skills for improvising IR as suggested by Lawal (2010) are as follow:

1. **Mechanical Manipulation:** This allows one to draw, sketch, cut, glaze and paint if need be.
2. **Reflective Thinking:** This allows one to think fast but critically about alternative resources in case of scarcity and their suitability.
3. **Gathering:** This puts one at an advantage to 'scout around' for relevant materials to be put together to produce improvised material.
4. **Locating Information:** This is a demonstration of currency as regards source(s) of information and materials that could be useful for prompt and easy development of the improvised teaching aids.
5. **Observation:** This concerns the alertness that could help to regularly discover the need for improvisation.
6. **Planning:** This concerns the ability to recognise the need for improvisation and work towards it systematically. It facilitates the successful production of the materials.
7. **Problem-Solving:** It is the "mother of all the skills." This is because it is that which encompasses all other skills. Good use of this skill increases the chances of producing useful and relevant improvised instructional materials.
8. **Organising:** This is closely related to the skill of planning. It depicts the teacher's ability to put everything being developed into proper shape for eventual use.
9. **Controlling Situation:** This is the skill that assists the teacher in managing a crisis situation that has to do with limited or scarce IR. With this skill, the teacher will not unnecessarily panic.

Summary of the Study (Novelty)

Professionalism requires the demonstration of high skills and expertise in a specific profession. Thus, professionalism in teaching Islamic studies would demand an Islamic studies teacher to be an embodiment of the wherewithal required to make teaching delivery efficient and effective. Part of these requisites is the knowledge of the principles guiding the selection and utilisation of relevant IR for teaching the subject matter.

Enhancing Professionalism in Teaching   121

It is on this premise that the present study was carried out. We are able to present, herein, the explanation of the essence and essentialness of IR, forms of IR, the principles guiding selection and utilisation of IR and some examples of relevant IR that could be adopted by Islamic studies teachers to enhance goal achievement and promote professionalism in teaching Islamic studies. The roles of IR have been extensively expounded upon globally, particularly by educationists and educational technologists. What makes the present study different and unique is its approach to explaining how directly IR and media could be applied to teaching Islamic studies.

The researchers are able to point out in this chapter that the notion that some aspects of religious studies, particularly Islamic studies, could be taught in abstraction should be disenchanted. Relevant IR ranging from audio, visuals, audio-visuals, print, projected, non-projected media, community resources and human resources are all resources that could be applied in teaching all aspects of Islamic studies. Some of the ways in which being cognizant of the essence of IR would improve the teaching performance of teachers in Islamic studies include the following:

a. Effective utilisation of IR is vital for encouraging and facilitating students learning.
b. Through the utilisation of IR, subject content can be more carefully selected and organised.
c. Through the utilisation of IR, subject content can be delivered in a well-organised, consistent, specific and clear manner.
d. The utilisation of IR can make instruction much more interesting and enjoyable.
e. Effective utilisation of IR makes classrooms interactive and cooperative.

Conclusion

It has been revealed in the study that there is a profusion of IR, which can be used by Islamic studies teachers to enrich their teaching performance in Islamic studies. This would afford them considerable opportunities to make their teaching more effective and efficient. Some of the IR identified in the study includes audio, visual audio-visuals media, print media, chalk and chalkboard, graphic materials, realia, still pictures, models and mock-ups, audio media, overhead projectors, slide projectors and filmstrips projectors, film projector and video player/projector and multi-media presentation. An Islamic studies teacher is therefore expected to key into the principles elucidated herein so as to enhance professionalism in his or her teaching activities.

References

Abdur-Rafiu, J. (2014). Effect of concept-mapping and guided-discovery methods on secondary school students' performance in Islamic studies in Oyo State, Nigeria, An Unpublished Ph.D. research proposal submitted to the Department of Arts and Social Sciences Education, Faculty of Education, University of Ilorin.

Abolade, A.O. (2004). Basic criteria for selecting and using learning and instructional materials. In Abimbola I. O. and Abolade A. O. (eds). *Fundamental principles and practice of instruction*. Published by University of Ilorin, Department of Curriculum Studies and Educational Technology.

Adedeji, L. L. (2000). A Critical Examination of the relevance of Instructional Materials to the Teaching and Learning of Islamic Studies. *NATAIS* (16) 15–19.

Adelodun, G. A. & Asiru, A. B. (2015). Instructional resources as determinants of English language performance of secondary school high-achieving students in Ibadan, Oyo State. *Journal of Education and Practice*, 16 (21) 195–200

Alabere, R. A. (2017). The importance of instructional materials in teaching English as a second language. *IOSR Journal Of Humanities And Social Science*, 6 (9) 2319–7714.

Amuzu, S. (2018). Bridging the gap between theory and practice; teachers' utilization of instructional resources in teaching social studies in basic schools in West Mamprusi district in Northern Region, Ghana. *International Journal of Education, Learning and Development*, 6 (1) 10–25.

Bisiriyu, A. A. (2016). Instructional materials as correlates of students' academic performance in biology in senior secondary schools in Osun State. *International Journal of Information and Education Technology*, 6 (9) 705–708.

Eny, S., Djamiah, H., Haryanto and Baso, J. (2013). A model of creating instructional materials based on the school curriculum for Indonesian secondary schools. *Journal of Education and Practice*, 4 (20) 10–18.

Koech, F. (2017). Instructional resources used in teaching and learning in pre-schools in Kenya. *IOSR Journal of Humanities and Social Science*, 22 (1) 79–87.

Kumar, K. L. (2012). *Educational technology—a practical textbook for students, teachers, professionals and trainers*. Delhi: New Age International (P). Limited.

Lawal, B. O. (2010). *Religion and moral education*. Lagos. National Open University of Nigeria.

Ogbaji, D. I. (2017). Teachers' perception of the utilization of instructional materials in teaching social studies in junior secondary schools in Calabar municipality, cross river state, Nigeria. *Global Journal of Educational Research*, (16) 95–100.

Onyia, M. N. (2013). Instructional materials and design: Issues and challenges. *Academic Journal of Interdisciplinary Studies*, 2 (6) 153–158.

Umar, M. (2010). Assessment of teachers' use of instructional media for teaching Islamic studies in secondary schools in Kano State. An unpublished M. Ed research project submitted to Department of Sciences Education, Faculty of Education, University of Ilorin, Ilorin, Nigeria.

10 Improving Islamic Self-Motivation for Professional Development (Study in Islamic Boarding Schools)

Muhammad Anas Ma'arif, Muhammad Mujtaba Mitra Zuana and Akhmad Sirojuddin

Introduction

The success of Islamic education in instilling character is influenced by several components of education. The most important element is the role, competence and personality of the teacher (Wangid, 2016). Teacher competence is capable of conducting the learning optimally, fostering a conducive classroom atmosphere, providing good examples to students and instilling character from an early age (Toom, Husu, & Tirri, 2015). Teachers do not only transfer knowledge but serve as innovative and positive role models for students (Abdullah, 2017; Ahmed, 2018; Memon, 2011). Recent research shows that student success still depends on the quality of human resources (Ciampa, 2015).

In Indonesia, it is still said that the level of education is low due to the absorption of graduates from both schools and universities still not ready to enter the workforce, including the lack of teacher competence, as seen from the human development index in 2015, which is still not optimal. It also includes the widely held conceptualisation that religious education in Islamic boarding schools is often considered old-fashioned and lacking innovation; consequently, it is felt to be underdeveloped and neglected in comparison to other fields of study and knowledge (Al Idrus, 2016; Fauzi, 2012). Islamic boarding schools in Indonesia should be able to improve their strategy, management and development of teacher's competencies so that they are better able to form graduates who are ready to work and have utilitarian competencies.

If some Islamic boarding schools still retain the old way of learning, it is different from the Islamic boarding school that will be examined—namely, the Amanatul Ummah Islamic Boarding School in Mojokerto Indonesia. Every year, approximately 1,000 students graduate and enter well-known tertiary institutions, both domestically and abroad (Maarif and Rofiq 2018). The school follows contemporary educational objectives by incorporating both a religious and modern curriculum. The most important aspect of the success of students at this Islamic boarding school is due to qualified human resource management and guaranteed teacher welfare (Chalim, Sujono, & Usman,

DOI: 10.4324/9781003193432-12

2020; Hasanah, 2020). It serves as an interesting case study with which to examine the processes by which teachers carry out self-development and increase their competence and professionalism in Islamic boarding schools.

The purpose of this study is to analyse and identify strategies implemented by the Amanatul Ummah Islamic Boarding School in Mojokerto, Indonesia, in improving teacher competence. The scope of this chapter is the strategy of the Amanatul Ummah Islamic Boarding School to improve teacher competence by (1) self-motivation in developing competence, (2) giving scholarships to teachers, (3) evaluating teacher discipline, (4) providing training and workshops to teachers, (5) improving the quality of teacher learning and (6) teacher professional development through self-motivation.

Method

This chapter is qualitative research using a case study approach. The place was conducted at the Amanatul Ummah Islamic Boarding School in Mojokerto, Indonesia. The school uses a combination of *salaf* and modern models—namely, the formal and *diniah* (Islamic aspect). The case of this research is that teachers undertake serious learning innovations and self-development, making students more accomplished at national and international levels.

A case study according to Yin (2013) is research that emphasises real-life context phenomena and makes use of multiple sources of evidence. The fact is that the Amanatul Ummah Islamic Boarding School educational institution implements various strategies in developing the professionalism of educators, such as giving rewards to teachers, providing opportunities for teachers to continue higher education and providing teacher welfare appropriately.

The method of collecting data used observation, interviews and documentation. The researchers conducted observations and participant observations in which they directly saw and followed the activity process at the Amanatul Ummah Islamic Boarding School. Interviews were conducted with informants including the head of the *madrasah* (school), the coordinator of Islamic boarding schools, the students, teachers and the deputy coordinator. The interviews were not structured and open in nature. Not all teachers became informants, meaning that the researcher chooses teacher informants on the recommendation of the head of the madrasah and the deputy coordinator of the Islamic boarding school education and teacher training sector.

Meanwhile, data analysis techniques were carried out by (1) collecting data in the field with observation and in-depth interviews with informants; (2) data reduction, eliminating unnecessary data and categories; (3) presenting data, explaining meaning; and (4) verification and drawing conclusions. The research was conducted from 29 July 2019 to November 2019.

The findings in this study are as follows:

1. The Amanatul Ummah Islamic Boarding School undertook a management process of professional development among teachers by (a) planning for individual teacher needs, (b) the recruitment and placement

of teachers, (c) fostering and developing the teacher profession, (d) increasing the ability of teachers in learning and (e) evaluating teacher performance

2. Strategies to improve teacher professional development in self-motivation in Islamic boarding school (*Pesantren*) *covered intrinsic and extrinsic factors*

3. Teacher professional development was conducted through self-motivation in learning in Islamic boarding schools

Professional Development of Human Resources at the Amanatul Ummah Islamic Boarding School

Since the teachers are considered the measure of success in implementing education, the Amanatul Ummah Islamic Boarding School takes several steps in developing the teaching profession to improve the learning processes:

1. *Planning and Determining the Teacher Needs*
   The Amanatul Ummah Islamic Boarding School carries out the planning by conducting an annual work meeting facilitated by the Foundation and followed by the institution's work meeting. The Foundation consists of Gus and Ning (sons and daughters of the Foundation owner). There are at least six institutions under the Foundation's control. Meanwhile, the planning for the teacher's needs is undertaken by the institution. It is done and adjusted to the number of students. Every year, it has additional students so that the need for teachers is always increasing. Teacher needs are carried out when a needs analysis has been undertaken by the leader. In line with Ibrahim (Bafadal 2003), we stipulate the following employee needs: (1) inventory the number of existing employees, (2) the workload in each unit and (3) the capacity of teacher performance by recruiting (Das, Halik, & Amaluddin, 2016). Planning for the needs of teachers at the Amanatul Ummah Islamic Boarding School was carried out carefully under the Teacher Welfare Division.

   At the beginning of each year, the work meeting is held and determines the analysis of teacher needs and placement of positions. Before carrying out the recruitment process, the manager looks at the analysis of the student's accepted needs. The ratio of students and the teachers must be balanced. The planning will be followed up in the recruitment process for education staffs and teachers.

   (Laksono, 2019)

2. *Teacher Recruitment and Placement*
   Teacher quality is of course the priority in the teacher recruitment and placement process (Rahman 2015). The quality teachers come from a good selection and recruitment process (Bustamar, Idris, & Khairuddin, 2016). Teachers are required to possess our competencies (professional,

126 *Muhammad Anas Ma'arif et al.*

pedagogic, personality and social), following the direction of the government (Ramayulis, 2013). However, it is certainly difficult to find teachers who have these four competencies. The Amanatul Ummah Islamic Boarding School maintains specific standards throughout the recruitment process. The selection process is strictly supervised by the Foundation and competency tests are conducted according to teacher placement needs (such as the results of an interview with the coordinator of the school).

The teacher selection process is carried out by the Foundation and supervised by Foundation stakeholders. Selection and competency testing processes and interviews are conducted at the Foundation office. Gus (Sons of the Foundation owner) or the Human Resources directly selects. Requirements to be accepted as a teacher The Amanatul Ummah Islamic Boarding School are: 1) Being Muslim and affiliated with Nahdlatul Ulama`. 2) Having pedagogical competence as needed. 3) Having a good character.

(Zein, 2019)

Basically, teacher recruitment and selection are orientated to improve the quality of the school (Tambak, Amril, & Sukenti, 2021). The selection process should be able to measure the applicant's motivation, commitment and personality. The selected applicants will be placed according to the required needs of the school, curriculum and pupils (Hasanah, 2020). Teachers are expected to be able to adapt to the culture of Islamic boarding schools both in terms of clothing, traditions and culture and language (no swearing, etc.). Islamic boarding schools uphold Islamic values (Fakhrurrazi & Sebgag, 2020). The teachers selected must be role models for their students.

3. ***Coaching and Professional Development of Teachers***
Improving the quality of teachers is undertaken regularly. The teachers certainly cannot develop if they are not supported by institutions and policies that buttress their development (Hardy, 2012). They also need time to pursue self-development, especially teachers with minimal experience and who have just passed the selection (Adey, 2004). Institutions need to have policies supporting the continued development of teacher skills.

The Amanatul Ummah Islamic Boarding School carries out professional development (Sahertian, 2000), which has three programmes, including (1) pre-service education, helping teachers to continue their studies to suit their skills and eligibility to further their teaching competencies. (2) In-service education, providing opportunities and recommendations for teachers who are interested in further studies. It is evidenced by the data from the Islamic boarding school that 60% of the teachers in Amanatul Ummah have obtained master's and doctoral degree certificates. (3) In-service training; Amanatul Ummah teachers are given training related to teaching skills, such as coaching in making teaching materials, syllabus and lesson plans, national seminars and *halaqoh* with *kiai* (the owner and leader) and *habaib*.

4. **Teacher Professional Development in Conducting Learning**
    The teacher is a reflection and role model for students. If students have a bad attitude, it is influenced by the teacher. Therefore Amanatul Ummah has a slogan that reads, "*Be a good teacher or not at all.*" This is in line with the hadith of the Prophet, which means "*I was sent to be an example for my Ummah.*"

    How teachers innovate learning methods and strategies can make the teaching and learning process interesting in the class (A. Rusdiana, 2014). Various methods and strategies are applied by the teacher so that students are not deliberately bored. The teacher interacts differently and does not stop (Abidin, 2014). Some Islamic boarding schools are famous for being old-fashioned because they do not apply technology and learning innovations. It is different at the Amanatul Ummah Islamic Boarding School, which provides novel educational methodologies and offers additional skills for students.

    The Amanatul Ummah Islamic Boarding School provides flexibility for teachers to carry out learning innovations, such as (1) learning is not always in the classroom; it can be outside or learning with nature; (2) developing teaching materials to facilitate learning; (3) the discipline of teachers (such as punctuality); (4) *istikamah* (continuously) following *istigasah* and praying every morning; and (5) the teacher is the role model in daily activities.

5. **Evaluation of Teacher Performance**
    The Amanatul Ummah Islamic Boarding School evaluates teacher performance through several aspects: pedagogical, social and personality. The performance appraisal conducted at the Amanatul Ummah is very objective because the assessment system is not only a review by the direct leader but also the appraisal of teachers is assessed by peers and students.

    The evaluation of teacher performance at the Amanatul Ummah Islamic Boarding School refers to the rules (Director General of Higher Education, Ministry of National Education, 2004)—namely, (1) evaluation of the mastery of material and subject areas being handled; (2) evaluation of the understanding of students socially, culturally and psychologically; (3) evaluation of the learning strategies and methods used; and (4) evaluation of the professionalism and personality of the teacher while in the Islamic boarding school.

Strategies to Improve Teacher Professional Development through Self-Motivation

Once achieved, a satisfactory improvement of teacher performance can improve the overall quality of the education provided if the ability and motivation factors are accommodated and facilitated by the institution in question (Mangkunegara, 2005). The ability of individual teachers is developed

128 *Muhammad Anas Ma'arif et al.*

within the framework of professional development activities supported by the institution. A teacher with a higher educational background who teaches according to their field will find it easier to implement their performance according to the institutional goals. Motivation is also an important factor in improving the quality of teacher performance. Recent research has elucidated how teacher motivation has a major influence on the achievement of teacher performance (Kusumawati, 2020; Mohtar, 2019; Pianda, 2018).

The self-motivation of teachers to develop their own professionalism cannot be separated from the stimulus provided by the institution. The stimulus in this case according to Hergenhahn and Olson (2016) and Hurlock (1981) is a reward given to the teachers for the performance that has been attained commensurately. Teachers experience a dilemma if their work is heavy while the compensation provided by the institution is only small (Darmadi, 2016; Kartiko & Azzukhrufi, 2019). This will affect the self-motivation of teachers in increasing their professionalism.

The Amanmatul Ummah Islamic Boarding School provides stimulus in the form of rewards to every employee and teacher, provided they evince good work performance and discipline. The rewards reflect a form of high appreciation and take multiple material and religious forms. The most important thing is that the compensation provided by the institution is very respectable. The compensation may be in the form of a decent salary, health insurance, incentives, holiday allowances and so forth. It is under the narration from *Fikih*, the teacher of Amanatul Ummah.

> The compensation provided by the institution is very decent, I also have not found an institution that provides high salaries and wages like Amanatul Ummah. With this compensation, I become more disciplined and improve my performance, high motivation to improve performance and quality performance. I am more focused on improving my performance in learning because I am no longer focused on looking for other sides.

The self-motivation of teachers cannot be separated from their personal needs. It is believed that a strong urge to act appropriately and professionally will arise when the teachers have fulfilled their personal needs. It cannot be separated from the theory that private needs must be primary or secondary (Maslow, 2014). The primary needs of teachers as educators must be achieved so that they are not distracted from more pressing personal concerns/priorities. Ideally, teachers should be focused on undertaking what will be taught tomorrow.

According to Mangkunegara, self-motivation for teacher professional development is divided into two components—namely, intrinsic (internal) motivation and extrinsic (external) motivation (Mangkunegara, 2005).

1. Intrinsic factors (from the teachers themselves) include the following:
   a. Teachers' intelligence and ability to perform tasks. The teachers' intelligence is the determinant in completing the tasks they are

doing. In this case, the Amanatul Ummah Islamic Boarding School gives great appreciation if teachers carry out tasks intelligently and deftly. Teachers will complete their assignments correctly and on time if they have intelligence and abilities above average. Here, Amanatul Ummah applies the principle that Rasulullah has, namely, the character of *Fatanah* (intelligent).

b. Skills and Prowess: This intrinsic factor can be fostered by providing assignments, experience and training to teachers. The more experienced, the more proficient and skilled in completing work. The Amanatul Ummah Islamic Boarding School provides flexibility for teachers to attend seminars, workshops, training and other activities to support personal skills.

c. Talent: The adjustment between talents and job choices can make a person work according to his/her choice, expertise and temperament. The Amanatul Ummah Islamic Boarding School provides assignments and lesson hours according to the abilities and expertise of the teacher. There is little utility in obliging an Islamic education teacher to instruct on profane/mundane economics and so on. A suitable academic placement, according to their field of temperament and training, will motivate staff towards further self-development (Harefa, 2020).

2. Extrinsic factors (from outside of the teacher) include the following:

a. Work Environment: A pleasant work situation will encourage a teacher to work optimally. The work environment here is a sense of security, adequate salary, opportunity to develop professionalism, co-workers who are intelligent and help each other. The work environment in Islamic boarding schools is different from the mainstream school environment or institutions in general. Islamic boarding schools prioritise Islamic values. The Amamatul Ummah Islamic Boarding School provides a positive environment that will be full of high Islamic values. Teachers consistently set an example to students, such as discipline, honesty, sincerity and mutual respect.

b. Communication with the Principal: The leadership aspect is needed to foster self-motivation for teachers. Meetings and activities with the principal always remind the aims of Amanatul Ummah's education and the high ideals of the Amanatul Ummah Islamic Boarding School caregivers.

c. Facilities and Infrastructure. The existence of adequate infrastructure helps teachers improve their performance in learning. The Amanatul Ummah Islamic Boarding School provides adequate facilities in each class for conducive and enjoyable teaching and learning processes.

d. Teacher Welfare: Income levels can affect the work performance of professional teachers In order that the teachers concentrate on teaching at the Amanatul Ummah Islamic Boarding School, the

130 *Muhammad Anas Ma'arif et al.*

Foundation discretely provides guarantees and welfare incentives, such as regular salary increases, health insurance, holiday allowances and so forth.

Teacher Professional Development through Self-Motivation in Learning

The increase in teacher professionalism is, of course, undertaken gradually. The development of teacher professionalism carried out in learning will not be meaningful if the management of the Islamic boarding school is not pursued properly. The good management of an Islamic boarding school infers that it will/may provide opportunities for teachers to increase staff creativity and credibility. The activities of the teacher in the classroom are as follows: (1) planning the lesson wisely and correctly, (2) communicating effectively with students, (3) developing learning strategies, (4) controlling the class and (5) mastering the evaluation of learning correctly.

Teacher competence is also sharpened and developed so that students can express themselves. The goals of Islamic education are achieved in learning. One of the factors in honing teacher competence and developing student creativity is providing motivation (Ahn, Chiu, & Patrick, 2021; Mohtar, 2019). The motivation here is an impulse arising in a person to achieve specified goals (Duncan, 1978; Koontz, 2010).

The most popular motivation is contained in the flow of behaviourism that a person needs work motivation when there is a stimulus and is followed by a response. In general, human motivation is widely used in several institutions. The Amanatul Ummah Islamic Boarding School also gives a reward to every teacher who is able to improve competence and have achievements. This nodal axiom is reinforced by the Maslow theory that a teacher will be motivated to increase their learning activities when their needs are met (Maslow 2014).

Practically, at the Amanatul Ummah Islamic Boarding School, the teachers carry out some activities to arouse students' motivation during the learning process—namely, the following:

1. Providing a pleasant atmosphere in learning.
2. Guiding students sincerely based on high affection. The guidance can be done in learning or outside learning, such as counselling.
3. Organising assignments by prioritising cooperation rather than individual abilities.
4. Honing students' potential (*fitrah*) according to their talents and interests.
5. Encouraging students' sense of knowledge to explore.
6. Giving constructive praise.

According to Abraham Maslow (2014), the motivation discussed here can be divided into three: biological, psychological and meta-motivation.

Improving Islamic Self-Motivation 131

According to some Muslim scholars, the world of Islam infers three similar motivations: *jismiah*, *nafsiyah* and *ruhaniyah* (Baharuddin 2007). The motivation applied by Amanatul Ummah is illustrated in Baharuddin's theory—namely, the following:

1. Self-motivation of the teacher in *jismiah*: The teacher will work optimally if the biological needs are met. The strong encouragement of teachers to increase effectiveness and creativity is based on economic improvement. The Islamic boarding school provides decent salaries and allowances, as well as high appreciation.
2. Teacher self-motivation in *nafsiyah*: The teacher is provided with a sense of security and a pleasant environment.
3. Self-motivation of the teacher in *ruhaniyah*: Motivation to work sincerely based on worship to Allah. The Islamic boarding school environment always emphasises this aspect. The highest motivation for self-actualisation in Islam is to do something to worship unto Allah.

Personality is a very influential factor in the success of a staff member as a human resource developer because a teacher is a role model and *uswatun hasanah* for the students. Therefore, in developing the potential of students, it starts with an example in the educator's personality. The personality is the main basis for self-realisation, both in carrying out professional duties in an educational and other living environments.

The Amanatul Ummah Islamic Boarding School develops teachers' abilities in learning by applying the following keys to success:

1. Being serious (*al Jiddu wal muadhobah*): Being serious in practicing their knowledge—namely, being able to apply and integrate knowledge or skills in certain populations and certain situations, as well as discipline in carrying out all teaching obligations in education.
2. Eating a little (*Taqlilu Ghida'*): Educators should not eat too much, in this case, to always maintain their health because eating a lot and being full is the origin of all sickness arising. Eating a little can be beneficial for maintaining health, keeping yourself from usury cases, not getting a lot of sleep, being able to share with needy people, and so on. Rasulullah said, "Allah hates three people who are full to eat, arrogant and stingy" (Abu Husain Muslim 2010).
3. Having a night prayer (*qiyamul lail*): *Qiyamul lail* prayer is very useful for physical and spiritual health, which is very important for educational process activities. *Qiyamul lail* that is undertaken by teachers routinely is the remedy for students who are less able to accept subject matter, have a lack of attention in learning and issues of delinquency. Educators performing the midnight prayer are asking Allah for help so that all personal treatment and activities in education can be forgiven and blessed so that everything can become good, and what is good becomes even better.

4. Keeping ablution (*Mudhawamatul wudhu*): Knowledge is the divine light which will not reach the hearts of students if their souls are dirty and immoral. Therefore, the teacher must be able to perpetuate ablution to consistently maintain this divine emission. The teacher requirements include good physical and mental health. Poor health in either of these categories will affect their abilities to implement educational activities or duties properly. Likewise, poor spiritual health is also unhelpful for the students. In addition to good health (physically, mentally and spiritually), ideally, the teacher should be clean in body, mind and appearance.
5. Reading the Holy Koran by looking at the text (*Qiratul Qur`an Nadran*): An educator should also be accustomed to reading the Holy Koran by looking at it. This point includes the recommendation of Prophet Muhammad SAW that reading the Holy Koran by sight is one of the features that makes a man intelligent. The teachers are required to be smart in educating so that they can use a variety of strategies and methods to make the learning process engaging.

Conclusion

A teacher is a significant figure in the educational process. Good teachers should be able to carry out the learning processes with great creativity. The professional abilities of teachers are developed so that the learning process is meaningful and has a certain quality. The Islamic boarding school provides something different to increase teacher professionalism—namely, by providing high motivation. It provides this motivation so that the teachers can undertake effective quality in learning. The self-motivation of the teachers in Islamic boarding schools evinces more Islamic values. Muslim boarding schools prioritise aspects of Islamic values rather than just basic teaching and assessing the cognitive skills of students. Therefore teachers are expected to set an example and serve as role models for students. The Amanatul Ummah Islamic Boarding School also provides complete self-motivation to teachers from *jismiyah* biological motivation, *nafsiyah* motivation (a sense of security and a pleasant environment) and *spiritual* motivation (sincerity to practice their knowledge with the intention of worship).

References

Abdullah, M. A. (2017). Islamic studies in higher education in Indonesia: Challenges, impact and prospects for the world community. *Al-Jami'ah: Journal of Islamic Studies, 55*(2), 391–426. doi:10.14421/ajis.2017.552.391-426

Abidin, Y. (2014). *Desain sistem pembelajaran dalam konteks kurikulum 2013* (Cetakan kesatu). Refika Aditama.

Abu Husain Muslim, A.-H. (2010). *Shahih Muslim* (3rd ed., Vol. 1–1). Dar al-Kotob Al-Ilmiyah.

Adey, P. (2004). *The professional development of teachers: Practice and theory.* Springer Science & Business Media.

Improving Islamic Self-Motivation 133

Ahmed, F. (2018). An exploration of Naquib al-Attas' theory of Islamic education as ta'dib as an 'indigenous' educational philosophy. *Educational Philosophy and Theory, 50*(8), 786–794. doi:10.1080/00131857.2016.1247685

Ahn, I., Chiu, M. M., & Patrick, H. (2021). Connecting teacher and student motivation: Student-perceived teacher need-supportive practices and student need satisfaction. *Contemporary Educational Psychology, 64,* 101950. doi:10.1016/j.cedpsych.2021.101950

Al Idrus, A. J. (2016). Modernisasi Sistem Manajemen Dan Kurikulum Pondok Pesantren. *Jurnal Penelitian Keislaman, 12*(2), 141–154.

Bafadal, I. (2003). *Peningkatan profesionalisme guru sekolah dasar dalam kerangka manajemen peningkatan mutu berbasis sekolah* (Cet. 1). Bumi Aksara.

Baharuddin. (2007). *Paradigma Psikologi Islami, Studi tentang Elemen Psikologi dari Al-Qur`an* (2nded.). Pustaka Pelajar.

Bustamar, B., Idris, J., & Khairuddin, K. (2016). Strategi Kepala Sekolah Dalam Pengembangan Profesional Tenaga Kependidikan Pada Sma Negeri 5 Darussalam Banda Aceh. *Jurnal Administrasi Pendidikan: Program Pascasarjana Unsyiah, 4*(1). http://www.jurnal.unsyiah.ac.id/JAP/article/view/2603

Chalim, S., Sujono, G., & Usman, F. (2020). Trend analysis based educator planning. *Nazhruna: Jurnal Pendidikan Islam, 3*(2), 273–284. doi:10.31538/nzh.v3i2.683

Ciampa, K. (2015). An investigation of teacher candidates' questions and concerns about occasional teaching. *Journal of Applied Research in Higher Education, 7*(2), 146–163. doi:10.1108/JARHE-06-2013-0026

Darmadi, H. (2016). Tugas, Peran, Kompetensi, Dan Tanggung Jawab Menjadi Guru Profesional. *Edukasi: Jurnal Pendidikan, 13*(2), 161–174. doi:10.31571/edukasi.v13i2.113

Das, S. W. H., Halik, A., & Amaluddin. (2016). Paradigm of Islamic education in the future: The integration of Islamic boarding school and favorite school. *Information Management and Business Review, 8*(4), 24–32. doi:10.22610/imbr.v8i4.1390

Duncan, W. J. (1978). *Organizational behavior*. Houghton Mifflin.

Fakhrurrazi, F., & Sebgag, S. (2020). Methods of learning Kitab Kuning for beginners in Islamic boarding school (Dayah). *Nazhruna: Jurnal Pendidikan Islam, 3*(3), 296–310. doi:10.31538/nzh.v3i3.838

Fauzi, M. L. (2012). Traditional Islam in Javanese society: The roles of Kyai and Pesantren in preserving Islamic tradition and negotiating modernity. *Journal of Indonesian Islam, 6*(1), 125–144. doi:10.15642/JIIS.2012.6.1.125-144

Hardy, I. (2012). *The politics of teacher professional development: Policy, research and practice*. Routledge.

Harefa, D. (2020). Peningkatan Prestasi Rasa Percaya Diri Dan Motivasi Terhadap Kinerja Guru Ipa. *Media Bina Ilmiah, 13*(10), 1773–1786. doi:10.33758/mbi.v13i10.592

Hasanah, M. (2020). Rekrutmen Dan Seleksi Tenaga Pendidikan (Guru) Untuk Meningkatkan Kualitas Pendidikan di SMA Unggulan Berbasis Pesantren Amanatul Ummah Pacet. *Al-Tarbawi Al-Haditsah: Jurnal Pendidikan Islam, 5*(1), Article 1. doi:10.24235/tarbawi.v5i1.6310

Hergenhahn, B. R., & Olson, M. H. (2016). *Theories of learning = teori belajar* (Triwibowo, Trans., 6th ed.). Prenada Media Grup.

Hurlock, E. B. (1981). *Developmental psychology: A life-span approach*. Tata McGraw-Hill.

134   *Muhammad Anas Ma'arif et al.*

Kartiko, A., & Azzukhrufi, R. (2019). Pengaruh Budaya Organisasi Dan Kompensasi Terhadap Kinerja Pendidik Di Madrasah Aliyah Nahdlatul Ulama Mazro'atul Ulum Paciran. *Nidhomul Haq: Jurnal Manajemen Pendidikan Islam*, 4(2), 207–226. doi:10.31538/ndh.v4i2.351

Koontz, H. (2010). *Essentials of management.* Tata McGraw-Hill Education.

Kusumawati, E. (2020). Telaah Hubungan Motivasi Diri dan Kinerja Pembelajaran Pada Guru SMK Pariwisata. *Altasia Jurnal Pariwisata Indonesia*, 2(2), 299–304. doi:10.37253/altasia.v2i2.678

Maarif, M. A., & Rofiq, M. H. (2018). Pola Pengembangan Kurikulum Pendidikan Pesantren Berkarakter: Studi Pondok Pesantren Nurul Ummah Mojokerto. *TADRIS: Jurnal Pendidikan Islam*, 13(1), 1–16. doi:10.19105/tjpi.v13i1.1635

Laksono, P. (2019). *Divisi Kesejahteraan Guru Amanatul Ummah Mojokerto* [Personal communication].

Mangkunegara, A. A. A. P. (2005). *Evaluasi kinerja SDM.* Tiga Serangkai.

Maslow, A. H. (2014). *Toward a psychology of being.* Van Nostrand.

Memon, N. (2011). What Islamic school teachers want: Towards developing an Islamic teacher education programme. *British Journal of Religious Education*, 33(3), 285–298. doi:10.1080/01416200.2011.595912

Mohtar, I. (2019). *Hubungan Antara Motivasi Kerja Dan Pengalaman Kerja Dengan Kinerja Guru Madrasah.* Uwais Inspirasi Indonesia.

Pianda, D. (2018). *Kinerja guru: Kompetensi guru, motivasi kerja dan kepemimpinan kepala sekolah.* CV Jejak (Jejak Publisher).

Rahman, K. A. (2015). Rekrutmen Tenaga Pendidik dalam Peningkatan Mutu Madrasah Aliyah Negeri Insan Cendekia Jambi. *Nadwa*, 9(1), 23–38.

Ramayulis. (2013). *Profesi dan Etika Keguruan.* Kalam Mulia.

Rusdiana, A.. (2014). *Konsep Inovasi Pembelajaran.* Pustaka Setia.

Sahertian, P. A. (2000). *Konsep dasar & teknik supervisi pendidikan: Dalam rangka pengembangan sumber daya manusia.* Penerbit Rineka Cipta.

Tambak, S., Amril, A., & Sukenti, D. (2021). Islamic teacher development: Constructing Islamic professional teachers based on the Khalifah concept. *Nazhruna: Jurnal Pendidikan Islam*, 4(1), 117–135. doi:10.31538/nzh.v4i1.1055

Toom, A., Husu, J., & Tirri, K. (2015). Cultivating student teachers? Moral competencies in teaching during teacher education. In *International teacher education: Promising pedagogies (Part C)* (Vol. 22C, pp. 11–31). Emerald Group Publishing Limited. doi:10.1108/S1479-36872015000026001

Wangid, M. N. (2016). Membentuk Guru Yang Bermoral, Humanis Dan Profesional Melalui Proses Psiko-Pedagogis. *Jurnal Pembangunan Pendidikan: Fondasi Dan Aplikasi*, 4(2), 145–153.

Yin, R. K. (2013). *Case study research: Design and methods.* SAGE Publications.

Zein, K. (2019). *Kordinator Muadalah MBI Amanatul Ummah Mojokerto* [Personal communication].

11 Islamic Teacher Professionalism

The Role of Family and Society in Teacher Professionalisation

Abulfazl Ghaffari and Dina Yousefi

Introduction

What is meant by teacher professionalism? How does a teacher learn to be a professional? Most teacher education programmes have the ultimate aim of producing professional teachers. However, the question is how and when the transformation of a teacher to a professional one happens (Creasy, 2015). Professionalism is a multifaceted concept and therefore difficult to define. According to Creasy (2015), professionalism is divided into three categories: (1) *professional parameters*, which focus on the legal and ethical issues to which a professional must adhere, such as the local and state laws pertaining to educational and instructional issues; (2) *professional behaviours*, which are observable actions that demonstrate the individual's appropriate behaviours, such as forming appropriate relationships with students, parents and colleagues or modelling of the appearance and attitudes of a professional; and (3) *professional responsibilities* for a teacher that include demonstrating responsibility to the profession, students, the school district and the community.

Teachers are highly recommended to upgrade their knowledge of pedagogy to prepare students for living with dignity in the modern world. They should tailor their teaching to the level of the students' cognitive, affective and psychomotor development. Teachers must constantly upgrade their knowledge and understanding of the field, change their professional interests and needs with new developments and be ready to have a personal and ongoing commitment (Hoesein, 2015; Sutomo, 2014).

Literature Review

Islamic Education

What is the definition of Islamic education? The term 'Islamic education' covers a variety of meanings (Berglund, 2010). Excellent quality in the teaching profession is highly demanded in Islam in line with the recommendations of the Qur'an (Qur'an, 39:9; Hussin, Noh, & Tamuri, 2014). Islamic pedagogy is currently a lively and international area of inquiry. Researchers

DOI: 10.4324/9781003193432-13

136 *Abulfazl Ghaffari and Dina Yousefi*

have raised specific concerns regarding pedagogical quality, responsiveness to students' needs and epistemological links between pedagogies and larger philosophies of education. Islamic education is a concern for many teachers, administrators and parents. Principles of Islamic education, derived from Islamic primary sources, should be delineated by research in this field (Alkoualti, 2018).

The Ultimate Goal of Islamic Education

In the Islamic view of teaching, the main purpose of education is the *regeneration of the soul*. The word 'soul' is mentioned many times in the Holy Qur'an. This shows the significance of the soul in Islamic teachings. According to one Qur'anic verse (Qur'an, 21:35), man's experience of death is an indication of his life and his being tested by Allah shows that it could be trained and disciplined. *Akhlaq* (moral character) is part of Islamic education. *Akhlaq* education needs a comprehensive approach: the involvement of the family and the community as the partners of the school, the creation of a positive moral culture in the school and the intensive supports in the classroom (Sutomo, 2014). For Al-Ghazzali, education is the disciplining of the self through religious knowledge and moral values (Abdalla, Chown, & Abdullah, 2018).

A Brief History of Islamic Teaching Philosophy

It is important to know the historical trends of Islamic education in order to understand the background and purpose of modern-day Islamic education. The history of Islamic education can be traced back to several Muslim scholars, such as Ibn Rusd, Ibn Sina, Ghazzali and Zarunji, whose works reflect the purposes of learning. Zarunji (2003) described some of the qualities of Islamic pedagogy, including the nobility of learning, the importance of intention when learning, the assiduity with which learning should be approached, and the purpose of learning is described as putting knowledge into action and controlling one's lower self through the very act of learning (Ahmed, 2018).

Al-Ghazzali proposed a comprehensive psycho-spiritual theory that is grounded in Islamic ideology. The theory of the soul is considered as his major contribution to Islamic psychology (Ahmed et al., 2019). Al-Ghazzali's rejected the views of other philosophers that only logic/reason could be a source of guidance for human beings. Through his intellectual contributions, he conceptualised and demonstrated the impact of Qur'anic teachings, under the command of Allah, on the human soul.

Method

This chapter enjoys a descriptive-analytic approach to Islamic teaching professionalism. It has a theoretical part which introduces Al-Ghazzali's concept of soul and a practical aspect which draws on the results and findings of the current literature in the domain of Islamic teaching. Everywhere in the chapter references are made to the Qur'an as the backbone of the principles and techniques introduced for the professionalisation of Islamic teaching.

Islamic Education Conceptualised as Soul Regeneration (The Qur'an, 2004, 5:32; 6:122; 8:24; 9:38; 16:97; 25:58; 36:33; 39:9)

God's call to man as the supreme being and as the first teacher of man and the appointment of Prophet Muhammad as the great teacher of humanity and the necessity of embracing this call as well as the Holy Qur'an's reference to giving life to a dead person (dead in the heart) and granting life (direction) to him, alludes to the fact that in Islam, soul regeneration is assumed to be the most significant job of the teacher. Giving life to a human being is important to the extent that it has been equated with granting everything to all humanity. In Islam, spiritual well-being is the natural state of humans. Man is an *a priori* spiritual being, as humans are endowed with the spirit of Allah. Man feels psychologically happy and satisfied only as long as he moves closer to his inner nature and feels unhappy and miserable at the time he deviates from it (Baba & Zayed, 2015; Egel & Fry, 2017).

Some Principles of Soul Generation

Given the importance of soul regeneration in Islamic education, Muslim scholars and teachers should provide an agenda for Islamic teaching which guarantees soul regeneration as an end in Islamic education. To come up with such an agenda, the principles of this kind of education should be provided as a starting point. Some principles of soul regeneration are as follows: (1) emphasis on innate human qualities and attributes, (2) focus on man's material and earthly life as a necessary component of one's pure life and (3) emphasis on the gradual progression of the upgrading of the soul (Ahmed, 2016; Lubis et al., 2010: Sahin, 2018).

Some Methods and Techniques for Soul Regeneration

Soul regeneration could be achieved through a number of ways and methods (Abdalla, Chown, & Abdullah, 2018; Adam, 2017; Al-Karasneh & Saleh, 2010; Alkoualti, 2018; Sahin, 2018). Some of which are as follows: *teaching of philosophy (wisdom)* (Qur'an, 22:46; 69:12), *empowering the unprivileged people and liberating them* (Qur'an, 21:92; 28:5; 49:13), *enlivening human noble status* (Qur'an, 17:70; 19:50; 36:11), *journey into the material and immaterial world* (Qur'an, 27:69; 29:20; 30:42; 34:18; 41:53), *reminiscence (of wisdom, prayer, Qur'an, death)* (Qur'an, 87:9; 6:126; 35:3; 16:17), *kindness and sympathy* (Qur'an, 16:125; 29:46), *taking individual differences into account* (Qur'an, 5:48; 2:286; 49:13) and *enjoining good and forbidding wrong* (Qur'an, 3:104, 110; 9:71, 112; 31:17).

138 *Abulfazl Ghaffari and Dina Yousefi*

The adherence to moral and religious virtues and constant practice in maintaining virtues is considered a necessary element in Islamic teacher professionalism (Qur'an, 5:1, 7–8; 8:27). Some of the most significant virtues and vices which are frequently stipulated in Islamic education are as follows: *brotherhood* (Elkaleh & Samier, 2013); *civic duty, humility, piety, sincerity, trust, truthfulness; moderation; patience, tawadu and Ta'zim (respect), tawakkol (submission to God), wara (keeping away bad deed)* and *zuhud (refraining from worldly life)* (Huda & Kartanegara, 2015) and *seeking knowledge* (Tamuri, Ismail, & Jazmi, 2012). Also, learners should also be taught to avoid such negative traits as lying, cheating, bullying, selfishness, intolerance, discrimination and the like Elkaleh & Samier, 2013).

Islamic Teacher's Responsibilities

Islamic teacher professionalism could be neatly categorised into four different responsibilities which are as follows: (1) *responsibilities towards Allah (God)*. The invitation to take Allah as one's Lord is regarded as central in Islam. Hence, Islamic education refers to the process of becoming divine (Bagheri & Khosravani, 2006). (2) *Responsibilities towards oneself.* A teacher has a dignified and honoured position in Islam. In line with this vital role, Islamic teachers are expected to equip themselves with knowledge, skills, personality, behaviour and propensity to project themselves as role models and as effective teachers. Also, professional teachers possess such characteristics as responsibility, matured and developed personality, morality and spirituality, commitment to the interests of students, ability to think reflectively and correctively, and having effective personality (Al-Karasneh & Saleh, 2010; Alkerden & Alqahtani, 2016).

As for (3) *responsibilities towards learners*, according to Ag (2014), Mustafa and Salim (2012) and Sutomo (2014), the responsibilities of an Islamic professional teacher towards the students consist of the following practices and activities: analysing students' participation in terms of content comprehension, encouraging participation from diverse student populations, recording and updating the results of students' assignments, collecting information about students' progress in a systematic manner, analysing the performance of students with diverse learning styles, maintaining confidentiality in all situations, communicating positive information and concerns to parents/caregivers and ensuring that all students receive an equitable opportunity to succeed. (4) *Responsibilities towards society.* According to Ag (2014), Al-Karasneh and Jubran (2013), Dean (2005), Huda (2017) and Keshavarz (2010), Islamic teachers need to take care of social aspects of education which comprise the following: seeking assistance from other professionals concerning teaching and learning; participating in school-related activities; participating in students' teaching seminars; attending all required school and district professional development programmes; showing evidence of participation in at least one professional organisation; integrating information from professional publications into daily instruction; assessing personal, cultural perspective and its influence on interactions with others; complying with school and class rules; using relevant codes of ethics for the teaching profession; following proper procedures for reporting students' welfare and safety; acting responsibly regarding school and personal property; and, finally, challenging stereotypical attitudes.

The Role of Family in Islamic Teacher Professionalism (Qur'an, 29:8)

Numerous studies have demonstrated the importance of home-school relationships and parental involvement in different school-related issues (Abdalla, Chown, & Abdullah, 2018; Baeck, 2015; Gorton & Schneider, 1991; Merry, 2005; Torre & Murphy, 2016). Owing to the fact that parents are authentic partners in home-school relationships, their voices are important in shaping school and classroom decisions. Parent voice includes opportunities to speak and the commitment of school staff to listen and hear (Shakeel, 2018; Torre & Murphy, 2016).

Gorton and Schneider (1991) suggest four things as the objectives of involving parents in school activities: (1) to give them more information about what students are learning in school; (2) to encourage parents to provide school facilities for supporting children's learning activities at home; (3) to offer them some chances to give input of ideas, expertise and human resources for school reform; and (4) to help them create effective school management (cited in Sumarsono et al., 2016).

What Muslim Parents Should Do

Based on Qur'anic teachings (9:119; 33:21), research findings in the field and taking into account the views of scholars working in the domain of Islamic teaching (Ahmed, 2018; Baeck, 2015; Badrasawi et al., 2017; Hamdan, 2014; Merry, 2005; Olsen & Fuller, 2003; Ng & Yuen, 2015; Shah, 2016; Sumarsono et al., 2016; Torre & Murphy, 2016, to mention just a few), the following list summarises what parents should practically do in order to assist teachers in the realisation of a true Islamic education. Hence, parents in Islamic education are supposed to

(a) communicate with school;
(b) help actual learning of individual children;
(c) take part in parent programme and organisation;
(d) assist in school operation;
(e) participate in decision-making;
(f) try to resolve value differences between teachers and parents;
(g) help their children to integrate positively with the wider society while maintaining their Islamic culture and identity;
(h) preserve honesty in the home-school relationship;

140 *Abulfazl Ghaffari and Dina Yousefi*

(i) phone calls to inform teachers of issues related to the education of their children;

(j) have email exchanges with teachers concerning issues related to the education of their children;

(k) direct parental involvement in their children's education;

(l) establish communal trust between themselves and teachers;

(m) foster personalisation through small schools or through a cohort system within a larger school;

(n) provide invaluable information to teachers about student interests, strengths and weaknesses that will enable teachers to better differentiate instruction;

(o) engage in two-way interactions with teachers to positively shape students' academic progress;

(p) to be actively involved in school-related things, such as learning, supervision, coordination and other services at the school;

(q) to be a resource person, prepare field trip programmes, develop an inspiring classroom, plan and evaluate the learning activities outside the classroom through *parenting day* activities; and

(r) be involved in planning and solving problems in the domains of curriculum or learning programmes or policies concerning students.

The Role of Society in Islamic Teacher Professionalism (Qur'an, 90:12–18; 89:17–24; 92:5–10)

The principle of systematic social work is emphasised in Islam. Social work is considered as *Ibadah* (worship of Allah) and principally whatever is done to acquire His satisfaction is considered as *Ibadah*. A whole chapter of the Qur'an, called *Al Ma'oon*, divinely mandates to fulfil the needs of others. As the *khalifa* of Allah, Muslims have to invent comprehensive and effective social work and services leading to 'excellence' (Abdalla, Chown, & Abdullah, 2018; Baba & Zayed, 2015; Hoesein, 2015; Rissanen, 2012). Students' learning is influenced by various factors, not least among them the social and educational context in which their learning takes place. Therefore, there is a constant interaction between what students are taught and the dominant social and political discourses that are embedded in the media and institutions in which they live (Revell, 2010).

According to some scholars, there are some deficiencies in the current practice of curriculum integration for Islamic universities; it does not focus on a particular topic selected by the teacher, and it does not involve the teacher in both planning and directing students in activities, which may enable a teacher to plan in advance and recycle units from year to year (Rufai, 2016). Today, generally speaking, educational curricula for Islamic disciplines in religious seminaries and increasingly in Islamic 'universities' do not seem to prepare educators to deal effectively with modernity, let alone the educational needs of a modern society (Saeed, 2006).

Islamic Teacher Professionalism 141

What Islamic Professional Teachers Should Do

One of the fundamental aspects of teaching is the effect of social factors and their contribution to the quality of teaching. A teacher who does not take social factors into account will lose the whole picture and will engage in teaching in a deficient way. Accordingly, the following principles and techniques and guidelines are suggested by a number of researchers and educationalists for Islamic professional teaching (Al-Karasneh & Saleh, 2010; Benn, Dagkas, & Jawad, 2011; Hoesein, 2015; Hussien, 2006; Noh et al., 2014; Nolan & Molla, 2019; Osmond-Johnson, 2016; Rishi, 2013). Islamic professional teachers are expected to do the following:

(a) Do not restrict their attention to the classroom alone, leaving the larger setting and purposes of schooling to be determined by others … they need to determine their own agency through a critical and continual evaluation of the purposes, the consequences and the social context of their calling.

(b) Be able to pursue what they value in their practice and "make choices, take principled action and enact change." This makes agency as a key element of teachers' professional capability.

(c) Provide leadership to a group of students.

(d) Provide direct, face-to-face instruction.

(e) Work with colleagues, parents and others to improve classrooms and schools as learning organisations.

(f) Pay a lot of attention to the content of the curriculum and critique it to improve it.

(g) Redesign or design curricula, including social justice issues.

(h) Build on students' cultural and linguistic resources.

(i) Promote critical thinking and deep questioning in students.

(j) Develop a culture of respect among students and between students and teachers.

(k) Engage in community work and get students engaged in these kinds of activities.

(l) Break down racial or class barriers for students.

(m) Teach students about civic engagement.

(n) Create learning opportunities for students to live a successful future.

(o) Make curriculum relevant and applicable to students.

(p) Know and understand students' social and cultural contexts.

(q) Be fair to all students in the classroom without showing favourites.

(r) Challenge students' stereotypes or biases related to race, class and gender.

(s) Value students' diversity and establish a caring and inclusive environment.

Discussion and Conclusion

According to Sahin (2018), the research into concepts of Islamic education or Islamic pedagogy, curriculum and teacher education–related issues have not been subject to proper research and development. One of the major drawbacks in the performance of Islamic teachers by which they come short of professionalism is that Islamic teachers usually lack the basic and working knowledge of critical thinking in terms of their inability to define critical thinking to students regardless of their educational levels. In order to remove this problem, it is suggested that universities and teaching training centres or school staffs try to create both short- and long-term programmes to equip Islamic teachers with the appropriate critical thinking skills and strategies.

Previous studies on the professionalism of teachers in Islamic education (e.g., Halim et al., 2004, 2006; Kamaruzzaman et al., 2003; Mohd, 2011) have found that the components of teaching practice which have obtained a large percentage of low and moderate accomplishment are the involvement of students; response to students; examples of contents, teaching materials and resources; and the implementation of content activities. The study by Ab. Halim et al. (2006) shows that out of 717 Islamic teachers, about 81.3% had never used video/CD, 82.7% never utilised the LCD (Liquid Crystal Devices), 85% had not used Islamic education software and 92.4% had never accessed the web during their learning and teaching. This is so while educators are rightly required to be skilled in communication and accessing information, and should know how to use various technologies that can be adapted within the teaching profession (cited in Hussin, Noh, & Tamuri, 2014).

Another crucial problem found in Islamic teaching centres relates to the fact that many teachers appear to be poor in the mastery of teaching methods, though undeniably they possess high character for the position of educators. This leads to a situation in which these poor teachers are still in service because schools need them, irrespective of their insufficient competencies demanded by the teaching-learning processes. Changes in the mentality of the teachers appear to be necessary to remedy the existing problems (Sutomo, 2014). Still another serious gap in the research on Islamic education is the lack of teachers' voices on their practices. Despite the exponential increase in the studies of Islamic education, studies of teachers' practices, roles and voices are relatively absent (Niyozov & Plum, 2009).

The literature on Muslim students' education shows that Islamic teachers' voices and practices remain marginalised (Niyozov & Plum, 2009). Impoverished understanding of how the teachers conceptualise and make meaning of particular aspects of their teaching has led to the rise of dubious assumptions about what teaching is. It seems that still we lack adequate definition or insights into how teachers perceive their own teaching in light of the Islamic teaching context, and the lines between religion and education seem to be blurred. Moreover, quality assurance in Islamic universities has not lived up to expectations, especially in terms of creative innovations and inventions. These weaknesses could be attributed to a lack of leadership quality to spearhead innovative projects and the subsequent brain drain of bright Muslim minds to more prosperous societies (Kayode & Hashim, 2014).

The professional Islamic teacher must review the learning experiences in the contents of the recent Islamic education body of research. The teacher should shun the use of the textbook as a single source of knowledge and try to embrace diverse, open, traditional and digital sources; encourage students to evaluate the sources of knowledge; and select different teaching tools. The search for the appropriate form of religious education, in the form of both content and pedagogy, which could not only address and satisfy the spiritual but also the practical needs of young Muslims, is among those challenges that ought to be of primary concern for Muslim schools, madrasahs and educators in the contemporary world.

References

Abdalla, M., Chown, D., & Abdullah, M. (2018). *Islamic schooling in the West: Pathways to renewal.* Switzerland: Palgrave MacMillan.

Adam, A. M. (2017). The concept of pluralism in Islamic teaching. *Ar-Raniry, International Journal of Islamic Studies,* 4(1), 71–86.

Ag, H. A. M. (2014). A study for searching new foundation of philosophy of Islamic education to revitalize the teacher roles and duties in globalization era. *International Journal of Social Science and Humanity,* 4(5), 391–396.

Ahmed, F. (2016). An exploration of Naquib al-Attas' theory of Islamic education as ta'dib as an 'indigenous' educational philosophy. *Educational Philosophy and Theory,* 50(8), 1–9.

Ahmed, J. M. (2018). *Stakeholder expectations of Islamic education.* Dissertations and Theses. Portland State University.

Ahmed, A., Arshad, M. A., Mahmood, A., & Akhtar, S. (2019). The influence of spiritual values on employees' helping behavior: The modeling role of Islamic work ethic. *Journal of Management, Spirituality, & Religion,* 16(3), 1–29.

Al-Karasneh, S., & Jubran, A. (2013). Classroom leadership and creativity: A study of social studies and Islamic education studies in Jordan. *Creative Education,* 4(10), 651–662.

Al-Karasneh, S. M., & Saleh, A. M. J. (2010). Islamic perspective of creativity: A model for teachers of social studies as leaders. *Procedia Social and Behavioral Sciences,* 2, 412–426.

Alkoualti, C. (2018). Pedagogies in becoming Muslim: Contemporary insights from Islamic traditions on teaching, learning, and developing. *Religions,* 9, 1–18.

Baba, S., & Zayed, T. M. (2015). Knowledge of *shariah* and knowledge to manage 'self' and 'system': Integration of Islamic epistemology with the knowledge and education. *Journal of Islam, Law, and Judiciary,* 1(1), 45–62.

Badrasawi, K. J. I., Preece, A. S., Hashim, C. N., & Azizi, N. M. S. (2017). The concept of murabbi in Muslim education with reference to selected teaching methods of the prophet Muhammad. *Al-Shajarah, Journal of Islamic Thought and Civilization* (Special issue), 22, 327–357.

Baeck, U. K. (2015). Beyond the fancy cakes: Teachers' relationships to home-school cooperation in a study from Norway. *International Journal about Parents in Education,* 9(1), 37–46.

Bagheri, K., & Khosravani, Z. (2006). The Islamic concept of education reconsidered. *The American Journal of Islamic Social Sciences,* 23(4), 88–103.

Benn, T., Dagkas, S., & Jawad, H. (2011). Embodied faith: Islam, religious freedom and educational practices in physical education. *Sport, Education and Society,* 16(1), 17–34.

Berglund, J. (2010). *Teaching Islam: Islamic religious education in Sweden.* Berlin: Waxmann.

Creasy, K. L. (2015). Fostering a culture of professionalism in teacher preparation programs. *Journal of Education and Human Development,* 4(4), 26–31.

Dean, B. L. (2005). Citizenship education in Pakistani schools: Problems and possibilities. *International Journal of Citizenship and Teacher Education,* 1(2), 35–55.

Egel, E., & Fry, L. W. (2017). Spiritual leadership as a model for Islamic leadership. *Public Integrity,* 19, 77–95.

Elkaleh, E., & Samier, E. A. (2013). The ethics of Islamic leadership: A cross-cultural approach for public administration. *Administrative Culture,* 14(2), 188–211.

Gorton, R. A., & Schneider, G. T. (1991). *School-based leadership: Challenges and opportunities.* Dubuque, Iowa: Wm. C. Brown Publishers.

Hamdan, A. (2014). Parental support as a driver for educational success among Arab Muslim Canadian women. *Pertanika Journal of Social Sciences & Humanities,* 22(2), 429–454.

Hoesein, M. H. (2015). Using mobile technology and online support to improve language teacher professionalism. *Procedia-Social and Behavioral Sciences,* 191, 491–497.

Huda, M. (2017). Understanding divine pedagogy in teacher education: Insights from Al-Zarunji's Ta'lim Al-Muta'Allim. *The Social Sciences,* 12(4), 674–679.

Huda, M., & Kartanegara, M. (2015). Islamic spiritual character values of al-Zarunji's Ta'lim al-Muta'allim. *Mediterranean Journal of Social Sciences,* 6(4), 229–235.

Hussien, S. (2006). *Towards the Islamization of critical pedagogy: A Malaysia case study.* Thesis, Department of Educational Studies, University of Sheffield.

Hussin, N. H., Noh, A. M. C., & Tamuri, H. (2014). The religious practices teaching pedagogy of Islamic education excellent teachers. *Mediterranean Journal of Social Sciences,* 5(16), 239–246.

Kayode, B. K., & Hashim, C. N. (2014). Quality assurance in contemporary Islamic universities: Issues and challenges. *ILUM Journal of Educational Studies,* 2(2), 40–58.

Keshavarz, S. (2010). Quran point of view on dimensions of reflections and its indications in education system. *Procedia Social and Behavioral Sciences,* 9, 1812–1814.

Lubis, M. A., Yunus, M. M., Embi, M. A., Sulaiman, S., Mahamod, Z. (2010). Systematic steps in teaching and learning Islamic education in the classroom. *Procedia Social and Behavioral Sciences,* 7, 665–670.

Merry, M. S. (2005). Advocacy and involvement: The role of parents in western Islamic schools. *Religious Education,* 100(4), 374–385.

Mohd A. C. N. (2011). The practice of teaching recitation of Quran: A review on the perception of teachers at daily secondary schools in Malaysia. *Journal of Islamic and Arabic Education,* 1(1), 57–72.

Mustafa, Z., & Salim, H. (2012). Factors affecting students' interest in learning Islamic education. *Journal of Education and Practice,* 3(13), 81–86.

Ng, S., & Yuen, G. (2015). Exploring teaching professionals' constraints in implementation of parental involvement in school education. *Procedia-Social and Behavioral Sciences,* 191, 1077–1081.

Niyozov, S., & Plum, G. (2009). Teachers' perspectives on the education of Muslim students: A missing voice in Muslim education research. *Curriculum Inquiry,* 39(5), 637–677.

Noh, M. A. C., Tamuri, H., Razak, K. A., & Suhid, A. (2014). The study of Quranic teaching and learning: United Kingdom experience. *Mediterranean Journal of Social Sciences*, 5(16), 313–317.

Nolan, A., & Molla, T. (2019). Supporting teacher professionalism through tailored professional learning. *London Review of Education*, 17(2), 126–140.

Olsen, G., & Fuller, M. L. (2003). *Home-school relations: Working successfully with parent and families* (2nd ed.). Boston: Allyn and Bacon.

Osmond-Johnson, P. (2016). Contextualizing teacher professionalism: Findings from a cross-case analysis of union active teachers. *Alberta Journal of Educational Research*, 62(3), 268–287.

Revell, L. (2010). Religious education, conflict and diversity: An exploration of young children's perception of Islam. *Educational Studies*, 36(2), 207–215.

Rishi, S. (2013). *Education and curricular perspectives in the Quran*. Dissertation. Arizona State University.

Rissanen, I. (2012). Teaching Islamic education in Finnish schools: A field of negotiations. *Teaching and Teacher Education*, 28, 740–749.

Rufai, S. A. (2016). The challenge of curriculum integration for Islamic universities: Setting the principles of curriculum integration. *IIUM Journal of Educational Studies*, 4(1), 46–77.

Saeed, A. (2006). *Islamic thought: An introduction*. New York: Routledge.

Sahin, A. (2018). Critical issues in Islamic education studies: Rethinking Islamic and western liberal secular values of education. *Religions*, 9, 1–29.

Shah, S. (2016). *Education, leadership and Islam: Theories, discourses and practices from an Islamic perspective*. New York: Routledge.

Shakeel, M. D. (2018). Islamic schooling in the cultural West: A systematic review of the issues concerning school climate. *Religions*, 9, 1–31.

Sumarsono, R. B., Imron, A., Wiyono, B. B., & Arifin, I. (2016). Parents' participation in improving the quality of elementary school in the city of Malang, East Java, Indonesia. *International Education Studies*, 9(10), 256–262.

Sutomo, I. (2014). Modification of character education into *akhlaq* education for the global community life. *Indonesian Journal of Islam and Muslim Societies*, 4(2), 291–316.

Tamuri, A. H., Ismail, M. F., & Jazmi, K. A. (2012). A new approach in Islamic education: Mosque based teaching and learning. *Journal of Islamic and Arabic Education*, 4(1), 1–10.

The Qur`an. (2004). A new translation by M. A. S. Abdel Haleem. New York: Oxford University Press.

Torre, M., & Murphy, J. (2016). Communities of parental engagement: New foundations for school leaders' work. *International Journal of Leadership in Education*, 19(2), 203–223.

Zarunji, I. B. (2003). *Instruction of the student: The method of learning* (G.E. Von Grunebaum & T. Abel, Trans.). Chicago, IL: Starlatch Press.

12 Teachers' Roles in Making Multiple Intelligences Work in Indonesian Muslim Schools

Muhammad Zuhdi and Erba Rozalina Yulianti

Introduction

Indonesian Islamic schools are known for their adaptability to changes in education theories. The long history of Indonesia's Islamic education shows that the variety of Islamic education institutions indicates that Islamic school continuously adapts to the changing education theories and practices. While a number of Islamic schools maintain their traditional ways of teachings, a number of new models of Islamic schools continue to exist, adopting new approaches in education. The development of some new models of Muslim schools reflects the sustainability of Indonesian Islamic education. While religion-based schools are assumed to be traditional and reluctant to change, a lot of Indonesian Muslim schools are open to modernisation and improvement. One of the most important factors in the development of Indonesian Islamic education is its openness to Western education theories that are based on empirical and scientific ideas. Theories such as Bloom's taxonomy, Piaget's cognitive development, Goleman's emotional intelligence and Dewey's pragmatic education have been popular and implemented in Indonesian Muslim schools.

Since the publication of *Frames of Mind* in 1983, Howard Gardner's multiple intelligences (MI) theory has spread all over the world and influenced schools everywhere. The theory explains that human beings have many cognitive abilities that can be enhanced through experiences. When nurtured in positive ways, these abilities can help individuals to achieve the best careers of their lives. Realising the complex structure of human cognitive abilities, it is unfair to judge a person based on his/her level of logical-mathematical abilities, like what the IQ test does. Those who have good mathematical and language intelligences will certainly perform better on IQ tests compared to students who have less mathematical and language abilities. The theory argues that human beings have different intelligences that they develop and use in their lives. Those who perform low in math may have better results in language or music.

Scholars and practitioners have published a number of books and articles discussing the importance of the theory and how it can be applied in schools. Armstrong (2017), for instance, elaborated on how curriculum development

DOI: 10.4324/9781003193432-14

incorporates the MI theory. The theory has changed the way teachers and schools view and treat their students. Moreover, the theory has also changed the definition of 'smart' to include various fields or disciplines, instead of focussing on logical, mathematical and verbal linguistics only. Students can now explore and develop their potential without being concerned that they are not very good at math and language.

While Islamic education tends to be open to accept Western ideas of a good education, not all Muslim educators are in agreement with applying MI theory in an Islamic education context. Turkish educators Akpunar and Dogan, for instance, maintain that MI theory is not relevant to be implemented in Muslim schools, as it is based on materialism, which contradicts Islamic teaching (Akpunar & Dogan, 2011). However, a lot of other Muslim educators find that applying MI theory in Islamic education will benefit Muslim students, and hence a lot of Muslim schools in various countries continue to apply the theory as the basis of their teaching and learning. In Indonesia, the use of the theory has been widely accepted by Muslim educators. Munif Chatib, for instance, promotes the application of the theory in a number of schools that he supervises (Chatib, 2015). Similarly, the MI theory is also widely accepted in Malaysia (Hamdan & Jamian, 2015).

The purpose of this chapter is to reveal how Indonesia's Muslim schools' teachers prepare themselves to implement this theory in Muslim school settings. While the main mission of Muslim schools is ensuring young generations know about and practice Islam, Muslim schools in Indonesia go beyond this. Most Indonesian Muslim schools are designed to help students learn various branches of knowledge and skills in addition to religion. Many Muslim schools adopt Western-oriented education models, such as Montessori and Cambridge curricula. The recent adoption of the MI theory has only increased these schools' adaptation of the Western education model.

This chapter explains how Muslim schools improve skills and professionalism in applying the MI theory in their classrooms. This study is composed of qualitative, multiple case studies conducted at Sekolah Menengah Umum (SMU) Plus Muthahhari (High School) in Bandung and Sekolah Menengah Atas (SMA) Lazuardi (High School) Depok. Both schools are located in West Jawa, Indonesia. Data were collected through documentary study and in-depth interviews with principals and teachers. Principals' and teachers' experiences in applying the theory in schools were major sources of information.

The Context of Indonesia's Muslim Schools

Islamic education has a long history in Indonesia. Its contribution to the country's human resource development is unquestionable. Indonesia's unique *pesantren* education was among the early forms of Islamic education institutions and still exists today. In addition to *pesantren, madrasah* is another form of Islamic education. While both are focussed on teaching Islamic knowledge and religious practices to students, *pesantren* (similar to boarding school) has a more intensive religious education since students normally stay at the *pesantren* during the course of their study. *Pesantren* was a place for young Indonesian Muslims to learn not only religious knowledge but also various life skills prior to the 19th century. *Madrasah*, unlike *pesantren*, is a day school that serves students to learn various branches of religious knowledge. *Madrasah* was first introduced to Indonesia at the beginning of the 19th century (Yunus, 1996).

Despite their long history and contributions, Islamic education institutions were not officially recognised until 1975, when the government released a three-minister decree on the improvement of the quality of Muslim schools (*madrasah*) (Zuhdi, 2006). After being in the peripheral of the national education system since the beginning of the country's formation, Indonesia's Muslim schools gained momentum in the late 1980s. The enactment of the 1989 National Education Law officially recognised *madrasah* as an integral part of the national education system (Zuhdi, 2006). Much later, *pesantren* was also recognised as a part of the national education system through the enactment of the 2003 National Education Law.

In addition to *pesantren* and *madrasah*, there is another type of Muslim school that is becoming more popular in Indonesia—namely, *sekolah Islam* (Islamic School). This is a day school that combines secular and religious education. The difference between *madrasah* and *sekolah Islam* is that the first is administered under the Ministry of Religious Affairs, while the second is overseen by the Ministry of Education. One notable *sekolah Islam* is the Al-Azhar school. It is noted that the number of Al-Azhar Islamic schools, a symbol of school for the Muslim middle class, grew significantly from 4 schools in 1975 to 8 schools in 1985 to 40 schools in 2000 all over Indonesia (Zuhdi, 2006, p. 147). Other similar schools are built in various cities in Indonesia following Al-Azhar's popularity, including *SMA Muthahhari* in Bandung, West Jawa (SMUTH) and *SMA Lazuardi* in Cinere, West Jawa (LAZ).

MI Theory and Education

Howard Gardner's MI theory is one of the most important findings influencing education in the 20th century. The theory explains that human intelligence is not singular but plural. It challenges the previous understanding of intelligence, whereby only human logical-mathematical, linguistic and spatial intelligences are measured through IQ tests (Davis et al., 2012). The theory explains that every human being has eight autonomous intelligences from which they develop ideas, perform activities and or solutions to problems in their lives (Gardner, 2000). The eight intelligences are linguistic, logical-mathematical, musical, visual-spatial, naturalist, bodily kinesthetic, interpersonal and intrapersonal (Gardner, 2011). There is an assumption of the existence of a ninth intelligence, known as existential intelligence (see, for instance, Husnaini et al., 2020), but Gardner confirms that the official MI theory remains consisting of eight intelligences. (Gardner, 2013). He did propose existential intelligence as the ninth in one of his works, but he is hesitant to include this as a full-fledged intelligence (Gardner, 2020).

As Gardner indicated, the MI theory conflicts with the existing IQ theory (Gardner, 2000) that undermines people who have less intelligence in math and language, which has many implications in education. Interestingly, Gardner argues that the IQ tests that focus on logical-mathematical, linguistic and spatial intelligences are relevant for the 20th century, while the MI theory is more likely to be relevant for 21st-century schools (Davis et al., 2012). Chatib draws an interesting example of how different intelligences can lead to different paths to success. He writes about an Indonesian lawyer who failed to influence his child to become a lawyer because the child loved music and chose to study music instead. The child became a productive songwriter and later became his father's client when he defended his son's musical work against plagiarism (Chatib, 2015, p. 77).

Munif Chatib is one of the proponents of the adaptation of MI theory in Indonesian schools. He argues that Gardner's theory is a breakthrough in education that redefines the meaning of intelligence. This has an important implication on a schooling ecosystem where people overvalue the IQ test and use it as a marker of success (Chatib, 2015). Thomas Armstrong has previously conducted some work on how schools can use MI theory in their classroom activities. Armstrong argues that the eight intelligences potentially exist in every individual, although some intelligences may work stronger than others. Interestingly, the different intelligences function together when a person does an activity or tries to solve a problem (Armstrong, 2017). Armstrong further asserts that children may begin to show a sort of orientation towards one or more intelligences at an early age. Therefore, understanding this theory will be beneficial for both teachers and students.

The key to the successful implementation of the theory into classroom practices relies very much on teachers' understanding of the theory and their capacity to translate the theory into teaching and learning activities. The explanation so far indicates the usefulness and importance of implementing the MI theory in the classroom. However, Hanafin emphasises that this is not an easy task. "Change takes place slowly and with difficulty" (Hanafin, 2014, p. 4). Campbell and Campbell illustrate that "[w]hen teachers adopt an MI approach to instruction, they confront unavoidable demands. Time is needed to develop multimodal lessons[,] to work as team members[, and] to incorporate the specialties of librarians" (Campbell and Campbell, 1999, p. 8).

Successful implementation of the theory needs teachers' commitment to change their teaching paradigm. Therefore, it is important to facilitate teachers in finding applicable teaching strategies, methods and approaches. It all should be able to make students feel appreciated (Hanafin, 2014). In other words, prior to the implementation of the theory, schools should ensure that teachers have sufficient knowledge of the theory, the school environment should support positive peer-group interactions and school administrations should provide spaces for teachers to explore various learning activities.

150 Muhammad Zuhdi and Erba Rozalina Yulianti

Classroom activities can take place anywhere. Teacher-student interactions can be more diverse and dialogical.

Report

MI Theory in Indonesia's Muslim School

SMA Muthahhari (SMUTH) is a private high school that provides education based on Islamic values. The school was built in 1991 as a *pesantren* but transformed into a high school a year later. While recognised as a general school within the Ministry of Education, the school proclaims itself as a 'plus' school, meaning that the school not only helps students to learn from the national curriculum but also provides them with local subjects concerning religion and Islam-based moral development (*akhlak*). The school identified itself as "a school of champions towards the 21st century." One of the characteristics of 21st-century learning is multiple ways of learning, which is very relevant to the MI theory.

Similar to SMUTH, *SMA Lazuardi* (LAZ) is a private high school that combines the national curriculum and religious education. Founded in 2003, the school promotes itself as a "global compassionate school." This means that the school has a global orientation and helps students to grow and optimise their unique potential.

Since their onset, the two schools have identified major problems in existing middle-class schools, including a heavily academically oriented curriculum. The MI theory significantly influenced the development of both schools. The principals of the two schools have clearly indicated that the schools recognise students' unique potential. Therefore, the schools have been eager to implement the MI theory in classroom activities.

The application of the theory of MI at SMUTH originated from the idea of its founder, Jalaluddin Rahmat, a notable Indonesian Muslim scholar (Yulianti et al., 2015). Rahmat has a philosophical view that every child is unique, and the purpose of education is to develop the unique, distinctive and extraordinary potentials that children have (Rakhmat, 2007). In short, every student is a champion, and the process of implementing the MI theory in learning is an effort to guide children to become champions in what they are good at. "The [school] of champions" became the motto of the school, designed to continuously motivate teachers and students to succeed.

The philosophical view mentioned previously became the basis for understanding students. The teachers believe that there are no stupid students in class, and they do not believe that some students are smart and some are not. They believe that every child is intelligent in different ways.

The influence of the founder's philosophical view towards this school's character is also found at the LAZ school. The founder, Haidar Bagir, a notable Islamic thinker in Indonesia, had a view that a school should become a place where children can learn happily. One of the sources of happiness is that children can learn whatever will help them further explore and develop their potential. A school should be able to meet the needs of every unique student. Therefore, the school regards itself as a "global compassionate school," meaning that the school, with a global perspective, aims to help students pursue their dreams. It is this basic view of schooling that makes the MI theory easily accepted in the LAZ school.

Teacher Training

Teachers are essential for the implementation of the MI theory. Without a proper understanding of the theory, teachers will not be able to proceed with teaching strategies and facilitate student learning. Although the MI theory has been around for more than two decades, teachers' understanding of the theory remains incomprehensive, especially in Indonesia. Faculties of education may have offered courses that introduce the theory, but having the theory implemented in the classroom is another story. The latter requires many other steps, including curriculum development, lesson plan creation, teaching strategies, classroom activities and student assessment. The substantial factor for successful implementation of the MI theory, according to Armstrong, is a fundamental change in school structure (Armstrong 2017, p. 122). All individuals involved in a school should be aware that they have to provide a learning environment, as well as learning experiences where students can activate and further develop their intelligences.

In SMUTH, the Muthahari Foundation (the umbrella institution for the school) had the teachers within the organisation learn about MI through internally conducted seminars and training. Sukardi, the vice principal for curriculum, explained during an interview that the training involved several experts on MI theory and practices. Teachers were exposed to the concept of MI in education and how their school can be transformed into an MI school. This is an important part and confirms Hanafin's explanation that says teachers' understanding of intelligence gives them more power to help students feel valued and get educated through the teaching and learning process (Hanafin, 2014)

Aya Sopia, a teacher of SMUTH, also explains that the most important part of implementing MI was their strategy in teaching and learning. Teachers' capacity to use various teaching strategies is developed through training and grows with experience. Further, the deepening of learning strategies will result in the teacher's ability to facilitate student interest and learning over a relatively fast period of time (Chatib, 2015). Importantly, teachers must be allowed to experiment and make new mistakes. As long as they know the principles and have clear objectives in their new approaches in teaching, teachers should not be blamed for making mistakes, as they will be able to learn from them, which will ultimately lead to better results (Hoerr, 2000).

At the LAZ school, new teachers have to learn about how MI works at school. Agung Purwanto, the principal of the LAZ school, explained in an interview that it is important for schools to ensure that teachers clearly understand the school culture and adapt to it, including the MI-based learning culture. From Agung Purwanto's explanation about how the school prepares the teachers to implement MI theory, it can be concluded that there are three important steps in personal development for teachers in applying the MI approach in teaching.

1. Reading. All teachers are required to read some references on MI, from basic theory to classroom practices and assessment.
2. Training and refreshing. New teachers should receive training about MI to be more familiar with how the theory works at school. Occasionally, schools should invite experts on MI to share their views, experiences or research results on the application of MI.
3. Support groups. Teachers can develop their knowledge and experience through daily interactions with other teachers.

Realising the importance of having teachers aware of the academic culture makes the LAZ school highly selective in finding new teachers. In fact, the school prefers to recruit fresh graduate students to become new teachers instead of accepting experienced teachers. Agus Purwanto argues that it is easier to train new graduates to adopt new behaviours at school and familiarise them with school culture than to hire experienced teachers who do not understand the MI concept.

Teaching Strategies and Classroom Activities

The MI theory changes not only the way people view student achievement but also the way teaching and learning are conducted. The theory has opened ample opportunities for teachers to execute and experiment with various teaching strategies. Some strategies, as Armstrong (2017) asserts, may have already existed and been popular among teachers, while others can be invented and used to nurture the different characteristics of students. The MI theory suggests that there is no single strategy that can be applied at all times and for all students. Therefore, teachers have to explore as many teaching strategies as possible to optimise their students' learning experiences.

In SMUTH, as Sukardi mentioned during the interview, teachers use multi-model teaching and learning. Teachers limit themselves in making presentations or lecturing and devote most of the allotted time to student activities. Aya similarly said in that interview that teachers only use at most 30% of the time to actively deliver material, while the remaining 70% is used for student activities. This means that students have more time to explore how they learn a certain lesson. In a more detailed manner, Agus Purwanto explains that, in LAZ, it all starts with a lesson plan that teachers create. The lesson plan should accommodate different ways of learning based on students' dominant intelligences. Hence, it is very likely that a lesson could involve different activities, as it is also possible that a teaching method is applicable in one class and not in others.

Fatma, a LAZ school teacher, affirms that that is exactly what makes the MI approach in teaching different from the conventional one. A teacher in a conventional class is normally using a certain method of teaching for everyone in the class, while an MI teacher will use various methods in a class to serve students with different intelligences.

The recent development of Indonesian education yields more opportunities for the application of MI approaches in classrooms. In 2014, the Indonesian government introduced the new curriculum, known as the 2013 curriculum. This is a mandated curriculum for all schools in Indonesia. One of the different features that the new curriculum offers is its 'scientific approach' to learning. The scientific approach to learning is an application constructivist theory of learning where students are encouraged to observe, question and make connections between what they are learning and construct their own understanding. This is very relevant to the MI approach to learning.

The variation of learning strategies that teachers apply in a classroom activity makes classrooms more flexible and adjustable. This exactly affirms Armstrong's assertion that, with the MI approach, schools need to restructure the conventional form of a classroom. Schools should provide a classroom environment that helps students with different intelligences (Armstrong, 2017). Classrooms need not be limited to a physical classroom, as teachers can take their students to the library, a garden or other places that can make students' learning experiences as close to reality as possible.

Sukardi, during the interview, shared his experience in teaching with the MI approach in SMUTH. He asserted that teachers should prepare various learning strategies that can help students of all different intelligences to learn effectively. At the same time, teachers can use the entire school ecosystem as a classroom. Classroom arrangements should be designed in some ways that can make students comfortable while learning, and hence teachers can have their classes in the laboratory, library, school playground or even outside of school. Certainly, there are limitations that teachers should be aware of, especially when taking students outside the physical classroom.

Student Assessment

In the era of accountability, student assessment plays an important part in any education process. Assessment is needed to ensure the effectiveness of the teaching-learning process. In general, good assessment results indicate the success of an education process and vice versa. The question is whether assessments reflect a student's general achievement compared to educational goals or whether they only reflect their comprehension at the time at which the test takes place. The MI theory problematises student assessments that have long been used. Various forms of student assessment cannot measure different intelligences. A single assessment procedure normally benefits a certain type of student and disadvantages others.

As there are a variety of teaching strategies that teachers can apply with the MI approach, there are also a number of ways teachers can assess student achievement. The main concern of MI-based assessment is its authenticity (Armstrong, 2017). This means that teachers are expected to witness student performance in a real setting and not in an artificial one. Therefore, authentic assessment becomes an important approach in pursuing MI theory in education. Armstrong further argues that the most important instrument of an authentic assessment is observation.

During the interview, Sukardi argues that children should not be judged solely on the results of their final tests. In SMUTH, teachers should pay attention to children's performances at school through observation of various activities. Similarly in LAZ, Fatima explains that she often uses group projects as a method of student assessment. She argues that, by having students working on a group project, students' strengths in both academic and non-academic aspects of learning can be seen. She further asserts that this model of assessment is more authentic than a test.

A variety of assessment methods are also applied in SMUT, as Aya Sofia explains during the interview. She said that teachers can employ a variety of assessments, such as wall galleries and exploration, where students expose their works and their explorations of various learning resources.

Implications for Teacher Professional Development

MI theory is a very important breakthrough in education that has a worldwide impact. Despite criticism that the theory receives, schools around the globe continue to apply the theory in their efforts to provide better education for their children. Likewise, educators and researchers continue to study the theory further to increase its positive impact on education.

Teachers are keys to any educational endeavour, and the application of MI theory is not an exception. Schools have to facilitate their teachers to understand the conceptual framework of the theory before asking them to apply the theory in their classes. This is a very crucial part of engaging teachers in changing the way they see students, the way they teach them and the way they assess their performances. Without a prior understanding of the theory, teachers will not be able to change their educational world view, and it will be impossible to apply the theory. Once the teachers understand the concept of the MI theory and renew their understanding of teaching and learning, teachers need to be guided to explore various teaching strategies, methods and approaches that are relevant to the theory through various workshops, internships or action research.

Following the workshops, the teachers will be ready to apply the theory in their respective classes. At this stage, it is very important for the schools to give support and more freedom to the teachers to explore and experiment with various strategies and methods. A peer support group is very helpful to build confidence among teachers. Likewise, giving certain freedom to the teachers is also very important to build self-confidence so that it can resonate the spirit of freedom in learning in students.

Conclusions and Recommendations

We have discussed how MI theory can be applied in Indonesian Muslim schools. While the theory has been employed in schools for more than two decades, its application in Indonesian Muslim schools is not so popular. The main challenge that most schools face in applying the theory to classroom practice is the preparation of teachers.

The two Muslim schools explored in the chapter show that Muslim schools are open to new ideas in education and that Islam-based schools can successfully implement the theory. The two schools, however, indicated that the decision of having the MI theory as a main reference for teaching and learning processes is derived from the schools' visionary leaders. The leaders helped the teachers to further understand the theory and facilitate them to further explore the application of the theory through trainings and workshops.

It is important to note that, in addition to the leaders' decisions to apply the MI theory in their schools, teachers' commitment plays a significant role. The application of the MI theory is largely dependent on teachers' readiness. They have to be ready to change the way they see their students, to redesign the way they teach and to renew the way they assess their students' performances.

Recommendations

1. The successful implementation of the MI theory in Indonesian Muslim schools indicates that the theory is applicable in the diverse Indonesian education system. Based on the benefits for both students and school governance, it is suggested that all schools should consider applying the theory in their classrooms.
2. Many questions have arisen from the implementation of the MI theory in Muslim schools. Schools must successfully educate their staffs and ensure a collective commitment to the theory.
3. Further research is necessary to further develop the MI theory and its implications.

References

Akpunar, B. and Dogan, Y. (2011). Deciphering the theory of multiple intelligences: An Islamic perspective. *International Journal of Business and Social Science*, 2(11), 224–231.

Armstrong, T. (2017). *Multiple intelligences in the classroom* (4th ed). Alexandria-Virginia: ASCD.

Campbell, L. and Campbell, B. (1999). *Multiple intelligences and student achievement: Success stories from six schools*. Virginia: ASCD.

Chatib, M. (2015). *Sekolahnya Manusia: Sekolah berbasis multiple intelligences di Indonesia (School for Human: Multiple Intelligences based school in Indonesia)* (republished edition). Bandung: Mizan.

156 *Muhammad Zuhdi and Erba Rozalina Yulianti*

Davis, K., et al. (2012). The theory of multiple intelligences. Retrieved from https://howardgardner01.files.wordpress.com/2012/06/443-davis-christodoulou-seider-mi-article.pdf

Gardner, H. (2020). A resurgence of interest in existential intelligence: Why now? *Howard Gardner (Blog)*, https://howardgardner.com/2020/07/08/a-resurgence-of-interest-in-existential-intelligence-why-now/ retrieved, February 20, 2021.

Gardner, H. (2013). Frequently asked questions—multiple intelligences and related educational topics, retrieved from https://howardgardner01.files.wordpress.com/2012/06/faq_march2013.pdf

Gardner, H. (2011). *Frames of mind: The theory of multiple intelligences* (3rd ed.). New York: Basicbooks.

Gardner, H. (2000). *The disciplined mind: Beyond facts and standardized tests, the K–12 education that every child deserves.* New York: Penguin Books.

Hamdan, A. and Jamian, J. (2015). *Integration of the multiple intelligence theory in Islamic education curriculum in matriculation programme ministry of education Malaysia. Proceedings of the 2nd International Conference on Education and Social Sciences (INTCESS15)*, 2–4 February 2015, Istanbul, Turkey.

Hanafin, J. (2014). Multiple intelligences theory, Action research, and teacher professional development: The Irish MI project. *Australian Journal of Teacher Education, 39* (4), 126–141.

Husnaini, M., Fuady, A.S., and Victorynie, I. (2020). Multiple intelligence in the perspective of the Qur'an. *IJIES*, 3 (2), 141–159.

Hoerr, T. (2000). *Becoming a multiple intelligences school.* Virginia, USA: ASCD.

Rakhmat, J. (2007). *SQ for kids: Mengembangkan Kecerdasan Spiritual Anak Sejak Dini (Development of kids spiritual intelligence).* Bandung: Mizan Pustaka.

Yulianti, E., Saepudin, D., and Ali, Y. (2015). Upaya Kepemimpinan Spiritual dalam Mengembangkan Budaya Mutu in SMA Plus Muthahhari Bandung (Spiritual leadership and quality culture in SMA muthahhari bandung). *Indo-Islamika*, 5 (2), 258–281.

Yunus, M. (1996). *Sejarah Pendidikan Islam di Indonesia.* Jakarta: Mutiara Sumber Widya.

Zuhdi, M. (2006). *Political and social influences on religious school: A historical perspective on Indonesian Islamic school curricula.* Canada: Published Heritage Branch.

13 Lifelong Learning among Islamic Studies Teachers

A Path for Professionalism

Merah Souad and Tahraoui Ramdane

Introduction

A generation ago, teachers could expect that what they taught would last their students a lifetime. "Today, because of rapid economic and social changes, schools have to prepare students for jobs that have not yet been created, technologies that have not yet been invented and problems that we don't yet know will arise" (Schleicher, 2013). In the last two decades, the challenges facing education have become various and complex. The intensity of the curriculum, fast technological development, multiple pedagogies, no 'empty vessels' students, well-informed parents, high level of competition in education due to globalisation and knowledge-based economies are some examples among many other challenges. Teachers find themselves on the front lines with the heavy task of finding a way to cope with new emerging situations and also to remain relevant to the educational exigencies of the time.

Teachers' readiness to face 21st-century educational complexities is a subject of debate among educationists and policymakers who think that it is a prerequisite tool that enables teachers to be more efficient in helping their students with equipping themselves with skills, techniques and strategies deemed fundamental to face the rapid changes societies are witnessing at all levels. It is proposed that lifelong learning is the best strategy to maintain continuous teacher development and ensure their readiness. Lifelong learning is usually defined as self-initiated education/training a person has to undergo for his/her personal development. It is generally used to indicate the learning that takes place outside formal learning institutions and is not limited to a certain period.

Lifelong learning is held by many as the "the new educational order" (Field, 2000). There has been a considerable debate over the past 20 years about lifelong learning to an extent in which continuing education should become mandatory for registration as a member of a professional occupation (Jarvis, 2004). Currently, lifelong learning has become human rights-based training (Elfert, 2019). This shows to what extent lifelong learning is needed

DOI: 10.4324/9781003193432-15

for all teachers regardless of their educational background and training and their field of specialisation. Therefore, how schools, educational directorates and other educational bodies facilitate teachers' professional development for lifelong learning and the main skills deemed essential to serve this purpose differ dramatically. For instance, for Islamic studies (IS)[1] teachers who are usually labelled as traditional in their teaching and also criticised for using outdated pedagogies and being generally untrained (Hashim, 2005; Adeyemi, 2016) due to the traditional training they have received, lifelong learning should be a mandatory activity for them to address the contemporary fundamental pedagogical skills in addition to many other crucial techniques, skills and information. This is to serve their professional development and also to improve their teaching skills and to keep them well informed and ready and help them with information management, especially with the evolution of the internet to be productive, relevant to the time's stipulations and, most importantly, effective in 21st-century classrooms.

The purpose of this chapter is to explain the concept of lifelong learning in IS and its importance in 21st-century educational attainment. It also explains lifelong learning's Islamic religious interpretation and how IS teachers should understand it. Besides, it highlights the importance of lifelong learning for the professional development of Muslim teachers, especially in what concerns teaching methods, mastery of teaching technologies and students' management besides the acquisition of different skills.

The Religious Foundation of Lifelong Learning in Islam

"In early centuries of Islam, the dissemination of knowledge was carried out voluntarily. It was a way to seek Allāh's pleasure. Muslims, in general, were motivated to pursue knowledge under the fundamental religious rule of *'fi sabil Allah'* (for the sake of God); financing education was provided under this rule as well. Spending on *'talabatul al 'ilm'* (students) was primarily from contributions given by princes, lords and rich merchants who were sensitive towards the needs of the poor and for socio-religious solidarity" (Merah & Tahraoui, 2017, p. 246). Drawing on this conceptual foundation, learning in Islam is not restricted to age, place, occupation or even to a social class. It is a flexible process that takes place wherever a learner is aspiring to learn and a teacher who is willing to embark on the journey of disseminating knowledge, skills and, most importantly, values—all should be done to seek the pleasure of God. From the first verse revealed to the Prophet of Islam to the prophetic tradition to the efforts and practices of Muslim *shuyukh* (teachers), seeking knowledge has become a faith-based activity. Therefore, many think that "knowledge is the twin half of the entire Islamic Message while the other twin half—which is based upon the former—is sanctifying and purity. It is not conceivable that purification and sanctification could be fruitful with ignorance" (Taher, 1997). While the Qur'anic verses and the prophetic sayings emphasise the importance of seeking knowledge (learning), it was never stated that this learning is confined to the early stages of

Lifelong Learning among Islamic Studies 159

humans' lives or that it should end at a certain age. Learning in Islam seems to be free from all restrictions; a person can always learn when he/she feels he/she should. This was always the case in the Islamic tradition of learning.

> Wherever a man who knew how to read met another who was not quite so fortunate, yet willing to learn, a school was organised. It may have been under a palm tree, in a tent or a private house; nevertheless, it was a school.
>
> (Totah, 1926, p. 12)

Thus, teaching, learning, spreading and sharing knowledge was a religious duty to prepare both young and adult Muslims for them to be capable of delivering the message of Islam to the world and also to implant into them faith in unity among mankind, not neglecting the fact that learning in Islam is also crucial to *tadabur* (contemplation/forethought) life affairs, as God will not change the condition of living of people unless they do it by themselves for themselves, as is clearly stated in the Qur'anic verse *"Allah does not change a people's lot unless they change what is in their hearts. But when (once) Allah willeth a people's punishment, there can be no turning it back, nor will they find, besides Him, any to protect"* (Ar Ra'd:11). Though Muslims have to practice *tawakul* (reliance) on God and seek His help through prayers and supplication, they remain the owners of their faith, and they are responsible for changing their lives and the conditions of their living. In the Islamic world view, the consciousness of the masses comes into existence not due to material economic conditions which then create their distinction from the rest who live in incompatible conditions with the masses (class struggle) as the Marxists claim, but the consciousness of people according to the Islamic perspectives comes into existence through education in general and the pursuit of knowledge (learning) in particular (Shariati, 1991). In this respect, knowledge would engender *istiqamah* (integrity) in his heart and mind. Integrity, that is, because of the rightness of conduct and behaviour. Thus, learning in Islam is free from any delimitations; it is open to all individuals, rich and poor, young and old and even Muslims and non-Muslims, at any time or place. It aims to keep Muslims enlightened about God, His creations, the secrets of life and, above all, to serve humans in their endeavour to become God's successful vicegerents, who can *imarah* (inhabit) Earth in the best ways. Therefore, "early Muslim education emphasised practical studies such as the application of technological expertise to the development of irrigation systems, architectural innovations, textiles, iron and steel products, earthenware and leather products; the manufacture of paper and gunpowder; the advancement of commerce; and the maintenance of a merchant marine" (Encyclopedia Britannica, 2021). In the Islamic tradition, teaching, spreading and sharing knowledge were regarded as a religious duty. "Some scholars used their influence to obtain funds, not for themselves but to distribute them among students ... pensions were offered by the sovereign to jurists, consults, learned men in general and to students" (Makdisi, 1981,

160 Merah Souad and Tahraoui Ramdane

pp. 162–163). Thus, learning was a tool to prepare the young Muslims so that they would be capable of delivering the message of Islam to the world and also to implant into them faith in unity among mankind (Merah & Tahraoui, 2017). From its inception, Islam considered/regarded lifelong education as the basis for education in the Islamic community. Islam thus preceded other civilisations in considering knowledge as a necessity of life which a person needs from the cradle to the grave, a meaning that has only recently been realised by human societies, and when a Muslim recites the verse "*and you are not given aught of knowledge but a little*" (Al-Israa: 85), he realises that Islam requires him to learn more throughout his life so that he acquires the largest possible amount of education that will benefit him in his life and enable him to achieve his mission on Earth as a successor to Allah. God also asked the Muslim to ask His Lord to increase him in knowledge: "*[A]nd say: O my Lord! increase me in knowledge*" (Taha: 114).

The Prophet urged to continue the pursuit of knowledge and made the scholars as heirs of the prophets, the noble Messenger: "*[K]nowledgeable people are the heirs of the prophets, and the prophets did not bequeath a dinar or a dirham, but rather they inherited knowledge, so whoever took it took ample luck*" (narrated by al-Tirmidhi). Islam has made beneficial knowledge among the things in which the reward of a person continues even after his death. Therefore, it is safe to conclude that learning in Islam is in fact lifelong learning.

The Necessity for Lifelong Learning among IS Teachers

> The only constant in the emerging world is change—and the accelerating rate of that change. Hierarchical corporate structures under the old economic order are being replaced by a spider web of activity whose strands reach all over the world. A technology-induced redefinition and reorganisation of work, coupled with the need to manage change will inevitably break up the present boxes of school, work and retirement. The coming interweaving of work, learning and life calls for new flexibility and a re-thinking of our industrial-aged institutions—political, economic and social.
>
> (Burton, 1992, p. xv)

Therefore, finding new mechanisms for adaptation in all fields, staying relevant and being able to develop are deemed crucial. For instance, in 21st-century education, the effectiveness of schools in general and teachers, in particular, is referred to—besides other criteria—by the exhibited level of flexibility and adaptation vis-à-vis the latest innovations and progress achieved at all societal levels. For the teaching profession, lifelong learning is more crucial than any other profession because "the nature of teaching demands that teachers engage in continuing career-long professional development but particular needs and how they may be met will vary according to circumstance, personal and professional histories and current dispositions"

(Day, 2002, p.1). Hence, all education-related bodies should plan, help and motivate teachers to become lifelong learners and also try to understand the obstacles which may prevent teachers from pursuing lifelong learning, especially what is related to the persona; differences, equal opportunity to learn, the availability of information; power and authority; and the nature of the self (Marshall, 1996, p. 268).

In many post-independent Muslim countries (though the comparison is relative), the educational sector in general and Islamic education, in particular, are facing many challenges, such as lack of funding and equipment, untrained teachers, unsuitable textbooks, poor management and, most importantly, the dilemma of dualism in education manifested in the 'religious versus secular.' Although education systems were 'nationalised' (Salleh, 2013, p. 2), in some Muslim countries, post-independent governments have reduced Islamic education (as an educational system) to an orphan subject in the school time table, which takes different labelling: IS, Islamic sciences, Islamic education and even Qur'anic sciences. This subject is mainly concerned with teaching Islamic rituals (*ibadat*) which are normally taught in a form of indoctrination (Tahraoui & Merah, 2019, p. 11) or what is coined the dissemination of "control beliefs that result in ideological totalism" (Tan, 2012) with the intention of making devoted worshippers. It is also observed that teachers usually receive traditional training besides being textbook-bounded and preachers for obedience and reverence (Sahin, 2018). This will have an impact on students' motivation to learn this subject on one side and how they perceive its importance on another side. On another note, there is an argument that the content and the methods used in teaching this subject are rigid and foster extremism by emphasising intolerance and animosity towards the 'Other' (Shea & Al Ahmed, 2006). Therefore, introducing some reforms in this subject is crucially needed and no doubt changing teachers' mindsets about learning and improving teaching quality is a top priority in this process. In this regard, lifelong learning seems to be the way for creating the needed paradigm shift, open teachers' minds to new perspectives and equip them with new skills and knowledge.

Although it is challenging to keep individuals' motivation to acquire knowledge and learn new things at an old age and to change the perception that learning is an activity that should be done at the first stage of an individual's life, lifelong learning is increasingly becoming a necessity at the present time. It is fundamental for IS teachers to learn to stay up-to-date, to be more productive in a very demanding and competitive work environment. Lifelong learning can also help IS teachers to improve their understanding of the world, living exigencies and also enable them to have better personal and professional opportunities by maintaining consistent development. Therefore, lifelong learning strongly stands as the only way to increase IS teachers' efficiency and keep them relevant to the time and social context of the educational activities, especially with the evolution of learning which becomes the constant striving for extra competencies and the efficient management of the acquired ones (Lambeir, 2005). It is a matter of survival in the workplace and staying relevant. Besides, lifelong learning will help IS teachers in having better interactions among environmental conditions, work on individual differences, cater to task demands, acquire educational technology and widen career opportunities across the lifespan.

In line with Delors' (1996) lifelong learning four main pillars, IS teaches will improve themselves on aspects that go beyond the main focus of the traditional schooling they have received throughout adult life or post-compulsory education. Besides sharpening their individual and professional skills by

> learning to know—mastering learning tools rather than the acquisition of structured knowledge. Learning to do also to be equipped with the types of work needed now and in the future including innovation and adaptation of learning to future work environments and above all learn to live together and with others peacefully resolving conflict, discovering other people and their cultures, fostering community capability, individual competence and capacity, economic resilience and social inclusion.
> (Delors, 1996, as cited in Duţă, & Rafailă. 2014, p. 802)

Therefore, the Islamic educational system urgently needs to be reformulated in accordance with the dynamics of times (Halik, 2016), and lifelong learning seems to be one of the ways to cope with all these transformations. This will require new forms of collaboration from business, labour, education and government stakeholders (World Economic Forum, 2019).

Lifelong Learning and IS Teachers' Professional Development

It is crucial, however, to mention that lifelong learning and professional development among teachers is strongly related to "the nature and operation of educational systems, policy environments and reforms, teacher working conditions as well as historic factors that determine what is accepted or not as suitable forms for professional development" (Avalos, 2011, p. 12), in addition to the support of their work culture, economic and social policies. Also, it is because of the nature of their jobs via which they are required to inspire and guide their students to become lifelong learners as well. IS teachers are not in any way an exception from this. It is on the contrary, as they are in a great need to keep on learning for self-development, progress and also to develop more skills to stay relevant to the time and to be more effective in their teaching.

> Private and government sector schools in most Muslim countries make Islamic Studies a compulsory subject for all Muslim students from elementary up to secondary school level. Usually, this subject is responsible for teaching students the Islamic faith (*aqidah*), law (*fiqh*) and the main traits of Islamic identity.
> (Tahraoui & Merah, 2019)

Lifelong Learning among Islamic Studies 163

It is also customary that Qur'an memorisation and *tafseer* (interpretation/exegesis) are parts of IS. Besides being considered a conventional-outdated educational subject, IS are usually critiqued for using teacher-centred textbooks, focussing on quantity and memorisation of facts, rather than the higher qualities of reflection, discussion, students' involvement, experiential discovery and lifelong skills (Mustafa & Salim, 2012). On *tête de liste* also comes the criticism of teachers' quality who are entrusted to teach this subject. Instead of being knowledge guides and co-learners who are fostering scientific scepticism, rationality and criticality, IS' teachers are revered as repositories of knowledge who disseminate via preaching and indoctrination, certainty, trust, purity and fidelity (Sahin, 2018). IS teachers are also known for working more within *taqlid* -unquestioning acceptance of the traditional corpus of authoritative knowledge. They are, in fact, working in the tradition of their teachers who in their turn have learnt from their teachers who have learnt from theirs, etc., in an unbreakable chain of traditions. Enshrined in the tradition of Qur'anic memorisation, it is believed that IS are also taught in the same fashion. In Mustaffa and Abd Rashid's (2019) study, it was found that IS teachers still use traditional methods in teaching which marginalise student's roles during the lesson. Hence, it was recommended that the teachers should encourage and promote the students to engage and participate in active learning or student-centred learning (p. 613). The exclusion of skills such as critical thinking, inquiry, creative thinking and problem-solving was also highlighted in other studies (Hashim, 2005; Sahin, 2018; Tahraoui & Merah 2019). In this case, opening the door for IS teachers to rejuvenate their teaching skills via lifelong learning will be of great help to them. Lifelong learning should comprise the following aspects.

Embracing Lifelong Learning as the Way for Self and Students' Development

To meet the requirements of 21st-century education, IS teachers should believe in lifelong learning as a way for their professional development and also the best way to guide their students to become lifelong learners; that is, "learners who have a wide repertoire of cognitive learning strategies, are metacognitive about learning and themselves as learners, are motivated to learn and can manage their feelings and available resources effectively" (De la Harpe & Radloff, 2000). A paradigm shift is needed on how IS teachers perceive learning and teaching and also the objectives of teaching IS. They have to understand that there is a need to form 'world citizens' as not a group of isolated believers who glorify and romanticise their Islamic heritage. "Dispositions and attitudes are often said to be more important than knowledge." Therefore, changing Islamic studies teachers' perception about the necessity of lifelong learning is crucial especially because lifelong learning relies on self-directed individual initiatives, whereby teachers should take by themselves a voluntary effort to develop and gain what is needed of knowledge and skills in their profession. Therefore, realising how important lifelong learning should be attained first. There is a need to create a "transformative educational culture" as expressed by Sahin (2018) among IS teachers. They should continue to learn, especially in learning how to learn, to transform their knowledge into a useful practice for their individual development and most importantly for the benefit of their students' growth (Avalos, 2011). IS teachers are in fact in great need of lifelong learning to master their subject, gain some soft skills (competencies) such as critical and creative thinking, problem-solving, managing one's learning, have a good command of research and investigation, communication and networking.

The Acquisition of Curriculum Knowledge and the 'How to Know'

In the case of IS teachers and as highlighted earlier, the trend is that these teachers are traditional in their teaching styles, they mainly depend on rote teaching, and they are ineffective in most cases (Tolchah & Mu'ammar, 2019; Ajmain et al., 2019; Sahin, 2018). Therefore, there is a great need to learn 'how to learn' and also how to make learners learn effectively. Drawing on the fact that the school curriculum is inherently a selection of knowledge, and also is a reflection of its social and historical contexts, this fact makes lifelong learning a mandatory activity that IS teachers should be involved with. Besides, IS's curriculum is usually criticised for being outdated (Sahin, 2018; Tahraoui & Merah 2019). An Islamic education teacher can display his interaction with lifelong education by continuing to train himself appropriately and equip his students with new skills and abilities. He needs to tirelessly search for strategies, approaches and methods appropriate for the era and environment in which he lives so that it does not become irrelevant or backward while the world around him is pulsing with progress and technical sophistication. IS teachers must be keen to develop their students' abilities to tackle new problems, move quickly and economise effort. Therefore, lifelong learning enables IS teachers to grasp all emerging pedagogical innovations consisting of new ways to be followed in the process of teaching and learning that promote effective, meaningful and up-to-date learning.

The Acquisition of Skills

Lifelong learning can help in developing many skills deemed crucial in 21st-century education and life in general. IS teachers are usually criticised for being heritage-bounded individuals (Sahin, 2018) who lack many skills that widen their scope, such as creativity, problem-solving and openness to the 'Other.' Hence, lifelong learning can help them acquire what was missed in their formal education and gives more opportunities to develop creativity, initiative and responsiveness in them and enable them to show adaptability in post-industrial society through enhancing skills to manage uncertainty, communicate across and within cultures, sub-cultures, families and communities and also negotiate conflicts. Also, there is the need to prepare them for using experiments, analogies, demonstrations, simulations, examples to provide experience for students to accelerate their understanding besides the usage of educational technology. No doubt that technology is shaping sociocultural practices and human behaviour at every level making it critical to understand its global influence on learning practices (Selwyn, 2017, as cited in Ferreira et al., 2017). The emergence of Information and Communication Technologies (ICT) and its expansion to the educational arena have led to the need to develop the digital competence of teachers in general and IS teachers in particular. Currently, it has become one of the educational challenges that teacher training has to tackle (Garzon Artacho et al., 2020). There is no doubt that in the teaching profession, using technology has become more crucial, and lifelong learning is regarded as the main way to master it. Therefore, it is recommended that technological literacy shall continue to be a key component in any IS teachers' continuous training and development, as it is indeed a fundamental pillar for promoting a new way of teaching and being the only way to develop a real teaching innovation panorama (Garzon Artacho et al., 2020) and to infuse technology in their teaching because teaching IS needs to adapt to the reality of today's globally networked knowledge society (Peters & Romero, 2019) and not to stay imprisoned in tradition. By learning how to learn and how to use ICT in their classrooms, IS teachers will be able to be creative in designing their lessons and all related activities such as being able to develop digital content, students' activities, assessment, better communication, searching and sharing knowledge using different platforms and pallets to conduct online learning when necessary.

Conclusion

Undoubtedly, lifelong learning provides an opportunity for IS teachers to work on their talents and develop themselves professionally. It enables them to create a learning environment in their classrooms that stimulates learners' interests and desires to create active, progressive and civic social actors. However, it will bear fruit only if they are provided with adequate opportunities for continuous training and they are fully engaged in designing lifelong learning agendas according to their needs. This chapter provides an argument about the importance of lifelong learning for IS teachers and some recommendations which could form the foundation for a workable strategy in maximising IS teachers' potential. Therefore, a key task for Muslim countries' leaders, educational institutions and society at large is to provide IS teachers with continuous educational opportunities that keep them updated about the challenges and choices in society beyond the school walls and enable them to navigate their professional life with confidence, open-mindedness and positive actions.

Note

1 Using the name, 'Islamic studies' in this context is in fact in reference to the school subject, regardless of the level in which it is taught that comprises knowledge and skills meant to enable Muslim students (or maybe others as well) to learn about the religion of Islam in terms of *aqidah* (Islamic faith), *fiqh* (Islamic jurisprudence), *adab* and *akhlaq* (Islamic morality), *sirah* (the prophetic life and tradition) and Qur'anic studies that includes *tahfeez* (memorization), *tafseer* (exegesis) and, in some cases, the Arabic language as the language of the holy text (refer to Adeyemi, 2016). In fact, there is a confusion or misuse of both Islamic education and Islamic studies. There is a "[l]ack of conceptual clarity in various current depictions of the field, including 'Muslim Education', 'Islamic Pedagogy', 'Islamic Nurture' and 'Islamic Religious Pedagogy', is outlined and the frequent confusion of Islamic Education with Islamic Studies is critiqued. The field of Islamic Education Studies has theological and educational foundations and integrates interdisciplinary methodological designs in Social Sciences and Humanities. The second part of the inquiry draws attention to the lack of new theoretical insights and critical perspectives in Islamic Education" (refer to Sahin, 2018).

References

Adeyemi, K. A. (2016). The trend of Arabic and Islamic education in Nigeria: Progress and prospects. *Open Journal of Modern Linguistics, 6*(3), 197–201.

Ajmain, M. T., Mahpuz, A. N. A., Rahman, S. N. H. A., & Mohamad, A. M. (2019). Industrial revolution 4.0: Innovation and challenges of Islamic education teachers in teaching. *BITARA International Journal of Civilizational Studies and Human Sciences (e-ISSN: 2600–9080), 2*(1), 38–47.

Avalos, B. (2011). Teacher professional development in teaching and teacher education over ten years. *Teaching and Teacher Education, 27*(1), 10–20.

Burton, L. E. (1992). *Developing resourceful humans. Adult education within the economic context.* Routledge.

Day, C. (2002). *Developing teachers: The challenges of lifelong learning.* Routledge.

De la Harpe, B. & Radloff, A. (2000). Informed teachers and learners: The importance of assessing the characteristics needed for lifelong learning. *Studies in Continuing Education, 22*(2), 169–182.

Duţă, N. & Rafailă, E. (2014). Importance of the lifelong learning for professional development of university teachers–needs and practical implications. *Procedia-Social and Behavioral Sciences, 127*, 801–806.

Elfert, M. (2019). Lifelong learning in sustainable development goal 4: What does it mean for UNESCO's rights-based approach to adult learning and education? *International Review of Education, 65*(4), 537–556.

Encyclopedia Britannica (2021). *Aims and purposes of Muslim education.* Retrieved from https://www.britannica.com/topic/education/Aims-and-purposes-of-Muslim-education.

Ferreira, G. D. S., Rosando, L., & Carvalho, J. (2017). Education and technology. Critical approaches. *Rio de Janeiro.*

Field, J. (2000). *Lifelong learning and the new educational order.* Trentham Books.

Garzon Artacho, E., Martínez, T. S., Ortega Martin, J. L., Marin, J. A., & Gomez Garcia, G. (2020). Teacher training in lifelong learning—the importance of digital competence in the encouragement of teaching innovation. *Sustainability, 12*(7), 2852.

Halik, A. (2016). Paradigm of Islamic education in the future: The integration of Islamic boarding school and favorite school. *Information Management and Business Review, 8*(4), 24–32.

Hashim, R. (2005). Rethinking Islamic education in facing the challenges of the twenty-first century. *American Journal of Islamic Social Sciences, 22*(4), 133.

Jarvis, P. (2004). *Adult education and lifelong learning: Theory and practice.* Routledge.

Lambeir, B. (2005). Education as liberation: The politics and techniques of lifelong learning. *Educational Philosophy and Theory, 37*(3), 349–355.

Makdisi. G. (1981). *The rise of colleges: Institutions of learning in Islam and in the West.* Edinburgh University Press.

Marshall, J. D. (1996). Education in the mode of information: Some philosophical considerations. *Philosophy of Education Archive,* 268–276.

Merah S. & Tahraoui R. (2017). Institutionalizing education and the culture of learning in medieval Islam: The Ayyūbids (569/966 AH) (1174/1263 AD) learning practices in Egypt as a case study. *Al-Shajarah, Special Issue: Education,* 249–280.

Mustafa, Z. & Salim, H. (2012). Factors affecting students' interest in learning Islamic education. *Journal of Education and practice, 3*(13), 81–86.

Mustaffa, A., & Abd Rashid, A. (2019). Teaching methodologies in Islamic education in 21st century; challenges and perspective. In *Proceedings of the 6th International Conference in Islamic Education: Rabbani Education 2018* (pp. 608–614).

Peters, M. & Romero, M. (2019). Lifelong learning ecologies in online higher education: Students' engagement in the continuum between formal and informal learning. *British Journal of Educational Technology, 50*(4), 1729–1743.

Sahin, A. (2018). Critical issues in Islamic education studies: Rethinking Islamic and Western liberal secular values of education. *Religions,* 9 (11).

Salleh, M. S. (2013). Strategizing Islamic education. *International Journal of Education and Research, 1*(6), 1–14.

Schleicher, A. (2013). The case for 21st century education. Organisation for Economic Co-operation and Development.

Shariati A. (1991). *On the sociology of Islam* (H. Algar, Trans.) Elhoda.

Shea, N. & Al-Ahmed, A. (2006). Saudi Arabia's curriculum of intolerance with excerpts from Saudi ministry of education textbooks for Islamic studies. *Center for Religious Freedom.*

Taher, M. (Ed.). (1997). *Encyclopaedic survey of Islamic culture.* Anmol Publications PVT. LTD.

Tahraoui R. & Merah S. (2019). Traditional morality and the depiction of non-Muslims in Islamic studies: An analytical account. *International Journal of Advanced Research in Islamic and Humanities, 1*(3), 9–19.

Tan, C. (2012). *Islamic education and indoctrination: The case in Indonesia* (Vol. 58). Routledge.

Tolchah, M., & Mu'ammar, M. A. (2019). Islamic education in the globalization era; challenges, opportunities, and contribution of Islamic education in Indonesia. *Humanities & Social Sciences Reviews, 7*(4), 1031–1037.

Totah, K. A. (1926). *The contribution of the Arabs to education.* Gorgias Press.

World Economic Forum. (2019). *A global standard for lifelong learning and worker engagement to support advanced manufacturing.* World Economic Forum, Geneva, Switzerland.

Part 3

Islamic Curriculum Reform, Assessment and Islamisation of Knowledge

14 Research-Based Reform of Madrasah Curriculum in Bosnia and Herzegovina and Its Implications for Fostering Teachers' Professional Development

Amina Isanović Hadžiomerović and Dina Sijamhodžić-Nadarević

Introduction

Change in education is inevitable, but it is seldom evident what drives the reform measures, how new values, models and practices are formulated to replace the previous ones. As it has been argued by Slavin (2019, p. 21), reforms in education are strongly influenced by "politics, financial considerations, or long-standing traditions," while the role of educational research remains marginal. Based on a thorough literature review, Hargreaves and Goodson (2006, p. 4) find that secondary schools "have proved especially impervious to change and to adapting to the changing learning needs" due to bureaucratic complexity, subject traditions and identifications and closeness to university selection. Furthermore, in the post-socialist societies such as the Bosnian, teachers have been characterised as having a "lack of preparedness for the liberal reforms" (Khavenson, 2018, p. 87), placing them in a position of low accountability and ownership over change processes. This is further shown in short-term professional development programmes that are primarily focussed on seminars and training in areas pre-defined by educational authorities rather than an investigation of actual learning needs. On the other hand, it is documented that teachers' participation in curriculum reforms is correlated with positive attitudes towards implementation of the measures (e.g., Fullan, 1993, 2006; Livingston, 2008; Turnbull, 2002) and that culture of participation and collaborative learning stimulates teachers' continuing professional development (Boeskens, Nusche, Yurita, 2020, p. 13–15).

This chapter describes the process of a recent research-based approach to the curriculum reform of madrasahs in Bosnia and Herzegovina (hereafter B&H), presenting the most critical implications of such an approach for fostering teachers' professional development. There is an accustomed, although artificial, divide between practice, theory and research in the educational

DOI: 10.4324/9781003193432-17

172   *Amina Isanović Hadžiomerović et al.*

domain. Practitioners are especially infrequently involved in theoretical reflections and research activities, leading to educational decisions' penurious groundedness and limited prospects for generating conceptualisations. However, professionalisation is based on a systematised and certain understanding of the nature of things, as well as the anticipating of repercussions. In light of this, the purpose of this chapter is to draw attention to the relevance of teacher engagement in research-based educational initiatives as a means of fostering their professional identity and accountability.

The chapter begins by situating madrasah reforms in the context of historic and contemporary needs in education and society. The succeeding section describes the process of developing a research-based approach to madrasah curriculum, which surfaced with the challenge of striking a balance between contemporary needs and the traditional educational matrix from which madrasah originated. The chapter closes with implications of such an approach to madrasah curriculum reform for fostering teachers' continued professional development for more effective implementation of innovative practices and change measures.

The General Framework for Positioning Madrasah Reforms between Traditional and Contemporaneous Demands

Given the unique characteristics of madrasahs in B&H compared to other regions of the world, this part provides a general framework for positioning madrasah between traditional Islamic knowledge and the social, political and methodological demands of delivering up-to-date knowledge in various disciplines.

Madrasahs in B&H are the longest-lasting educational institutions in this country, but whose curriculum, teaching practices, teachers, student body and status within the wider social and educational systems has witnessed changes over the course of the centuries. Madrasahs' 600-year history is a turbulent one marked by radical political and social changes and varying ideologies represented by different political forces that either ruled or waged war in the country. The different socio-political and cultural milieus that emerged have strongly impacted the madrasah, challenging its status, structure and curriculum and affecting reform (Sijamhodžić-Nadarević, 2018, p. 240–241).

Madrasahs in B&H as an educational model were created in the Islamic cultural and civilisational framework during the Ottoman rule (from 1463), with the educational process taking place in the traditional way, familiarising students with basic Islamic knowledge and sciences. The penetration of Western European civilisation into B&H through the rule of the Austro-Hungarian administration (1878), after four centuries of Ottoman rule, also brought a major challenge to madrasahs in this area. It was primarily reflected in the urge of preserving the elementary values of Islamic teaching and value systems and the need to adapt to the concepts of the pro-European school system. In this change of the cultural-civilisational basis of

Research-Based Reform of Madrasah Curriculum   173

life, madrasahs endured and fitted into the new, essentially the non-Islamic cultural-civilisational model without losing much of the basic matrix of their being and continued to carry out an important mission for Bosnian Muslims (Bosniaks; Karčić, 1999). On one hand, conservative ulama showed the resistance to reforms, but on the other hand, the resistance emerged also due to the broader political and cultural motives and attempts of the Austro-Hungarian government to control the madrasahs' activities through the inclusion of secular subjects in the curriculum apart from the traditional religious subjects.

With the change of governments and the enactment of new social and political institutions between the two world wars—the Kingdom of Serbs, Croats and Slovenes; the Kingdom of Yugoslavia; and the Independent State of Croatia—Bosnian Muslims entered a new state-legal and especially cultural-civilisational framework whose main determinant, in addition to the previous Western-Catholic, is the Christian-Orthodox ideological concept, with pronounced national-religious characteristics and exclusivity, so the system of Islamic education in general and madrasah education, in particular, suffered also as a result. The policies of the government of the Kingdom of Yugoslavia prevented madrasah graduates from continuing on to secular higher education in the country in the way that the curriculum excluded a number of secular subjects. Later, during the communist regime, with its state policies during the first decade of communist Yugoslavia, abolished numerous Islamic institutions and closed all madrasahs by force except the one in Sarajevo, which has been continuously operating since the Ottoman time (Bušatlić, 2002).

New legislation in the country that was passed during the war (1992–1995) and in the post-war period secured greater religious freedom and thus paved the way for a greater manifestation and practice of religion. This resulted, among other things, in the re-establishment of five traditional Islamic madrasas which were closed during the socialist regime. In addition to those six madrasahs, one more madrasah has been established in 2020.

Education in B&H has been an arena of various experimentations over the past decades, which were based on the attempts of policy borrowing from successful education systems throughout Europe. Conversely, educational changes were not based on actual needs analysis and evaluation of existing practices in the local context. Madrasahs, in particular, were in the position of experimenting with different models of integrating general and religious subjects into their curricula.

Over the past two decades, the madrasah curriculum has evolved substantially, transforming them from institutions that primarily produced *imam* and religious teachers into general high schools with religious components, whose graduates could pursue higher education in a variety of disciplines.

Madrasahs, nowadays, are the secondary Islamic educational institutions (International Standard Classification of Education level 3) organised around a group of Islamic disciplines in addition to courses in humanities, sciences, social studies and a multidisciplinary field of knowledge (information

174 *Amina Isanović Hadžiomerović et al.*

technology, physical and health education, democracy and human rights). The current curriculum of the madrasah is compatible with the gymnasium curriculum, encompassing mandatory and elective subjects.

Although the curriculum of madrasahs opens opportunities for their graduates to a variety of study fields, there are still certain challenges concerning the perception of the traditional matrix of madrasahs and its adjustment (in organisational structure, duration of study, subject offerings and time allocation to different fields of knowledge) with trends in society, science and technology. Hence, those perceptions and dilemmas have been reflected in the reform project initiated in 2017, following the *Strategic Plan for the Development of Madrasahs (2014–2024)*.

Research-Based Reform of Madrasah Curriculum

The initiative to change the madrasah curriculum was founded on a study of the educational process, which included identifying needs and devising actions. It also claimed the active role of teachers in educational needs diagnosis and formulating suggestions for curriculum change. As a result, such an approach was innovative in and of itself, given that the previous curriculum reform which took place in 2003 was detached from teachers' practical experiences, limiting their role to that of consumers rather than initiators of innovation processes.

In contrast to the earlier reforms, when study content was the central referential point, this one put teachers' and students' learning needs in the centre of further action. This is reflected in the two main aims of the reform actions (Sijamhodžić-Nadarević, Slatina, Isanović Hadžiomerović & Avdić, 2018, p. 27). The first aim was to ensure high-quality education to students, granting them the best possible preparation for continuing their education on the tertiary level in an array of disciplines, beyond solely theological faculties. It was first necessary to revisit teachers' competencies for new curriculum planning to create conditions for more future-relevant learning outcomes. The second aim was to ensure the ongoing implementation of quality standards by empowering madrasah principals and teachers for critical examination of their own practices and formulating the necessary innovations on the site. To this end, it was required to set up a framework that would enable practitioners' participation in tailoring the current reform actions by including their assessments and organising training in the areas of identified learning needs.

Although the expert team headed the project,[1] all other relevant stakeholders, including academics and representatives from all six madrasahs operating inside the Islamic Community of Bosnia and Herzegovina (ICBH), were included in various project stages. This was the first time in the ICBH that academics, practicians, students, parents and stakeholders from the community were included in the curriculum reform. In a sense, this approach promoted a different paradigm of curriculum change, given that prior studies at the global level show that "principals and teachers pay little attention to research and rarely consult it to improve their practices" (Slavin, 2019, p. 21). Contrary to this, the project was designed from the onset as research-based (cf. Greany & Maxwell, 2017), meaning that decisions regarding further curriculum planning were based on data obtained from research and discussed in groups with madrasah representatives.

Intending to make the curriculum change natural and sustained, principals' and teachers' participation in the current project was indispensable. Their practical knowledge, assessments and recommendations were encouraged and served for planning further steps. To address the two aims of curriculum reform, the four main segments of the project were defined. Results from each stage served as a basis for further actions (see Table 14.1).

Results obtained in the strengths, weaknesses, opportunities, threats (SWOT) analysis clearly indicated five developmental areas where change was needed (Sijamhodžić-Nadarević et al., 2018, pp. 34–36):

1. Identifying students' actual learning needs, offering guidance and a stimulating environment for students in order to address their needs and help them accomplish the desired developmental results
2. Improving the quality of the curriculum and teaching process by raising awareness of learning outcomes and training teachers for implementation of innovative practices
3. Adopting the strategy of continuing teachers' professional development
4. Investing in high-quality school infrastructure
5. Establishing stronger cooperation with students' parents by involving them more in school curricular and extra-curricular activities

Further action was targeted at identifying needs for improving the madrasah curriculum. In the large-scale research that included both quantitative and qualitative questionnaires and a total of 763 participants, a set of four curriculum elements were precisely extracted as domains of further needed improvement:

1. Teachers' teaching competencies
2. Modernisation of study content (the need for problem-based instead of subject-based teaching materials)
3. Modernisation of textbooks and better integration of religious and general knowledge subjects
4. Reorganisation of elective subjects in order to serve the self-actualisation of students

Varieties in participants' perceptions of the madrasah curriculum conceptual framework were identified, which was also reflected in the debates arising during the project. Some madrasahs did not advocate for significant change of the existing educational matrix for fear of violating the traditional concept of the madrasah and its centuries-old recognisability in B&H, which was also unique in the European educational space. One of the factors influencing

176 *Amina Isanović Hadžiomerović et al.*

Table 14.1 The structure of a research-based approach to madrasah curriculum reform

Activity	Participants	Resulting actions
SWOT analysis of priority areas of change	School principals Teachers Students Students' parents/ guardians	• Results indicate five priority areas of change • Dissemination of obtained results in discussion groups within the expert team, counselling and visits to madrasahs • Targeting a further action plan on curriculum improvement
Large-scale, mixed-methods research (evaluation of current madrasah curriculum and identifying needs for improvement)	School principals and representatives of school administration (N = 25) Teachers (N = 140) Students (N = 350) Parents (N = 120) Alumni (N = 98) Local community representatives (N = 30)	• Compilation of report • Discussion in the round table with representatives from the madrasahs in ICBH • Identified learning needs of madrasah principals and teachers • Organising trainings for madrasah staffs
In-house trainings for madrasah staffs in the implementation of curriculum change, new teaching approaches and strategies	School authorities and all teachers in every single madrasah Expert team	• Instructional material designed for trainings was co-created by the participants whose additions were included • Discussion among school practitioners was open about the change; they were free to discuss their concerns and ask for support • Local particularities of every single madrasah were traced • Teachers reported having identified further learning needs and being empowered for further professional development
Compiling the document *Guidelines for Designing and Evaluating the Madrasah Curriculum*[2]	Members of the expert team coming from the academic community	• Compilation of research results and best practices to serve in the process of madrasah curriculum reform • The document offers guidelines for systematic reform, starting from revisiting the madrasah vision and mission and continuing with key competencies, standards, learning outcomes, innovative teaching and assessment methods and closing with future challenges

Research-Based Reform of Madrasah Curriculum   177

such a commitment is the fact that today madrasahs operate in a highly decentralised education system in B&H, where ministries of education at the cantonal levels allocate certain finances to madrasahs and also prescribe curricula and textbooks for all areas of knowledge except Islamic. This limits the autonomy of madrasahs to some extent.

The project's subsequent step was to develop training for madrasah staff, which was carried out by a team of trainers who paid visits to madrasahs and conducted instruction on the spot. This provided a unique glimpse into the varieties of organisational cultures and climates existing in different madrasahs. Training also gave the possibility to test the prepared instructional material and open the space for madrasah teachers to contribute with their ideas and experiences. As the final step in the project, the report *Guidelines for Designing and Evaluating the Madrasah Curriculum* was formulated by the expert team. The document was an important innovation, for it did not contain pre-defined, ready-to-use prescriptions on what to change, but it was instead an instruction on how to administer the process of curriculum reform, what elements should be included and what role school authorities and teachers can play. The document was designed as a workbook with specific activities for teacher teams to work on to come to relevant conceptualisations and practical implementation of the new curriculum.

Debates drawn from the research results indicate that some madrasahs and religious authorities predominantly perceive the existing traditional educational matrix in the ICBH as a concept mainly compatible with trends in society, science and technology. However, those debates left some room for every single madrasah's autonomy in creating a curriculum (around 15%), unlike the current unified curriculum for all madrasahs operating under the ICBH. To a certain extent, this would emphasise specific profiles of individual madrasahs and urge for more commitment of school management and teachers in designing the individual and specific curriculum features in their respective madrasahs.

The project's implementation has revealed that there are differences amongst madrasahs in terms of willingness to change. While some madrasahs refused to make significant changes to their existing curriculum concept, others argued that the current unified curriculum should be changed so that the Islamic field of knowledge remains a core for all madrasahs and that specific fields of knowledge need to be strengthened in individual madrasahs. In practice, this means that some madrasahs specialise in, for example, the language field, others in natural sciences and mathematics, social sciences and Islamic sciences. This kind of specialisation in the madrasah curriculum is anticipated to better equip students to compete for enrolment in various study programmes both in the country and abroad. Students' and teachers' mobility across madrasahs was proposed as an additional innovation to foster the active exchange of experiences and successful practices. All of the proposed innovations would necessitate additional effort in terms of teachers' professional development, mobility between madrasahs, participation in joint programmes and international collaboration.

Implications for Fostering Teachers' Professional Development

The real effects of teachers' participation in the research-based madrasah curriculum reform are yet to be measured, and it should be conducted in two complementary ways. Short-term effects should be tracked by indicators of teachers' further effort in professional learning and development. Long-term effects would be identifiable in students' learning outcomes and adaptation to tertiary education. However, some indices of the benefits that this project has brought along have been already observable during the implementation process, and they are summarised in this section in the form of lessons learned.

During the round-table sessions, discussions and training, teachers were asked to reflect on their personal role and the meaning of the process to them. Based on the qualitative analysis of teachers' accounts, three central benefits of the project concerning teachers' professional role were identified:

- more informed participation in curriculum reform processes,
- acquiring up-to-date knowledge on the teaching process and
- facilitation from the expert teams and opportunities for peer-learning.

Teachers' participation in the project was seminal for its vitality and further implementation. However, at the same time, it acted as a motivator for professional learning in order to better respond to the demands of current and future processes in curriculum reform. During the process, both teachers and school authorities were in the position of re-examining existing practices and imagining what would be the desired outcomes for themselves and their students. Evidence-based educational reforms (Slavin, 2017, 2019) use specific data sets obtained from rigorous experimental designs as grounds for shaping the reform measures. In research-based reforms (Turnbull, 2002; Cordingley, 2008), on the other side, assessment, inquiry and evaluation processes serve as the basis for decision-making. Turning to the inquiry, teachers took critical stances and evaluated the ideas concerning the madrasah's mission and the developments in society and knowledge. One of the most important lessons learned is that teachers are willing to re-evaluate traditional and accepted educational models in the light of current demands. In doing so, they are safeguarding for what madrasah essentially represents but also looking at the current needs and developments. Experiences of this project showed that teachers should be more encouraged to speak openly about the teaching philosophies underlying their practices.

It has been already argued (Richardson, 2003, p. 401) that teachers' participation in research-based reforms, among other benefits, has the potential to encourage collegiality, to foster agreement among participants on goals and vision and to acknowledge their existing beliefs and practices. This rests on the "naturalistic sense of teacher change" (ibid., p. 403), for teachers are in the position of changing and adapting their practices all the time, and what they need is strategic leadership in outlining the change directions and professional development trajectories. As it can be discerned from Table 14.1, the present project was tailored to offer guidance, training and direct support, which are found to be seminal for the teachers' development (Orr, Rimini, & van Damme, 2015) but also left space for adaptability and creativity of an individual teacher and madrasah. Teachers recognise the lack of democratic culture in educational change processes and maintain that their participation should be guided and facilitated by relevant experts. This is also supported by the finding from the substantive review of relevant research conducted by Boeskens et al. (2020, p. 10), showing the benefits of external expertise in teachers' professional learning in introducing teachers to new perspectives and challenging established beliefs about teaching and students.

Addressing teachers' identified needs and adopting the attitudes about teachers as the main change agents puts them in the position of improving their own competencies and practices. This would require continuing professional learning in various formats besides the most common short-term training. This implies that the process which has been conceived as the research-based reform of madrasah curriculum needs to be transformed into the process of research-based teacher professional development. In order for currently observable positive implications for teachers' active engagement in professional learning and development to become a long-term process, additional initiatives are needed from the ICBH authorities. It should be a meticulously planned and supported process to continuously improve teachers' competencies for better student learning outcomes and fulfilment of the madrasah's purpose and mission.

Conclusions

In this chapter, we intended to describe how research, participation and teacher's professional development could be integrated to elicit more natural and sustained change processes in the institutions balancing between the inherited centuries-long tradition and emerging modern-time challenges. As Nasr (2016) argues, Islamic education should be designed in such a way that it encourages diversity and decentralisation of curriculum planning, teaching approaches, ideas and educational practices. The classical educational system offered vast possibilities to madrasah teachers (*mudarrisun*) to create and re-design curricula respecting specific features of culture and social conditions. Islamic schools throughout the world, by implementing a research-based approach to curriculum reform and teacher professionalisation, which makes teachers directly involved and puts them in the position to create key educational processes, are thus respecting the unifying Islamic classical heritage and the contemporary educational approaches.

Based on what has been said thus far about the process of madrasah curriculum change, it can be concluded that a research-based approach to curriculum planning showed the potential to produce scholarly relevant and, at the same time, practice- and needs-oriented insights. Such an approach is innovative since it challenges madrasahs to open up to recent trends, stepping out from the accustomed content-based thinking about the curriculum. Teachers were encouraged to critically examine their previous practices, to identify their needs for professional development and to question ways of framing their teaching approach in contemporary trends, such as outcomes-based curriculum planning; enhancement of the science, technology, engineering, arts and mathematics area; better integration of Islamic studies and general subjects (e.g., science, geography, arts); and better linking of madrasahs with the world of work and the wider society.

All those questions further yield re-conceptualisation of teachers' training and question their professional profiles, given the fact that madrasah teachers teaching subjects beyond Islamic disciplines are trained in purely secular contexts with no formal Islamic training. It is also seen how previous change initiatives in madrasahs have shaped the educational needs of madrasah teachers. Earlier madrasah curriculum reforms had resulted in more teachers pursuing postgraduate qualifications (master's and Ph.D.) in their respective content fields. It can also be expected that the new approach to madrasah curriculum change would prompt new waves of professional development, which should also be supported by the relevant expert guidance and strategic commitment of the ICBH authorities.

The post-pandemic educational landscape will be intensively searching for innovative practices and new teaching paradigms. The research-based curriculum reform presented in this chapter provided a snapshot view of how teachers can search for new practices when encouraged in critical questioning and researching their practice. Religious schools are oft-times sceptical to changes, especially those coming from secular circles. One way to overcome scepticism is by empowering teachers to initiate changes by questioning the existing practices and models.

Notes

1 Members of the expert team coordinating and directing the development of the new madrasah curriculum are Prof Dr Mujo Slatina, Prof Dr Dina Sijamhodžić-Nadarević and Dr Amina Isanović-Hadžiomerović.
2 The document was compiled by the expert team members and submitted to the Office for Science and Education of ICBH in December 2019.

References

Boeskens, L., Nusche, D., & Yurita, M. (2020). Policies to support teachers' continuing professional learning: A conceptual framework and mapping of OECD data, *OECD Education Working Papers*, No. 235, OECD Publishing, Paris, https://dx.doi.org/10.1787/247b7c4d-en [accessed November 20 2020].

Bušatlić, I. (2002). Programske i organizacijske reforme vjersko-obrazovnog sistema islamske zajednice u 20. Stoljeću. [Program and organisational reforms of the Islamic Community educational system in the 20th century]. *Novi Muallim* [*The New Teacher*], 3(8), 45–50.

Research-Based Reform of Madrasah Curriculum   181

Cordingley, P. (2008). Research and evidence-informed practice: Focusing on practice and practitioners. *Cambridge Journal of Education*, 38(1), 37–52.

Fullan, M. G. (1993). Why teachers must become change agents. *Educational Leadership*, 50(6), 12–17.

Fullan, M. (2006). Educational change over time? The sustainability and nonsustainability of three decades of secondary school change and continuity. *Educational Administration Quarterly*, 42(1), 3–41.

Hargreaves, A., & Goodson, I. (2006). Educational change over time? The sustainability and nonsustainability of three decades of secondary school change and continuity. *Educational Administration Quarterly*, 42(1), 3–41.

Greany, T., & Maxwell, B. (2017). Evidence-informed innovation in schools: Aligning collaborative research and development with high quality professional learning for teachers. *International Journal of Innovation in Education*, 4(2/3), 147–170.

Karčić, F. (1999). *The Bosniaks and the challenges of modernity: Late Ottoman and Habsburg Times*. Sarajevo, El-Kalem.

Khavenson, T. (2018). Postsocialist transformations, everyday school life, and country performance in PISA: Analysis of curriculum education reform in Latvia and Estonia. M. Chankseliani & I. Silova (eds.), *Comparing post-socialist transformations: Purposes, policies, and practices in education* (pp. 85–103). Oxford: Symposium Books.

Livingston, K. (2008). New directions in teacher education. T. Bryce & W. Humes (eds.), *Scottish education* (pp. 855–863). Edinburgh: Edinburgh University Press.

Nasr, S. H. (2016). Philosophical considerations of Islamic education – past and future: Interview with professor Hossein M. Zaman & N. A. Memon (eds.), *Philosophies of Islamic education: Historical perspectives and emerging discourses* (pp. 17–25). New York & London: Routledge, Taylor & Francis Group.

Orr, D., M. Rimini and D. van Damme (2015), *Open educational resources: A catalyst for innovation, educational research and innovation*. Paris, OECD Publishing https://dx.doi.org/10.1787/9789264247543-en [accessed November 21, 2020]

Richardson, V. (2003). The dilemmas of professional development. *Phi Delta Kappan*, 84(5), 401–406.

Sijamhodžić-Nadarević, D. (2018). Development of madrasah education in Bosnia and Herzegovina. Abu Bakar, M. (ed.), *Rethinking madrasah education in a globalised world* (pp. 228–243). London & New York: Routledge.

Sijamhodžić-Nadarević, D., Slatina, M., Isanović Hadžiomerović, A., & Avdić, E. (2018). SWOT analiza prioritetnih područja poboljšanja kvaliteta odgojno-obrazovnog rada u medresama [SWOT Analysis of Priority Fields for Improving the Quality of Educational Work in Madrasahs]. *Novi Muallim*, 19(73), 27–37.

Slavin, R. E. (2017). Evidence-based reform in education. *Journal of Education for Students Placed at Risk (JESPAR)*, 22(3), 178–184. doi:10.1080/10824669.2017.1334560

Slavin, R. E. (2019). How evidence-based reform will transform research and practice in education. *Educational Psychologist*, 21–31. doi:10.1080/00461520.2019.1611432

Turnbull, B. (2002). Teacher participation and buy-in: Implications for school reform initiatives. *Learning Environments Research* 5, 235–252.

15 Arabic Teaching at Australian Islamic Schools

Working with Student Diversity and Curriculum Challenges

Nadia Selim

Introduction

The nature of linguistic, cultural and social diversity in many societies has been transformed by the unparalleled levels of people's movement (Blommaert & Rampton, 2011, 2012). Some researchers use the term superdiversity to describe the great differences that can emerge in migrant communities in terms of nationality, ethnicity, language, religion and motives, as well as patterns and itineraries of migration (Blommaert & Rampton, 2011, p. 1). These diversities (and others) manifest in language classrooms and compel researchers and educators to ponder some established concepts, frameworks and pedagogical approaches (Conteh & Meier, 2014a; Scarino, 2012, 2017, 2019).

A serious issue that emerges in connection with diversity in language classrooms is the degree to which teachers are willing to and capable of responding to diversities (Conteh & Meier, 2014a; Galante, 2018; Little et al., 2014). For instance, it was stated that language teachers might be unprepared to deal with the linguistic diversities of learners even if they have received specialised training in language education or applied linguistics (Galante, 2018, p. 324). More research on Arabic learning is needed in Australia (Selim, 2019), but data imply that some Arabic teachers at Australian Islamic schools (AIS) might not be certified teachers or sufficiently trained to teach Arabic (Jones, 2013). For instance, Jones (2012) noted that "the main issue when it came to Arabic classes was the standard of teaching" because in "the early schools, virtually anyone who spoke Arabic was enlisted as a teacher, often when they were not trained as teachers in the first place" (p. 42). For example, Jones (2012) mentioned that imams often assumed the mantle of an Arabic teacher (p. 42).

Therefore, this chapter aspires to help AIS Arabic teachers in their educational efforts. The chapter's key objective is to inform the teachers' approach. It urges teachers to focus on learners and partner with them to generate more meaningful learning experiences that could inspire them to become lifelong learners of Arabic. To this end, the chapter introduces three principles: *at-taʿāruf* (knowing one another), *at-tšāwur* (consultation) and *taš-jeeʾ al-istiklāliy-ya* (encouraging autonomy). The chapter seeks to work

DOI: 10.4324/9781003193432-18

Arabic Teaching at Australian Islamic Schools 183

with some ideas from the literature on education and language education in a contextually sensitive way.

Background

In the early 1980s, some Australian Muslims established AIS as an alternative to secular public education (Clyne, 2001). These Muslims wanted their children to be educated in environments that permit them to learn about Islam and practise it freely (Ali, 2018). Abdullah (2018) noted that Muslims felt that "a quality Islamic religious, cultural and Arabic/ethnic language experience could be more readily realized by the establishment of full-time Islamic schools" (p. 196). AIS are non-governmental providers of primary and secondary education that exhibit an Islamic ethos but are like other Australian schools in terms of curriculum (Clyne, 2001; Saeed, 2004). That is, they teach the Qur'an, Islam and Arabic in addition to the Australian curriculum (Jones, 2012). AIS fees are kept low so "parents (who are often recent migrants or from working-class backgrounds) can afford to send their children to these schools" (Saeed, 2004, p. 56).

AIS school populations manifest the diverse nature of the Australian Muslim population. About 37% of Australian Muslims are born in Australia, and the remainder comes from 183 countries (Hassan & Lester, 2018). Muslims speak many languages, such as Arabic, Turkish, Farsi, Bosnian, Bahasa Indonesia, Bengali, Malay, Dari, Albanian, Hindi, Kurdish and Pashtu (Hassan & Lester, 2018, p. 8). The socio-economic profiles of Muslims vary. Some are highly accomplished, and some struggle with resettlement (Casimiro et al., 2007; Colic-Peisker, 2005). Many Muslims experience economic disadvantage and "earn significantly less, both at the household and individual levels" than other Australians (Hassan & Lester, 2018, p. 12). It was estimated that a "quarter of all Muslim children in Australia are living in poverty, compared with 13% of all Australian children" (Hassan & Lester, 2018, p. 12).

Therefore, a cohort of Muslim learners at any Australian Islamic school could have vastly different profiles that influence their learning abilities, needs, motives and preferences. The students' language profiles alone have many implications for Arabic language learning classrooms. Students bring a range of languages, proficiencies and language learning experiences into the classroom depending on their backgrounds, migration stories and individual situations. Arab students can bring different dialects (e.g., Lebanese, Egyptian, Iraqi), levels of exposure to Arabic (or other languages) and English proficiencies into the classroom. Non-Arab students can bring a range of languages, abilities in these languages, familiarity with Arabic and English proficiencies into the classroom. Additionally, some non-Arab learners' home languages have more in common with Arabic than others. As Scarino (2012) identified, this diverse nature of Australian language classrooms contrasts with standardisation trends in state and national frameworks of Australian K–12 language education.

184   *Nadia Selim*

The range of learners attending AIS is not well captured in the Arabic curriculum released by the Australian Curriculum, Assessment and Reporting Authority (ACARA). The context statement (CS) explains that the curriculum "is pitched to background language learners" because they are the dominant cohort of learners in Australia (ACARA, 2021a). It recognises that these learners are diverse but adds that they "have exposure to Arabic language and culture" and "may engage in active but predominantly receptive use of Arabic at home" (ACARA, 2021a). The CS further stipulates "the place" of Arabic in Australian education, noting that the "study of Arabic provides background students with the opportunity to connect with their family heritage and to communicate with speakers of Arabic in Australia and around the world" (ACARA, 2021a).

The conception of Arabic learners used in the curriculum is narrow (Selim, 2019) and has attracted some criticism. The outcomes of a consultation report published by ACARA (2016) show that the West Australian School Curriculum and Standards Authority made two critical statements. First, the curriculum "only addresses students with a background in the language and does not cater for the range of students currently learning the language" (ACARA, 2016, p. 58). Second, the "curriculum is pitched at too high a level and assumes students are first language learners" (ACARA, 2016, p. 58).

Additionally, faith-based motives and orientations can emerge in connection with Arabic learning at AIS because Arabic is the language of the primary Islamic religious texts. Research suggests that AIS can be religiously oriented in their introduction of Arabic programmes. For instance, Campbell et al. (1993) stated that the Al-Noori Islamic school launched their Arabic programme in 1983 and believed that "a sound understanding of Islam rests on the knowledge of Arabic" (p. 4). However, religious orientations to Arabic learning might not be easily reconcilable with the current Arabic curriculum, given its emphasis on connecting "Arab" background learners with their "family heritage" and other speakers of Arabic (ACARA, 2021a). The sequence of content and achievement documents posted by ACARA shows subject matter that reflects this emphasis (ACARA, 2021c). The CS states, "Classical Arabic and its successor, Modern Standard Arabic, have been and continue to be the language of religious texts as well as the basis for a rich heritage of classical poetry and literary prose" (ACARA, 2021a). This statement constitutes the extent of recognition given to the connection between Arabic and religion, which draws many Muslim learners to learning it.

Furthermore, ACARA foregrounds three types of diversities: learners with disabilities, gifted or talented learners and learners who are taught with English as an additional language or dialect (ACARA, 2021b; Scarino, 2019) and relegates the management of these diversities, and all others, to the teachers. ACARA states that teachers need to "take account of the range of their students' current levels of learning, strengths, goals and interests and make adjustments where necessary" (ACARA, 2021b). Relegating the responsibility for bridging the gaps between the curriculum and the needs of diverse Arabic learners means that the quality of Arabic learning experiences is highly contingent on the talents and training of the Arabic teachers. This underscores the importance of supporting AIS Arabic teachers in their efforts to meet this responsibility.

Making Arabic Learning Meaningful

The New London Group (1996, 2000) emphasised that if educators want to make learning relevant to learners, then learning processes should not attempt to ignore or erase the subjectivities, interests, purposes, commitments, aspirations and intentions learners bring to learning; rather, they need to harness them. If Arabic teachers acknowledge learners' diversity and collaborate with them, they are more likely to create opportunities for meaningful Arabic language learning. For instance, the teacher's focus on working with the curriculum should not lead them to disregard the abilities, needs and interests of non-Arab Muslim students. In other words, as Conteh and Meier (2014b) identified, although educational authorities often determine curricula, teachers and learners can "find and make spaces to interpret curricula in their own ways in the actions they take in their classrooms" (p. 7). This means that the learners' needs and interests can be incorporated into learning through classroom negotiations. These in-classroom actions are underpinned by a type of pedagogy that: (1) sees learning as a partnership between teachers and learners, (2) believes that peers can learn from each other (3) and accepts that learners bring valuable linguistic, cultural and other knowledge into the learning context (Conteh and Meier, 2014a, p. 293).

The following sections outline three principles to inform the Arabic teachers' approach and encourage their partnerships with learners.

at-taʿāruf (Knowing One Another)

Muslims are encouraged to engage with different groups of people respectfully to come to know them. From an Islamic educational perspective, concern for students' welfare, sensitivity to their needs, response to their experiences, recognition of differences and respectfulness and acceptance of learners are important aspects of pedagogy that draw on the practices of Prophet Muhammad (peace be upon him: *pbuh*; Abdullah, 2018; Abdullah et al., 2015). Furthermore, literature on Islamic education suggests cultivating and nurturing the child's character, self and identity is an important outcome of the educational process (Abdullah et al., 2015; Ahmed, 2021). Achieving such outcomes necessitates understanding the child or learner. This is no less important in Arabic teaching, especially when one views Arabic as fundamental to the Islamic identity AIS are trying to develop.

This invites the notion of *at-taʿāruf,* which means coming to know one another. Knowing who the learners are is fundamental to the success of educational efforts. This idea is established in the literature on education and language education. A good teacher knows their students and optimises instruction based on their knowledge (Zinn & Scheuer, 2006). Likewise, a good language teacher will develop a rich understanding of the learners' profiles and incorporate this understanding into the teaching process (Scarino & Liddicoat, 2009, p. 52). Scarino (2017) identified that learning begins with the nature of the learner and their lifeworlds, which necessitates a sound understanding of their linguistic and cultural profiles because these can be constitutive of learning (p. 168). Incorporating this understanding of learners into the curriculum is crucial because nothing is more demotivating to a learner than learning something that "they cannot see the point of because it has no seeming relevance whatsoever to their lives" (Dörnyei, 2001, p. 63).

A teacher needs to ask themselves four critical questions: (1) Who are these learners, and what meaning do they make of what we are doing? (2) How does this intended learning relate to who they are, and how does it connect with their previous experiences? (3) How will this intended learning contribute to the students' trajectory of learning? (4) How will this learning contribute to the development of the student's identity (Scarino & Liddicoat, 2009, p. 51)? In doing this, Arabic teachers recognise that learners are social beings who bring linguistic, cultural, ethnic, socio-economic diversities, personal histories and ways of knowing into the classroom (Scarino, 2019; Scarino & Liddicoat, 2009). Moreover, the teachers recognise that learners are not only Arabic learners; they are 'real' children or young people (Scarino & Liddicoat, 2009; Ushioda, 2009). This may seem 'self-evident,' but curriculum teaching, learning and assessment, which constantly foreground standards, skills, tasks and outcomes, have arguably become 'de-peopled' (Scarino & Liddicoat, 2009, p. 51).

Rather than rushing into teaching aspects of the curriculum or units from a textbook, Arabic teachers need to spend time getting to know their learners because each learner's biography will impact why they learn, what they learn and how they learn (Scarino & Liddicoat, 2009). In other words, the teacher should care about learners as real people first and foremost (Dörnyei, 2001). Knowing the learners will help the teacher in building positive relationships with them. This process takes time and will involve an ongoing engagement with the emerging profiles of the students. However, in the initial stages, Arabic teachers can design various activities to acquaint themselves with the individual learners and the overall cohort's diversities. Naturally, such activities will also be mindful of learners' ages and developmental levels. These activities can also be used as an impetus for building relationships with the learners and for encouraging them to build relationships with one another. The teacher should encourage learners to get to know one another and engage with each other's diversities (Scarino & Liddicoat, 2009, p. 52). If the teacher feels that there is a need to imbue activities with an Islamic perspective, they can use verses from the Qur'an or sayings of the Prophet Muhammad (*pbuh*) to inspire students (Tables 15.1 and 15.2).

Arabic Teaching at Australian Islamic Schools · 187

Table 15.1 Examples of activities to help teachers become acquainted with the learners

	Icebreakers	Initial Learner Profiles
Name	"My favourite things."	"All about ME" poster.
Tools	Spinner (manual or virtual) marked with categories, portable devices or laptops for students.	Poster paper, scissors, sticky notes, markers, stickers, portable devices or laptops for students.
Description	Teachers ask students to prepare a list of their favourite things across a set of categories— e.g., games, books, foods, places. They can use Google Translate to find the Arabic words they need. Next, students sit in a half-circle facing the board. The teacher prepares a spinner marked with categories of favourite things—e.g., games, books, foods, places. Each student spins the spinner and tells the group about their favourite item in the category on which the spinner lands. Students can tell each other the meaning of the Arabic words.	Students make a personal profile of themselves. They are given free rein with the design and structure but are asked to address three key points. The first is the important things in their life. The second is about the languages they know and how they use them. The third is their encounters with and interests in Arabic. After creating the poster, the students can use the Arabic dictionary or Google Translate to find the relevant Arabic words and add them to the poster. They can add these words to a list entitled "My Words."
Online resources	http://www.superteachertools.com/spinner/	https://edu.glogster.com/

at-tšāwur (Consultation)

Listening to students is a fundamental aspect of getting to know them and has implications for the success of Arabic educational efforts in contexts of high diversity. The notion of consultation expressed by the word *at-tšāwur* has strong foundations in the Noble Qur'an and the life and sayings of Prophet Muhammad (*pbuh*) (Al-Raysuni, 2011). Therefore, initiating Muslim children into this consultation practice is recommended, particularly if they are of a discerning age (Al-Raysuni, 2011, p. 5). Al-Raysuni (2011) explains that *šūrā* (*shūrā*) has various benefits, such as elevating a person to a new level when managing their affairs and developing their intellect and capacity to serve their needs and others' to an optimal level (p. 146). Therefore, training children to engage respectfully with others to negotiate better outcomes for their classroom community is important.

Like other Muslim groups, if students share a common problem, they are entitled to consult among themselves, and "they all have the right to be consulted concerning the best way or ways of dealing with the issues or

188 *Nadia Selim*

Table 15.2 Encouraging learners to know each other in a Qur'an-inspired activity

| Name | *Qur'an-Inspired Activities* | |
	"Recognise one another."	*"Meet my tribe."*
Qur'an verse	The Holy Qur'an [49:13]: "People, We created you all from a single man and a single woman, and made you into races and tribes so that you should recognize one another. In God's eyes, the most honoured of you are the ones most mindful of Him: God is all knowing, all aware." (Abdel Haleem, 2005)	
Tools	Interview cards and journals	Presentation software
Description	The teacher prepares interview cards with some guiding questions and space for students' questions. Next, students are asked to interview two of their peers and write what they have learnt in their journals. The teacher should follow this with classroom discussion, in which the students discuss what they have learnt. Finally, students reflect in their journals on interesting similarities and differences they encountered.	Students are asked to create three-minute-long presentations or audio-visual content about themselves and their 'tribes.' They decide the means of presentation, design and structure of the content they create. For example, they can create an avatar that speaks in their stead or create a video about themselves. First, however, they are asked to acquaint their classmates with the ethnolinguistic and cultural profiles of the tribe to which they belong.
Online resources		https://www.voki.com/ https://www.powtoon.com/

problems that concern them" (Al-Raysuni, 2011, p. 55). Moreover, classroom discussions can generate practical solutions for issues (Abdullah et al., 2015, p. 521). Therefore, in models of Prophetic pedagogy, students' constructive suggestions are encouraged and accepted (Abdullah et al., 2015, p. 522). However, for students to feel comfortable sharing their perspectives, teachers must create a safe environment for the learners in which they are not shamed or put down and so feel that their views are respected by the teacher and their peers alike (Abdullah, 2018; Abdullah et al., 2015). In other words, as Al-Raysuni (2011) explains, consultations ideally occur in an atmosphere of freedom, safety and confidence (p. 97).

This notion resonates with arguments that have been made in education literature for the importance of students' voices. The term "student voice" is used to describe various adult-student consultations and partnerships focussed on improving students' educational experiences in schools (Cook-Sather, 2006, 2018; Mitra & Gross, 2009; Pearce & Wood, 2019; Pekrul & Levin, 2007; Rudduck, 2007; Smyth, 2007). In this discussion, voice refers to communications of all students' purposes, intentions, perspectives and world views (Ranson, 2000, p. 265) concerning Arabic language learning within the classroom context. Listening to students helps teachers develop clearer understandings of students' learning needs and preferences (Joseph, 2006), which can inform teaching processes, differentiation and adaptations of curriculum content.

The literature suggests that making space for students' voices helps them discover and affirm their perspectives (Ranson, 2000) and develops their social skills (Joseph, 2006; Ranson, 2000). Moreover, such initiatives are likely to increase students' commitment to learning and doing well, albeit indirectly (Rudduck & McIntyre, 2007). Therefore, learners need to be actively involved in contributing to the nature of their Arabic learning experiences. That is, they need to be involved in the decision-making processes of the classroom (Brown, 2008). In connection with Arabic learning at AIS, consultations can reinterpret the curriculum because even if the curriculum is non-negotable, how curriculum goals are pursued and the teacher's interpretation of the curriculum are always open to negotiation (Little, 1991, 2007).

Undertaking student voice initiatives can be challenging. For instance, it can be difficult to include the voices of students who exclude themselves, manage the overrepresentation of more confident high-achieving students and engage the voices of younger primary students (Mayes et al., 2019). Therefore, this practice involves teachers' investing time and energy in creating activities that solicit students' perspectives and then translating their outcomes into action. Additionally, the teacher will need to work with their community of learners to arrive at a common voice or shared agreement "about the learning process, its purposes, beliefs and activities" (Ranson, 2000, p. 266). "This shared system of meaning will need to be negotiated to enable mutual appropriation of ideas" (Ranson, 2000, p. 266). However, the benefits of consulting students far outweigh the challenges (Tables 15.3 and 15.4).

taš-jee' al-istiklāliy-ya (Encouraging Autonomy)

Nurturing Muslim children's capacity for conscious thinking, rigorous examination of their intentions and sense of responsibility is an important outcome of Islamic education (Abdullah et al., 2015, p. 522). Ahmed's (2021) articulation of the "Shakhsiyah Islamiyah" is useful in explaining the importance of developing the child's personality, character, individuality and subjectivity Islamically (p. 10). According to Ahmed (2021), an individual who embodies Muslim selfhood submits to the will and law of Allah (*SWT*) but will also be a critical thinker, as well as reflexive, active and autonomous in their learning (Ahmed, 2021, p. 10). This individual will also seek knowledge and avenues for personal growth (Ahmed, 2021, p. 10). In this sense, it is important to encourage young Muslim learners to own their Arabic language learning journey and make it a lifelong one.

Learners of any age are capable of high levels of autonomous behaviour outside of the classroom (Little, 2011). The role of teachers is to harness learners' pre-existing capacity for autonomy and channel it into their

190   *Nadia Selim*

Table 15.3 Consultation activities for secondary students

Name	Planning Arabic Learning	Evaluating Arabic Learning
Description	Teachers invite students to contribute to the planning of their course. First, the teachers give students a list of topics/units they intend to cover from the curriculum. Second, they ask students to offer their perspectives on how the topics can be covered in ways that will engage them. Third, the teacher asks students to add one topic that they would like to cover. Finally, teachers work with students to plan strategies, activities, resources and material they want to incorporate into their learning experiences.	Outward manifestations of engagement and disengagement are observable. However, to better gauge these phenomena, teachers can invite students to rate their experiences and provide suggestions for improvement regularly. The teacher sets up an anonymous suggestion box and provides students with lesson evaluation cards. Students drop their ratings and suggestions for improvement into the box at the end of every lesson. The teacher then tallies ratings and discusses suggestions where necessary.

Table 15.4 Consultation activities for primary students

Name	Planning Arabic Learning	Evaluating Arabic Learning
Description	Teachers invite students to contribute to the planning of their course. First, the teachers create several learning stations (Schweitzer, 1995). "Learning stations are physical locations in the classroom where students are asked to solve a problem and answer some questions using the materials provided" (Schweitzer, 1995, p. 336). The stations will include learning games, activities and resources corresponding to the work units they intend to cover. Second, they give the students happy, neutral and sad emoji cards. Third, they ask the students to try the different stations and use their emoji cards to indicate their preferences.	For teachers to gain insights into students' feelings about their learning, the students can be given printed packs of emojis that represent degrees of satisfaction with lessons. Students can drop their selected emoji (and ideas) into an anonymous box at the end of every lesson. The teacher can tally the emojis and discuss ideas with the students where necessary.

language learning efforts (Little, 2011). Encouraging autonomous learning does not mean that the teacher needs to relinquish their initiative in the classroom (Little, 1991) but that they should encourage learners to do things for themselves (Little, 2007). The teacher needs to foster the learners' autonomy (Ismail & Yusof, 2012) by creating an autonomy-supportive learning context (Dincer et al., 2012). Fostering the learners' autonomy is important because some learners are unlikely to embrace autonomous learning without active encouragement (Little, 1991). However, the teacher needs to recognise that autonomy is not something that they can do to the learners; that is, they cannot programme autonomy development into a sequence of lesson plans (Little, 1991, p. 3).

Fostering learner autonomy requires allowing learners to exert some measure of conscious control over their learning process (Little, 1991, p. 52). If learners are accustomed to a passive learner role, they could be reluctant to take ownership of their learning and could even be wary of the responsibility of setting learning targets, selecting materials and activities (Little, 2007, p. 17). Therefore, to a great extent, the encouragement of autonomy depends on the initiatives the teacher takes (Little, 1991). Closely connected with the second principle of consultation, encouraging learners' autonomous learning can begin by involving them in a reinterpretation of the curriculum (Little, 1991, 2007). Learners can decide their learning objectives, define the content, select methods, techniques or strategies, monitor progress and evaluate what has been learnt (Little, 1991).

A classroom that promotes learner autonomy will "create the conditions in which learning proceeds by negotiation, interaction, and problem-solving, rather than by telling and showing" (Little, 1991, p. 48). The learning content in the classroom will be a combination of teacher-selected and learner-selected material (Little, 1991). Learners would also be encouraged to maintain a "journal in which they record what they have done, how well they think they have done it, and what they think they have learned" (Little, 1991, p. 52). The teacher will need to support the maintenance of the diary by scaffolding the learners' reflection as necessary (Little, 1991, p. 52). In such a classroom, learners will be given various opportunities to interact with Arabic in ways that suit them and their learning styles. These opportunities will be considerate of their language learning levels. Moreover, learners' profiles will be welcomed as part of learning and reflection. Scarino and Liddicoat (2009) explain that making learning meaningful extends to creating space "for learners to make their own connections with the topic and explore their own ideas, reactions and interests" (p. 85). In other words, the learning context creates space for students to develop a perspective on what they are learning rather than passively assimilate content (Scarino & Liddicoat, 2009, p. 85). Teachers need to resist the tendency to feel that a certain amount of ground needs to be covered (e.g., grammar, vocabulary) before encouraging learner autonomy (Little, 1991, p. 42). Furthermore, and despite the need for a strong focus on using Arabic in the classroom (Little, 2007), the 'multilingual turn' in language acquisition suggests the classroom does not have

192 *Nadia Selim*

to be a total immersion context but can involve activities in which learners use their diverse languages as needed (Kramsch, 2019).

Naturally, as Egel (2009) highlights, when the teacher encourages autonomous learning, "a phase of relative anarchy typified by uncertainty of purposes and responsibilities" arises (p. 2025). However, promoting learner autonomy has important benefits. First, there is a strong possibility of increased motivation in language learners who perceive themselves as autonomous (Dörnyei & Ushioda, 2011; Little, 2011; Noels, 2001; Noels et al., 2019; Noels et al., 2000). If learners feel that they have chosen to do an activity, they are more likely to become intrinsically motivated than if they feel that the activity is imposed (Deci & Ryan, 1985). Second, promoting autonomy can counter the imposition of the curriculum on learners without regard for their experiences, needs, interests or goals (Little, 1991, p. 7). An autonomous learner generates their learning purposes, decides on the content and ways of learning and determines the successfulness of learning (Little, 1991, p. 7). "In other words, the curriculum now comes from within the learner, as a product of his past experience and present and future needs," and learning is "deinstitutionalized" (Little, 1991, p. 7; Tables 15.5 and 15.6).

Table 15.5 Ways of encouraging autonomous learning in older learners

Name	Description
Al-'aqd (language learning contract)	Language contracts can be developed between the teacher and the individual student. In the contract, the student and their teacher can negotiate what the learner will learn, how they will do so and how the learning will be measured (Ismail & Yusof, 2012). The contract should also include the partnerships students think they will need to facilitate their learning (e.g., working with a friend on a project). The contracts can also include the elective topics that a student selected. This elective can be added to the student's outcomes as extra credit points.

Table 15.6 Ways of encouraging autonomous learning in younger learners

Name	Description
As-souq (market)	The teacher organises learning stations for the students. These are vetted during the consultation process. Each learning station is designed to be a *dukkan* (stall) at the *souq* (market). During the lesson, students can travel between the stalls and engage in the language learning activities, solve the problems or answer the questions that they choose (Schweitzer, 1995). The learners can also decide to engage in the activities individually, in pairs or in groups.

Conclusion

Unparalleled movement of people has heightened the levels and natures of diversities in many societies, including Australia. Diversity has altered the nature of Arabic language classrooms in AIS. Arabic teachers at AIS work with learners whose profiles can be vastly different. Moreover, they need to attempt to reconcile these learners' language levels, learning needs and interests with the national curriculum for Arabic. The responsibility relegated to AIS Arabic teachers is huge, especially when some teachers might not be adequately trained or certified. Therefore, there is a need to support teachers in their Arabic educational efforts.

Accordingly, this chapter encourages AIS Arabic teachers to focus on students and partner with them to create language learning experiences that are more meaningful. To this end, the chapter proposed a simple framework: *at-taʿāruf* (knowing one another), *at-tšāwur* (consultation) and *tašjeeʾ al-istiklāliy-ya* (encouraging autonomy) to inform the teachers' stance and approach. The framework synthesises work from the areas of education and language education while remaining sensitive to the AIS context of the application. The arguments made in the elaborations of the framework urge the teachers to focus on the learners throughout the learning process and partner with them to generate more meaningful learning experiences and perhaps inspire them to become lifelong learners of Arabic.

References

Abdel Haleem, M. (2005). *The Qur'an*. Oxford University Press.

Abdullah, M. (2018). A pedagogical framework for teacher discourse and practice in Islamic schools. In M. Abdalla, D. Chown, & M. Abdullah (Eds.), *Islamic schooling in the West: Pathways to renewal* (pp. 195–226). Palgrave Macmillan. doi:10.1007/978-3-319-73612-9

Abdullah, M., Abdalla, M., & Jorgensen, R. (2015). Towards the formulation of a pedagogical framework for Islamic schools in Australia. *Islam and Civilisational Renewal (ICR)*, 6(4), 509–532.

Ahmed, F. (2021). Authority, autonomy and selfhood in Islamic education—theorising Shakhsiyah Islamiyah as a dialogical Muslim-self. *Educational Philosophy and Theory*, 1–16. doi:10.1080/00131857.2020.1863212

Ali, J. A. (2018). Muslim schools in Australia: Development and transition. In M. Abdalla, D. Chown, & M. Abdullah (Eds.), *Islamic schooling in the West: Pathways to renewal* (pp. 35–62). Palgrave Macmillan. doi:10.1007/978-3-319-73612-9

Al-Raysuni, A. (2011). *Al-Shura: The Qur'anic principle of consultation, a tool for reconstruction and reform* (N. Roberts, Trans.). International Institute of Islamic Thought. doi:https://doi-org.access.library.unisa.edu.au/10.2307/j.ctvkc67gn

Australian Curriculum, Assessment and Reporting Authority/ACARA. (2016). *Australian curriculum: Languages consultation report version 2.0 (August 2016).* https://www.acara.edu.au/docs/default-source/default-document-library/20160916-australian-curriculum-languages---consultation-report---v2.pdf?sfvrsn=2

194 *Nadia Selim*

Australian Curriculum, Assessment and Reporting Authority/ACARA. (2021a). *Arabic: Context statement*. Retrieved from https://www.australiancurriculum. edu.au/f-10-curriculum/languages/arabic/context-statement/

Australian Curriculum, Assessment and Reporting Authority/ACARA. (2021b). *F-10 Curriculum languages: Student diversity*. https://www.australiancurriculum. edu.au/f-10-curriculum/languages/student-diversity/

Australian Curriculum, Assessment and Reporting Authority/ACARA. (2021c). *The sequence of content and achievement PDF documents*. https://australiancurriculum. edu.au/f-10-curriculum/languages/arabic/pdf-documents/

Blommaert, J., & Rampton, B. (2011). Language and superdiversity. *Diversities*, *13*(2), 1–21. www.unesco.org/shs/diversities/vol13/issue2/art1

Blommaert, J., & Rampton, B. (2012). *Language and superdiversity* (2192–2365). (MMG Working Papers WP 12-09, Issue. https://www.mmg.mpg.de/59855/wp-12-09

Brown, J. K. (2008). Student-centered instruction: Involving students in their own education. *Music Educators Journal*, *94*(5), 30–35.

Campbell, S., Dyson, B., Karim, S., & Rabie, B. (1993). *Unlocking Australia's language potential: Profiles of 9 key languages in Australia. Volume 1—Arabic*. National Languages and Literacy Institute of Australia Limited. https://eric.ed.gov/?id=ED365111

Casimiro, S., Hancock, P., & Northcote, J. (2007). Isolation and insecurity: Resettlement issues among Muslim refugee women in Perth, Western Australia. *Australian Journal of Social Issues*, *42*(1), http://dx.doi.org/10.1002/j.1839-4655.2007.tb00039.x

Clyne, I. D. (2001). Educating Muslim children in Australia. In A. Saeed & S. Akbarzadeh (Eds.), *Muslim communities in Australia* (pp. 116–137). University of New South Wales Press. https://search.ebscohost.com/login.aspx?direct= true&AuthType=cookie,ip,shib&db=nlebk&AN=75478&scope=site&au-thtype=ip,shib&custid=s3684833

Colic-Peisker, V. (2005). 'At least you're the right colour': Identity and social inclusion of Bosnian refugees in Australia. *Journal of Ethnic and Migration Studies*, *31*(4), 615–638. doi:10.1080/13691830500109720

Conteh, J., & Meier, G. (2014a). Conclusion: The multilingual turn in languages education. In J. Conteh & G. Meier (Eds.), *The multilingual turn in languages education: Opportunities and challenges*. Multilingual Matters. doi:10.21832/9781783092246

Conteh, J., & Meier, G. (2014b). Introduction. In J. Conteh & G. Meier (Eds.), *The multilingual turn in languages education: Opportunities and challenges*. Multilingual Matters. doi:10.21832/9781783092246

Cook-Sather, A. (2006). Sound, presence, and power: "Student voice" in educational research and reform. *Curriculum Inquiry*, *36*(4), 359–390. doi:10.1111/j.1467-873X.2006.00363.x

Cook-Sather, A. (2018). Tracing the evolution of student voice in educational research. In R. Bourke & J. Loveridge (Eds.), *Radical collegiality through student voice: Educational experience, policy and practice* (pp. 17–38). Springer. doi:10.1007/978-981-13-1858-0_2

Deci, E. L., & Ryan, R. M. (1985). *Intrinsic motivation and self-determination in human behavior* (1st ed. 1985. ed.). Springer Science+Business Media. doi:10.1007/978-1-4899-2271-7

Dincer, A., Yesilyurt, S., & Takkac, M. (2012). The effects of autonomy-supportive climates on EFL learner's engagement, achievement and competence in English speaking classrooms. *Procedia - Social and Behavioral Sciences, 46*, 3890–3894. doi:10.1016/j.sbspro.2012.06.167

Dörnyei, Z. (2001). *Motivational strategies in the language classroom.* Cambridge University Press. doi:10.1017/CBO9780511667343

Dörnyei, Z., & Ushioda, E. (2011). *Teaching and researching motivation* (2nd ed.). Pearson Education Limited. doi:10.4324/9781315833750

Egel, I. P. (2009). Learner autonomy in the language classroom: From teacher dependency to learner independency. *Procedia—Social and Behavioral Sciences, 1*(1), 2023–2026. doi:10.1016/j.sbspro.2009.01.355

Galante, A. (2018). Linguistic and cultural diversity in language education through plurilingualism: Linking the theory into practice. In P. P. Trifonas & T. Aravossitas (Eds.), *Handbook of research and practice in heritage language education* (pp. 313–329). Springer. doi:10.1007/978-3-319-44694-3_13

Hassan, R., & Lester, L. (2018). *Australian Muslims: The challenge of Islamophobia and social distance.* https://www.unisa.edu.au/contentassets/4f85e84d-01014997a99bb4f89ba32488/australian-muslims-final-report-web-nov-26.pdf

Ismail, N., & Yusof, M. A. M. (2012). Using language learning contracts as a strategy to promote learner autonomy among ESL learners. *Procedia—Social and Behavioral Sciences, 66*, 472 – 480. doi:10.1016/j.sbspro.2012.11.291

Jones, P. (2012). Islamic schools in Australia. *The La Trobe Journal, 89*, 36–47. https://www.slv.vic.gov.au/sites/default/files/La-Trobe-Journal-89-Peter-D-Jones.pdf

Jones, P. D. P. (2013). *Islamic schools in Australia: Muslims in Australia or Australian Muslims?* [University of New England]. Armidale, Australia. https://hdl.handle.net/1959.11/13607

Joseph, R. (2006). The excluded stakeholder: In search of student voice in the systemic change process. *Educational Technology, 46*(2), 34–38.

Kramsch, C. (2019). Between globalization and decolonization: Foreign languages in the cross-fire. In D. Macedo (Ed.), *Decolonizing foreign language education: The misteaching of English and other colonial languages* (pp. 50–72). Routledge.

Little, D. (1991). *Learner Autonomy 1: Definitions, issues and problems.* Authentik.

Little, D. (2007). Language learner autonomy: Some fundamental considerations revisited. *International Journal of Innovation in Language Learning and Teaching, 1*(1), 14–29. doi:10.2167/illt040.0

Little, D. (2011). *Language learner autonomy: What, why and how?* Empowering Teachers and Learners, *Proceedings of the Oman International ELT Conference,* 20–21 April 2011, ed. N. McBeath, Muscat, Oman: Sultan Qaboos University, The Language Centre.

Little, D., Leung, C., & Van Avermaet, P. (2014). Introduction. In D. Little, C. Leung, & P. Van Avermaet (Eds.), *Managing diversity in education: Languages, policies, pedagogies* (pp. xvii–xxv). Multilingual Matters.

Mayes, E., Finneran, R., & Black, R. (2019). The challenges of student voice in primary schools: Students 'having a voice' and 'speaking for' others. *Australian Journal of Education, 63*(2), 157–172.

Mitra, D. L., & Gross, S. J. (2009). Increasing student voice in high school reform: Building partnerships, improving outcomes. *Educational Management Administration & Leadership, 37*(4), 522–543. doi:10.1177/1741143209334577

196 *Nadia Selim*

Noels, K. A. (2001). Learning Spanish as a second language: Learners' orientations and perceptions of their teachers' communication style. *Language Learning*, *51*(1), 107–144. doi:10.1111/0023-8333.00149

Noels, K. A., Lou, N. M., Lascano, D. I. V., Chaffee, K. E., Dincer, A., Zhang, Y. S. D., & Zhang, X. (2019). Self-determination and motivated engagement in language learning. In M. Lamb, K. Csizér, A. Henry, & S. Ryan (Eds.), *The Palgrave handbook of motivation for language learning* (pp. 95–115). Palgrave Macmillan. doi:10.1007/978-3-030-28380-3_5

Noels, K. A., Pelletier, L. G., Clément, R., & Vallerand, R. J. (2000). Why are you learning a second language? Motivational orientations and self-determination theory. *Language Learning*, *50*(1), 57–85.

Pearce, T. C., & Wood, B. E. (2019). Education for transformation: An evaluative framework to guide student voice work in schools. *Critical Studies in Education*, *60*(1), 113–130. doi:10.1080/17508487.2016.1219959

Pekrul, S., & Levin, B. (2007). Building student voice for school improvement. In D. Thiessen & A. Cook-Sather (Eds.), *International handbook of student experience in elementary and secondary school* (pp. 711–726). Springer Netherlands. doi:10.1007/1-4020-3367-2_28

Ranson, S. (2000). Recognising the pedagogy of voice in a learning community. *Educational Management and Administration*, *28*(3), 263–279. doi:10.1177/0 263211X000283003

Rudduck, J. (2007). Student voice, student engagement, and school reform. In D. Thiessen & A. Cook-Sather (Eds.), *International handbook of student experience in elementary and secondary school* (pp. 587–610). Springer. doi:10.1007/1-4020-3367-2_23

Rudduck, J., & McIntyre, D. (2007). *Improving learning through consulting pupils* (Taylor & Francis e-Library ed.). Routledge. doi:10.4324/9780203935323

Saeed, A. (2004). *Muslim Australians: Their beliefs, practices and institutions*. Canberra, Australia: Department of Immigration and Multicultural and Indigenous Affairs, and the Australian Multicultural Foundation, in association with the University of Melbourne. Retrieved from https://minerva-access.unimelb.edu. au/handle/11343/34592

Scarino, A. (2012). A rationale for acknowledging the diversity of learner achievements in learning particular languages in school education in Australia. *Australian Review of Applied Linguistics*, *35*(3), 231–250. doi:10.1075/aral.35.3.01sca

Scarino, A. (2017). Assessing the diverse linguistic and cultural repertoires of students of diverse languages. In S. Coffey & U. Wingate (Eds.), *New directions for research in foreign language education* (1 ed., pp. 167–182). Routledge.

Scarino, A. (2019). The Australian curriculum and its conceptual bases: A critical analysis. *Curriculum Perspectives*, *39*(1), 59–65. doi:10.1007/s41297-019-00066-4

Scarino, A., & Liddicoat, A. (2009). *Teaching and learning languages: A guide*. Melbourne Curriculum Corporation. https://tllg.unisa.edu.au/uploads/ 1/2/7/6/127656642/gllt__1_.pdf

Schweitzer, J. (1995). The use of learning stations as a strategy for teaching concepts by active-learning methods. *Journal of Geological Education*, *43*(4), 366–370. doi:10.5408/0022-1368-43.4.366

Selim, N. (2019). Will Arabic survive in Australia? Participation and challenges. *Islam and Civilisational Renewal (ICR)*, *10*(1), 85–105. https://icrjournal.org/index. php/icr/article/view/73

Smyth, J. (2007). Toward the pedagogically engaged school: Listening to student voice as a positive response to disengagement and 'dropping out'? In D. Thiessen & A. Cook-Sather (Eds.), *International handbook of student experience in elementary and secondary school* (pp. 635–658). Springer Netherlands. doi:10.1007/1-4020-3367-2_25

The New London Group (1996). A pedagogy of multiliteracies: Designing social futures. *Harvard Educational Review, 66*(1), 60–92.

The New London Group (2000). A pedagogy of multiliteracies: Designing social futures. In B. Cope & M. Kalantzis (Eds.), *Multiliteracies: Literacy learning and the design of social futures* (pp. 9–36). Routledge.

Ushioda, E. (2009). A person-in-context relational view of emergent motivation, self and identity. In Z. Dörnyei & E. Ushioda (Eds.), *Motivation, language identity and the L2 self* (pp. 215–228). Multilingual Matters.

Zinn, C., & Scheuer, O. (2006). Getting to know your student in distance learning contexts. In W. Nejdl & K. Tochtermann (Eds.), *Innovative approaches for learning and knowledge sharing: First European conference on technology enhanced learning, EC-TEL 2006 Crete, Greece, October 1–4, 2006 proceedings* (pp. 437–451). Springer-Verlag Berlin Heidelberg. doi:10.1007/11876663_34

16 Islamisation of Knowledge
A Critical Integrated Approach

Alhagi Manta Drammeh

Introduction

The chapter aims at examining the concept of Islamisation of knowledge with references to its main proponents and their different approaches and theoretical frameworks. It also examines the importance of appreciating the synergies between reason and revelation in Islamic education that should motivate students to develop critical thinking. "Then they found one of Our servants upon whom We had bestowed Our mercy, and whom We had taught knowledge from Us" (18:66 and 35:28 and 29). The significance of the research lies in highlighting the importance of examining both the traditional and modernist approaches to the study of Islam to be able to respond to new challenges. I will also highlight the institutional frame of Islamisation as the International Institute of Islamic Thought (IIIT) and the International Islamic University in Malaysia. Finally, I will assess the contemporary context of Islamisation. The methodology of the research is focussed on critical textual analysis of the works on Islamisation of knowledge with regards to reflective learning and teaching in light of teachers' professionalisation. This allows me to compare the approaches developed by proponents in light of educational contemporary challenges.

Historical Development of Islamisation of Knowledge

Early writers on Islamisation of knowledge had the perception that regardless of multiculturalism, cultural peculiarities cannot be ignored (Abd al-Ghani, 1989). Reading books on Islamisation of knowledge, one can sense the frustration of some of the proponents with the way in which aspects of human and social sciences have been presented.[1] The proponents have been critical of both the traditional Muslim methods of scholarship and the secular articulation of ideas in relation to social and human sciences. The traditionalist approach was mainly literalist without considering societal dynamics. On the other hand, the secularist approach was bent on the denial of revelation because of the historical experiences and contradictions in modernism during the medieval period. Thus, the development of the critique of conventional theories within subject areas such as political sciences psychology, sociology and anthropology.

DOI: 10.4324/9781003193432-19

Islamisation goes as far back as the 1960s when Mawdudi (1903–1979) laid the foundations of the Islamic Research Academy in Pakistan to examine the relationships between secular and religious knowledge (Yusuf, 2012). Later, Al-Faruqi (1921–1986) buttressed the thought in his paper "Islamization of Knowledge: A Work Plan" at a conference at the International Islamic University in Islamabad in January 1983. The paper outlined the vision and philosophy of Islamic education with emphasis on its ethical and universal values.

In *Social and Natural Sciences: The Islamic Perspective*, Al-Faruqi, emphasises that knowledge must be structured under the Islamic concept of *tawhid* (Al-Faruqi & Naseef, 1981; Al-Faruqi, 1982, 1992, 1995). The idea of tawhid has been amplified in Al-Faruqi's, *Al-Tawhid: Its Implications for Thought and Life* arguing that tawhid is the essence of Islamic civilisation and gives Islam its identity binding the different constituents (Al-Faruqi & Naseef, 1981).

Proponents

Ismail al-Faruqi was born in 1921 and died in 1986. He was recognised as an authority on Islam and comparative religion. He promoted intellectual, cultural and religious engagement between the Western world and the Muslim world. At the Faculty of Divinity, McGill University, he was offered a fellowship between the years 1958 and 1959. In 1964, at Syracuse University's department, he taught Islamic studies and the history of religion. He was professor of religion at Temple University, where he chaired the Islamic studies programme. Among his works are *Christian Ethics: A Historical and Systematic Analysis of Its Dominant Ideas*. Despite all this academic activity, he managed to establish the Islamic Studies Group of the American Academy of Religion and chaired it for ten years. He also served as the vice-president of the Inter-Religious Peace Colloquium, the Muslim-Jewish-Christian Conference and as the president of American Islamic College in Chicago. His early emphasis was on Arabism as the vehicle of Islam and Muslim identity. He was also one of those who proposed the idea of Islamization of knowledge and founded IIIT together with Taha Jabir Al-Alwani and Abdul Hamid AbuSulayman, former Rector of the International Islamic University, Malaysia. Al-Faruqi also employed methods of comparative religious studies in Islam and other religions, particularly the Abrahamic faiths. He was instrumental in creating momentum for a new awareness about Islam in both North America and Europe in the 1970s (Al-Faruqi, 1991).

Al-Faruqi's methodology was influenced by events and experiences in his life journey. He began his works on the history of religion exploring ecumenical issues in dialogue as reflected in his book *Christian Ethics*. He later explored the area within the philosophical foundations of religion, examining methodologies of engagement with others. Finally, he investigated how to implement those ideas into a model as reflected in the institutional framework of Islamisation of knowledge (Al-Faruqi, 1991). His

200 *Alhagi Manta Drammeh*

grounding in critical philosophy enabled him to contribute greatly to education (Imtiaz, 2012).

Naquib Al-Attas (b. 1931) is a prominent Muslim thinker. Al-Attas' philosophy and methodology of education have one goal: Islamisation of the mind, body and soul and its effects on the personal and collective life of Muslims as well as others, including the spiritual and physical non-human environment. He is the author of works on various aspects of Islamic thought and civilisation, particularly on Sufism, metaphysics, philosophy and Malay literature. He was exposed to Malay literature, history, religion and Western classics in English. This nurtured in Al-Attas the style that was unique to his Malay writings and language. In 1987, Al-Attas founded the IIIT and Civilization (ISTAC) in Kuala-Lumpur. This institution strives to bring an integrated approach to knowledge. He argues that Islamic metaphysics reflects that reality is composed of both permanence and change; the underlying permanent aspects of the external world are perpetually undergoing change (Al-Attas, 1993). For al-Attas, Islamic metaphysics is a unified system that discloses the ultimate nature of reality in positive terms, integrating reason and experience with other higher orders in the supranational and trans-empirical levels of human consciousness.

AbdulHamid AbuSulyman,[2] renowned scholar and chairman of IIIT, took the responsibility of the International Islamic University, Malaysia in the initial stage. AbuSulyman has written several publications of which *Towards an Islamic Theory of International Relations* and *Crisis in the Muslim Mind* are widely acclaimed. He lamented the backwardness of the Muslims and blamed it on their educational crisis. He asserts that the main cause of the ills of the Muslims can be attributed to their failure to restructure education. AbuSulayman believes that Islamisation should not be seen merely as a muscle flexing. He notes the centrality of knowledge reformation for any meaningful transformation in the Muslim world (AbuSulayman, 1994). This requires the need to redefine thought regarding what is the essence of knowledge and what methods can be utilised to shift from the literalist approach in engaging with traditions and classical jurisprudence. This necessitates the urgency of clarifying the relationship between revelation and reason in order to orient the methodology of Islamic education that breaks the "confused dualism" that mechanistically classifies knowledge into 'religious' and 'secular' (AbuSulayman, 1994). Divine revelation embodies the ultimate objectives of human reason and serves as a control mechanism against excesses spiritually or intellectually. Divine revelation is not meant to cancel reason. Rather, they work to complement one another (AbuSulayman, 1997). AbuSulyman stresses that the alleged conflict between revelation and reason is an illusion emphasising that the realm of reason is to compare contradictory views in order to determine the degree of harmony. Indeed, the Qur'anic world view is an ethical, purposeful and monotheistic perspective on the world seeking to reflect a balanced individual. This Qur'anic educational view articulates a vision of love, dignity, peace and mutual respect (AbuSulayman, 2011).

Approaches within Islamisation

Islamisation is in fact a response to the intellectual challenges imposed on the Muslims through colonisation. As opposed to the reactionary response by rejecting the Western education or the adoption of it to perpetuate the colonial structures, Islamisation of knowledge was to create independent thinking and holistic approach to knowledge. This paradigm questions the modernist dualistic model that has its own prejudices (Imtiaz, 2012). Reading the literature of IIIT, one can identify three salient approaches:

Academic and Educational Approach

The academic and educational approach is geared towards reviewing programmes at institutions of higher education. This was successful with the establishment of international Islamic universities. The Malaysian model seems to be the most successful, where leading academics converged between the 1980s and 1990s to examine the different aspects of education in Muslim majority countries. The proponent of this approach has been mainly AbuSulyman, who complained of crisis in the Muslim mind (*azmat al-'aql al-Muslim*). Equally, Al-Attas and Al-Faruqi could be part of this approach, but theirs was focussed more on philosophical and theological issues. Wan Sabri et. al. believe that Al-Faruqi's approach to Islamisation was to argue that Islamisation needed four constituents. First, there was a need to appreciate the principles and essence of Islam as a civilisation. Second, to examine the historical development of Islam and its encounter with others. Third, they considered comparing Islamic civilisation with others to appreciate the strengths and weaknesses and areas of critical engagement (Sabri et al., 2015). Al-Attas emphasised the need to move away from the secular world view that declared the "death of God" in its paradigm.[3]

Philosophical and Theological

It employs an exploratory approach to knowledge on the basis of argumentation. The tools employed are used to help one interpret the text and relate those interpretations considering the challenges and new developments (Daun & Arjumand, 2018). The theological and philosophical approaches to education inquire about perfecting the person through knowledge (Daun & Arjumand, 2018). On the other hand, Al-Attas is concerned about the critique of Western modern philosophy in relation to the theory of knowledge, religion and modernity. Thus, he pioneered the establishment of IIIT and civilisation.

Quasi-political and Social Approach

The third approach is related to the concept that in order for any academic work to have relevance, it must have a social and political bearing. Although

202 *Alhagi Manta Drammeh*

the proponents of IIIT may not be politically active, some of them would like to see positive societal transformation in their countries. It is believed that through academic development and intellectual debates a proper methodology could be developed in order to overcome the crisis in the Muslim mind. The theoretical positions were tested in an institutional setting of the IIIT in the United States of America with branches in many parts of the world and the academic institution in the name of International Islamic University of Malaysia. Although there are similar institutions in Pakistan, Malaysia, Nigeria and Uganda, the International Islamic University Malaysia (IIUM) has been the most successful. While IIIT focusses on the critical review of education in the Muslim world, IIUM emphasise developing scholars with an integrated approach to education to respond innovatively to contemporary challenges. Similarly, the ISTAC was established in Malaysia under the leadership of Al-Attas to pursue the Islamisation agenda. His focus is on education and thought (Solihah & Yahya, 2017). Al-Attas focusses on an Islamic metaphysics that has implications for the conception of knowledge (Solihah & Yahya, 2017).

Despite the different approaches of the aforementioned scholars, they all concur on the need for developing a knowledge that will enable learners to be critical going beyond the dichotomous reading of the scripture. In their representations, they encourage teachers to embrace diversity to enrich academic and intellectual discourse. Nonetheless, one can observe from their works their critique of both the biased modernist approach on one hand and the traditionalist literalist and legalistic perspective on the other. It is believed that both approaches should be combined. Without the complementary combination of the two readings, one can distort the wider picture. This is to highlight the important nature of a multidisciplinary and interdisciplinary approach to education that would provide both learners and teachers a broader perspective.

Islamic Education

Education is not simply duplicating many learning institutions. It is the capital of any society to progress at all levels. Education reflects the world view of a civilisation on society, politics and economics. Thus, the constant evaluation of education to achieve the aforementioned in terms of content, delivery and quality is important. It is a complex process of creativity and innovation. It is one geared towards creating a generation culturally and morally strong. This is understood as the influence of the environment upon the individual to produce a permanent change in their behaviour and thought. From the previously noted conceptualisation of education, it can be observed that the social reality in which an educator or learner lives is crucial in shaping their thoughts and directing the values. The foundations laid in education, from an Islamic perspective, are associated with the prophetic traditions such as, "Wisdom is the goal of the believer and they must seek it regardless of its source," and "Quest for learning is a duty incumbent on every Muslim."

Islamisation of Knowledge 203

These emphasise that education must be sought from multiple sources for the benefit of humanity. They also stress the fact that everyone is entitled to knowledge. It can therefore be assumed that education is a social system that emanates from the philosophy of each nation, enabling a person to be critical and interactive (Fred, 2008).[4] Ibn Khaldun points out that education is a social phenomenon and is influenced by the nature of the material, intellectual and spiritual forces of the civilisation in which they live (Tibawi, 1979). Thus, education must create in the individual a sense of resilience and the ability to adjust to new circumstances. Essentially, education helps one to know oneself and to equip one with the necessary tools to develop themselves and harness their latent potentials (Islamiyiyat al-ma'rifah, 2006b, vol. XII).

Islamic Methodologies and Educational Implications

Al-Attas believes that education must aim at developing a good person. He emphasises that the basic element of that process is the inculcation of *adab* encompassing the spiritual, material and emotional aspects of life. Therefore, the aims of Islamic education are not simply to satisfy an intellectual curiosity but also to develop rational and righteous individuals.

It will be pertinent for Islamic education to achieve purposefulness, understanding of the reality, adding value to the learner, needs of the learner and the importance of the integration between knowledge and action. Basically, education from an Islamic perspective has a triangular relationship in light of three pillars—namely, *tarbiyyah, ta'dib* and *ta'lim. Tarbiyyah* refers to the development of the individual. *Ta'dib* menas to be refined and disciplined. It also alludes to character development and provides a basis for moral and social behaviour. On the other hand, *ta'lim* is originated from *'alima*, meaning to know. It also means to receive and impart knowledge. Education should therefore refine the person and make them develop intellectually, spiritually and ethically in a manner that is critical. Education is not merely the acquisition of knowledge but also the ability of the person to utilise that knowledge in the best manner for their betterment (Al-Attas, 1993; Tibawi, 1979).

AbuSulyman is critical of blind following of both the foreign solution and the historical solution. While the former springs from the cultural and colonial encounter with the West, the latter is the emphasis on the Islamic historical experience regardless of the consideration of time and space (AbuSulayman, 1997) This critical thinking will allow learners to evaluate their intellectual legacy to differentiate between the fundamental principles and changing circumstances, as noted next (AbuSulayman, 1997).

Purposefulness in the sense that the theory should be informed by reality and vice versa. This means that the aims of any subject matter must be clear about what it aims to achieve. This may be related to the dialectical relationship between reality and the text. Students should be challenged positively to relate their theoretical knowledge to their reality.

204 *Alhagi Manta Drammeh*

Finally, knowledge and action must be integrated into a broad framework of life reflecting the complementarity between reason and revelation or the so-called combination of the two readings (*al-jam' bayna al-Qira'atayn*; Al-Faruqi & Naseef, 1981).

Islamisation and Its Relevance to Teachers' Professional Development

The aforementioned theories and philosophical positions on Islamisation help teachers to engage critically with the sources in a way that will lessen biases and prejudices. They also help them to adopt a multidisciplinary approach to scholarship, enabling them to relate religious knowledge with reality to respond creatively to challenges. Thus, the students will be able to adjust to new circumstances. Education can fulfil its role in today's complex world only when learners are equipped with general and relevant skills to deal with complicated moral and philosophical challenges. In addition, teachers would be able to teach their students to relate the theory to the practice in a creative and innovative manner. In this way, teachers will be able to impart to their students the positive perspectives of both modernity and tradition in the socio-economic development of communities and societies. Thus, teachers would be able to enlighten their students about the futility and superficiality of antagonism between religion and aspirations to excel and develop at all levels. This integrated approach to knowledge and education can allow students to become partners in teaching and learning. One of the fundamental values of Islamisation of knowledge is to allow teachers to develop their students' moral and spiritual values in a holistic manner, enabling them to participate fully in the development of their societies. The significance of inculcating values cannot be understated amid the forces of globalisation that have turned the world into a so-called global village. With information explosion and interdependence between people of different ethnic, racial and religious backgrounds, teachers have a great role to impact their students in a way they will have a global perspective on one hand. On another, they should be aware of cultural and religious differences, despite shared commonalities. As a result, teachers would be equipped with the educational tools to go beyond ideological and extremist views. Teachers are to educate and not to indoctrinate to allow their students to be critical and positive partners in learning.

Contemporary Context: Going beyond Theorising

Islamic education is required to respond to the challenge of globalisation (Smith, 2006).[5] Therefore, there is a need to develop a vision for educational development in response to changing circumstances (Daun & Arjumand, 2018). There are two main responses to approaching education in Islam. First, there is the outright exclusivist response that sees anything external to Islam to be rejected. On the contrary, there is the modernist response that believes that the educational system must be completely overhauled without the religious framework of Islam (Tan, 2014). The former believes that authenticity is found exclusively within Islam, and the latter rejects Islamic education as antithetical to modernity. Instead of the duality of exclusivism and rejection, there is a need for complementarity that necessitates the combination of the ethical, moral and spiritual aspects of education that can benefit from an Islamic world view while focussing on new challenges that require innovative responses through critical thinking. Therefore, there is a need to shift from the stage of theorising to the stage of developing practical models in response to social, educational, political and economic challenges (Niyozov & Memon, 2011). The practical approaches may involve allowing the students to think critically. The Islamic sources have references to observation, reflection and critical engagement. As students are at the centre of teaching, they should be taught to be proactive. Consequently, I can argue that this compartmentalisation of knowledge into religious and secular may not be helpful. Rather, there is a need to approach knowledge in a holistic methodology. This integration between reason and revelation, and between theory and practice, is ever required. Any imbalance in the aforementioned regarding the way education is approached will have implications. Learners should not be subjective recipients of knowledge.

Islamisation and Professional Development of Islamic Studies Teachers

One of the key areas that require consideration is to explore ways to enhance the professional delivery of Islamic teachers in terms of curriculum development, delivery of teaching material and the use of the appropriate methodologies in teaching and learning. Efforts should be exerted to shift from the 'banking system' of learning to critical learning. Professional development through 'action research' enhances teacher adaptability and hence. This helps teachers respond effectively to the needs of the learners. Teachers must demonstrate innovative skills in coordinating and organising the resources at their disposal. The role of the teacher must potentially result in an increase in the value of the product (Drucker, 2011). This can be achieved by the changes the teacher introduces (Hisrich et al., 2010). A teacher is someone who has a vision and creates an action plan in order to attain it. The focus is on the 'innovation and vision' instead of 'organisation and coordination of resources.' "Hisrich et al. 2010" emphasise "the process of creating something new with value by devoting the necessary time and effort; assuming the accompanying financial, psychic, and social risk and uncertainties; and receiving the resulting rewards of monetary and personal satisfaction". According to Bornstein (David, 2004), self-correction, breaking barriers and a multidisciplinary approach to learning will help in developing engagement.

It is inspiring for a teacher to seek to excel, resulting in the creation of high-achieving students who will never settle for anything less in life. Finally, teachers must use their classes as experiments of improving subsequent classes. This point underscores the essence of what is often referred to as action research. The primary purpose of action research is to create knowledge that is practically driven and knowledge that could potentially help individuals. Action research provides a platform for practitioners to discover which aspects of their theories find no application in the practical realms. In this way, it bridges the boundary between theory and practice. The chapter will also allow teachers to adopt the perspective on Islamic education that primarily aims at developing a balanced human being morally, spiritually and intellectually. In addition, it will orient Islamic education to universality and human commonalities based on justice, equity and morality.

Conclusion

The chapter concludes that education is a holistic behaviour anchored on the combination of sciences and values of revealed knowledge that emphasise critical thinking and innovation. The state of education of a society can be a good measure of its standard of civilisation (Islamiyiyat al-m'rifah, 2006b, vol. XII). Education should not be treated from an ideological perspective. Rather, it should be examined as an attempt to review issues of knowledge and methodology critically without any doctrinaire constraints, creating space for innovative thinking. I have shown the importance of shifting from a narrow legalistic approach in the human and social sciences to a broader hermeneutic approach that can incorporate Islamic primordial principles (Islamiyiyat *al-m'rifah*; Fall 2006a; Winter 2007). Education should be geared towards developing the individual student intellectually, morally and spiritually. The self-made division between secular education and religious education is an innovation.

I have also indicated that social interaction in teaching involves dealing with different people with different attitudes. Thus, a teacher must be sensitive to the different demography of students in order to make scholarship as creative as possible and, at the same time, enable learners to think critically. Learning and knowledge creation do not only tap into the stock of human knowledge but also prepare the whole intellectual learning environment. The teacher should therefore be conversant with the factors that influence student learning to be able to build in them the capacity for their individual development. The teacher needs to identify unique student characteristics, such as student understanding of the subject, individual differences and previous learning experience of the students. Overall, Islamisation with its theoretical and philosophical principles, can play a key role in helping teachers to develop critical approaches to dealing with sources of knowledge whether revealed or human. Islamisation can help teachers to be professionally objective in transmitting knowledge. Teachers should not be influenced by ideology or other subjective biases. Rather, teachers should be objective in a way to help their students to become independent, critical and innovative.

Finally, Islamisation is not to produce individuals with mere information. In fact, the proponents of Islamisation emphasise the need for teachers to

Islamisation of Knowledge   207

be both creative and innovative. Moreover, it should enable both learners and teachers to have a critical mind in approaching the body of knowledge. As part of their professional development, Islamic studies teachers should indeed make use of technological advancement in teaching. Moreover, disciplines in social sciences and humanities can be helpful in broadening one's perspective, as well as help one to understand one's tradition much better.

Notes

1 Anthropology helps us understand our culture and other cultures because people, regardless of their differences, have common ambitions and aspirations. It is concerned with the understanding of all the non-biological human activities, human ethics and values. It also looks into relationships between human societies. See ibid. pp. 28–30.
2 Professor AbuSulyman passed away on 18 August 2021 and is buried in Makkah.
3 In his *Islam and Secularism*, Al-Attas presents a detailed understanding and definition of secularism. He argues that secularism sees society as ever evolving and developing, whereby metaphysics transits from theology to science. See pp. 1–17.
4 Being critical is foundational to education as it enables one to creatively imagine circumstances and conditions different from those which prevail or known to one. See, Fred Inglis, *Key Concepts in Education*, London, Sage, 2008, pp. 57–8.
5 Globalisation focusses on market opportunities, business interests and access to key material resources for technological and scientific development in terms of international money movement, in search of new energy sources and cheap labour as much as possible. Globalisation is also about the gradual creation of links between groups and societies. These links have become extensive, complex and dynamic, see, Smith, Dennis, *Globalisation: the hidden agenda*, Cambridge, Polity, 2006, pp. 1–19.

References

Abd al-Ghani, K. A. (1989). Nahw 'Im al-insān al-islamī. IIIT.
AbuSulayman, A. H. (1994). *Islamization: Reforming contemporary knowledge*. Virginia: International Institute of Islamic Thought (IIIT).
AbuSulayman, A. H. (1997). *Crisis in the Muslim mind*. Virginia: International Institute of Islamic Thought (IIIT).
AbuSulayman, A. H. (2011). *The Qur'anic worldview: A springboard for cultural reform*. Surrey.
Al-Attas, S. N. (1993). *Islam and secularism*. Kuala Lumpur: International Institute of Islamic Thought and Civilisation.
Al-Faruqi, I. R. (1982,1992,1995). *AL tawhid: Its implications for thought and life*. Virginia: IIIT.
Al-Faruqi, I. (1991). *The trialogue of the Abrahamic Faiths*. Virginia: IIIT.
Al-Faruqi, I., & Naseef, A. O. (1981). *Social and natural sciences: The Islamic perspective*. Jeddah: King Abdul Aziz University.
Bradbury, P., & Reason, H. (Eds.). (2007). *The sage handbook of action research participative inquiry and practice* (Second ed.). London: SAGE Publications.
Daun, H., & Arjumand, R. (Eds.). (2018). *Handbook of Islamic education*. Sweden: Springer International Publishing AG.

208 *Alhagi Manta Drammeh*

Davidson, C. N., & Goldberg, D. T. (2010). *The future of thinking: Learning institutions in a digital age.* Cambridge: The MIT Press.

Drucker, P. F. (2011). *The five most important questions you will ever ask about your organization.* New York: Vol. 90. John Wiley & Sons.

Fred, I. (2008). *Key concepts in education.* London: SAGE.

Halstead, J. M. (2004). An islamic concept of education. *Comparative Education, 40*(4), 517–529.

Hawitng, G. R. (Ed.). (1993). *Approaches to the Qur'an.* London: Routledge.

Heller, F. (1993). Another look at action research. *Human Relations, 46*(10), 1235–1242.

Hisrich, R. D. et al. (2010). *Entrepreneurship.* New York: Mc Graw Hill International.

Imtiaz, Y. (Ed.). (2012). *Islam and knowledge.* London and New York: I.B. Tauris.

Inglis, F. (2008). *Key concepts in education.* London: SAGE.

Inglis, F. *Key concepts in education.* London: SAGE.

Islamiyiyat al-M'rifah. (Fall 2006a, Winter 2007). *Vol. XII* (46–47; 144)

Islamiyiyat al-M'rifah, vol. XII. (2006b). *XII* (46–47), 144.

Khalil, 'Imad al-Din. (1991). *Islamization of knowledge: A methodology.* Herndon: IIIT.

Lahmar, F. (2011). Discourses in Islamic educational theory in the light of texts and contexts. *Discourse: Studies in the Cultural Politics of Education, 32*(4), 479–495.

Martin, R. (Ed.). (2001). *Approaches to Islam in religious studies.* Oxford: Oneworld Publications.

Newble, R., & Cannon, D. (2006). *A handbook for teachers in universities and colleges: A Guide to improving teaching methods.* London and New York: Routledge.

Niyozov, S., & Memon, N. (2011). Islamic education and Islamization: Evolution of themes, continuities, and new directions. *Journal of Muslim Minority Affairs, 31* (1), 5–30.

Parsons, A., Ward, J., Ankrum, W., & Aimee, M. (2016). Professional development to promote teacher adaptability. *Theory into Practice, 55*(3), 250–258.

Robert, H., Micheal, P., & Dean, S. (2010). *Entrepreneurship.* New York: Mc Graw Hill International.

Roldan, M., Strage, A., & David, D. (eds.) (2004). "A framework for assessing academic service-learning across disciplines." *New perspectives in service-learning: Research to advance the field*, 39–59.

Sabri, W. et al. (2015). Islamic civilization: Its significance in al-Faruqi's Islamization of knowledge. *International Journal of Islamic Thought, 7*, 51–54.

Safi, L. (1996). *The foundation of knowledge.* Kuala Lumpur: International Islamic University.

Sarfaroz, N., & Nadeem, M. (2011). Islamic education and Islamization: Evolution of themes, continuities and new directions. *Journal of Muslim Minority Affairs, 31*(1), 5–30.

Smith, D. (2006). *Globalisation: The hidden agenda.* Cambridge: Polity.

Solihah, Z., Yahya, B.H.. (2017). A comparative analysis of the conceptions of Muhammad Naquib al-Attas and Ismail al-Faruqi in Islamisation of knowledge. *Journal of Islamic Studies, 2*(1).

Tan, C. (Ed.). (2014). *Reforms in Islamic education.* London: Bloomsbury.

Tibawi, A. L. (1979). *Islamic education.* London: Luzac & Company LTD.

Warren, S. (2009). *An introduction to education studies.* London & New York: Continuum International Publishing Group.

Yusuf, I. (Ed.). (2012). *Islam and knowledge al-Faruqi's concept of religion in Islamic thought.* London: I.B. Tauris.

17 Maktab Teachers and Behaviour Education

Ruminations from a Teacher Education Programme in the UK

Imran Mogra

Introduction

The interest to learn about Islam has experienced exponential growth in the United Kingdom (UK). There has been a proliferation of Islamic courses which some Muslims are accessing both online and in residential institutes. In addition, many local centres of learning have been set up in various communities offering part-time and full-time courses, some of which are limited to topics or texts while others authorise their attendees to graduate as scholars (*'Ulāmā'* and *'Ālimāt*). In this expanding educational landscape, this chapter aims to show how the *maktab* is also undergoing transformation.

It begins by briefly charting the history of the *maktab*. Thereafter, it highlights its main salient features in the UK, discusses key terms and celebrates some of its main contributions. Insights from *maktab* teachers, trained by the author, are then offered. The last section focusses upon behaviour education as part of an original contribution to the still underdeveloped area of research in this important sector.

Maktab Education in Islam

The '*maktab*' appeared during the time of Prophet Muhammad (ﷺ). The earliest educational setting was the house of Zaid, son of Arqam, in Makkah. After migration to Madinah, a veranda, called *al-suffah*, was created next to the Prophet's (ﷺ) mosque for teaching and, thereafter, other venues followed (Boyle, 2004; Mogra, 2004). As Islam expanded, it became necessary to create uniformity in the teachings of Islam and to formalise these settings. Henceforth began the worldwide phenomenon of *makātib*. Muslims in the UK have upheld this uninterrupted tradition and this system continues to exist in many parts of the world in its own local variations with many similar features.

Maktab Education in the UK

The word *maktab* (pl. *makātib*) is derived from Arabic, *ka-ta-ba*, meaning to write. In contemporary usage, it means a place of primary learning. Often,

DOI: 10.4324/9781003193432-20

210   *Imran Mogra*

in the UK, *madrasah*, a place for studying (pl. *madāris*), derived from Arabic, *da-ra-sa*, meaning to study, is applied for *maktab*. Hence, due to this interchangeable application, it is important to distinguish it from a *madrasah* when it refers to higher institutes of learning. Furthermore, it is important to note other variants used in other parts of the world, including *Msid* and *kuttāb* (Boyle, 2004), *pondok* (Mohd. Nor Wan Daud, 1989) and *malcaamado* (Kahin, 1997), which reflect their respective linguistic traditions.

This chapter prefers the term *maktab* as a collective term for those studies that Muslim children undertake outside full-time mainstream state education. They are held mainly in the evening ranging from one hour to two hours. Often, children will refer to the *maktab* as a 'mosque school.' It has been suggested that in the UK, the establishment of the 'Qur'anic School' commenced during the 1960s (Noh, Tamuri, Razak & Suhid, 2014). Some offer community languages such as Arabic, Bengali, Somali, Turkish, Urdu and others (Cherti & Bradley, 2011; Gent, 2018). Many settings are multi-ethnic communities where children and adults gather for worship, education, social celebrations, family events and youth clubs.

There are many variations in these settings. In West Africa, most of the Islamic learning in *maktab* has a narrow focus (Hardaker & Sabki, 2019). In some UK settings, children are taught a more comprehensive curriculum which typically includes, in addition to the Qur'ān and *tajwīd*, the biography of the Prophet ﷺ)), *fiqh* (jurisprudence), *aḥādith* (sayings of the Messenger ﷺ)), Islamic history (*tārīkh*) and social and moral values (*akhlāq*) (Mogra, 2007). Many of these *makātib* offer a *hifḍ* class for those wishing to memorise the Qur'ān.

They are held in mosques, community centres, former church halls, school halls which are hired outside regular school hours, or in private homes. Many are registered charities and often run through mosques (Cherti, Glennie, & Bradley, 2011). A large population of Muslim children attends them, although not all do so in all areas. For the community, it is important to recognise that the age profile is much younger (MCB, 2015), and, therefore, continued attention needs to be paid to the quality of provision in the *maktab* sector and to expand these facilities.

Beyond these academic pursuits and, in view of some concerns related to the quality of provisions, attempts have been made in recent years to further enhance *makātib* by providing training on child protection, safeguarding, health and safety and behaviour management (Mogra, 2005; Siddiqui, 2006; Cherti & Bradley, 2011). Among all these collaborations, reforms and research studies, the perspective of the personnel at the heart of these *makātib* has seldom been explored (Gent, 2006).

The subject of improving the quality of the management of *makātib* and their associated classroom practices has been an area of discussion among researchers, practitioners and members of the community for some time (Siddiqui, 2006; Ahmed and Riasat, 2013; Scourfield, Gilliat-Ray, Khan, & Otri, 2013; Mogra, 2018). Moreover, teachers demonstrate many ways of teaching. Teachers in an Irish study act autonomously to some degree in their approaches (Sai, 2018). That said, some have noted concerns about health and safety issues and the potential risk of being radicalised (Waghid, 2009; Cherti, Glennie, & Bradley, 2011; Ryan, Last, & Woodbury, 2012).

Recently, the UK government proposed to legislate out-of-school settings (Mogra, 2018). This initiative was not only a concern for some Muslim communities, but other faith groups also had reservations. The proposal included a requirement on settings to register, supply basic information, a power for a body to inspect and a power to impose sanctions where settings would fail to promote the welfare of children. This could include barring individuals from working with children and the closure of premises (DfE, 2018). However, following a nationwide consultation, the government did not find it favourable. Nevertheless, it proposed a consultation on a voluntary code of practice to set out clear standards for providers so that they could meet their existing legal obligations in relation to child welfare, health and safety, governance, suitability of staff, teaching and financial management (DfE, 2018). Generally, some of the fears about *makātib* are not based on extensive and rigorous research; instead, they appear to be based on intermittent reporting and speculation in the media. Thus, Cherti, Glennie and Bradley (2011) expressed the need for better understanding of them. This chapter contributes towards this end.

Contributions of *Makātib*

Maktab education is significant for philosophical and religio-cultural reasons. Elicitation exercises during training sessions with teachers, most of whom were Imāms and *'Ulāmā'*, both male and female, from various ethnicities, reveal that they have a deep concern for the faith development, social welfare and knowledge acquisition of their pupils.

Faith Development

Education in a *maktab* links Muslim pupils to God and to their application of the teachings of Islam. An Imām succinctly declared, "If a child does not receive the learning in maktab then s/he will not recognise the teachings of Allah and His Messenger ﷺ)), in fact, his/her faith will be in danger then how will he perform his/her worship." *Makātib* are set up as a matter of priority, almost anywhere and everywhere that Muslims have settled. Internationally, they assist in preserving and transforming social, educational and religious practices (Boyle, 2004; Brenner, 2008).

Environment

In the absence of a secure foundation, some Muslim children would become more susceptible to being manipulated by external pressures and may have their courage challenged in resisting peer and social pressures. Participating

212 *Imran Mogra*

teachers recognised the significance of equipping children to be resourceful, self-regulatory and to resist negative influences as best as they can. According to an Imām, a child "will be influenced by the environment and will be involved in all sorts of vices, a means of menace for all" should they miss *maktab* education.

Society

The social context in which Muslim children are growing up and what it means to be a Muslim has been put under renewed scrutiny considering national and international events (McKenna & Francis, 2019). Some experience tensions between Islam and secular Western entertainment, while others are clear about their Muslim faith but also enjoy aspects of secular culture without seeing conflicts between the two (Scourfield, Gilliat-Ray, Khan & Otri, 2013). Therefore, these teachers feel that *maktab* education enables some children to see the "difference between right and wrong." Some *'Ulāmā'* and *'Ālimāt* asserted that children may "disrespect their parents, teachers and others" and experience a "loss of self-discipline." Some felt children will "remain uninformed and ignorant of the basic information."

Identity

Some Muslim children live a life of split identities (Ali, 2020), and with the majority (73%) of Muslims seeing their foremost national identity as 'British' (MCB, 2015), the establishment of *makātib* serves the purpose of transmitting language and cultural aspects. Thus, the absence of the 'cultural' content in the state curriculum is addressed via the structured teachings and socialisation at the *maktab*. This reality seems to be acknowledged by some participants, who are anxious that, without a firm familiarisation with Islam, some pupils "will be affected by the western life more" and the "Islamic identity of the children will be lost." Specifically, there is anxiety about assimilating to the conditions of their surroundings. Children who spend time in Islamic places (including homes) are likely to have their faith and ethnicity become central to their identity, and, being in a minority, especially when there is some hostility towards Muslims, this may enhance their identification with Islam (Cherti & Bradley, 2011; Scourfield, Gilliat-Ray, Khan & Otri, 2013).

Spirituality and Emotional Development

Muslim pupils begin to develop a relationship with Allah and gain a sense of purpose in life. In the absence of this, a child, some teachers argue, will have "no sense of direction." Their spiritual and emotional development may diminish. A female teacher observed, "The *noor* [spiritual light] and the feelings will disappear." Psychologically, another teacher noted, an "inferiority complex in matters of Islam" could grow. Consequently, "peace will slowly leave their lives." Thus, *makātib* are seen as compensators for the failure of state schools in providing an essential part of moral and spiritual education (Gent, 2018).

McKenna and Francis (2019) found that the majority of female students in their study felt the importance of religion in their daily lives. It played a leading role when making important decisions, and their lives had been shaped by their religious faith (p. 394). Thus, the *maktab* plays a significant role in contributing to this religious and spiritual awareness. Indeed, it is the main way for most Muslim children across the UK to access the teachings of the Qur'ān (Noh, Tamuri, Razak, & Suhid, 2014).

First Steps in Professionalism

There were several motivating factors which prompted the initiation, design and delivery of this training programme. Discussions with some children revealed a need to enhance their confidence to express their learning in *maktab* in their school and other social contexts, and to apply their skills of memorising and intense learning in *maktab* to their school contexts so that they achieved higher in both settings (Berglund & Gent, 2019). Furthermore, Noh, Tamuri, Razak and Suhid (2014) noted criticism of some outdated modes of teaching among some Imāms and the need for teacher training in the existing courses which prepare '*Ulāmā*' (Scott-Baumann & Cheruvallil-Contractor, 2017). Specifically, in relation to behaviour, many staff in *makātib* and parents admitted that behaviour is an issue in some mainstream schools. A non-ministerial department of the UK government responsible for inspecting a range of educational institutions judged a third of schools as not having good enough behaviour (DfE, 2019). Behaviour is still a significant challenge for many schools (Bennett, 2017). Equally, many *maktab* teachers admitted some challenges in addressing inappropriate behaviour.

Synopsis of the Training

A training initiative for *maktab* teachers across the UK and beyond is delivered by the author in an independent capacity. Over 15 years, several hundred have attended a variety of training sessions. This chapter is based on selected post-training anonymous questionnaire evaluations received from 410 (male 303, female 107) participants.

The programme covers several areas of teaching and learning to enrich their knowledge, skills and lifelong learning. This includes the aims and purposes of a *maktab* in a post-secular and postmodern society; revisiting the teaching methods of the Prophet Muhammad (ﷺ) (Abu Ghuddah, 2017); understanding a Muslim child; considering theories informing modern pedagogies; the use of visual and multi-media resources; being a Muslim teacher from theological, sociological and psychological perspectives; curriculum design; pupil-teacher relationships; nature of the classroom environment; and addressing additional learning needs of individual pupils.

214 *Imran Mogra*

Behaviour Education

The Context

Some concerns about the use of corporal punishment in some *makātib* have been featured (Siddiqui, 2006; Mogra, 2018). Nevertheless, *makātib* are consistently seen as centres for instilling discipline and a sense of duty in Muslim children. Most research participants who had attended *maktab* felt that the strict environment and religious context led them to monitor and control their own behaviour. Some felt that this instilled a sense of 'spiritual fear' which meant they would behave better in the *makātib* than in their mainstream school. However, in a small number of cases, the discipline used within a *makātib* was seen to be detrimental to the welfare of children (Cherti & Bradley, 2011). Thus, a key element of their training development was to critically evaluate the issues of corporal punishment from a theological, historical and Muslim juristic position, coupled with social and legal expectations.

The rest of the chapter offers a reflective analysis of the selected sessions, the pedagogical approaches adopted and their impact.

Behaviour Education and the Qur'ān

Teachers begin to reflect on the broad teachings of the Qur'ān and how some principles and practices for behaviour education are presented there. Thereafter, a rehearsal of specific *aḥādith* to help in delineating appropriate approaches for the UK context is conducted. This stresses 'the teacher as a model of the Prophet' concept so that teachers become concerned not only with behaviour issues but also with all aspects of pupils being Muslim. To this end, teachers recognise how to respond appropriately to pupils' physical, emotional, mental, spiritual and social needs and how they can promote healthy bodies, minds and souls.

Behaviour Education and Muslim Scholarship

In another session, participants read texts from classical and contemporary scholars as accumulated knowledge to explore the nature of behaviour and the gradual and systematic way they approached behaviour education (Mogra, 2007). This collective reading attempts to create 'communities of practice' within their local areas (Wenger, 1998). From this, teachers learn how to prioritise pupils' safety and welfare. They review their attitudes, systems and policy. Thereafter, they learn and understand their statutory safeguarding duties and child protection responsibilities as outlined by regulatory bodies in England.

The Challenges

A matrix is used to examine the seriousness and frequency of some behaviours considered to be challenging by these teachers. Consequently, many realise that, generally, the behaviour of some of their pupils in their classes, in contrast to some behaviours in mainstream schools, as noted earlier, is usually better. They conclude that what they consider to be serious are low-level behaviours, although their frequency is sometimes high. For example, pupils showing a "bad attitude," "coming late to class," "calling names" and "not doing what they are told." Following a detailed deliberation, they begin to see their pupils in a new light and review their attitudes to some behaviours and how they deal with them.

Policy

Headteachers bring their behaviour policy to the training session. The aim is to show the importance of respecting the decisions made by management teams, to evaluate their effectiveness, to examine their contents and to recognise the importance of having a consistent approach across all classes. The critical analysis involves teachers from different settings studying a single policy. From this, they recognised that

> a uniform policy of behaviour management should be implemented.
>
> (BHM25E/32)

They also learn that policies can be different for each setting with some similarities. The trainer emphasises that policies need to be reviewed regularly (O'Brien, 2020) and be developed in conjunction with parents. Teachers must respect the policy and not criticise it in the presence of their pupils; otherwise, pupils will undermine it.

Rules

Teachers share their classroom rules to demonstrate the commonality and distinctiveness of the number, nature, categories and the process of developing these rules in each setting. Thereafter, they learn the significance of establishing and reinforcing routines which set the tone of learning. Following the training, some mentioned that they would be more responsive to their legal contexts:

> laws and rules are changing day by day in the UK. The *maktabs* need to adapt according to these laws.
>
> (BHM24E/31)

Others suggested that they would improve by introducing

> reward systems for well-behaved children.
>
> (OM2E/358)

216   *Imran Mogra*

Teachers are taught that class rules are a means for religious, moral, social, spiritual and personal development, and, as such, they ought to be used to serve the purposes for which they have been designed; otherwise, they should be changed and not be treated as ends in themselves.

Sometimes, it transpires that some settings do not have routines. Thus, from this analysis, they learn several ways of setting up routines in and out of classrooms, which creates order, calmness and minimises the repetition of instructions by teachers.

The Powerful Language

Teachers must understand that language is a powerful tool for their teaching and behaviour education. Participants examine the kind of language used in various settings by sharing some terms used to describe pupils, their work, effort and behaviour. These are listed under a positive and negative heading, respectively. Following this, a deeper analysis of the frequency of positive and negative phrases is undertaken to illustrate the dominant feature and, significantly, the nature of these phrases is scrutinised. Thereafter, the potential emotional and psychological impact of using these terms is highlighted. A teacher wrote that they would

> show love and mercy, no abuse.
>
> (BDM27E/68)

The power of language also lies in bringing about the desired changes in a classroom. To facilitate cognisance of this feature, attendees are provided with a set of sentences to interpret and conduct textual analysis. Thereafter, they are asked to offer alternative phrases to use in their own classes. Moreover, they practise these phrases with each other to appraise the potential impact of positive and constructive phrases. This activity made some participants

> more conscious of words used when addressing children.
>
> (BDM24E/68)

Others suggested that they would enhance their quality of teaching by

> [l]isten[ing] to their problem, try[ing] to understand them, if anyone does anything mention what he has done, not him.
>
> (OLM46E/394)

Consistency and Integrity

Some pupils are acutely alert to matters of fairness. Thus, it is vital for teachers to be consistent in their use of language, recognition and sanctions. Some pupils are apt at noticing favouritism, which can sometimes manifest in an unusual way a teacher might rebuke or praise two pupils for an identical misdemeanour or effort. Thus, these teachers discuss and receive feedback on how they could improve their responses and feedback to their pupils in a consistent manner. A teacher declared they would show

> more love and affection and have a discussion with "d" children.
>
> (BDM28E/72)

Moreover, teachers learn that their language should be a means to influence pupils' resilience, resourcefulness and self-belief about their ability to succeed. They are reminded to ensure that all should experience meaningful success through positive reinforcement and praise and celebration of their achievements, efforts and personal development. When asked what changes they would introduce after the training, a teacher recorded

> build pupils' self-esteem by praising them occasionally.
>
> (DWF2E/89)

The message to give attention to individual pupils resonated with some teachers who suggested that they would

> talk to children individually.
>
> (BHF3E/3)

Consider Life Experiences

Teachers need to understand the importance of developing a positive and predictable strategy to manage excessive talk and disruptions. Thus, they predict what they would expect to be the main concern in the minds of their pupils as they arrive at the *maktab* following a win by their local football team, for example. Teachers discuss how they would manage the inevitable excessive discussions. They offer examples such as "remind them of rules," "tell them not to talk about the game," "separate them from their best friend" and so forth. They are then informed that, first, they must be prepared for the obvious—i.e., unavoidable discussions about the game (or any other important event for pupils). They should consider giving pupils time at the start of the lesson to talk about the matter and to join in their conversation. Thereafter, expectations should be set for the rest of the lesson. This helps to explore their emotions and build good relationships, as pupils see that their life experiences are understood, and the teacher is interested in what happens in their lives.

On return to their classes, some wrote they would now

> make them laugh (share a joke).
>
> (BDM25E/69)

218   *Imran Mogra*

> I intend to change my attitude and behaviour and attention towards my pupils. Also, I intend to help them through making it easier for them.
>
> (DWF7E/94)

> [Create a] friendly atmosphere.
>
> (OLM62E/410)

Monitoring Emotions

A role play is used to stress the importance of self-regulating emotions, which can affect pupils in many ways. The Qur'ān expects control of anger (Ali-'Imrān, 3:134). Prophet Muhammad (ﷺ) advised against becoming angry (Al-Bukhārī, 8:76:137). In the role play, a teacher, representing a child, pretends to arrive late. The trainer, representing a teacher, shouts, insults the whole family for such behaviour, loses control and seeks no explanation for the lateness. Thereafter, teachers analyse all aspects of the behaviour of both. They examine the character shown and the potential physical, psychological, social and emotional impact on both parties. They explore the options available for dealing with latecomers, the importance of modelling good etiquette and of asking for explanations for their lateness. Some teachers professed that they would avoid

> [s]houting, calling them by bad name, i.e., donkeys etc.
>
> (OLM51E/399)

> Sanctions which could lead to inferiority.
>
> (DWF3E/90)

Since recourse is made to the Qur'ān and *ḥadīth*, others felt that

> child behaviour needs to be studied and seen in the eyes of our religion.
>
> (DWM6E/100)

Attractors and Distractors

A *maktab* should be a place where pupils feel that they belong. To understand pupils' sensitive nature and to find multiple ways of encouraging their attendance, love for their *maktab* and their engagement in lessons, participants from different settings work collaboratively. They create a list of factors which they think attract and distract Muslim pupils. The trainer facilitates an evaluation of these features. They learn to improve their setting by establishing a positive, supportive and inclusive classroom with a clear system of rewards and sanctions. The ensuing discussion is then taken deeper to examine the role of intrinsic and extrinsic motivation for learning and behaving.

They think about how they could move pupils from needing extrinsic motivation to being motivated intrinsically.

A significant shift was detected. Some teachers envisaged to make

enjoyment factors for children.

(BDM24E/68)

[G]ive them some time during the lesson to do what they want.

(WF3E/79)

[D]on't avoid and neglect their thoughts but try to be part of them and talk to them about their thoughts.

(OLM37E/392)

[T]ry to understand the child's problems (at maktab/home) and take necessary steps.

(OLM47E/395)

Conclusion

In general, teachers are under continuous pressure to deliver the elementary educational programme of Islam to Muslim children within various constraints. In this context, the dedication of teachers and Muslim communities to arrange essential faith-based religious education for their children is praiseworthy.

This chapter made an original contribution in outlining an innovative training programme designed to enhance the professionalism of *maktab* teachers in the UK. The programme shifts their theorisation and praxis of being a didactic pedagogue to one of being collaborative, reflective and transformative. They recognise their curriculum and methodologies are a means to serve the pupil, rather than exclusive ends in themselves. They begin to view the Muslim child as an active learner rather than solely being a *tabula rasa*. They grapple with the affective, cognitive and spiritual aspects of learning as well. Teachers come out of their silos and recognise the importance of networking and involving parents and the community in nurturing Muslim pupils to become faithful, lifelong learners and good members of society.

Recommendations

These findings offer lessons at three levels to assist Muslim teachers around the world in improving their *makātib*. To begin with, with regards to the welfare of children, all *makātib* should have health and safety, mental health

220 *Imran Mogra*

and well-being, safeguarding and child protection policies. These should be enacted in their local contexts. The curriculum on offer must cater for their holistic development. This means it should go beyond knowledge and rituals and incorporate explicitly the spiritual, moral, social, cultural and personal development and be responsive to their lived realities. To this end, teachers should receive regular training facilitated by organisations and management boards.

In terms of behaviour education, teachers should reflect upon the Qur'ān to derive theories, principles and practices to enhance their behaviour management and understanding of children. They should be well-versed with the manners in which the Prophetic teacher (ﷺ) interacted with his Ṣaḥābah as learners. Teachers should be familiar with their scholarly traditions to inform their ongoing reflections to enable them to be responsive in their own cultural contexts. Importantly, they should use respectful language and enact their policies in a fair and consistent manner.

Specifically, in terms of teacher development, it is recommended that teachers are involved in a continuous cycle of reflection to improve their practice. Teachers should conceptualise their roles and become mentors and agents of transformation in addition to knowledge transferers. Muslim teachers should recognise that their accountability in relation to the treatment meted out to their pupils lies with Allah and extends beyond their employees and community.

References

Abu Ghuddah, A. (2017). *Prophet Muhammad the teacher*. Claritas Books.

Ahmed, I., & Riasat, A. (2013). *Children do matter*. Council for Mosques Bradford.

Al-Bukhārī, M. I. (1986). *Ṣaḥīḥ Al-Bukhārī*. Translated by M.M. Khan. Kazi Publications.

Ali, S. (2020). The Politics of Islamic identities. In A. Elliott (Ed.), *The handbook of identity studies* (2nd ed., pp. 325–346). Routledge.

Bennett, T. (2017). *Creating a culture: How school leaders can optimise behaviour.* Crown Copyright.

Berglund, J., & Gent, B. (2019). Qur'anic education and non-confessional RE: An intercultural perspective. *Intercultural Education, 30*(3), 323–334.

Brenner, L. (2008). *Controlling knowledge: Religion, power and schooling in a West African Muslim society*. Hurst & Co.

Boyle, H. N. (2004). *Quranic schools: Agents of preservation and change*. Routledge Farmer.

Cherti, M., Glennie, A., & Bradley, L. (2011). *'Madrassas' in the British media*. Institute for Public Policy Research.

Cherti, M., & Bradley, L. (2011). *Inside Madrassas understanding and engaging with British-Muslim faith supplementary schools*. Institute for Public Policy Research.

DfE. (2018). *Out-of-school education settings. Report on the call for evidence conducted November 2015 to January 2016*. Crown Copyright.

DfE (2019). *Schools backed to tackle bad behaviour*. Press Release. Crown Copyright. https://www.gov.uk/government/news/schools-backed-to-tackle-bad-behaviour (Accessed 19-09-2020).

Gent, B. (2006). The educational experiences of British Muslims: Some life-story images. *Muslim Education Quarterly, 23*(3&4), 33–42.

Gent, B. (2018). *Muslim supplementary classes: And their place within the wider learning community.* Beacon Books.

Hardaker, G., & Sabki, A. A. (2019). *Pedagogy in Islamic education.* Emerald Publishing.

Kahin, M. H. (1997). *Educating Somali children in Britain.* Trentham Books.

McKenna, U., & Francis, L. J. (2019). Growing up female and Muslim in the UK: An empirical enquiry into the distinctive religious and social values of young Muslims. *British Journal of Religious Education, 41*(4), 388–401.

MCB (2015). *British Muslims in numbers.* The Muslim Council of Britain.

Mogra, I. (2004). *Makātib* education in Britain: A review of trends and some suggestions for policy. *Muslim Education Quarterly, 21*(3 & 4), 19–27.

Mogra, I. (2005). Moving forward with *Makātib*: The role of reformative sanctions. *Muslim Education Quarterly, 22*(3 & 4), 52–64.

Mogra, I. (2007). Moral education in the *makātib* of Britain: A review of curriculum materials. *Journal of Moral Education, 36*(3), 387–398.

Mogra, I. (2018). Religious education at crossroads in the United Kingdom: Muslim responses to registration, regulation and inspection. *Journal of Muslim Minority Affairs, 38*(2), 198–217.

Mohd. Nor Wan Daud, W. (1989). *The concept of knowledge in Islam and its implications for education in a developing country.* Mansell.

Noh, M. A. C., Tamuri, A., Razak, K. A., & Suhid, A. (2014). The study of Quranic teaching and learning: United Kingdom experience. *Mediterranean Journal of Social Sciences, 5*(16), 313–317.

O'Brien, J. (2020). *Leading better behaviour: A guide for school leaders.* SAGE.

Ryan, J., Last, K., & Woodbury, J. (2012). *Independent evaluation of the ASDAN Islam and citizenship short course.* University of the West of England.

Sai, Y. (2018). Teaching Qur'an in Irish Muslim schools – curriculum, approaches, perspectives and implications. *British Journal of Religious Education, 40*(2), 148–157.

Scott-Baumann, A. & Cheruvallil-Contractor, S. (2017). *Islamic education in Britain: New pluralist paradigms.* Bloomsbury.

Scourfield, J., Gilliat-Ray, S., Khan, A., & Otri, S. (2013). *Muslim childhood: Religious nurture in a European context.* Oxford University Press.

Siddiqui, G. (2006). *Child protection in faith-based environments.* The Muslim Parliament of Great Britain.

Waghid, Y. (2009). Education and madrassahs in South Africa: On preventing the possibility of extremism. *British Journal of Religious Education, 31*(2), 117–128.

Wenger, E. (1998). *Communities of practice: learning, meaning, and identity.* Cambridge University Press.

18 Islamic Religious Education (IRE) Teachers in the Netherlands[1]
From Tradition-Based to Modern Teaching

Ina ter Avest

Introduction

In the 1960s, 'guest workers' from Turkey and Morocco were recruited to contribute to the post-war reconstruction of the Netherlands. In the 1970s, the families that many guest workers left behind—women and children—began to arrive in the country. As a result, the Dutch public and denominational schools were overtaken by the arrival of pupils with Islamic backgrounds. At the time, Islam was an unknown life orientation in the secularised Christian Dutch context. Different methods were explored to include these children in Dutch school culture (Ter Avest, 2009). However, the schools did not meet the Muslim parents' needs in terms of the religious education (RE) they wished for their children.

In 1988, pioneering Muslim parents founded the two first Islamic primary schools in the Netherlands (Budak et al., 2018). While the pupils in these schools all had a Muslim background, most teachers—due to a lack of Muslim professionals—were of Dutch origin. Since 1988, the number of Islamic primary schools in the Netherlands has risen sharply (*Dienst Uitvoering Onderwijs*, Organisation for the Realisation of Education). This creates a high demand for qualified Muslim or Islam-dedicated teachers, who possess the competencies to instruct Muslim children in Islamic religious education (IRE) and non-religious subjects (such as languages, biology, geography and mathematics) from an Islamic perspective.

When the first Dutch Islamic primary schools were founded, Muslim parents were concerned about the RE given to their children, especially the dress codes at school. Nowadays, sex education is a hot topic. This chapter focusses on this last topic and on the issue of adequate teacher training.

In this contribution, first, the Dutch 'pillarised' education system is presented, together with an outline of the ideas on sex education recently presented by the Ministry of Education. This is followed by an outline of the discussion on 'Islamic pedagogy' and 'Islam *and* pedagogy.' The core subject of this contribution is sex education in Islamic primary schools. Teaching materials developed for this education are described and reflected upon from a constructivist point of view, taking 'Islamic pedagogy'/'Islam and

DOI: 10.4324/9781003193432-21

pedagogy' into consideration. The chapter concludes with recommendations for the training and professionalisation of teachers.

The Dutch Pillarised Education System

As the Netherlands moved into the 20th century, 'pillarisation' became the core characteristic of its education system. Education was separated into three 'pillars': Catholic, Protestant and humanistic. In the schools belonging to these pillars, a distinct Catholic, Protestant or humanistic 'flavour' permeated the lessons (Ter Avest et al., 2007). In Christian schools (both Catholic and Protestant) the day began with prayer, and during the week Bible stories were told and hymns sung in class. In humanist schools, no attention was devoted to any world view, as the school was seen as a neutral environment, where every child was welcome irrespective of its background. These pillars not only marked the boundaries that ran through the education system: other institutions like the media, health organisations and sports clubs were also organised according to these pillars. Nowadays people would call these the 'bubbles' they live in.

As a result of secularisation most denominational schools (Protestant and Catholic) have become liberal Christian schools by 2020, where school rituals are restricted to the Christmas and Easter season. Public schools nowadays do pay attention to world views following a pedagogical strategy of 'teaching about,' under the subject of citizenship education.

Islamic Education in the Netherlands

A history of Islamic education and the foundation of Islamic education in the Netherlands is described by Wilna Meijer (2006) and Ter Avest & Bakker (2018) respectively. A challenging factor for the two pioneering Islamic schools in 1988 was that most of the available teachers were of Dutch origin, adhering to a Christian denomination (Budak, in progress 2022). In 2020, of the total of 6,268 primary schools in the Netherlands, 54 were Islamic schools. This creates a high demand for qualified Muslim or Islam-dedicated teachers, who possess the competencies to instruct Muslim children in IRE in the Dutch plural context. Teachers are expected to guide their pupils in the process of becoming literate in Islam as part of their religious identity development, with a focus on making pupils well aware of their own identity and open to others.

When Islamic primary schools were first founded in the 1980s—nearly 40 years ago—a particular concern of the parents was the RE given to children, especially the culturally and religiously inspired dress codes at school. Nowadays, in the postmodern Dutch society, sex education has become a hot item. It is on this issue that this chapter focusses.

224   *Ina ter Avest*

Sex Education in the Netherlands

The *'Rutgers Kenniscentrum Seksualiteit'* defines sex education as

> coaching the child in its sexual development from birth onward. Children under 12 are assisted in discovering their bodies, their feelings, what they like and don't like, and in forming relationships. Children older than 12 are coached in making their choices regarding their sexuality.
> (*Rutgers Kenniscentrum Seksualiteit*; Rutger Knowledge Centre of Sexuality; www.rutgers.nl)

In 2012, the Dutch Ministry of Education published primary objectives for sex education based on the "Standards for Sexuality Education in Europe" (WHO, 2018). In general, the Ministry's aim is to prevent sexual harassment and misconduct, as well as 'gay-bashing.' Pupils must be educated about the core aspects of the world view movements that are prominent in the Dutch multicultural society, and they must develop a respectful attitude towards the different sexualities in Dutch society (primary educational objective no. 38; www.sexuelevorming.nl). Various school subjects can serve as a point of departure for sex education, like 'biology' and 'social studies.'[2] The European guidelines and those of the Ministry of Education function as minimal guidelines for the implementation of sex education. Although RE is not explicitly mentioned as a possible starting point, in the actual practice of Islamic primary schools, sex education falls under IRE.

> [C]oaching the child in its sexual development from birth onward. Children under 12 are assisted in discovering their bodies, their feelings, what they like and don't like, and in forming relationships. Children older than 12 are coached in making their choices regarding their sexuality.
> (*Rutgers Kenniscentrum Seksualiteit*; Rutger Knowledge Centre of Sexuality; www.rutgers.nl)

Slamic Pedagogy/Islam *and* Pedagogy

As outlined by Kaplick and Skinner, 'Islamic pedagogy' is an interdisciplinary field that explores education in relation to Islamic sources, using this knowledge to bring human beings into flourishing—cognitively, emotionally and spiritually (cf. Kaplick & Skinner, 2017). Although these authors focus on *psychology* and Islam, in our view, their approach is also interesting for the relationship between *pedagogy* and Islam—as these fields of research are intertwined. Islamic pedagogy is therefore an academic pedagogy rooted explicitly and solely in Islamic sources.

Building on this, 'Islam *and* pedagogy' refers to a relationship between Islamic sources and (Western) social sciences as practiced in academia.

The focus of 'Muslim pedagogy,' thirdly, lies on the daily behavioural practices, patterns therein and religious experiences of faithful Muslims (cf. ibid., p. 199).

In her study of the different ways in which IRE is taught in schools, Uçan (2020) refers to confessional IRE as "teaching according to Islam" (Uçan, 2020, p. 2). In the approach of confessional IRE, Uçan states—following Al-Attas (1979)—all knowledge comes from God, while human beings are expected to receive this knowledge. The goal here is *tarbiyah*, the socialisation of the learner in Islam. The main teaching methods to achieve this objective are repetition and memorisation (see also Meyer, 2006, p. 71ff.). The focus lies on the delivery and transmission of knowledge—the knowledge of texts and shared Muslim practices. Uçan points to the difference with teaching methods based on a constructivist approach, which are commonly used in Western countries. In this approach, the pupils' autonomous religious development is the objective. A critical stance towards diversity—both within Islam and between different traditions—is understood as a condition *sine qua non* for the development of pupils' individual religiosity (Uçan, 2020, p. 4). Both of these educational goals, an autonomously developed individual religiosity and a critical stance, constitute a challenge for contemporary IRE according to Uçan. Inspired by the work of, among others, Bilgin (2007), Selçuk (2012, 2020) and Sahin (2013), Uçan introduces the concept of critical religious education (CRE), which encourages "pupils to engage in an attentive, intelligent, reasonable, and responsible learning process" that aims at the development of "new and powerful ways of perceiving an object or phenomenon by introducing students to varied accounts of it." According to Uçan, this means that CRE "can create possibilities for Muslim pupils to develop a deeper discernment of Islamic knowledge through the use of variation" (ibid., p. 12).

Teaching Materials for Sex Education in Islamic Schools

In 2019, two booklets were published for pupils of Islamic primary schools, which give information on topics like puberty, bodily changes, purity, relationships, sexuality, etc. A separate booklet was made for boys and girls (Claassen 2019a, 2019b).[3] The title of the workbook for girls is "*Help! Ik word volwassen. Mijn lichaam, mijn sieraad*" ["Dear Me! I'm Growing Up. My Body, My Pride"]. For boys, the title is "*Help! Ik word volwassen. Mijn lichaam, zo werkt dat dus*" ["Dear Me! I'm Growing Up. My Body, So That's How It Works"]. The two booklets are structured in a similar way (Claassen, 2019a, 2019b). Sources used for these two publications are the Qur'an, the Islamic jurisprudence treatise *Fiqh us Sunnah* by Sayyid Sabiq (1992), the Dutch info website *Mens en Gezondheid* ("Humanity and Health") and a 1993 report on youth prostitution in the city of Rotterdam *Het zal je zusje maar zijn* ("Imagine It Is Your Little Sister").

Dear Me! I'm Growing Up

The cover of the girls' booklet shows a girl wearing a colourful headscarf and backpack, looking at a daffodil on her shoulder, turning her head away

226 *Ina ter Avest*

from three boys in the background who are silhouetted in black against a grey-and-white drawing of a school. The boys' booklet shows two boys, one wearing a green hoodie and the other a green backpack, talking to each other, with two girls silhouetted in the background against a light green-and-white drawing of a school.

The preface to the booklets states that, for many years, information on sexuality was pussyfooted around in Islamic schools, with the result that teachers developed *ad hoc* lesson plans on this sensitive subject. Because of profound differences between the Islamic and the secular-society approach to sexuality, the publication of sound teaching material on sexuality was seen as a necessity to protect children from the pitfalls of the society they live in. It is stated that the content of the two booklets is published as a tool for the education of pupils into Muslim adults (ibid., p. 5). The point is made that, since the Islamic primary school is for most children the only environment where they can be clearly informed about these issues from an Islamic perspective, it is important to already touch upon the topic of sexuality in primary school. The content of the booklets conforms to the compulsory educational objectives formulated by the Ministry of Education for primary school children aged 10–12 and secondary school children aged 13–15. It is further explained that a separate booklet for girls and boys is published since in most schools boys and girls are separated for lessons on sexuality. The booklets are structured in the same way, except that in the girls' booklet, a section of one lesson is dedicated to "the monthly period and the religious duties that go with it," while for boys, the emphasis is on "issues that are particularly relevant for boys." Finally, it is emphasised that all lessons were piloted in Islamic primary schools and that comments from pupils, RE teachers and critical friends were incorporated into this second edition (ibid., p. 5).

The two booklets consist of 11 lessons: "Introduction," "Puberty," "Bodily Changes," "Purity and Hygiene," "More Things to Know about Growing Up," "*Zina* (Illicit Sexual Relations)," "How Babies Are Made (!)," "Relationships and Sexuality in Western Society and in Islam," "Homosexuality in Islam," "Not Feeling Well," "Loverboys and Prostitution: Don't Fall for It!"

Each chapter begins with an introduction to the theme. This is followed by information, interspersed with different texts: verses from the Qur'an, sayings by the prophet or his wife (from the *Hadith* and the *Sunnah*), or statements by Islamic scholars. The texts taken from tradition, in Arabic or Dutch, emphasise the Islamic foundations of the presented information, or function as illustrations of what was known in Islamic tradition long before social sciences scholars in the West recovered this knowledge. Assignments are given to the pupils to test their understanding of the presented information, to relate the information to their own lives, to initiate conversations with classmates, etc.

Puberty

The content of the second chapter—on puberty—differs for boys and girls. To begin with, hormonal activity is explained to boys and girls, followed by a fact-checking assignment: what are hormones, and what do they do? By way of a case study, 'falling in love' is discussed—for boys the example of a boy is considered, for girls the example of a girl. In an assignment, the pupils are invited to give advice to the character in the example.

For girls, this is followed by information about 'friends' on social media, accompanied by warnings about what could go wrong, summarised in five rules: (1) don't add 'friends' to your account that you don't know; (2) never show yourself (in real life or social media) in a way that would make you feel ashamed; (3) don't keep anything from your parents; (4) don't chat privately with boys, unless it is necessary for your schoolwork; and (5) take care of each other, and give good advice to your friends about social media.

For boys, the introductory part is followed by a paragraph on 'sexual attraction,' illustrated by the story of Yusuf. This is followed by seven lessons that must be retained: (1) sexual feelings are normal; (2) Yusuf's strong will is a gift from Allah; (3) it's difficult to say 'no' to something you might like (for example when a girl is inviting you); (4) don't get yourself into trouble, never isolate yourself with a girl; (5) illicit behaviour will bring you from bad to worse; (6) don't judge others—you never know what you might end up doing in a tempting situation; and (7) illicit behaviour is never so bad that Allah won't forgive you. The next paragraph focusses on the question, "Would you want your sister to be approached in that way?," referring to a newspaper article about the sexual harassment of a pop star. Here a link is made to key lessons that can be learned from Yusuf's story. This section is then followed by the paragraph on social media.

Bodily Changes

In the third chapter, "Bodily Changes," the focus for girls is on the monthly period and the religious duties that go with it; for the boys, the focus is on wet dreams. In the introduction to the fourth chapter on 'purity and hygiene,' both sexes are advised to remove pubic and armpit hair to prevent unpleasant smells, or to use a neutral deodorant, or—even better—"to mix 100 grams of coconut oil with 1 teaspoon of bicarbonate of soda and a few drops of lavender oil, and to rub a fingertip of this mixture into the armpit daily" (p. 30 boys, p. 34 girls). After these practical matters, the *Sunan Al-Fitrah* is introduced—cleanliness habits that fit the natural constitution of boys and girls. In both booklets, circumcision is presented as a hygienic measure (for boys) and as a culture-related (not religiously based!) habit (for girls). Subsequently, key concepts such as *ghusl* (full-boy ritual purification), *janabah* (state of ritual purity after sexual intercourse) and *mukallaf* (the accountable person) are introduced and the comprehension thereof tested.

228   *Ina ter Avest*

Chapter 5, entitled "More Things to Know about Growing Up," provides more in-depth knowledge about puberty. For boys and girls, additional information is given on the development of the other sex. Dress codes for men and women in regard to covering intimate parts of the body

> (*awrah*) is the main topic of this chapter, a topic covered in greater detail for girls than for boys. Chapter 7, "*Zina*, Illicit Sexual Relations," has the same content for boys and girls. AIDS is mentioned as one of the consequences of *zina*, being a sexually transmitted disease. Chapter 8, "Relationships and Sexuality in Western Society and in Islam,"

focusses on differences between Islamic values and secular-Western values. Giving in to illicit feelings is explained as the work of Shaitan.

Concrete Regulations

Chapter eight gives regulations on how to look for a partner, together with some advice: (1) think about the question: is this the person you want to share your life with?; (2) attach more importance to character than attractiveness; (3) is this a person you can trust and respect?; (4) don't get married just because you think the other will make you happy!; (5) if you want to marry a girl who has not been married before, you need the permission of her (Muslim) father. This chapter ends with the reassuring affirmation, "Don't worry, Allah already decided long ago who you will marry" (p. 68 for boys, p. 72 for girls). The title of Chapter 9 is "Homosexuality in Islam." This theme is introduced with the story of Loet. In both booklets, a case about a lesbian who is insulted invites pupils to talk about this issue and to relate this to what Islam says about "gay-bashing" (p. 27 for boys, page 78 for girls). The Qur'anic texts quoted here centre on the message not to use violence in case of severe disagreement. Chapter 10 focusses on "not feeling well" about your figure and appearance. Key here is the message that Allah created human beings as 'good.' In Islam, changing one's appearance or—in the case of drug and alcohol abuse—one's behaviour is condemned. The same prohibition applies to men who behave like women, and vice versa.

Don't Fall for It!

The theme of the final chapter is 'loverboys and prostitution,' whereby the subtitle contains a warning: 'don't fall for it!' The introduction in both booklets consists of two parts: the story of Doenia broaches the theme, followed by information about the percentage of young people in Rotterdam who have come into contact with loverboys or prostitution. A conversation in smaller groups about the pupils' own experiences and convictions, followed by a class discussion, is one of the assignments. The chapter—and the booklets as a whole—ends for boys and girls with a knowledge test on sexual development: knowledge derived from sayings of the prophet on biological facts (gender-specific) and from Islamic precepts on homosexuality.

In what follows, the described teaching materials become the object of reflection, taking the point of view of 'Islamic pedagogy'/'Islam *and* pedagogy.'

Reflection on "Dear Me! I'm Growing Up"

Striking are the covers of the booklets: a girl with a headscarf, turning her head away from a trio of boys, and two boys talking to each other, not paying attention to two girls. This sets the tone for a first impression of the material. An impression triggered by the drawings (what about the identification of girls who do not wear headscarves—for example, Alevi Muslimas?) but also by the subtitles of the booklets. For girls, their bodies are something to be proud of, to care for, like jewellery. For boys, their bodies are something of which they need to know how it works. The covers and subtitles give a first glimpse of the gender-specific approach used in the teaching material—for example, in Chapters 2 ("Puberty") and 3 ("Bodily Changes").

In the introductory chapter, an opposition is articulated between the Islamic and secular-Western attitude (here in the Netherlands) towards sexuality: "It cannot be but necessary to tell our children that Islam looks at this from a different angle, before they take as their norm what they see and hear around them" (p. 5). This position makes it understandable that sex education in these booklets is directly linked to the sayings of the prophet Muhammad, taken from the *Hadith* and the *Sunnah*. The texts, especially those on falling in love, are characterised by a cautionary tone.[4]

Taking a closer look at the didactics, the material shows a child-centred approach in establishing a relationship with the pupils' lifeworld: introducing newspaper items, inviting the pupils to discuss a topic, linking Qur'anic texts to their everyday lives. The focus is on texts from the Islamic tradition. The material is text-centred, testing the pupils' correct understanding of the presented information and/or Qur'anic texts (instruction, response, evaluative approach).

From the viewpoint of the *minimal* guidelines for sex education stipulated in the "Standards for Sexuality Education in Europe" and the corresponding educational criteria of the Dutch Ministry of Education, the "Dear Me!" teaching material meets the requirements of helping children to "discover their bodies, their feelings, what they like and don't like" and transmitting knowledge to them about "sexuality and diversity in the Dutch society, including diverse sexualities." Minimal sex education focusses on knowledge of facts—biological facts, facts about Islam and Western societies. *Maximal* sex education is about the whole person, including their consciousness of emotions evoked in various relationships (falling in love) and their solidarity and respect for the 'otherness' of others. Maximal sex education creates a space for bonds of mutual affection and love in relationships, including in sexual intercourse.[5] Maximal sex education is similar to Uçan's recommended

230 *Ina ter Avest*

approach in RE, called CRE, which she sees as a challenge for contemporary IRE teachers (Uçan, 2020, p. 11ff). Meeting this challenge is quite a task!

Recommendation

IRE teachers in Dutch Islamic primary schools have passed their primary school teacher exams and have a degree in theology. During their studies, they are not explicitly trained in classroom conversations on the tense issue of sex education. For (future) teachers active in this area of education, this chapter recommends personal reflection—in a systematic way—on their individual cognitive and affective relation with Islam and sex education. Such self-reflection creates resources for integrated sex education in the way this is offered in "*ZelfVerbinderOnderwijs*" (Self-Connector Education; Holman, 2020), an instrument based on the Valuation Theory and the Self-Confrontation Method (Hermans & Hermans-Jansen, 1995). Building on this, the exchange of these personal reflections with colleagues is recommended, in structural team conversations, with a focus on the religious, ethical and moral consequences of the school's vision and mission in concrete classroom situations—so-called Narrative Moral Consultations (Ter Avest, 2019).

To develop the dialogue competency of teachers in regard to sex education, both in the classroom and in teacher teams, Hargreaves and Fullan (2012) point to different 'capitals' a teacher must be able to use. They interpret capital as "one's own or a group's worth, particularly concerning assets that can be averaged to accomplish desired goals" (Hargreaves & Fullan, 2012, p. 1). Hargreaves and Fullan distinguish between different types of capital, emphasising the importance of decisional capital. Decisional capital can be defined as "the capacity to judge and judge well in situations of unavoidable uncertainty when the evidence or the rules aren't categorically clear" (ibid., p. 93). In order to deploy this capability, a moral compass—rooted in the Islamic world view, for example—is essential, a *sine qua non*. The significance of a moral compass brings us to the concept of normative professionalism (NP) (Van Ewijk & Kunneman 2013). The concept of NP points to a professionalisation that goes beyond the technical aspects of teaching, which provides room for professionals' personal values and norms, and their life orientation (Bakker & Montesano Montessori, 2016).

To make IRE professionals aware of their capabilities, deep reflection is recommended during teachers' first years of practice, focussing on their own and their colleagues' value orientation—a process of NP. This reflection, first of all, should explore their own positionality—as a teacher, as a religious person, as a loving and beloved person-in-context. In this reflection should be included the variety of 'voices' in the Islamic tradition on the issues of 'sex' and 'gender'—taking into account—as Selçuk suggests—the context and the origin of the respective texts (Selçuk, 2012). From a deeper understanding of these texts a moral compass develops. In addition, the teacher must be aware of the mission and vision of the school community (including both teachers and parents) in which s/he is appointed. Last but not least, s/he must be well informed about the cultural context and the accepted ideas about sex and its representations in the media. In deep reflection of this type, the complexity of the issue-in-context is taken seriously, and consciousness is reached about the role the different aspects play in the final normative positionality of the teacher in her/his classroom conversations. Taking up this challenge in modern teaching is a considerable task (!) for an interdisciplinary team of scholars and teachers alike.

Notes

1 The author would like to thank Stijn van Tongerloo (M.Phil) for the critical proofreading of the text.
2 The Dutch website www.seksuelevorming.nl offers 'examples of good practices' in primary schools for the subject of sex education.
3 The method caused a great deal of commotion in the Dutch educational world because of its negative tone in regard to Dutch views on sex education. This was reason enough for the Inspectorate to conduct a further investigation. In 2020, the Inspectorate declared that this method complies with the legal requirements of sex education in the Netherlands.
4 For a detailed account of love and sexuality, see Van Bommel (2003).
5 For this interpretation of minimal and maximal sex education, we follow McLaughlin's line of thought on minimal and maximal citizenship (McLaughlin 1992, p. 236-237; see also Miedema & Ter Avest 2011).

References

Al-Attas, S. M. (1979). *Aims and objectives of Islamic education*. Jeddah: Hodder & Stoughton.
Bakker, C., & Montesano Montessori, N. (2016). *Complexity in education. From horror to passion*. Rotterdam/Boston/Taipei: Sense Publishers.
Bilgin, B. (2007). Some thoughts on the contribution of religious education to the formation of a culture of tolerance and respect towards 'the other'. In: R. Kaymakcan & E. Leirvik (Eds). *Teaching for tolerance in Muslim majority societies*. Istanbul: Centre for Values Education, pp. 51–77.
Budak, B., Bakker, C., & ter Avest, I. (2018). Identity development of the two first Islamic primary schools in the Netherlands. In: J. Berglund (Ed.). *European Perspectives on Islamic education and public schooling*. Sheffield: Equinox, pp. 78–105.
Budak, B. (2022). The contribution of non-Muslim teachers to the identity of Islamic primary schools in the Netherlands. *Religions, Special Issue Islam in/and Education in the Netherlands* (Eds. Ter Avest & Budak).
Claassen, A. (2019a). *Help! Ik word volwassen. Mijn lichaam, mijn sieraad. Voorlichting over puberteit voor moslimmeisjes* [Dear me! I'm growing up. My body, my pride. Sex education for girls]. Amersfoort: ISBO.
Claassen, A. (2019b). *Help! Ik word volwassen. Mijn lichaam, zo werkt dat dus. Voorlichting over puberteit voor moslimjongens* [Dear me! I'm growing up. My body, so that's how it works. Sex education for boys]. Amersfoort: ISBO.
Hargreaves, A., & Fullan, M. (2012). *Professional capital. Transforming teaching in every school*. New York: Teachers College Press & Toronto: Ontario Principal's College.

232   Ina ter Avest

Hermans, H.J.M., & Hermans-Jansen, E. (1995). *Self-narratives. The construction of meaning in psychotherapy.* New York/London: The Guilford Press.

Holman, B. (2020). Focus in het mentorgesprek met de ZelfVerbinder Onderwijs [Focus in the mentoring conversation with self-connector education]. *Narthex, 20*(4).

Kaplick, P.M., & Skinner, R. (2017). The evolving 'psychology and Islam' movement. *European Psychologist, 22*(3), 198–204.

McLaughlin, T.H. (1992). Citizenship, diversity and education. A philosophical perspective. *Journal of Moral Education, 21*(3), 235–249.

Meijer, W.A.J. (2006). *Traditie en toekomst van het islamitisch onderwijs* [Tradition and future of Islamic education]. Amsterdam: Bulaaq.

Miedema, S., & ter Avest, I. (2011). In the flow to maximal interreligious citizenship education. *Religious Education, 106*(4), 410–424.

Sahin, A. (2013). *New directions in Islamic education. Pedagogy & identity formation.* Leicestershire: Kube.

Selçuk, M. (2012). How does the Qur'an see 'the people of the book'? An example of the communicative model of Islamic religious education. In: E. Bouayadi-van de Wetering & S. Miedema (Eds). *Reaching for the sky. Religious education from Christian and Islamic perspectives.* Amsterdam/New York: Rodopi, pp. 11–34.

Selçuk, M. (2020). *Teaching Islam within a diverse society* (taaruf). Pegem Akademi.

Ter Avest, I. (2009). Dutch children and their God. The development of the 'God' concept among indigenous and immigrant children in the Netherlands. *British Journal of Religious Education, 31*(3), 251–262.

Ter Avest, I. (2019). Provocative guidance: A practice of narrative leadership. In: H. Alma & I. Ter Avest (Eds.). *Moral and spiritual leadership in an age of plural moralities.* London/New York: Routledge, pp. 91–106.

Ter Avest, I., & Bakker, C. (2018). Islamic Education in the Netherlands. In: H. Daun & R. Arjmand (Eds). *Handbook of Islamic education.* Cham: Springer, pp. 873–887.

Ter Avest, I., Bakker, C., Bertram-Troost, G., & Miedema, S. (2007). Religion and Education in the Dutch Pillarized and Post-Pillarized Educational System: Historical Background and Current Debates. In: R. Jackson, S. Miedema, W. Weisse & J.-P. Willaime (Eds.). *Religion and education in Europe. Developments, contexts and debates.* Munster/New York/Munster/Berlin: Waxmann, pp. 203–221.

Uçan, A.D. (2020). *Improving the pedagogy of Islamic religious education in secondary schools. The role of critical education and variation theory.* New York/London: Routledge.

Van Bommel, A. (2003). *Islam, liefde en seksualiteit* [Islam, love and sexuality]. Amsterdam: Bulaaq.

World Health Organisation (2018). *International technical guidance on sexuality education.* https://www.who.int/publications/m/item/9789231002595

19 The Role of Supplementary Schools Education in Shaping the Islamic Identity of Muslim Youths in Europe

Mohammad Mesbahi

Introduction

In light of recent Muslim migration to Europe, an avalanche of studies on Muslim identity formation has been written. Also, literature on 'Islamic education' has increased, with many raising concerns about their impact on community cohesion and radicalisation. By exploring both topics of identity and education through a sample of published research, Islamic supplementary education is flagged as an area of concern, although research in this area is limited. Nevertheless, the potentiality of supplementary education to "enhance and improve learning outcomes" (Nwulu, 2015; p. 11) and "develop a positive sense of identity and belonging" (Evans & Gillan-Thomas, 2015, p. 7) is neglected. This failure is essentially because of the difference in the two education traditions, each with their own "aims, philosophical underpinning structures, pedagogies and learning process" (Berglund & Gent, 2018, p. 126). Thus, the intention behind this research is to fill this knowledge gap in line with the awakening theme of this book, and the questions that shape this study are as follows: what do Muslim pupils gain from their experiences in supplementary schools? What potential contribution can Muslim supplementary schools make to benefit the wider educational community?

This discussion is based on research that examines the supplementary educational provision by different Muslim ethnicities in the United Kingdom, indicative of Muslim community activities in Europe. By working with a series of Muslim schools that are linked through umbrella bodies, such as the Association of Muslim Schools and Muslim Council of Britain (MCB), this study highlights the discourse on supplementary education from "the insider's perspective." Considering the fundamental themes of institutional structure and individual actions, a case study is made and appropriately adapted. This methodological method offers a flexible and interpretive research approach to enable the understanding behind the pedagogy at such Muslim supplementary schools and also allows for reflections on the way pupils, parents and teachers view the provision and its enhancement. The presentation of this chapter will initially review the discourse of religion and identity within the literature, with a focus on the British Muslim perspective on education. Thereafter, it will address the issue of supplementary schooling, based on

DOI: 10.4324/9781003193432-22

234 *Mohammad Mesbahi*

surveys, interviews, workshops and reviewed documentation. By identifying the scale of the provision, the variety of purpose and the nature of pedagogy involved, this chapter analyses points of success and failure in educational structure for pupils within supplementary schools. The significance of this approach lies in the attempt to draw attention to the role traditional supplementary schools continue to play in shaping the Islamic identity of Muslim youths in Europe.

The Discourse of Religion and Identity

Islam is not limited to one particular region or centre based on its "intrinsic universality" which Islam shares with Judaism and Christianity (Hirschkind, 2001, p. 3). Subsequently, within the literature, there is the recognition that "Islam can be entirely re-territorialized" (Kahani-Hopkins & Hopkins 2002, p. 288), making the approach to its practice fundamentally imperative. This is particularly concerning for the European communities, considering that Europe is experiencing one of the most significant influxes of migrants and refugees in its history. In fact, according to the Pew Research Center, the Muslim share of Europe's total population as of mid-2016 was estimated to be 25.8 million (4.9% of the overall population), increasing from 19.5 million (3.8%) recorded in 2010. This figure is expected to increase to 14% of Europe's population by 2050 (Pew Forum, 2010; Pew Forum, 2017) in view of the high migration rates continuing. Nevertheless, religious profiling would be different across countries in Europe, and the levels of religious commitment and belief among the Muslim population would also vary. Other factors such as differences in fertility rates, the size of youth populations and the people switching faiths would also need to be taken into consideration (Pew Forum, 2015). Yet there is a growing body of research noting an increase in the prominence of religion as a 'key marker of identity,' particularly when religious groups are reconciling themselves with a secularist environment (Hashemi, 2009, p. 2).

Although the sense of religious identity can influence Muslims both positively and negatively, it has been the source of increased anxiety in Europe, with discourse around the "Muslim question" (Norton, 2020, p. ix), and the term 'Muslimness' is often used in the recent research literature. Such references consist of three separate yet inclusive categories: a person's own understanding of their Islamic identity, their association with the larger Muslim community and the visible display of practice of commitments to their faith within society (Shah, 2019, p. 344). However, religious identity shapes the daily lives of Muslims differently; it provides some Muslims in Europe with a "sense of belonging and self-worth" (Modood, 2005, p. 31), but for other 'secular Muslims' (Panjwani, 2017, p. 601), it may not be so salient. Moreover, Muslims "include people of many nations and colours, who speak many languages" (Meer & Modood 2009, p. 483), with differences in "social class, ethnicity, gender, sexuality, country of origin, educational attainment, language proficiency, occupation and many other factors" (Merry, 2018, p. 168). "Since the ethnic or the religious affiliation of Muslims, are not fixed, nor internally homogeneous, and not necessarily an easily identifiable entity," their ability to negotiate circumstances being encountered would also be different (Mesbahi, 2020, p. 32). For example, religious identity is regarded as more salient for the second- and third-generation European Muslims than other ethnic or regional affiliations. For them, "multiple identifications" are present and "different identifications would be prioritised within different situations" (McLoughlin, 1996, p. 227). Stakeholders within this study have reaffirmed this point, indicating that the crucial test for the Muslim community is to see whether the commitment to Islamic beliefs and practices is "maintained in a non-Muslim environment" particularly by the youth (Anwar, 1981, p. 17).

Consequently, the role of education is regarded as essential in the shaping of such religious identity for the next generation of Muslims. Thus, the issue of Muslimness within the educational context has emerged as the subject of intense suspicion and debate, often constructed as the 'complex problem' in Europe (Shah, 2016, p. 175). The growing significance of this issue has led to a 'religious turn' in educational debates in Europe. This is as a direct recognition of Islam's role in shaping the "discourses, social change, and practices" within a "variety of cultural contexts" (Panjwani & Moulin-Stożek, 2017, p. 519). Countries such as France with a large Muslim minority population have been contemplating radical steps in defence of secularism with proposals of allocating 'identification numbers' to Muslim children to ensure their attendance of secular schools and restricting their home-schooling (BBC, 2020). However, the capacity for European schools to support the needs of Muslim pupils and the extent to which secular education can attend to their identity needs is debatable. In light of the youthful demographic of Muslim communities, the educational discussion is regarded as 'a proxy' for the 'wider tensions' between Islam and the European society (Shah, 2016, p. 175). This is particularly evident because schools are envisaged as sites of "differentiation of identity," where the "interplay of class, lifestyle and taste" comes into full view (Ismail, 2004, p. 627).

British Muslims and the Educational Perspective

Within the European context, Britain is recognised as an "inclusive multi-faith country," with Muslims accounting for the second-largest religious group after Christianity (Mesbahi, 2020, p. 32). The large Muslim presence in Britain is "inevitably linked with the British Empire" (Samad, 2004, p. 2) and initially accommodated through an easier settlement process, although the recent influx has led to similar concerns, as elsewhere in Europe. The 2011 census[1] has shown there to be 2.7 million Muslims living in England and Wales, which equated to 4.8% of the total population (Census, 2011). This number is estimated to have increased to 6.3% of the total population in 2016 and is projected to reach 9.7% by 2050 in a zero-migration scenario (Pew Forum, 2017). Nonetheless in 2011, the British prime minister

236   *Mohammad Mesbahi*

declared the doctrine of 'multiculturalism' to have failed and proposed, thereafter, to abandon it altogether. Additionally, he instructed the Muslim population to embrace 'British values' (Cameron, 2011), raising the controversial issue of ethno-religious groups leading parallel lives, warning of Muslims failing to integrate with the wider society. An aspect that underlined this unease had been the youth issue. Since the 2011 census had shown approximately half of the Muslims to be under the age of 25 and a third under the age of 15 (Census, 2011), the "Muslim question within the educational context" (Modood, 2006, p. 37) has been tagged as alarming within the growing tensions over the Muslim integration into the British society. Added to this debate is the recent controversy around the 'Trojan Horse' affair, which makes reference to the suspicion of an Islamist plot to take over a series of Muslim majority state schools in Birmingham. Although the investigations that followed found "no evidence," the report maintained that there was still an "ideological threat" (Clarke, 2014, p. 95). This led to the Counter-Terrorism Security Act of 2015 that aimed to redefine the Muslim question around "liberal ideas of value and culture" in Britain (Miah, 2017, p. 5). In terms of education, the Act now requires all teachers operating in Britain to understand 'Prevent,' a mechanism to recognise pupil's vulnerability to radicalisation and know where to go to in order to report or seek further help (HM Government, 2015).

Muslim leaders in Britain, including those in the umbrella bodies of the schools involved, have highlighted the point that such 'secular perspective' by the government is not useful. We are reminded by stakeholders involved in this study that the approach taken by the British government complicates Muslim teachers' roles and their capacity to adopt 'impartial' or 'dialogical' pedagogical positions (Everington, 2014, p. 167). Furthermore, it questions their professionalism with the capacity to act as 'counter-terrorism agents' (Revell & Bryan, 2018, p. 63). The government has claimed to be aiming at creating "autonomous and critical individuals" but fails to approach "the divine" and excludes the "religious principles and priorities" (Nielsen, 2004, p. 58). Subsequently, their approach securitises Muslim identities and denies Muslims the capacity to incorporate Muslimness within their school context. We are also reminded by all schools visited that there is an "increase in vulnerability of the Muslim youth" to factors such as radicalisation and violent extremism, juvenile delinquency and gang crime and ethical concerns. Such undesirable outcomes of identity crisis reduce the impact of parental and community bonds more than ever before (Bellis, 2017, p. 41). Parents, in particular, are troubled by such complicated issues, seeking the use of supplementary education in the pursuit of inculcating good moral characters within their children during their formative years. The response by Muslim supplementary schools to the circumstances before them focusses on the use of religious reflective practice and the teachings of faith for accommodating such ethical and learning needs of the youth. However, such shaping and preserving of Islamic identity through supplementary schooling requires a realignment of the educational provision to include the modern theories

The Role of Supplementary Schools Education   237

of learning for managing pupil behaviour and highlights the importance of instructor professional development.

The Questions around Supplementary Schooling

Islamic education is a generic term, and the ambiguity with its use quite often revolves around the type of educational activity involved and its objective. These can be summarised into three categories that are readily available in Europe, although a fourth strand is also distinguishable. "Education of Muslims in their Islamic faith" refers to the community's efforts to educate the next generation by passing along the heritage of Islamic knowledge in educational settings where the emphasis is placed on religious instruction. "Education for Muslims which includes the religious and secular disciplines" refers to a mainstream faith-based school setting that embraces a much broader curriculum of both secular academic and religious instruction. "Education about Islam within a set curriculum" refers to education about Islam in a mainstream secular school setting often delivered as part of the religious studies subject using resources that serve as the medium for educating pupils about Islam. The fourth type, "education in an Islamic spirit and tradition," refers to the traditional concepts of the Islamic spirit of education, where knowledge is sought without making a distinction between religious and secular knowledge (Douglass & Shaikh, 2004, p. 7). The term 'religious school' also needs clarity; its use by Muslims can be summarised into three categories: the mainstream faith-based Muslim schools, the Islamic seminary schools—*darul uloom*—and the Muslim supplementary schools—*madrassa*. However, with literature, reference is made to such religious schools as Islamic schools and Muslim schools, but the terms are used interchangeably. Islamic schools are those aiming to define "the school ethos, curriculum and pedagogy through the traditional sources of Islamic knowledge." While Muslim schools are those with no reconstruction of the "educational philosophy or curriculum" but providing a provision of learning with an Islamic perspective to the content, conducive to Islamic standards of "dress, diet, and other religious observance" (Memon, 2019, p. 6). The debate around Islamic or Muslim schools in Europe has been polarised and essentially circles around parental choice and the Muslimness criteria. While Muslims point out the potential in promoting 'diversity and tolerance' alongside their spiritual environment, the host communities often view them with suspicion of their social impacts and of "segregating young people" (Ichijo, 2014, p. 101). Others have argued that the failure to address ethnic diversity in mainstream schooling is the cause of "a disproportionately high percentage of children from ethnic minority backgrounds being allocated to lower streams" (Gillborn & Gipps, 1996, p. 80), thus adding to the popularity of these faith-based schools which focus their provision in catering for the community. Nevertheless, the Western concern is pronounced with regards to Islamic or Muslim schools, mainly because they "operate in the independent sector," and therefore are not subject to the same 'oversight' as

238 *Mohammad Mesbahi*

state-funded educational institutions (Cherti & Bradley, 2011, p. 14). The discourse of Islamic, cultural and linguistic identities has placed particular scrutiny on the role that such schools may play in "facilitating the radical-isation of young Muslims towards violent extremism" (Cherti & Bradley, 2011, p. 1).

The Muslim supplementary school provision, *madrassa*, is traditionally located within or very near to a mosque, operating in the evenings or at weekends often by registered charities, although informal supplementary classes are possible and commonly found in Europe. The *madrassas* teach either a range of mother tongues and doctrines of faith or both by the tradi-tional methods of textbooks and memorisation and are frequently delivered by the clergy—*imams* or volunteers. There is no accurate data on the num-ber of *madrassas* in the United Kingdom or the number of young Muslims attending, but a report on British Muslim faith supplementary schools by the Institute for Public Policy Research in 2011 has used an estimate of 2,000 *madrassas*, with over 250,000 Muslim children attending (Cherti & Bradley, 2011, p. 3). There is no doubt that these numbers, if accurate, have increased, but their structure remains the same. Recently, *madrassas* have used volunteers who also teach in the mainstream schools, thereby an opportunity has arisen for utilising modern teaching methods within these traditional settings. The suspicion with regards to Islamic or Muslim schools is particularly evident for the *madrassas* because, unlike the mainstream Muslim faith-based schools that operate under regulatory supervision and have limitations on access, the supplementary Muslim schools do not. These are formed based on the community's needs and function based on the prin-ciple of inclusion of all, operating in the traditional format. Subsequently, these are viewed in Britain with a sense of 'an anomaly' within ethnic edu-cation (Reay and Mirza, 1997, p. 478), and their "traditional pedagogical methods and discipline" are being openly questioned (McLoughlin, 2011, p. 605).

The *Madrassas* in the United Kingdom

The work behind this chapter is based on a detailed study that benefitted from access to over 50 *madrassas* from a range of ethnic backgrounds through the support of their umbrella organisations. This provided an opportunity to survey and coordinate discussions and workshops with former and current pupils and parents, as well as teachers and volunteers. Importantly, over 90% of Muslim supplementary schools that were involved operated either from or linked to a local mosque. This is representative of the overall picture of *madrassas* in the United Kingdom; the MCB has indicated "94% of mosques in England and Wales providing some kind of education for young peo-ple" (Cherti & Bradley, 2011, p. 18). The *madrassas* set up is governed by the religious institutes for the sole purpose of teaching the Qur'an, Islam and basic Arabic language. However, the study also constituted just under 10% of Muslim supplementary schools that were run by volunteers or set up by a religious or cultural charity that are crucially outside the mosque in a mainstream school location or a local community centre. These were set up independently and regarded as more culturally oriented and geared towards the teaching of mother languages, alongside religious and ethical studies. This study did not involve informal classes held in people's homes, despite interest in this provision increasing, particularly by migrants. The range and size of *madrassas* encountered differed, but the overwhelming majority could be considered as large, with over 100 pupils attending each week. These often-convened classes from the youngest to the oldest by dividing pupils into single-sex classes with their own teachers; females teach the girls and male teachers teach the boys, but more mixing of sexes occurred in the culturally oriented schools or at an early age. The classes were not always arranged according to age group, but at times, depending on the subject or the institute, they were separated according to the pupils' abilities in the Qur'an or Arabic. A flexibility approach catered for the case of pupils who are learning either more quickly or more slowly than their peers in each group. Within the *madrassas* run by the mosques, a learning circles arrangement was in place in which the child sits directly on the carpet behind a wooden bench Qur'an-stand, and delivery was often in the mother languages. For other teaching locations, a chair and desk were used to provide the main context of learning similar to the mainstream school settings, and the delivery was regularly in English. Other than traditional textbooks, which are strongly oriented towards the teaching of Islam, there is an insufficiency of other teaching material, with little or no access to digital resources and computers. Over 80% of *madrassas* involved in this study used the *imams* to teach or required their teachers to have recognised theological training. However, the Qualified Teacher Status (QTS) was not a requirement, but over 20% of teachers had professional teaching qualifications, essentially because they also taught in the mainstream faith-based school for which QTS would be a requirement. A minority of institutions commented that there are limits to the extent to which they can demand qualifications because they depend on voluntary teachers. Additionally, there were a small fraction of *imams* who also possessed British academic and professional qualifications.

Within the *madrassas*, teachers taught all the pupils in the class as a whole, with occasional direct addressing of pupils, but the use of differentiated small groups within a class was less prevalent if not rare. However, the physical layout of the classroom environment enabled teachers to also call or address pupils individually to sit before them at the front. This one-to-one, individual contact between the student and the teacher, similar to the memorisation requirements, are 'classical' forms of learning and transmission of knowledge (Berglund & Gent, 2018, p. 129). Pupils were frequently given homework based on textbooks or memorisation of text but returned homework was not always checked by teachers. Pupils complained of being overwhelmed by homework from both their mainstream schools and the *madrassa*, subsequently failing to complete them due to time constraints. Within classes, the teachers often tested pupils on their progress; this is based on a policy of using tests, grading, competitions and rewards for 'motivating pupils,' particularly for the memorisation of the Qur'an (Cherti & Bradley, 2011, p. 44). All *madrassas* involved the parents in their pupils' learning processes and development; this was done through formal and informal channels for communication. This reflects other research that has identified 'parental involvement' and 'community links to parents' as a positive influence of supplementary school education (Cabrera & Leyendecker, 2017, p. 184). Over 90% of parents noted the *madrassas'* ethos of curriculum positively impacting upon their children's behaviour and self-esteem, but around 50% noted that the ability to develop academic reasoning was not a priority at their school, and its occurrence depended greatly on the subject, the teaching material and the professional ability of the teachers involved.

A clear distinction was made by all concerned between those teachers teaching entirely through memorisation and storytelling and those encouraging critical thinking about the material being taught. Almost all pupils in this study indicated their preference for *madrassas* that incorporate the modern approach to learning because they tend to engage all pupils in the teaching-learning process. Likewise, all teachers involved with mainstream education, and over 50% of teachers not involved, indicated the same preference. The motivation for such an approach was regarded as essential by teachers because they sought to go beyond memorisation and create a culture of learning. Teachers also benefit from peers with QTS who can support them based on their working experience in mainstream education by being introduced to new skills or applications. Teachers suggested that the use of the modern approach to learning empowered the pupils to make their own decisions, be respected as individuals and be trusted with personal responsibility. However, there was hesitation to use such an approach that involved outside bodies for the professional training within the *madrassas* in fear of a move away from the traditional approach; the modern pedagogy of secular mainstream schools is seen by some clergy as oppositional to the *madrassa's* ethos, and counter-resistances can also be anticipated at secular mainstream schools. Also, there was alarm over the possible involvement with the Prevent mechanism and its requirements, which complicated the teacher's role. For pupils, parents and the teaching staff, there is no doubt that the *madrassas'* achievements could be enhanced by access to modern teaching techniques, resources and pedagogies. Nevertheless, professional development of teachers can provide the *madrassa* with an understanding of the countless ways of benefitting from such facilitated learning. Moreover, the successful learning outcomes set by dedicated Muslim teachers for their pupils would in turn provide better Muslim youth identity formation. Facilitated student learning is not just a set of strategies and tools but also an approach that addresses ways teachers could encourage pupils to learn and absorb information in ways that are meaningful and relevant to them and their Muslim identity. This complements rote memorisation with critical thinking, comprehensive understanding, imaginative learning and appreciation for subtlety. These valuable strategies support and encourage students to learn for themselves and

The Role of Supplementary Schools Education   241

provide them with tools that will benefit them for the rest of their lives as they encounter the many hurdles they will face in Europe as Muslims.

Conclusion

Discourses on the integration of minority ethnic communities such as the Muslims are sprinkled throughout the literature on religious identity. British Muslims have been confronted by two challenges, one of "commonality, cohesion and integration" and the other of "fluidity, multiplicity and hybridity" (Meer & Modood, 2009, p. 490). The provision of supplementary schools has made a unique contribution towards addressing the requirements of such challenges. The discussions throughout this chapter have provided a wider understanding of this provision through the scope of an extensive participative study that included a wide variety of Islamic supplementary education in the United Kingdom. Subsequently, it is concluded that British Muslim youth have gained positively from their experiences of *madrassa* supplementary schools. The European education systems are at times explicitly oriented towards Christianity or are comparatively secular education. Thus, the *madrassas* are immensely important to Muslims residing in Europe, particularly with regards to the complex topic issue of Muslim identity formation.

Nonetheless, stakeholders have requested such *madrassas* to broaden their curriculum and work with mainstream schools to strengthen this valuable provision. Considering the inclusivity and diversity apprehensions, Muslim supplementary schools are also regarded as having a high potentiality of contributing extensively to the wider educational community. However, this again requires the *madrassas* to link and collaborate with mainstream schools, particularly when many are faith-based, and identify with the Muslim community's sensitivities. Additionally, instructor professional development within such institutions is deemed to be essential, and there are now ample opportunities for *madrassas* to join support networks in order to expand the way they operate and improve their teaching quality and instructor professional development. It is thereby concluded that the understanding of strategies in facilitating learning within *madrassas* would provide the Muslim community with choice, variation, connection, conversation and better use of available resources. This forms as a key indicator for a purposeful education programme, enabling the shared and cumulative transmission of knowledge, which in turn improves the teaching practice and delivery while addressing Muslim identity concerns. Partnerships and enhanced communication between *madrassas* and mainstream schools could help everyone concerned and lessen the lacuna that is regularly referred to within the discourse around religion and identity. Moreover, it could standardise the pedagogy and curriculum of *madrassas* by making them contextually relevant to today's youth and provide them with the necessary skills to handle a range of modern-day issues. Finally, the COVID-19 pandemic requirements that were faced during the last couple of years further highlighted the need

242   *Mohammad Mesbahi*

for the *madrassas* to move forward from their traditional stance. The digital availability of teaching materials, resources and support has been proven to be the pivotal factor for the continued existence of *madrassas*, which are greatly valued by the Muslim community in Europe for the shaping and preserving of their Islamic identity.

Note

1 Censuses were taken every ten years, 2001, 2011 and 2021. Although the Census has been taken, its results have not yet been published, possibly due to the COVID-19 pandemic problems.

References

Anwar, M. (1981). Young Muslims in Britain: Their educational needs and policy implications. In M.W. Khan (ed.), *Education and society in the Muslim World.* (pp. 100–121). London: Hodder and Stoughton.

BBC. (2020). *France's macron issues 'republican values' ultimatum to Muslim leaders.* London: British Broadcasting Corporation. Retrieved on 19 November 2020, from http://www.bbc.com/news/amp/world-europe-55001167

Bellis, M. A. (2017). *Preventing violence, promoting peace: A policy toolkit for preventing interpersonal, collective and extremist violence.* London: Commonwealth Secretariat. Retrieved from http://www.wales.nhs.uk/sitesplus/documents/888/Preventing%20Violence%20Main%20Report.pdf

Berglund, J., and Gent, B. (2018). Memorization and focus: Important transferables between supplementary Islamic education and mainstream schooling. *Journal of Religious Education,* 66(2), 125–138.

Cabrera, N. J., and Leyendecker, B. (2017). *Handbook of positive development of minority children and youth.* New York: Springer.

Cameron, D. (2011). *PM's speech at the Munich security conference* (Delivered on the 5 February 2011). London: The Prime Minister's Office. Retrieved from http://www.number10.gov.uk/news/pms-speech-at-munich-security-conference

Census.(2011).*ReligioninEnglandandWales2011.*London:OfficeforNationalStatistics. Retrieved from https://www.ons.gov.uk/peoplepopulationandcommunity/culturalidentity/religion/articles/religioninenglandandwales2011/2012-12-11

Cherti, M., and Bradley, L. (2011). *Inside madrassas: Understanding and engaging with British-Muslim faith supplementary schools.* London: Institute for Public Policy Research. Retrieved from https://www.ippr.org/files/images/media/files/publication/2011/11/inside-madrassas_Nov2011_8301.pdf

Clarke, P. (2014). *Report into allegations concerning Birmingham schools arising from the 'Trojan horse' letter.* London: Her Majesty's Stationary Office. Retrieved from https://assets.publishing.service.gov.uk/government/uploads/system/uploads/attachment_data/file/340526/HC_576_accessible_-.pdf

Douglass, S. L., and Shaikh, M. A. (2004). Defining Islamic education: Differentiation and applications. *Current Issues in Comparative Education,* 7(1), 5–18.

Evans, D., and Gillan-Thomas, K. (2015). *Supplementaryschools.* London: Paul Hamlyn Foundation. Retrieved from https://www.phf.org.uk/wp-content/uploads/2015/05/PHF-supplementary-schools-analysis-final-report-alt-image.pdf

The Role of Supplementary Schools Education 243

Everington, J. (2014). Hindu, Muslim and Sikh religious education teachers use of personal life knowledge: The relationship between biographies, professional beliefs and practice. *British Journal of Religious Education*, 36 (2), 155–173.

Gillborn, D., and Gipps, C.V. (1996). *Recent research on the achievements of ethnic minority pupils*. London: Her Majesty's Stationery Office.

Hashemi, N. (2009). *Islam, secularism, and liberal democracy: Toward a democratic theory for Muslim societies*. Oxford: Oxford University Press.

Hirschkind, C. (2001). Civic virtue and religious reason: An Islamic counter public. *Cultural Anthropology*, 16(1), 3–34.

HM Government. (2015). *Counter-terrorism and security act 2015*. London: Her Majesty's Stationary Office. Retrieved from http://www.legislation.gov.uk/ukpga/2015/6/contents/enacted

Ichijo, A. (2014). Religion in education: The faith debates in contemporary Britain. In M. Topić and S. Sremac (eds.), *Europe as a multiple modernity: Multiplicity of religious identities and belonging*. (pp. 92–108). Cambridge: Cambridge Scholars Publishing.

Ismail, S. (2004). Being Muslim: Islam, Islamism and identity politics. *Government and Opposition*, 39(4), 614–631.

Kahani-Hopkins, V., and Hopkins, N. (2002). Representing British Muslims: The strategic dimension to identity construction. *Ethnic and Racial Studies*, 25(2), 288–309.

McLoughlin, S. (1996). *In the name of the umma: Globalisation, race relations and Muslim identity politics in Bradford*. (Vol. 1, pp. 206–228). The Netherlands: Kok Pharos, Kampen.

McLoughlin, S. (2011), United Kingdom. In J. Nielsen, et al. (eds.). *Yearbook of Muslims in Europe*, (Vol. 3, pp. 595–618). Leiden: Brill.

Meer, N., and Modood, T. (2009). The multicultural state we're in: Muslims, 'multiculture' and the 'civic re-balancing' of British multiculturalism. *Political Studies*, 57(3), 473–497.

Merry, M.S. (2018). Indoctrination, Islamic schools, and the broader scope of harm. *Theory and Research in Education*, 16(2), 162–178.

Mesbahi, M. (2020). The Mosaic of Muslim identity in Britain. In N. Khanfar (ed.), *Islam, Muslims in Britain: Radicalisation, deradicalisation, and human rights* (pp. 24–40). London: Center for Arab Progress.

Miah, S. (2017) *Muslims, schooling and security: Trojan horse, prevent and racial politics*. London: Palgrave Macmillan.

Modood, T. (2005). *Multicultural politics: Racism, ethnicity, and Muslims in Britain*. Edinburgh: Edinburgh University Press.

Modood, T. (2006). British Muslims and the politics of multiculturalism. In T. Modood, A. Triandafyllidou and R. Zapata-Barrero, *Multiculturalism, Muslims and citizenship* (pp. 37–56). London: Routledge.

Memon, N.A. (2019). *A history of Islamic schooling in North America: Mapping growth and evolution*. London: Routledge.

Nielsen, J. (2004) *Muslims in Western Europe*. Edinburgh: Edinburgh University Press.

Norton, A. (2020). *On the Muslim question* (Vol. 19). Princeton: Princeton University Press.

Nwulu, S. (2015). *Beyond the school gates*. Developing the roles and connections of supplementary schools. London: The Royal Society for Arts.

244 *Mohammad Mesbahi*

Panjwani, F. (2017). No Muslim is just a Muslim: Implications for education. *Oxford Review of Education*, 43(5), 596–611.

Panjwani, F., and Moulin-Stozek, D. (2017). Muslims, schooling and the limits of religious identity. *Oxford Review of Education*, 43 (5), 519–523.

Pew Forum. (2010). *Global religious futures*. Washington, D.C: Pew Research Center. Retrieved from http://www.globalreligiousfutures.org/religions/muslims

Pew Forum. (2015). *Religious composition by country, 2010–2050*. Washington, D.C: Pew Research Center. Retrieved from https://www.pewforum.org/2015/04/02/religious-projection-table/

Pew Forum. (2017). *Europe's growing Muslim population*. Washington, D.C: Pew Research Center. Retrieved from http://www.pewforum.org/2017/11/29/europes-growing-muslim-population/

Reay, D., and Mirza, H. S. (1997). Uncovering genealogies of the margins: Black supplementary schooling. *British Journal of Sociology of Education*, 18(4), 477–499.

Revell, L., and Bryan, H. (2018). *Fundamental British values in education: Racialisation, national identity and Britishness*. Bingley: Emerald Publishing.

Samad, Y. (2004). Muslim youth in Britain: Ethnic to religious identity. Muslim Youth in Europe: *Typologies of Religious Belonging and Sociocultural Dynamics*. Edoardo Agnelli Centre for Comparative Religious Studies.

Shah, S. (2016) *Education, leadership and Islam: Theories, discourses and practices from an Islamic perspective*. London: Routledge.

Shah, S. (2019). "I Am a Muslim First…" Challenges of Muslimness and the UK state schools. *Leadership and Policy in Schools*, 18(3), 341–356.

20 Crafting a Strategy to Assess the Learning of Islamic Studies in Elementary Schools

Tahraoui Ramdane and Merah Souad

Introduction

While pedagogy can be simply defined as the art of instruction, assessment and evaluation are essential components to judge the attainment of instruction. Along with planning and teaching, assessment is generally considered one of the three aspects of instruction. No doubt that during teaching and learning processes, the instructor needs to know whether students are learning. The latter also needs to find out how they are doing and how to use the information to study more effectively (Brookhart, 1999). Anyway, evaluation is commonly known as "a process in which the teacher uses information derived from many sources to arrive at a value judgement" (Burden & Byrd, 2019, p. 318), and assessment is "a process used by teachers and students to recognise and respond to student's learning in order to enhance that learning during the learning" (Cowie & Bell, 1999, p. 32, as cited in William, 2011, p. 9). Assessment is also perceived as a constructed, systematic and criteria-based process of using empirical data on the knowledge, skill, attitudes and beliefs to assess learning in general and students' performance in particular which means that assessment requires gathering evidence of student's performance over a period of time to improve student's learning, and evaluation is the final outcome because it occurs when a mark is assigned after the completion of a task, test, quiz, lesson or learning activity (Islamic Studies Teacher, 2012). In every school subject/course, evaluation and assessment are used to determine the degree to which educational aims have been attained. They are used as indicators to identify where learners are in their learning, where they need to go and how to get there. Practising this in the classroom "reveals a complex weave of activities involving pedagogic style, student-teacher interaction, self-reflection (teacher and student), motivation and a variety of assessment processes" (Gardner, 2012, p. 3). It is worth mentioning that learning assessment is usually conducted as a formal classroom-based assessment that emphasises the grading function of evaluation (Crooks, 1988, as cited in William, 2011, p. 5) and applies what has been learnt.

Islamic studies[1] are usually criticised for being stagnant, dormant and incapable of coping with educational transformations taking place in the

DOI: 10.4324/9781003193432-23

contemporary world. Critics of the curriculum of Islamic studies highlighted that it is theoretical and neglects other activities related to learners' lives. Furthermore, attention is focussed solely on cognitive aspects of learning, neglecting individual differences among learners, limiting students' tasks in the reception of information and passing the exams. As such, learners are rendered as passive recipients who are unable to carry out any external activity that helps them develop the spirit of innovation and creativity. The curriculum of Islamic studies is developed in advance, and instructors are restricted by what is stated, hence unable to carry out any additional activity that might guide learners towards innovation and connect with the local environment in which they live.

As a result, most Islamic studies teachers lack fundamental pedagogical skills of planning and delivering lessons, as well as proper evaluation and assessment of students. They are also criticised for failing to nurture students with much-needed skills. such as creative and critical thinking (Rosnani, 2005; Ramadan, 2004, as cited in Ashaari et al., 2012, p. 619). This criticism carries further weight in the area of assessment and evaluation, perhaps because similar to other components of Islamic education, it suffered—due to historical, political and economic factors in the last two or three centuries—from acute deficiencies and missed the chance to benefit from tremendous developments in the area of instruction and educational assessment.

Taking the condition of instruction in Islamic education into account, the purpose of this chapter is basically to craft a strategy for assessment and evaluation to be used in the Islamic studies subject at the elementary level. It also explains the necessity of tailoring different assessment and evaluation tools for the different segments that make this elementary school subject. Simultaneously, the chapter highlights the uniqueness of the evaluation and assessment's aims of this subject.

General Objectives of Teaching Islamic Studies in Elementary Schools

They can be divided into three major domains:

1. Cognitive: which seeks to cultivate learners' minds with factual, conceptual, procedural and metacognition of knowledge that allows them to process, remember, understand, apply, analyse and evaluate issues related to *aqidah* (Islamic creed), *fiqh* (Islamic jurisprudence), *akhlaq* (ethics and character) and the Islamic world view in general.
2. Affective: which aims to nurture noble human emotions and motivations in the learners, such as sentiments of religiosity, devotion, loyalty and belonging, as well as developing new human emotions approved by Islam such as selflessness, kindness, generosity and every attitude or value that aims to benefit the individual and community and fight unwanted emotions, attitudes and values not sanctioned by the religion.

Crafting a Strategy to Assess the Learning   247

3. Behavioural: by accustoming learners to the desired good habits and applying them in their lives and by training them to memorise parts of the Holy Qur'an and the *sunnah* of the Prophet (pbuh), which would ultimately develop their positive religious attitudes so that they adhere to the religion encompassing all matters of their lives.

Accordingly, the objectives of teaching Islamic studies at the elementary level can be divided as follows:

1. Producing learners who worship and fear Allah by conviction
2. Educating learners to attain virtues and piety
3. Achieving happiness in this world and the hereafter
4. Teaching learners the principles of Islam
5. Nurturing learners' righteousness so that they can positively interact with their social environment and value social responsibility
6. Educating the personalities of learners mentally, spiritually, emotionally, physically and socially
7. Refining morals and character of learners by monitoring their behaviour in accordance with the teachings of Islam
8. Developing learners' abilities to cultivate the earth and utilise what is in it for their benefit
9. Constructing human universal values and love towards mankind that Islam instils in the hearts of its adherents by respecting others and dealing with them in dignity and honour regardless of colour, gender or faith

Characteristics of the Islamic Studies Teacher in Elementary School

Instructors of Islamic studies should have the following characteristics:

1. Strong-willed, intelligent, objective, fair, firm, self-confident, active, social and considerate of circumstances and motives of others
2. A cultured, broad-minded person who has interests in reading, arts and culture in general
3. Physically fit, free from certain defects and disabilities; has a clear voice; and possesses adequate knowledge of the conditions and problems of the society
4. Likes to work with his students and form a good relationship with them, as well as with colleagues, superiors and members of the local community outside the school
5. Qualified and well versed in the subjects he teaches

Evaluation and Assessment in Islamic Studies

Islamic studies is a sensitive subject of the elementary school curriculum, and offering it as a school subject engages students with a range of complex, challenging, alien, provocative information, morals and values. Questions such as what should students learn, with what objectives, via which pedagogy, how assessment should be conducted, are among many crucial issues of concern for stakeholders (educational managers, teachers, students and parents). While in other subjects, students acquire different skills and information related to numeracy and literacy in a fairly neutral fashion, in Islamic studies, students are theoretically able to formulate personal aesthetical, ethical, epistemological, metaphysical and logical convictions and beliefs according to the guidelines of the Islamic world view. Still, issues may arise about which values should be prioritised and how they should be taught. Because Islamic pedagogies are transformative with the ultimate goal of changing people (Sahin, 2018), the primary goal of the Islamic studies curriculum should be to guide learners in internal self-investigations towards appropriating this vision. The transformative quality of Islamic pedagogies suggests that they may be catalysts of learning and developing, that ways of teaching and learning are themselves educational and may be as important as what is taught (Sahin, 2018). What is certain, however, is that teaching the subject of Islamic studies requires maximum effort and adequate preparation from instructors. It also requires them not only to master the content of Islamic studies subjects but, therein, prior to mastering original Islamic pedagogy of teaching those subjects including the use of best methods of assessment. A test in an Islamic pedagogy is, first and foremost, a means for the student to become aware of his or her accomplishments and challenges. As a result, students view tests and exams not as a threat challenging their performance but rather as an opportunity to identify their areas of weaknesses to overcome them (Ajem & Memon, 2011, pp. 45–46). Students who learn Islamic studies in an elementary school are not expected to only memorise and understand concepts; rather, they are also required to internalise all that they learn to strengthen their religious worship and practice. For instance, in subjects of Qur'an and prophetic traditions (*hadith*), learning objectives are not limited to the lower thinking order of memorising some designated portions of the Holy Qur'an or recalling certain bodies of prophetic sayings, deeds and approvals. Rather, developing a comprehensive understanding of those texts by formulating, analysing, evaluating and creating values that can be reflected and applied in different situations. In other words, to elevate students' thinking to a higher order, which involves internalisation and categorisation of related knowledge into the abstract that feeds reason and practicality that can guide their morality and way of life. After designing the curriculum of Islamic studies, teachers should be trained about the fundamental difference between conventional pedagogies which can fit easily with other academic subjects in the school and special pedagogies which are compatible with the special nature of Islamic studies subject. For instance, evaluation and assessment styles in Islamic studies will necessitate a clear understanding of two main contributing factors. First, the implemented teaching pedagogies and teachers' selection of the strategies and techniques in disseminating lessons' content to their students. Looking at the teaching of Islamic studies and based on the outcomes of some research (Boyle, 2006; Wagner & Lotfi,

Crafting a Strategy to Assess the Learning 249

1980; Memon, 2021), there is a heavy emphasis on conventional methods of teaching based on memorisation and direct indoctrination. Islamic studies teachers are usually criticised for failing to effectively face contemporary educational challenges and contending with negative rejectionist resistance (Ashaari et al., 2012). Second, the nature of different sections that make up this course, considering that every section needs a special way of assessment. It is customary that school subjects consist of *aqidah* (creed), *fiqh* (Islamic jurisprudence), *adab* and *akhlaq* (Islamic morality), *sirah* (prophetic biography and life) and Qur'anic studies that include *tahfiz* (memorisation) and *tafsir* (exegesis). In this regard, assessment styles adapted by Islamic studies teachers should be tailored according to the nature of each religious subject and also according to pedagogies used in teaching these subjects. As stated earlier, much research highlighted the fact that Islamic studies teachers confined instruction of religious subjects to rote teaching, indoctrination and preaching which rendered their methods of delivery outdated and bare (Ramdane & Merah, 2020; Tan, 2012). Similarly, evaluation and assessment methods employed by Islamic studies teachers are also outdated and rely on memory testing as the main tool. Therefore, Islamic studies teachers have to adopt new approaches in teaching, evaluation and assessment. They have to shift their minds and accept that evaluation is not a single rigid and unchangeable method but rather is a flexible decision that is necessitated by the nature of the subject and existing conditions in the learning process in the classroom. They have to accept that assessment should be performed continuously to determine students' academic attainment, progress and development and also to generate their enthusiasm for learning. Besides, it is necessary to realise that evaluating learning in Islamic studies is a process that covers learners' spiritual and social attitudes, knowledge, morals, skills and other competencies. Because what matters the most is that students show what is deemed the right attitude (Kristiawan et al., 2016) and demonstrate a strong desire and high commitment to understand and apply Islamic teachings (Mawardi & Supadi, 2018, p. 213). Drawing on available literature and current practices, the following aspects of learning should be assigned different evaluations according to each one's sought learning outcomes.

Evaluating Information

This type of evaluation refers to the process of measuring and judging 'what to know' in the area of Islamic studies. In evaluating information, Islamic studies instructors seem to have a long list of various assessment tools with different formats and styles. Timed and untimed written tests, open books tests, cooperative or individual assignments, factual and high-order tests, etc., are a few examples to mention here. Assessing information varies from recalling facts to creating new ideas. No doubt that "all learning implies that students retain the information and ideas they acquire; that is the heart of the education process. Memory is needed for students to possess knowledge and to comprehend, apply, analyse, synthesise and evaluate" (Burden

& Byrd, 1999, p. 296). Generally, memorisation is looked upon in the West as an instrument to indoctrinate memorisers of Islamic religious education into the practices and beliefs of Islam (MacDonald, 1911). This is a notion that is too simple and does not accurately represent the role of memorisation in Islamic schooling (Boyle, 2006). It is clearly reflected in the type of assessment Islamic studies teachers usually opt for. Most—if not all—formal written assessments, including tests, quizzes and examinations, are usually designed to test students' memories and their ability to recall information. In certain Islamic studies subjects, such as the Qur'an, assessing information seems legitimate and effective. For instance, assessing learners' retention of portions or even the entire Qur'an can still be associated with the cognitive domain, although not in the Western sense of being able to understand and explain it but in the sense of being able to recite it. Other Islamic studies subjects which require some level of memorisation assessment include *hadith* (prophetic traditions) and *sirah* (prophetic biography). However, not the same can be applied in subjects such as *aqidah* (Islamic creed), *fiqh* (Islamic jurisprudence) or *akhlaq* (ethics and character) in which students' assessment should focus on cognitive, affective and behavioural domains.

Evaluating the Practise of Religious Rituals

In Islamic studies, 'knowing what' and 'knowing how' are crucial objectives. Students should learn all necessary information and understand both the importance and rationale of *ibadah* (worshipping rituals) before practising them. Once theoretical and practical learning is attained, students' performance on 'how to do' should be conducted. Studies have shown that Islamic studies teachers are still lacking in assessing this aspect. For instance, in a study conducted in Indonesia titled "Teachers' Unpreparedness in Carrying Out Islamic Education Learning Using the Revised 2013 Curriculum in Elementary School," one of the major findings stated, "Islamic Education (PAI) teachers are not ready to conduct lesson assessments. It is caused by the complexity of the existing assessment flow where it includes aspects that are assessing both the fields of knowledge, attitudes and practices" (Husna et al., 2020, p. 1524).

At an early age, elementary students should be able to master the basic rituals that make them practising Muslims. In the Islamic tradition, learning how to pray was always the first ibadah the Muslim family or the school takes care of. Islamic studies teachers should train their students how to perform salah, ablution and doing zikr (repetition of the name of God or His attributes). In this aspect, teachers should observe their students, encourage and guide them by using individual appraisal because students differ in their performance due to their prior knowledge and family background. As for the steps of assessing students' ritual practices, first, teachers should know what it is that is being assessed be it the concept of procedural understanding, process skills or practical skills (Abrahams et al., 2013) because assessing practical skills aims to uncover whether the acquisition of these practical skills

Crafting a Strategy to Assess the Learning   251

would enhance both procedural and conceptual understanding. Therefore, the steps of assessing students' ritual practices should be as follows:

1. First, it should be a direct assessment whereby teachers prepare an observation sheet per student.
2. It also should be an individual assessment.
3. Brief the students on what is expected from them.
4. Create a simulation situation.
5. Use an observation form.
6. Teachers should encourage students to practice self-assessment. This is in line with the Islamic tradition of _muhasabah al nafs_ (self-reckoning).

Evaluating One's Religiosity

To prepare Muslims to be successful in this world and the hereafter (Munastiwi, 2019), developing religiosity within Muslim learners is fundamental in Islamic studies for all levels. It is essential here to clarify that in contrary to the conventional definition of religiosity/spirituality as "a subset of deeply religious people who have dedicated their lives to the service of their religion and their fellow human and whose lives exemplify the teachings of their faith traditions" (Koenig, 2008, p. 350), which is usually reflected in the attitudes of monks and nuns, in Islam, a person's spirituality/religiosity is the attainment of a moderate state of belief and practice that enables a Muslim to live his life according to his religious teachings. It is mentioned in the Qur'an

> _But monasticism they invented—We ordained it not for them—only seeking Allah's pleasure, and they observed it not with right observance. So We give those of them who believe their reward, but many of them are evil-livers._
> (57:27)

In Islam, the religiosity of an individual is a personal matter related to his faith and how close he is to Allah. It is strongly founded on _"ma waqara fi alqalb wa sadakahu al amal."_ Therefore, it should be demonstrated in his actions, attitudes and how he presents himself in the social arena. Starting with his relationship with Allah and demonstrated through his beliefs and rituals' practices, his relationship with fellow Muslims via communication, transactions and participation in supporting the group's collective sentiments and values. As for his relationship with humanity at large, it is subjected to the observation of Islamic humanistic morals and values. The scope of religiousness according to Kadir (2003, as cited in Zurqoni, 2016) is not ended in speculative understanding or only normative concept but it must be in concrete daily life behaviour. That's why someone's commitment to his religion can be seen from the realisation of religious elements including knowledge, belief, attitude and behaviour (Kadir, 2003, pp. 277–278, as cited in Zurqoni, 2016). The whole Islamic educational process is held to create a spiritual and intellectual human ready to serve God's will (Zurqoni, 2016). To serve these objectives, the different aspects of a Muslim's personality should be taken care of in the process of socialisation in general and in Islamic studies in particular. Those religious elements according to Fuaduddin and Hasan (2002, as cited in Zurqoni, 2016) are connected, but they are non-linear, and their realisation appeared to not always be the same among individuals. This will create a real dilemma in its assessment. Although someone's religiosity is an individual affair, and it is hard for others to realise its level, tensity and genuineness, some argue that Islamic studies is a legitimate venue to instil religiosity into students and assess it (Zurqoni and Muhibat, 2013; Muhaimin, 2003; Kadir, 2003; Fuaduddin & Hasan, 2002, as cited in Zurqoni, 2016). In this regard, teachers can assess students' understanding of how a person becomes religious and a devoted practitioner/religious seeker through students' reflective writing, discussions and inquiry. In this regard, teachers should use an observation sheet to measure the developing patterns of the spiritual and social behaviour of students (Kristiawan et al., 2016) through students' views and reflections. For instance, using a customised Religious Orientation Inventory[2] to evaluate students' diary entries and logs can serve this purpose. These assessment tools could be used to measure the different dimensions of one's religiosity—namely, knowledge, belief, ritual, experiential and consequential dimension (Abdullah & Karim, 1990, as cited in Zurqoni, 2016, p. 227). Evaluating religiosity is essentially evaluating "the occurrence of the spiritual experiences" (Spilka et al., 1985) because these experiences play such a formative role in the development of religious attitudes (Batson & Ventis, 1982; Clark, 1958; Glock, 1962, as cited in Kass et al., 1991, p. 204). In relation to assessing religiosity and in the spirit of Omar ibn al-Khattab's (second rightly guided caliph) saying, "Judge yourselves before you are judged, weigh your deeds before they are weighed for you". It is also suggested that students should be trained to the practice of self-assessment. It could be done via the processes of planning, acting, reflecting and revising. Besides embedding it (self-assessment) in all aspects of the classroom culture in which teachers are also required to participate as role models, teachers should evaluate religiosity (mainly in *aqidah* and *ibadah*) based on

1. organisational religious activities (religious sacrifices, congregational prayers, Halaqah's attendance);
2. non-organisational religious activities, private and personal behaviours; and
3. subjective or intrinsic religiousness—namely, the extent to which religion is the primary motivating factor in people's lives, drives, behaviour and decision-making.

Evaluating One's Morality

Contrary to the conventional dilemma and inevitable questions: if we are going to teach values, whose values are we going to teach? What method(s) shall we employ? What would be the intended outcomes? In Islamic studies, the values to be disseminated to students are clearly defined. They must encompass the Islamic morals and values as determined by the Qur'an, prophetic tradition and the historical practices of Muslims. The only issue of concern here is related to what method shall we employ? And how students' performance should be assessed? In this regard, Luma (1983) proposed that evaluating pupils on ethics should be based on observing attitudes, interests and problems and close association with the pupils to know that these aspects are so important for learning.

In addition to the usage of situational test where the pupil's behaviour is observed in a given life situation; observational test where the child's behaviour and attitudes are constantly evaluated by his associate teachers as he is in action to make an anecdotal recording of any incidents as they occur; diary records of activities engaged in self-report inventories of the interests, preferences, attitudes and feeling of the person are evaluated. (Luma, 1983, as cited in Bipoupout, 2018, p. 40).

Therefore, assessing Islamic ethics requires adequate preparation from teachers using up-to-date assessment methods, knowledge of moral education theories, an understanding of the roles of the different players in the moral drama not only the propagation of a fixed set of morals that differentiate between what is right and wrong, normal and deviant and halal and haram. Students are not only expected to merely memorise and understand the concept of Islamic ethics; rather, they are also required to internalise and practice the concept in their lives. This will only be achieved if Islamic studies teachers focus on coaching students for improving their value judgements via an ethical inquiry and a reflective intelligence to revise one's judgements because "the moral life is lived only as the individual appreciates for himself the ends for which he is working and does his work in a personal spirit of interest and devotion to these ends" (Dewey, 1993, as cited in Westbrook, 2015). Drawing on his criticism of the traditional morality and its reliance on teaching morals and values via direct commands reinforced by 'fear' and 'bribes,' Dewey has proposed an inquiry-based method that aims at teaching students how to think morally, instead of supplying them with fixed moral packages. The assumption is that reasoning skills are best developed when young people are involved in open-ended and peer group discussions of ideas in which they are interested (Sutcliffe, 2015). Dewey called it Philosophy for Children (P4C). P4C aims at identifying a supreme principle that can serve as a criterion for ethical evaluation and value judgements. The latter are tools for enabling satisfactory redirection of conduct when the habit no longer suffices to direct it. This method is regarded as effective because students and teachers who teach the subject come from different social backgrounds, thus, they are expected to have different abilities and motivations towards moral values. In P4C, children learn to become more and more critical in a process that involves consistent practice to improve the habits and tools of critical thought. This also goes along with the general Qur'anic command of inquiring. The Qur'an "puts the responsibility on every individual to personally question, analyse and verify" (39:18, 17:36, 5:105), as this could have a great impact on learning, understanding the self, others and also to shape the relationship of a person with his God and the Islamic tradition of discussion and debate. It is also proposed that the success of disseminating Islamic values to learners should be performed and continuously followed by examples or models (Munastiwi, 2019, p. 4). The Islamic morality is not just a personal concern but a mechanism that aims "to regulate and coordinate various social relations and deal with various discords which usually include the interpersonal relationships and the relationships between individuals and society" (LIU, 2011, p. 18). Thus, evaluating students' morality should be done at two levels: individually and in a group. The second level should be used to evaluate how Muslim students "carry out social coordination through their judgment of right and wrong and a self-perfection practice as well" (LIU, 2011, p. 19). Thus, inquiry-based and cooperative learning seems to be the best way to conduct lessons and at the same time to evaluate students' morality because in these two methods, learning and assessment form one entity. An Inventory of Positive Attitudes (IPA)[3] should be utilised to record and follow up on students' progress.

Strategy for Assessment in Islamic Studies for Elementary Schools

Objectives: This plan provides a practical strategy to be applied in assessing students' learning in Islamic studies subjects for elementary schools. It also highlights the usage of summative in the form of exams, tests, quizzes,

Table 20.1 Assessment methods according to Islamic studies' different segments

Islamic Studies Segments	Content	Proposed Method of Assessment
aqidah (creed)	Information	• Summative: Tests, quizzes, homework and exams • Formative: Inquiry-based learning
fiqh (Islamic jurisprudence)	Information and skills	• Summative: Tests, quizzes, homework and exams • Formative: Practice-based testing
adab and akhlaq (Islamic morality)	Information, morals and skills	• Formative: Inquiry-based learning and cooperative learning (assessment and learning take place at the same time), diary writing, role-play and descriptive progress reports
sirah (the prophetic biography) and Islamic history	Information and morals	• Summative: Tests, quizzes, homework and exams • Formative: Inquiry-based learning
Qur'anic studies: Hifz (memorisation)	Skills	• A diagnostic early evaluation should be conducted to identify students' individual level of competence • Formative: Descriptive progress reports • Summative: Tasmmii' (oral testing)
Qur'anic Studies: tafseer (exegesis)	Information	• Formative: Discussion and reflective writing

Crafting a Strategy to Assess the Learning   255

homework and final projects and formative assessment, such as discussion-based activities, research-based activities, role-play and diary writing. These assessment methods are classified according to Islamic studies' different segments. This should serve as a guide to Islamic studies teachers to change their strategy in assessing students' morality that is usually criticised for being memory-tested, outdated, irrelevant and bare (Table 20.1).

Conclusion

Undoubtedly, Islamic studies as a school subject offer a different instructional challenge compared to other subjects because learning outcomes in Islamic studies are related directly to learners' faith and understanding of Islam expands their scope beyond 'how much a student should know' to how much religiosity and morality he should acquire in order to attain right character and piety. The broadness of this learning outcome renders the duty of Islamic studies teachers closer to Islamic missionary assignment which transcends the domains of instruction. One way to help fulfil this assignment is for Islamic studies to blend their teaching styles with effective modern teaching pedagogies. The resistance of Islamic studies teachers towards the adoption of modern instructional strategies, evaluation and assessment included has been a weakness mostly highlighted by critics. For instance, Rosnani (2005) argued that the "methodology of teaching the Islamic sciences is plagued with weaknesses and is, in fact, the greatest hindrance to developing wisdom and building Muslim students' character". This weakness probably explains why Muslim students or young people are easily swayed by those Western cultures and values that contradict Islamic culture and values. This phenomenon reflects their fundamental weakness of character. Providing teacher training via lifelong learning is a good alternative to fill in the gaps left by conventional training most of these teachers were exposed to. Once able to use effective teaching and learning strategies, Islamic studies teachers will be able to select proper methods and procedures for evaluating and assessing their students in a way that serves the learning. The proposed strategy in this chapter could help teachers to conduct effective evaluation and assessment strategies, use the latest methods, create dynamism in their lessons and enable them to detect areas in which learning should be improved. As for students, these proposed methods of evaluation and assessments will allow students to reflect on their learning and identify areas of strength and weakness and offer them the chance to set their personal goals and advocate for their own learning.

Notes

1 The name 'Islamic studies' in this context refers to the school subject, regardless of the level at which it is taught. That comprises knowledge and skills meant to enable Muslim students—or maybe others as well—to learn about the religion of Islam in terms of *aqidah* (Islamic theology), *fiqh* (Islamic jurisprudence), *adab* and *akhlaq* (Islamic ethics and morality), *sirah* (the prophetic biography)

256 *Tahraoui Ramdane and Merah Souad*

and Qur'anic studies that include *tahfiz* (memorisation) and *tafsir* (exegesis) and in some cases the Arabic language as the language of the holy text (refer to Adeyemi, 2016). Sometimes, the terms 'Islamic education' and 'Islamic studies' are confusingly used. In fact, there is a "[l]ack of conceptual clarity in various current depictions of the field, including 'Muslim Education', 'Islamic Pedagogy', 'Islamic Nurture' and 'Islamic Religious Pedagogy', is outlined and the frequent confusion of Islamic Education with Islamic Studies is critiqued. The field of Islamic Education Studies has theological and educational foundations and integrates interdisciplinary methodological designs in Social Sciences and Humanities. The second part of the inquiry draws attention to the lack of new theoretical insights and critical perspectives in Islamic Education" (refer to Sahin, 2018).

2 In light of the tools developed to measure one's morality used in some psychological studies to measure spirituality, Islamic Studies teachers can tailor ROI to be used to evaluate their students' religiosity. For more details, refer to Kass et al. (1991).

3 In light of the tools developed to measure one's morality used in some psychological studies to measure spirituality, Islamic Studies teachers can tailor IPA to be used to evaluate their students' morality. For more details, refer to Kass et al. (1991).

References

Abdullah, T., & Karim, M. R. (1990). Metodologi Penelitian Agama: sebuah pengantar (Cet. 2). Yogyakarta: Tiara Wacana.

Abrahams, I., Reiss, M. J., & Sharpe, R. M. (2013). The assessment of practical work in school science. *Studies in Science Education*, 49(2), 209–251.

Ajem, R., & Memon, N. (2011). Principles of Islamic pedagogy: A teacher's manual. *Islamic teacher education program*. Toronto: Canada Razi Group.

Ashaari, M. F., Ismail, Z., Puteh, A., Samsudin, M. A., Ismail, M., Kawangit, R., & Ramzi, M. I. (2012). An assessment of teaching and learning methodology in Islamic studies. *Procedia-Social and Behavioral Sciences*, 59, 618–626.

Batson, C. D., & Ventis, W. L. (1982). The religious experience: A social-psychological perspective. New York: Oxford University Press.

Bipoupout, M. R. L. (2018). Evaluation of learning in moral education and pupils' behavior. *World Journal of Research and Review (WJRR)*, 6(2), 39–44

Boyle, H. N. (2006). Memorization and learning in Islamic schools. *Comparative Education Review*, 50(3), 478–495.

Brookhart, S. M. (1999). *The art and science of classroom assessment. The missing part of pedagogy. ASHE-ERIC Higher Education Report, Volume 27, Number 1*. ERIC Clearinghouse on Higher Education, One Dupont Circle, Suite 630, Washington, DC 20036–1183.

Burden, P. R., & Byrd, D. M. (2019). *Methods for effective teaching*. Boston: Allyn and Bacon.

Clark, W. H. (1958). *The psychology of religion*. New York, NY: McMillan.

Cowie, B., & Bell, B. 1999. A model of formative assessment in science education. *Assessment in Education: Principles, Policy & Practice*, 6(1), 101–116. https://doi.org/10.1080/09695949993026

Crooks, T. J. 1988. The impact of classroom evaluation practices on students. *Review of Educational Research*, 58(4), 438–481

Dewey, J. (1972). Ethical principles underlying education. In J. A. Boydston (Ed.), *The Early Works, 1882–1989* (Vol. 5, pp. 54–83). Carbondale: Southern Illinois University Press. (Original work published 1897).

Fuaduddin, Bisri, & Hasan, C. (2002). PENDIDIKAN AGAMA ISLAM, Dinamika Pemikiran Islam di Perguruan Tinggi: Wacana tentang Pendidikan Agama Islam / editor Fuaduddin & Cik Hasan Bisri (Vol. 2002). Jakarata: Logos.

Gardner, J. (Ed.). (2012). *Assessment and learning*. Sage.

Glock, C. Y. (1962). *On the study of religious commitment. Religious Education*, 57, S98–S110.

Husna, S. A., Ritonga, M., Lahmi, A., Saputra, R., & Ayu, S. (2020). Teachers' unpreparedness in carrying out Islamic education learning using the revised 2013 curriculum in elementary school. *European Journal of Molecular & Clinical Medicine*, 7(2), 1520–1528.

Islamic Studies Teacher. (2012). Retrieved from ps://www.slideshare.net/islam-icteachereducation/assessment-and-evaluation-in-an-islamic-pedagogy-isnaed-west-coast04jan12.

Kadir, H. M. A. (2003). Ilmu Islam Terapan: Menggagas Paradigma Amali dalam Agama Islam. Pustaka Pelajar dan STAIN Kudus.

Kass, J. D., Friedman, R., Leserman, J., Zuttermeister, P. C., & Benson, H. (1991). Health outcomes and a new index of spiritual experience. *Journal for the Scientific Study of Religion*, 203–211.

Koenig, H. G. (2008). Concerns about measuring "spirituality" in research. *The Journal of Nervous and Mental Disease*, 196(5), 349–355.

Kristiawan, M., Jumeldi, A., Ahmad, S., & Asvio, N. (2016). The implementation of affective assessment for Islamic education in high school 1 pariangan. *Research Journal of Social Sciences*, 9(4), 1–8.

LIU, Y. (2011). The coordination function of Islamic ethics in transforming Islamic societies. *Journal of Middle Eastern and Islamic Studies (in Asia)*, 5(3), 17–36.

Luma, L. E. (1983). *The education of African teachers*. Yaounde, Cameroon: SOPECAM

Macdonald, D. B. (1911). *Aspects of Islam*. New York: Macmillan.

Mawardi, D., & Supadi, S. (2018). Concentration on Learning Program Development in Islamic Education. *AL-HAYAT: Journal of Islamic Education*, 2(2), 213–230.

Memon, N. (2021, March 25). Islamic Pedagogy for Islamic Schools. In *Oxford Research Encyclopedia of Education*. Retrieved 30 November 2021, from https://oxfordre.com/education/view/10.1093/acrefore/9780190264093.001.0001/acrefore-9780190264093-e-1515.

Muhaimin. (2003). *Wacana Pengembangan Pendidikan Islam*. Surabaya: Pustaka Pelajar.

Munastiwi, E. (2019). Islamic education in Indonesia and Malaysia: Comparison of Islamic education learning management implementation. *Jurnal Pendidikan Islam*, 8(1), 1–26.

Ramadan, T. (2004). *Western Muslims and the Future of Islam*. UK: Oxford University Press.

Ramdane, T., & Merah, S. (2020). Islamic curriculum. In *Oxford research encyclopedia of education*.

Ramdane, T., & Souad, M. (n.d.) Islamic Curriculum. *Oxford Research Encyclopedia of Education*. Retrieved 30 November 2021, from https://oxfordre.com/education/view/10.1093/acrefore/9780190264093.001.0001/acrefore-9780190264093-e-216.

Rosnani H. (2005). Rethinking Islamic education in facing the challenges of the twenty-first century. *American Journal of Islamic Social Sciences*, 22(4), 133–147.

258 Tahraoui Ramdane and Merah Souad

Sahin, A. (2018). Critical issues in Islamic education studies: Rethinking Islamic and Western liberal secular values of education. *Religions, 9*(11).

Spilka, B., Shaver, P., Kirkpatrick, L. A. (1985). A general attribution theory for the psychology of religion. *Journal for the Scientific Study of Religion,* 24, 1–20.

Sutcliffe, R. (2015), *Presentation at philosophy for children (P4C) workshop at the Kulliyyah (faculty) of education,* International Islamic University Malaysia, 10 February 2015.

Tan, C. (2012). *Islamic education and indoctrination: The case in Indonesia* (Vol. 58). Routledge.

Wagner, D. A., & Lotfi, A. (1980). Traditional Islamic education in Morocco: Sociohistorical and psychological perspectives. *Comparative Education Review, 24*(2, Part 1), 238–251.

Westbrook, R. B. (2015). *John Dewey and American democracy.* Cornell University Press.

William, D. (2011). What is assessment for learning? *Studies in educational evaluation, 37*(1), 3–14.

Zurqoni, Z. (2016). *Menilai Esensi dan Modernisasi Pendidikan Islam.* Syamil: Jurnal Pendidikan Agama Islam (*Journal of Islamic Education*), *4*(1), 107–121.

Zurqoni, & Muhibat. (2013). *Menggali Islam Membumikan Pendidikan: Upaya Membuka Wawasan Keislaman dan Pemberdayaan Pendidikan Islam.* (S. Susmiyati, Ed.) (2nd ed.). Jogjakarta: Ar-Ruzz Media.

Index

15th century 98
19th century 148
2011 census 235
20th century 223
21st century 70, 92
21st-century classrooms 158
2nd century 19
5th/11th century 21
60,000 institutions 47
610 CE 18

A'ak Abdullah Al-Kudus 36
'Abbasid caliph al-Qadir bi'llah 22
'Abbasid caliphate 19, 21
'Abbasids 23
Abd Rashid 163
Abdul Hamid AbuSulayman 199
Abdullah 18
Abid's pedagogical approaches 11
Abrahamic faiths 199
absolute source of knowledge 18
Abu al-Faraj ibn al-Jawzi 22
Abu Hanifah 22
academic achievements 48
ACARA 184
accurate reproduction 18
Aceh 47
active 14
active engagements 66
active explorers 18
adab and *akhlaq* 249
Adam 18
ADDIE model 85
adl 38
administrative strategies 47
aesthetic 69
Afghanistan 24
African countries 25
agency 7
aḥādith 210

Ahl Al-Kalaam 62
Ahl al-Sunnah and *al-Jama'ah* 22
Ahmad ibn Hanbal 21, 22
AIMS 98
Akhlaq 136
akhlāq 210
Akpunar 147
al Jiddu wal muadhobah 131
Al Ma'oon 140
al- Mas'udi 22
Al-'aqd 192
Al-Azhar school 148
Albanian 183
Alevi Muslimas 229
al-Fara- bi 59
al-Faruqi 25
Al-Ghazali 59
Al-Ghāzālī 99
Al-Ghazzalī 136
alienation 28
'alim 20
Alimāt 212
al-I'tiqad al-Qadiri 22
Allah 8, 18
alliance 22
Al-Majiri system 99
Amanatul Ummah Islamic Boarding
    School 124
Amtsal 59
analytic skills 14
analytical method 111
Analytical Procedures 50
ancient irrelevance 5
Angel Gabriel 18
angels 18
Annuqayah 34
Annuqayah's educational mission 40
Annuqayah's zero-plastic initiative 38
ANOVA 103
antiquated image 5

260   *Index*

anti-rationalist 22
appreciation 64
appreciation of media 12
aqidah 6, 162, 246
Arabic 6, 18, 183
Arabic curriculum 184
Arabic language 58, 83
Arabic language classrooms 193
Arabic language learning classrooms 183
Arabic teachers 185
archipelago 31
argumentative debates 22
Aristotle 98
artificial intelligence 82
Asia 47
Asifa's 9
As-souq 192
ASSURE model 85
astronomy 19, 23
at- taʿāruf 185
at-tćawur 187
attitudes 4
attractive and creative 9
Audio Media 113
Audio-Visual Media 113
Australian curriculum 183
Australian K –12 language education 183
Australian Muslims 183
Australian schools 183
authentic choice 7
azmat al-ʿaql al-Muslim 201

backbone of secularism 26
backgrounds 4
Baghdad 19, 20
Bahasa Indonesia 183
balanced human 206
Bandung 147
bank sampah 35
Barmak 19
Barmaki 19
Basic Education Curriculum 2008 47
Bayt al-Hikmah 19
bedtime 11
Behaviour Education 214
Bengali 183
Bible 223
biblical traditions 38
biological 130
bio-rational pluralist education 27
bio-rational pluralist education' 27
Birmingham 236
black holes 14

black-and-white 26
blessing 11
blind 22
Bodily Changes 227
body language 11
bookmark 90
Bosnia 174
Bosnian 183
bounteous act of God 18
brick-and-mortar 92
Britain 236
British Council 41
British educational context 10
British educational model 24
British government 236
British prime minister 235
broader framework 27
broader religious objectives 64
bureaucratic competence 33

Caliph al-Maʾmun 19
Caliph Harun al-Rashid 19
Cana dian Sunni Muslim 4
Canadian culture 4
Canadian context 12
caring' thinking 69
case study approach 124
Catholic 223
cave 18
CDs/DVDs, 63
Central Asia 24
central pillars 19
Centre for Teaching Thinking 69
chalkboard 121
challenge of modernity 26
challenges 8
changing contexts 4
child 8
child-centred 59
child-centred approach and psychological principles 59
child-centred education 59
children critically discern 11
children's formative 7
choice 7
Christian Ethics 199
Christianity and Judaism 39
Christian-Orthodox ideological concept 173
civic duty 138
Climate Change 31
Climate Change Institution 41
Coaching 126
coercive questions 7
cognitive 12

Index 261

collaborative 60
collaborative problem-solving 40
colonial empires 24
colonial structures 201
commentary 23
communication skills 69
Communication Technologies 63, 165
communist Yugoslavia 173
community capability 162
Community Engagement 39
community engagement efforts 31
community of philosophical inquiry' 69
Community Resources 113
Community Service Bureau 39
comparative religion 199
con temporary debates 18
conceptual change 84
conceptual framework 15
conceptualisations 10
confused dualism 200
congregational prayers 252
Constructive Alignment 83
constructive feedback 59
constructive instruction 60
constructive praise 130
constructivism 58
Constructivism 60
constructivist approach 69
constructivist theory 153
constructivist viewpoint 87
contemporary Abrahamic 28
contemporary Arabic media 5
contemporary culture 9
contemporary Islamic education 18
Contemporary Islamic Education 25
Contemporary Muslim communities 18
Contemporary Muslim educators 12
contemporary pedagogical
    approaches 10
contemporary perspectives 27
contemporary realities 27
contemporary world 246
Content Knowledge 82
context matters 12
continuing professional learning 179
continuous educational opportunities
    165
contrary 21
Controlling 111
cooperative learning 60
COPI 69
COPI discussions 78
correct path 21
counterproductive results 29
counter-terrorism 236

COVID-19 82, 92
COVID-19 pandemic 241
craft 246
creativity 5
credibility 22
creed 6
critical disposition 70
critical engagement 205
critical thinkers 18
critical thinking 24, 163, 205
criticality 163
Croats 173
cross-cultural knowledge 53
cultivating Islamic analysis 12
cultural 183
cultural and inner circle ethnic 49
cultural assimila tion 49
cultural beliefs 46
cultural content-knowledge 54
cultural context 12
cultural diversity 48
cultural knowledge 48
Cultural Reflection 48
cultural relevance 6
cultural representation 53
cultures 18, 46
curiosity 59
current diversity 46
Curricular 31
curriculum 20, 183
curriculum design 213
curriculum designers 49
curriculum develop- ment 205
Curriculum Knowledge 164
curriculum planning 175
curriculum reform 174

daily instructional activities 100
Dalia 8
Dar al-Khilafah 22
Dar al-Tarjumah 19
Dari 183
Darse Nizami 24
darul uloom 237
Darul Uloom of Nadwat al-ᶜUlama 24
Dayah 47
decentralised education system 177
deductive 58, 59
deen 5
deep knowledge 59
deep understanding 59
deeper mindset 8
Deforestation 31
delinquency 25
democracy 174

262 Index

democratic culture 179
democratic transition 33
Denge Shunni 100
denominations 20
Deobandis 24
deplete carbon storage 31
derse 69
developmental 25
devotional spirituality 15
dialogic halaqah 4
dialogic relationships 4
dialogue 14
dictators of knowledge 18
differing value 7
digital age need 82
digital native learners 82
digital practices 64
diniah 124
disconnection 7
Discovery Learning 10
disintegration 28
diverse linguistic backgrounds 46
diversity 27, 185
divine 8
divine challenges 9
divine pedagogy 9
divine revelation 19
divine revelations 21
Doenia broaches 228
Dogan 147
double-consciousness 10
Dualism Education 48
Dutch Ministry 224
Dutch Ministry of Education 229
Dutch multicultural 224

East Java 31
eco-justice 40
ecological challenges 31
ecosystems 31
education system 223
educational heritage 15
educational intention 7
educational systems 172
educational technology 162
educational technology adoption 82
educationists 25
educators' pedagogies 4
effective learning 60
efficient management 161
eight autonomous intelligences 148
Electronic portfolios 92
ELT pedagogies 46, 48
ELT Textbook 48

emergent approach 10
emerging pedagogical innovations 164
emotional development 212
endeavour 12
endured 9
engagement 69
English communication 47
English diversity 49
English idealisation 49
English language 112
English language learners 48
English language learning 48
English language skills 46
English proficiencies 183
environmental awareness 32
environmental destruction 31
environmental education 32, 34, 42
Environmental Education 31, 32
environmental exploitation 33
environmental problems 31
environmental sensibilities 32
environmental stewardship 33, 42
environmental-friendly 42
environmentally responsible
    citizens 32
epistemological 69, 136
e-portfolios 92
equivocal pedagogies 7
Equivocal Pedagogies 7
esoteric 5
ethical thinking 69
ethics and character 246
ethnic diversity 27
ethnic language experience 183
ethnicities 46
European context 235
European educational 24
European educational space 175
European modernity 24
European supremacy 24
Evaluation and Assessment 247
everyday life 9
Evidence-based educational reforms 178
exemplary leaders 12
exemplary method 59
expansion' and 'contraction 23
exploiting 31
explora tion 15
extra-curricular environ- mental training
    camps 37
extremist 24
extremist and radical religious groups 24
extrinsic 128
Extrinsic factors 129

facilitators 18
factual situations 60
Faculty of Divinity 199
fair choice 8
faith 10
faithful young Muslims 12
Faizi's Islamic rationale 38
False Choice and Rewards 7
family fragmentation 25
family heritage 184
Faris 14
Faris' approaches 11
Farsi 183
Fatanah 129
Fatima 9
Fatimid al-Azhar 19
Fatimid era 23
Fatimid Shi'i Ismaili 22
Fatimid's *Jami' al-Azhar* 19
Fatimid's Khazana al-Kutub 19
Fatimids 19
fatwa 5
fatwas 5
Fikih 128
fiqh 22, 162, 210, 246
Fiqh 116
first university 19
first verses 18
First World Congress 25
fitra 7
fitrah 130
fixed curriculum 20
flexible classroom environment 112
Flipgrid 91
fluidity inherent 46
fluidity, multiplicity and hybridity 241
force 7
Forcing 6
foreign culture 47
foreign language 53
forgive 7
forgiveness 14
formative 255
fostering scientific scepticism 163
foundation 18
freelance basis 4
fun-based 62
fuqaha 21

Gagi and Wammakko 100
gamification 89
Gender diversity 27
general knowledge 46, 58
general theories 60
Generation Z 87

ghaybiat 5
global citizens 12
global content 54
Global North 32
global online learning market 82
global sustainability 40
global system 31
globalisation 15, 58, 204
Globalisation 63
gnostic approach 26
God 7, 18
God's prophets 18
God-consciousness 6
good 12
good citizens 28
good men' 28
Google Drive 92
Google Forms 91
government leadership 31
government-accredited curriculum 34
grand legal 23
graphic materials 121
Great Expectations 50
Greek 19
green movement 33
green party 33
Green Pesantren initiative 42
Green Pesantren Initiative 31
Green Pesantren programme 31
greenhouse gases 31
grooming 58
guaranteeing 8
guidance 15
guides 18
guiding principles 18
gymnasium curriculum 174

habituation method 59
hadith 21
Hadith 116, 229
Hala 8
halal al-dam 22
halal and haram 253
halaqah 10
Halaqah's attendance 252
halaqat circles 4
Halima 8
halqa 20
Hamza 9, 10
Hanbalite 21
haram 10
hardships 8
hating 8
heart 7
heaven 8

264 *Index*

heterogeneous ummah 4
Hierarchical corporate structures 160
hierarchy 40
higher learning 19
higher-order thinking 59
highly mindful 12
hijra 19
hill of books 23
Hindi 19, 183
history 5
Hiwar 59
holistic curriculum 31
holistic development of children 58
holistic pedagogies 4
Holy Qur'an 58
Homosexuality 228
Howard Gardner 148
human logical-mathematical 148
human rational thinking 21
human rational inquiry 21
human rights 174
humanistic 223
humanities 25
hybrid framework 18

Ibadah 140
ibadat 161
IBADAT 118
Ibn e Sina 59
Ibn Khaldun 59, 203
Ibn Rusd 136
Ibn Sina 136
idealisation 46
identities 48
Identity 234
ideological 20, 25
ideological threat 236
IIIT 199
IIUM 202
ijaza 25
ijtihad 22
ʿilm 18
imam 173
imams 238
īmān 77
imarah 159
in practice 6
inclusive society 28
indigenous cultures 18
Indonesia 31, 47, 83, 124, 147
Indonesian 112
Indonesian Muslim schools 155
Indonesian *pesantren* 31
inductive 58, 59
Ineffective Methods 6

ineffective pedagogies 7
Ineffective pedagogies 5
Information technology 92
informational stuffing 7
infuse technology 165
Infusing Technology 85
infusion of technology 92
ingredients 6
inherent agency 7
innate human qualities 137
Inner and Outer Circle nations 54
inner dynamism 20
innovative pedagogy 31
inquiry 163
inquiry-based instruction 59
insidious type 7
Institute for Disaster Response 33
institutionalising 23
institutions 18
Instructional Approaches 58
instructional design 84
Instructional Design 84
instructional materials 112
instructional objectives 58
instructional strategies 58
instructional styles 64
instructional technology 82
instrumental perspective 8
integration of religious 46
intellectual 19
intellectual capabilities 59
Intellectual Tradition 20
intellectual traditions 18
intended learning outcomes 84
intercultural citizens 53
interdisciplinary 32
inter-generational problem 7
Internal Dynamism 18
internal conflicts 49
internal contradiction 7
internal dynamism 20
international challenges 58
international collaboration 177
international communicative
    encounters 46
International Institute of Islamic
    Thought 25
International Islamic Universities in
    South Asia 25
International Islamic University in
    Islamabad 199
International Islamic University
    Malaysia 69
international Muslim ummah 12
international standards 61

Index 265

international target culture materials 49
interpersonal relationships 254
interpersonal skills 9
interpretation 18
interpretive study 4
intrinsic 10, 128
Intrinsic factors 128
intrinsic quality 15
Inward Dynamism 20
IQ 149
IQ tests 149
Iqbal Muzafar 24
IR 111
IR 4.0 82
IS 163, 165
Islam's doctrine 82
Islamic boarding schools 31, 124, 127
Islamic civilisation 201
Islamic civilisations 18
Islamic Community 174
Islamic creed 246
Islamic cultures and values 47
Islamic doctrines 62
Islamic education 7, 9, 23, 28, 173
Islamic Education 20, 136, 202
Islamic education institutions 148
Islamic education teachers 84, 92
Islamic Education Teachers 70
Islamic Environmental Ethos 38
Islamic ethical norms 24
Islamic ethical principles 39
Islamic ethics 253
Islamic feasts 52
Islamic frame 9
Islamic humanistic 251
Islamic identities 46
Islamic identity 242
Islamic ideology 65, 136
Islamic institutions 173
Islamic jurisprudence 246
Islamic knowledge 48
Islamic leadership 42
Islamic legal principles 33
Islamic literacy 15
Islamic material 6, 14
Islamic metaphysics 200
Islamic morality 254
Islamic norms 46
Islamic pedagogies 248
Islamic pedagogy, 4 58, 136, 248
Islamic perspective 58
Islamic Perspective 199
Islamic practices 46
Islamic psychology 136
Islamic reasoning 14

Islamic religious 158, 183
Islamic Research Academy 199
Islamic resilience perspective 9
Islamic scholars 41
Islamic spirit of edu cation 237
Islamic standard viewpoint 25
Islamic studies 47, 158
Islamic Studies 247
Islamic Studies Classroom 114
Islamic studies programme 199
Islamic teacher education programme 4
Islamic teachers 58
Islamic Teaching Philosophy 136
Islamic teaching pro fessionalism 136
Islamic teachings 11
Islamic thought 200
Islamic tradition 4
Islamic traditions 18
Islamic values 48
Islamic way of life 46
Islamic world view 246
Islamic-approved codes 46
Islamisation 199, 204
Islamisation agenda 202
Islamisation of knowledge 25, 26
Islamisation of the mind 200
Islamization of Knowledge 199
Islamizing 25
Ismail al-Faruqi 199
Ismaili Raji al-Faruqi 25
ISTAC 200
istigasah 127
istikamah 127
istiqamah 159

Jahannam 7
jalasa 20
Jannah 8
Java 47
Jennah 5
jidal 22
Jigsaw 65
Jina 5
jismiah 131
job market demands 64
John Biggs 83
jurisconsults 21
jurisprudence 22
jurisprudential schools of thought 24
jurists 22

kafir 22
Kahoot 82
kalam Allah Ta'ala ghayr-e makhluq 22
Kalimantan 47

266 *Index*

Kalpataru 34
Kenya 112
khaira ummah 76
Khalid 19
khalifa 38
Khazanat al-Hikmah 19
Khurasan 20
kiai 34
King Abdul Aziz University 25
Kingdom 173
knowledge 18
knowledge as problematic 59
knowledge management 18
Kuala-Lumpur 200
Kulliyyah of Education 69
Kurdish and Pashtu 183

language education 183
Laskar Hijau 36
lawmakers 21
Lawrence Kohlberg 38
Layla 9
LAZ school 150
leadership 14, 15, 39
Leading 111
learn and love Islam 7
learner autonomy 191
Learner Characteristics 86
Learner Uniqueness 9
learner-centred 69
learner-led 14
learners' cultures 51
learners' English proficiency 48
learning practices 165
learning styles 191
Learning Styles 87
left long- term 22
legacy 15, 23
Lembaga Penanggulangan Bencana 31
liberal Christian 223
liberal education 26
liberal student-centred approach 29
libraries 19
life circumstances 4
lifelong learning 61, 158
Lifelong Learning in Islam, 158
lifestyles 49
lingua franca 49
linguistic conventions 47
linguistic landscapes 49
literalist approach 200
living it 9
living rational 27
local context 10
local Melayu 46

local non-native English learners 46
Locating Information 120
logical 69
longer historical timeline 9
losing Islam 7
love 7
Lucknow 24
luxuries 8

ma waqara fi alqalb wa sadakahu al amal 251
madaris 113
madrasa 4
madrasa and *madrasa*-style 27
madrasa curriculum 23
madrasah 124, 147, 172, 210
madrasah curriculum 173, 174
madrasah curriculum reform 178
madrasah's autonomy 177
madrasahs 143, 172
*madrasa*s 20
madrassa 237
mainstream English varieties 46
majlis 20
major intellectual developments 19
makātib 214
maktab 210
Malay 183
Malay literature 200
Malaysian model 201
Malik 22
management of diversity 28
Manuel dos Santos 50
Marifa 59
marine 31
Marxists 159
Marya 9
Masjid Jamiᶜ 19
Masjid Rasul Allah 19
Maslow theory 130
materialism 5
mathematical equations 14
mathematics 23
mature faith formation 15
Mawlana Abu'l Hasan ᶜAli Nadwi 24
Mawrizi's 19
McGill University 199
McGraw Hill 50
Mecca 25
Mechanical Manipulation 120
medical knowledge 23
medicine 23
medieval Muslim tradition 25
meditation 18
memorisation 4, 59, 83, 249

memorize 6, 15
mentally and emotionally satisfied 5
Mentimeter 88
mentors 58
merciful 11
mess up 7
meta-language teaching methods 59
meta-motivation 130
metaphysical 69
metaphysical, knowledge 26
metaphysics 19, 200
methodologically effective 5
MI approach 153
MI theory 147, 153
MI-based assessment 154
middle-class individuals 49
mihnah 21
Ministry of Education 50, 224
minority ethnic communities 241
minority-Muslim 4
miracle of Qur'an 11
mis-pedagogies 4
mis-pedagogy of teaching 7
mixed Islamic 54
mizan 38
mobile devices 82
mobilisation 32
models 58
moderate 24
moderate reformists 24
modern 18
modern era 24
modern national economic-
    development 47
modern pedagogies 59
modern sciences 25
modern scientific developments 25
modern social sciences 25
modern subjects 25
modern systems 48
modern-day Afghanistan 19
modern-day Islamic education 136
Modernisation 175
Mojokerto 124
monopolise 20
Montclair State University 69
Moosa 19
moral balance 47
moral character 136
moral communities 38
moral education 38
moral judgements 69
moral responsibility 7
Moral Teachings 116
morality 11
Morocco 5

mosque 14
mosque centres 47
mosque/weekend schools 4
mosque-school 4
Motivation 128
Mount Hira 18
Mount Lemongan 36
mu'alim and mu'alimah 82
Mu'amalat 116
Mu'atazi 21
mudarrisun 179
Mudhawamatul wudhu 132
Mughal emperor 52
muhadath 21
Muhammad 18
Muhammad 'Abduh 24
Muhammad Iqbal 24
Muhammad's pedagogy 10
Muhammadiyah 33
multicultural background 58
multicultural contexts 47
multilingual 47
Multi-media Presentation 115
munazirah 22
Munif Chatib 147
Mushthafa 36
music 10
Muslim children 219
Muslim civilisations 23
Muslim community 235, 242
Muslim countries 161
Muslim edu cational and intellectual
    traditions 20
Muslim Education 25
Muslim educators 12
Muslim intellectual 18
Muslim intellectual traditions 18
Muslim learner 15
Muslim learners 47
Muslim learners' cultural contents 51
Muslim majority 26
Muslim mausoleum 52
Muslim minority population 235
Muslim pedagogy 224
Muslim Scholarship 214
Muslim School 150
Muslim teachers 220
Muslim world 199
Muslim youth identity formation 240
Muslim-Jewish-Christian
    Conference 199
Muslimness criteria 237
Muslims 7, 9
Muslims experience economic
    disadvantage 183
Muslims inhabit 12

268 *Index*

Muslims' intellectual and educational traditions 19
Mustaffa 163
Muʿtazilite 21
Mutwakkil 21

naʾma 11
Nadwat al-ʿUlama 24
nafsiyah 131
Nahdlatul Ulama 31, 33
Naquib al-Attas 25
Naquib Al-Attas 200
Nar 5
Narathiwat 47
Nasr 12
national curriculum 83
National Education Law 148
National Geographic 37
national stability 31
national-religious characteristics 173
Native cultural imperialism 54
native cultures 51
natural 59
natural disasters 32
natural resources 31
natural sciences 25
nature 18
negative consequences 22
neighbourhoods 12
Netherlands 223
new consciousness 25
new Islamic education 25
New Jersey 69
New London Group 185
new scientific achievements 18
New World 50, 53
NGOs 33
Nigeria 98
Nile 23
Nizam al-Mulk 20
Nizamiyya 20
Nizamiyya system 20
non-Abrahamic discourses 28
non-Islamic 11, 24
non-Islamic belief systems 28
Non-Muslims 92
noor 212
normative Islamic principles 39
Nour 11
Novelty 120
nuanced pedagogies 5
nurtures 10

Omar ibn al-Khattab 252
Open Educational Resources 89

Operating Facilities 115
opposite effect 7
ordinary scholastic towards 9
organic 7
Organising 111
orientation 49
orthodoxy 22, 25
orthodoxy's viewpoint 24
Ottoman rule 172
outcomes-based curriculum planning 180
outdated 5
outdated rulings 5
outdoors 9
over diversities 4
overarching themes, 4

P4C 71
Pakistan 199
paradigm 26
Parallel Education 48
paramount 18
Parent voice 139
parents 7, 8
Pasantren 47
passive recipients 18
patience 9
Pattani 47
pedagogic 126
pedagogical approaches 9, 18, 214
pedagogical change 4
pedagogical competence 126
pedagogical framings 4
pedagogical history 15
Pedagogical Innovation 31, 40
pedagogical knowledge 58
pedagogical practice 54
pedagogical quality 136
pedagogical recommendations 12
pedagogy 18, 224, 234
Pedagogy 25
Peer observation 59
Pendidikan Lingkungan Hidup (PLH) 36
Pengabdian Masyarakat 39
Persia 20
Persian 19
personality 64, 126
Personality 131
Perubahan Iklim 31
perversion 25
pesantren 34, 147
Pesantren 125
Pesantren Annuqayah 31
Pesantren Annuqayah, Sumenep 34

Pesantren Annuqayah's educational model 37
Pesantren Hijau 31, 34
Petronas Tower, Kuala Lumpur 53
Phaedo 98
philosophers 22
Philosophical 201
philosophical and historical underpinnings 24
philosophical foundations 48
philosophical problems 69
philosophical themes 72
philosophy 19, 23
Philosophy for Children 69
philosophy of Islamic education 199
physical classroom 153
physical non-human environment 200
physical, psychological, emotional and intellectual 58
physicians 23
physics 19
physiognomies 98
physiognomies of Islamic teachers 98
physiognomy' 98
pillarisation 223
Placement 125
planners 18
Planning 111
pluralism 27
pluralist teacher education concept 29
pluralist teacher education model 29
plurality of interpretations 28
pluricentricity 49
policymakers 49
political leadership 33
political systems 24
Pondok Madrasah institutes 47
Pondoks 47
pop culture 14
positive attitude 54
positive emotions 6
positive impression 23
post-pandemic educational landscape 180
Practitioners 172
prayer time 8
prayers 10
pre-colonised identities 25
preschool 25
prevailing cultural moment 12
principles 12
prior knowledge 87
private Islamic schools 47, 69
pro fessional qualities 100
problem-based learning 65
problem-solving 163

Problem-Solving 120
pro-environment behaviour 34
pro-environmentally 32
professional development 58, 177
Professional Development 205
Professional Development of Human Resources 125
Professional Development of Teachers 126
professional development trajectories 179
professional dispositions 98
professional growth 66
professional Islamic teacher 143
professional learning 178
professional Qur'anic memoriser 117
professional Qur'anic reciter 117
professional responsibilities 98
professional training platform 58
professional training programmes 66
professionalisation 137, 223
professionalism 111
Professionalism 213
professionalism' 98
Professor Rosnani Hashim 69
project-based instruction 60
Prophet 18
Prophet Muhammad 18, 62, 82, 186
Prophet's manner of living 19
Prophet's Mosque 19
Prophet's religious authority 20
prophetic biography 250
prophetic instruction approach 66
prophetic instructional strategies 59
Prophetic pedagogy 188
prophetic traditions 250
prophets 9
prostitution 228
protagonists 25
Protestant 223
pseudonyms 4
psychological 130
psychological perspectives 213
psychological principles 59
psychology 224
Puberty 227
public institutions 39
public speaking 14
punishment 6
pupils' mental capacity 59
pupil-teacher relationships 213
puzzle builders 89

qaba'il 28
qadim 21

270 Index

Qadirite Creed 22
qibla 23
Qiratul Qur`an Nadran 132
qiyamul lail 131
Qiyamul lail 131
qualitative content analysis 50
Qualitative criteria 50
qualitative research 124
quality teachers 125
Quasi-political 201
questioning 63
Quizizz 82
Quizlet 90
quizzes 250
Qur'an 6, 8, 70
Qur'an and Sunnah 64
Qur'an memorisation 163
Qur'anic pedagogy 10
Qur'anic sciences 161
Qur'anic studies 83
Qur'anic teachings 136, 139
Qur'anic verse 14
Qur'anic world view 200
Qur'an 19
Quran education 47
Qur'anic commentators 21
Qur'anic exegesis 21
Qur'anic verses 18

Ramifications 37
Raosoft sample size calculator 100
Rashid Rida 24
rational sciences 23
rationalism 23
rationalists 21
rationality 163
real life 11
real-life English encounters 46
recitation 6
reclaimed 15
recommendations 14
refinement 15
reflection 69
Reflective Thinking 120
reformists 24
relativism 28
religion 6
Religion 234
religion and spiritual morality 26
religious education 63
religious engagement 199
religious instruction 237
religious knowledge 199
religious plurality 26
religious sacrifices 252

religious teachers 173
Reorganisation 175
research-based instruc- tion 59
research-based instruction 59
research-based reform 179
Research-Based Reform 174
Resource Persons 113
responsibility 14, 15
Responsiveness 9
revolution 65
rewarding 8
rewards 8
rich mosaic 26
rightful global ownership 46
rigorous process 19
ritual practices 7
rivalry 21
Role play 65
role-playing 11
Rotterdam 228
Rubbaa 58
Rubban' 58
ruhaniyah 131
rural poor 31

Saba 11
Sahin's 10
Sahl bin Mu'adh bin Anas 92
salaf 124
Salafists 24
Salah al-Din Ayubi 22
salient factor 38
Satisfaction Guar- anteed 50
savvy generation 5
Sayyed Hossein 25
Sayyid Jamal al-Din al-Afghani 24
scaffolding 58
Scaffolding 62
schol arship 34
scholarship 206
scholarships 20
school community 42
school curricula 15
school curriculum 112
School Curriculum 112
school environment 29
schoolteacher 5
scientific 19
scientific knowledge 48
scientific theory 37
Second World War 25
secondary Islamic educational
  institutions 173
sectarian 20
secular academic 237

Index 271

secular approach 24
secular disciplines 48
secular education 48
secular epistemic hegemony 5
secular public education 183
secular reform 24
sekolah Islam 148
Sekolah Menengah Atas 147
Sekolah Menengah Umum 147
self-centred rivalry 21
self-confidence 69
self-confident 9
self-learners 5
self-motivation 124
Self-Motivation 127
self-reflection/expression 14
self-styled thinkers 26
self-transformation 9
Seljuqid 20
semi-structured interviews 4
Serbs 173
set of information 9
settings 7
Sex Education 224
Sexual Relations 228
Seyyed Vali Reza Nasr 26
Shafiʿ 22
share sound 9
shariʿah 21, 28
sheikhs 5
Shiʿi and Sufi schools 22
Shiʿi Ismaili caliphate 19
shuʿub 28
shuyukh 158
Sideen 10
single-sex education 25
Sites of Islamic education 14
Skills 6
Slamic Pedagogy 224
Slovenes 173
SMA Lazuardi 150
SMA Muthahhari 148
SMUTH 150
Social Approach 201
social awareness 14
social etiquette 10
social phenomenon 203
social progression 47
social relationships 20
social sciences 25
social-emotional 12
societies 18
sociocultural 46
socio-economic 31
socio-economic profiles 183

sociolinguistic cultural content analysis rubric 50
sociolinguistic landscapes 46
sociological 213
Socratic dialogue 69
soft skills 70
Sokoto State 98
Somali 210
Soul Generation 137
sound pedagogies 4, 9
Sound pedagogies 4
sound pedagogy 12
source culture materials 49
source of wisdom 11
Southeast Asia 47
South-East Asian countries 48
southern border provinces 46
Southern Thailand 47
spirit 21
spiritual 26, 212
spiritual being 137
spiritual development 10, 12
spiritual obligation 61
spotlight 29
springboards 14
state leadership 42
State of Croatia—Bosnian Muslims 173
Statistical Package for Social Sciences 101
stewardship 31
stimulus material 72
student assessment 153
student-centred 58
student-centred learning 163
student-centred learning approach 59
student-oriented 62
Students' Development 163
students' motivation 130
student-teacher-centred education 29
stuffing 7
Stuffing 6
substantive conversation 59
Sufism 200
Sumenep 34
summative 254
Sunan Al-Fitrah 227
Sunna 19
Sunnah 70, 229
Sunni educational institutions 22
Sunni Islam 22
Sunni orthodox 23
Sunni schools of *fiqh* 22
Sunni traditionalist 21
suppression 23
Surah Al Nahl 11

272   Index

Surah Al-Alaq 73
Surah Al-Baqarah 90
Surau 47
sustainability 33
sustainable consumption 31
sustainable development 32
SWOT analysis 176
Syed Ahmed Khan 24
Syed Ali Ashraf 25
synthesise 249
Syracuse Univer sity 199
Syriac 19
Systematic Analysis 199
systematic social work 140
systematic world 70

ta'dib 83
ta'lim 83
tabula rasa 219
tać-jee' al-istiklāliy-ya 189
Tadika institutes 47
tafseer 163
tafsīr 21
Taha Jabir Al-Alwani 199
Tahdhib 116
TAHDHIB 118
tahfiz 83, 249
tahqiq 23
tajwid 6
tajwīd 210
talabatul al 'ilm' 158
Taleem 58
talib 20
Tanzimat 24
taqlid 22, 23
Taqlilu Ghida 131
taqwa 6
tarbiyah 225
Tarbiyya 58
tarbiyyah, ta'dīb and ta'līm 203
tarbyah 83
target culture materials 49
Targhib and Tarhib 59
Tarikh 116
tārīkh 210
Ta'rikh Tabari 19
Tarjumah 19
tawakkol 138
tawhid 26, 199
Tawhid 116
tawhidic 70
tawhidic educational concept 26
Tbilisi Declaration of 1977 32
teach Islam 4
teacher competence 124

Teacher competence 130
teacher education certificate 29
Teacher Needs 125
teacher performance 127
Teacher Performance 127
Teacher professional development 125
Teacher Professional Development 154
teacher professionalisation 179
teacher professionalism 130
Teacher Professionalism 139
Teacher quality 125
Teacher Recruitment 125
teacher training 58
Teacher Training 41, 151
teacher training programmes 33
Teacher Welfare 129
Teacher Welfare Division 125
Teacher's Capability 115
teacher-centred 58
teachers based on gender 29
teachers threaten 6
teachers' classroom management 98
teachers' continued professional
    development 172
teachers' mobility 177
teachers' personalities 98
teachers' professional development 69
Teachers' Professional Development
    178
teachers' professional learning 179
teachers' professionalism 71, 99
Teachers' teaching competencies 175
teacher-student relations 98
teaching models 46
teaching profession 165
teaching styles 164
teaching-learning process 112
technicality 6
technological advancement 207
technological literacy 165
technological world 4
technology 25
Technology-Based Instruction 62
technology-infused classrooms 82
technology-infused pedagogies 82
Telegram 91
Temple University 199
tertiary education 178
textbook cultural contents 46
Textbook Sample 50
textbooks 20
Thai ELT practitioners 46
Thai Islamic cultures 54
Thai private Islamic schools 46
Thai Wattana Panit 50

Thailand 46
Thailand's ELT 46
the Centre for Philosophical Inquiry in Education 69
the ory 6
The Qur'an 116
the talk-and-chalk 112
thematic treasure 11
thematically analysed 4
theological 20
Theological 201
thinking 12
thinking skills 69
tourism 49
traditional informal pattern 20
Traditional Islamic Boarding Schools 31
traditional Islamic education 18
traditional Islamic knowledge 172
traditional Islamic madrasas 173
traditional matrix 174
traditional religious subjects 173
traditional versus 48
traditionalist leaning 33
traditionalists 21
traditionalists' 22
traditions 18
traditions of learning 22
trajectory 46
trans-disciplinary 41
transformation 15, 63
transformative education 84
transformative learning goals 40
transformative pedagogy 4
transmitted sciences 21
transmitter of knowledge 29
tried-and-true 9
triumph of Sunni Islam 23
Turkey 24
Turkish 183, 210
Turkish educators 147

UK 49, 210
Ulāmā' 211
ʿulema 21
ʿulema's quest 20
ʿulema-caliph alliance 21
ʿulema-caliphate 22
uncritical acceptance 22
undervalue environmental hazards 32
UNESCO 32, 41
United Kingdom 46, 238
United States 46
United States of America 202
unity of God 26
university 25

Unorthodox 46
Urdu 210
US Air Force 85
USD$350 billion 82
U-shaped 71
ushering humanity 12
uswatun hasanah 131

vast space 14
verses 11
vibrant educational institutions 18
vibrant Islamic education 18
vicegerents 12, 26
video games 14
virtual reality 82
virtual wor 92
vision 14
visionary leaders 155
Visual Media 113

Wahabis 24
wara 138
Way for Self 163
wealthy figures 49
welfare 58
West Africa 210
West Australian School Curriculum 184
West Jawa 148
West Sumatra 47
Western consumerism 49
Western education 201
Western influence 25
Western liberal education system 26
Western modern philosophy 201
Western philosophy 48
Western science 26
Western secularism 26
Western world 199
Western-Catholic 173
Western-oriented 147
Westernised educational paradigms 48
whiteboard 14
Whole-School Approach 37
widespread 7
Wi-Fi 91
Workshop 65
world 8
World Bank 31
world views 15
world wars 173
wudu 7

x-ray films 116

274 *Index*

Yahia Baiza 19
Yala 47
Yassine 8
yoga 7
Young Bukharan and Jadidi 24
young Muslims 14
young person 7
Young Turk 24
youth identity formation 4
YouTube 89

Yugoslavia 173
Yusr 8

Zarunji 136
zawiya 20
ZelfVerbinderOnderwij 230
Zina 226
zoom 90
Zopyrus 98
zuhud 138

Printed in the United States
by Baker & Taylor Publisher Services